SNAPSHOTS

an introduction to tourism sixth Canadian

norma polovitz nickerson | UNIVERSITY OF MONTANA

paula kerr | ALGONQUIN COLLEGE

william c. murray | MOUNT SAINT VINCENT UNIVERSITY

PEARSON

Toronto

Vice-President, Editorial Director: Gary Bennett
Editor-in-Chief: Michelle Sartor
Acquisitions Editor: Carolin Sweig
Marketing Manager: Jennifer Sutton
Supervising Developmental Editor: Suzanne Schaan
Developmental Editor: Christine Langone
Project Manager: Ashley Patterson
Production Editor: Nidhi Chopra, Cenveo® Publisher Services
Copy Editor: Judy Sturrup
Proofreader: Joe Zingrone
Compositor: Cenveo® Publisher Services
Photo and Permissions Researcher: STILLS Permissions and Research
Art Director: Julia Hall
Cover and Interior Designer: Martyn Shmoll
Cover Image: Getty Images/Randy Lincks

5 6 7 8 9 V0UD 19 18 17 16 15

Library and Archives Canada Cataloguing in Publication

Murray, William C.
    Snapshots : an introduction to tourism / William C. Murray,
Norma Polovitz Nickerson, Paula Kerr.

Includes bibliographical references and index.
ISBN 978-0-13-260516-8

    1. Tourism—Textbooks.   2. Tourism—Canada—Textbooks.
I. Nickerson, Norma Polovitz— II. Kerr, Paula, 1944–   III. Title.

G155.C2N56 2013   338.4'791   C2012-905435-6

ISBN 978-0-13-260516-8

CONTENTS

During times of prosperity, the ability to travel, whether for business or leisure, is seen as a valuable part of an industrial nation's lifestyle. During periods of economic uncertainty, the value of the tourism industry to a nation's economy cannot be overlooked. In Canada, tens of billions of dollars are generated in tourism revenue every single year. The industry employs 1.6 million Canadians and creates opportunities for increased government revenue from international visitors, stimulating our economy. While the instability of the international economy over the last few years continues to take its toll, tourism continues to thrive as the number-one global sector.

The world has seen many disasters since 2000, from terrorist attacks to devastating weather patterns. The events of September 11, 2001, clearly demonstrated the interconnection of all aspects of the global tourism industry: an event in one part of the world can have far-reaching—but unpredictable—effects. The tsunami that hit Southeast Asia was overwhelming and deadly, but the tourism industry bounced back with amazing fortitude. In North America, New Orleans was devastated by Hurricane Katrina and Toronto was stunned by the effects of a small SARS outbreak; it has taken these areas much more time to rebound to full tourism strength.

Other problems continue to trouble tourism. Airlines are struggling to survive the high costs of fuel and additional security. Crossing what was once the longest "unguarded border" in the world now requires full documentation, which means long border delays during the hot summer months. That has caused a serious erosion in tourism from our major foreign market, the United States. Still, Canada is fortunate. Tourists travel safely and easily through our country as Canada maintains a worldwide reputation for being friendly and welcoming. The 2010 Vancouver Winter Olympic and Paralympic Games were a success on the world stage, running safely and smoothly.

Most tourism textbooks tend to focus on one or two areas of tourism, such as hospitality, travel, event planning, or marketing. This book views the industry as a whole, demonstrating the interrelatedness of the components with each other. Earlier versions of this text focused on the eight core sectors of tourism that were initially segmented in the mid-1990s. At the turn of the millennium, North American countries reviewed all of their business dealings. At that time, the North American Industry Classification System, or NAICS, was developed to allow for increased comparability of country statistics; the implementation of the NAICS reduced the number of tourism industry sectors to five: transportation, accommodations, food and beverage services, recreation and entertainment, and travel services. This version of *Snapshots* has been revised to reflect this commonly used NAICS classification system.

The text is divided into three parts. Part 1 includes topics such as reasons for the growth of tourism, theories about why people travel, the impact of tourists on a culture, tourism planning and development, and the marketing of tourism. It is important that students understand these basic concepts before exploring the five NAICS components of tourism, which are fully discussed in Part 2. Part 3 looks at the issues, challenges, and future of tourism in Canada.

New to This Edition

Key revisions to this edition include the following:

- Transition from the eight components of tourism to the more commonly accepted five components of the North American Industry Classification System (NAICS)
- Expanded coverage of recent occurrences affecting tourism, including technological advances, safety and security, as well as ongoing severe weather events
- Information from research papers discussing the cultural impacts of tourism, tourism's effect on the ecosystem (its carbon footprint), and new green programs being used by the sector
- Updated Footprints, Snapshots, and Case Studies
- Additional discussion of travel patterns, including a closer look at ethics and how to serve travellers who have disabilities
- Travel statistics updates
- More comprehensive coverage of e-commerce and technology

Text Contents

Part 1 comprises three chapters. Chapter 1 introduces the Canadian tourism sector and provides general knowledge of tourism as a whole, including the North American Industry Classification System (NAICS) and the impact on tourism from the Western Hemisphere Travel Initiative (WHTI). Chapter 2 deals with the "people factor" of tourism—guests and hosts. Included in this section are theories of motivation that affect travel and a summary of the positive and negative effects of tourism on a city, region, province, or country. Chapter 3 looks at planning for, developing, and marketing tourism, the various stages that are required during planning, and some fundamental communication tools used in tourism.

Part 2 looks more closely at each of the five core sectors of the Canadian tourism industry as outlined by NAICS. Chapter 4 discusses transportation by land, sea, and air. It reviews the organizations, legislation, and trends that influence the transportation industry, as well as the theory behind travel choice. Chapter 5 explores the accommodation industry, including its variety, its organization, and its marketing techniques. Chapter 6 reviews the food and beverage industry, examining the spectrum of full-service and fast-food restaurants, and the contract food service business.

The next two chapters examine recreation and entertainment—specifically attractions (Chapter 7), and adventure tourism and outdoor recreation (Chapter 8). Chapter 9 focuses specifically on events, a field that overlaps somewhat with entertainment, but also includes factors that make it unique in tourism. The subsequent two chapters deal with tourism services: Chapter 10 discusses the important role of travel services, tourism's channel of distribution, and Chapter 11 highlights how tourism is supported by indirect industries such as the media, the government, and organizations and associations.

Finally in Part 3, Chapter 12 examines the current challenges and issues facing the industry, including the anticipated future of tourism in Canada, how tourism projects and communication are evolving, and the role that tourism may play in Canada's prosperity.

We hope that the variety of teaching opportunities provided with each chapter will make this introductory course an exciting one for both instructors and students.

How to Use This Text

Most chapters in this text contain a historical component, explaining how the industry as we know it today has developed. History roots tourism within a context, frequently demonstrating how key portions of the industry grew from the growth of trade between regions and the growth of the manufacturing and industrial sectors, not to mention military actions and the corresponding needs that come with supply lines. Not all important dates are covered, so students should feel free to add dates identified by their instructors as significant. Short biographies, called "Snapshots," are interspersed throughout the book and introduce students to some important movers and shakers in the industry. These Snapshots focus both on early pioneers of the tourism sector and on Canadians making a difference in tourism today.

"In Practice" segments, short case studies, and the "Footprint" discussions offer opportunities for in-class discussion. Chapters contain an array of features that provide extra resources to both the instructor and the student. Learning objectives and key terms are set out at the beginning of the chapters, while case studies and summary points end each chapter. There are also questions at the end of each chapter that are based on chapter material and may be used as out-of-class assignments, quiz questions, or small-group discussion questions. Weblinks can now be found in the margins for additional information on important topics.

Supplemental Materials

The **Companion Website** for *Snapshots* will benefit students and instructors alike. For students, this website provides timely updates, self-assessment quizzes for each chapter, and links to other internet resources. Go to www.pearsoncanada.ca/nickerson.

The **Instructor's Manual**, provided free to adopters, includes lecture outlines, topics for discussion, and suggested projects and research assignments. In this new edition, suggested online research activities have been added. This supplement is available online and can be accessed through the instructor link on the Text Enrichment Site or through Pearson's Instructor Central site at www.pearsoncanada.ca/highered.

MyTest includes multiple-choice, true/false, and essay questions for each chapter and is available in both print and computerized formats.

Each chapter of the text is also outlined in a series of **PowerPoint Presentations**, which include key points, figures, and tables.

Pearson's **Technology Specialists** work with faculty and campus course designers to ensure that Pearson technology products, assessment tools, and online course materials are tailored to meet your specific needs. This highly qualified team is dedicated to helping schools take full advantage of a wide range of educational resources by assisting with the integration of a variety of instructional materials and media formats. Your local Pearson Canada sales representative can provide you with more details on this service program.

CourseSmart is a new way for instructors and students to access textbooks online anytime from anywhere. With thousands of titles across hundreds of courses, CourseSmart helps instructors choose the best textbook for their classes and gives students a new option to buy the assigned textbook as a lower-cost eTextbook. For more information, visit www.coursesmart.com.

Acknowledgments

The effort of crafting an up-to-date textbook is truly a team endeavour, without which this book would not have been possible. First of all, I must thank Paula Kerr for her guidance and counsel over the past two decades; every student should be lucky enough to find such a trusted mentor who becomes both a peer and a friend. Being invited to collaborate on the new edition of this text, a project she has helmed since 2001, is truly an honour. Thanks also go out to my colleagues at the Canadian Tourism Human Resource Council and the Canadian Tourism Commission whose influence and support is evident in the content throughout this book. The team at Pearson Canada has shown great support and patience throughout this revision cycle and have set a very high bar in publishing support. David Le Gallais and Kathleen McGill were fantastic resources early in the project, helping a novice author to navigate the world of textbooks. The guidance of both Megan Burns and Christine Langone kept this project (and me) on track and on schedule; working with them has been nothing short of a pleasure. Deep thanks go to my wife, Andrea, who read each page of this text with me. Her keen editorial eye, understanding of textual flow, and her patience in lending an ear whenever I needed to talk through issues are appreciated more than she'll ever know. My two young sons, Austin and Zachary, showed uncharacteristic patience while, in their words, "Daddy worked on his book"; they have many outstanding IOUs to the ice cream store.

A final thanks to our reviewers, who included the following:

June Alton, College of the North Atlantic

Jane Banks, Georgian College

Pierre Deslauriers, Concordia University

Susan Gray, Fanshawe College

Kim McLeod, Capilano University

Ken Reynolds, St. Clair College of Applied Arts and Technology

L. Graham Smith, University of Western Ontario

Kim Wilmink, Fanshawe College

Steve Yurkiw, Red River College

William C. Murray
Mount Saint Vincent University

Understanding Tourism

Key terms

agritourism
common currency
culinary tourism
domestic tourist
ecotourism
excursionist
foreign tourist

inbound tourist
leakage
le grand tour
LGBT tourism
medical tourism
multiplier effect
outbound tourist

same-day visitors
sector
spa tourism
tourism
tourist dollars
travel deficit
trip

Learning objectives

Having read this chapter you will be able to

1. Describe the historical beginnings of the tourism industry.

2. Discuss the importance of tourism to the overall economic well-being of Canada.

3. Identify and explain the sectors of tourism as designated by the North American Industry Classification System.

4. Illustrate reasons for growth in the tourism industry over the past 100 years.

5. Explain the roles played by key Canadian and international tourism organizations.

6. Identify key issues faced by the tourism industry, both presently and in the future.

There are few places in the world today where the tourism industry does not play a major role. Tourism encourages people within a country to spend money, it brings in travel dollars from outside a country, and it provides a significant level of employment. In 2010, in Canada, all of the various sectors of the tourism industry employed over 1.6 million Canadians,[1] approximately one in every ten Canadians looking for work. Much of the world's population has had experience with some part of the tourism industry and many nations depend on tourism as one of their biggest sources of revenue.

In this text, you will learn about the scope of the tourism industry and explore each of the sectors that combine to make up this industry. The historical building blocks will be uncovered, along with the key areas of change and the speed with which these changes are fundamentally altering our industry. By examining our roots and understanding our present situation, we will be able to look ahead at the future opportunities available in the Canadian tourism industry.

At the turn of the twentieth century, your life would have been very different from the one you live now. Your great-grandparents likely heard about the Wright brothers' marvellous accomplishment—the first flight of an aircraft in 1903—but it would have taken weeks to see a picture of the event. Instantaneous communication had not yet materialized; the first radio news program was not transmitted until 1920 and television for the masses was still fifty years away.

The speed of development since that first flight has been intense. In just sixty-six short years, we have not only built aircraft that can fly faster than the speed of sound, but have also placed people on the moon, the kind of feat of which fairy tales were once made. Just as impressive, the first moon landing made by Neil Armstrong was watched and listened to, live, by millions around the world because television sets and radios had become standard household items.

The speed of advancement continues at a staggering rate. Today, the very beginning of space tourism has become a reality. Seven "tourists" have already visited the International Space Station and over 400 people have paid deposits for a suborbital flight on SpaceShipTwo, currently being constructed by Virgin Galactic.[2] The speed of communication has also followed suit, with instant sharing of live video and messages on mobile phones and through social media such as Twitter and Facebook.

Although tourism has undergone major transitions over the last millennium, with changes in technology, transportation, and social organization, the fundamental conditions of the development of tourism still exist: travellers must have both the ability and the willingness to travel.

THE EARLY BEGINNINGS OF TOURISM

As an industry, tourism is relatively young; however, the building blocks of tourism go back almost to the beginning of civilization. The infrastructure of early tourism originally occurred as a by-product of planning and development in other areas, including military, economic, and religious activities. For thousands of years, people did not have the funds much less the time to travel. And even if they had the ability, travelling far from home was too dangerous—so, early in our history, people kept close to home and focused on food and family. The world remained a mysterious place.

In the early days of civilization, people seldom travelled unless it was to search for food sources; to adjust to climate changes; or to escape other stronger, threatening tribes. They travelled on foot and were exposed to many dangers. Historical research suggests that some people in early civilizations, often linked by marriage and common ideals, did travel occasionally for the purpose of business and pleasure. Archaeologists have unearthed artefacts from digs in North and South America, Europe, and Asia that indicate that tribes would meet at certain times of the year to perform religious celebrations, to conduct tribal business, to trade, and to dance and socialize.

As civilizations developed, the strongest tribes would seek to control the resources of an area. Armies conquered entire regions, enslaving the inhabitants and taking their possessions, which increased not only the conquering tribe's influence, but their wealth as well. Traders travelled to different lands to find goods to sell at home. At a basic level, these could be considered the original business travellers. Two peoples of ancient times who became noted as traders, rather than warriors, were the Sumerians and the Phoenicians. They focused on industry to increase their wealth, and they established early trade routes in the African and southern European corridors. The Sumerians were the first nation to develop coinage, used as payment for goods. The Phoenicians, noted sailors, were responsible for creating some of the first maps, showing their system of water routes, to help guide others.

Three major civilizations dominated the world between 4800 BCE and 300 CE: the Egyptians, the Greeks, and the Romans. Each civilization in its own way provided for the advancement of travel activities. Ancient people travelled frequently to conduct trade; to complete government business; and for educational, religious, and social reasons. The Egyptians developed strong central governments and large, flourishing cities, which attracted travellers. Many of their cities were built along the Nile River, with its northward currents and southward breezes. Travel by boat was easy and safe, making these urban centres accessible.

By 900 BCE, groups of Greek-speaking peoples had formed a network of city-states that exchanged goods and maintained open ports and roads. Researchers, explorers, traders, and philosophers, the Greeks made travel part of their education and way of life. City-states and shrines flourished, becoming destinations in themselves. As tourists do today, the Greeks loved to shop, eat, and drink. They loved the theatre and spectator sports, and they travelled great distances to partake of these forms of entertainment.

By 400 BCE, a new culture was on the rise that would grow into one of the most successful empires in the history of the Western world. Starting at the tail end of the Republic and continuing into the rise of the Empire, the Romans developed a travel infrastructure, constructing roadways that allowed for the consolidation of their growing realm. These roads were originally designed for both commercial needs and the swift movement of military troops and equipment. The Romans established colonies across Europe, ranging from North Africa and Asia Minor to France, Germany, and Great Britain, and wherever they moved, they built roads. At the height of the roadway system, it spanned over 400 000 km and over 20% of roads were paved.

The roads also transported the Roman civilization, including culture, language, and way of life. A strong, central government and well-established Roman laws and local magistrates provided peace and security for the empire for many years. Roman coinage became the universally accepted currency. Travel became easier and safer.

Lodging and taverns sprang up to care for travellers in towns that developed along the roads. Food service, bars, and a wide variety of entertainment flourished in the cities. Roman shrines and baths became destinations for recreational travellers, and Roman business people established some of the first fast-food-style restaurants to accommodate them.

In sum, more than any other ancient civilization, the Roman Empire clearly illustrates the conditions under which tourism may flourish—peace and prosperity. Travel modes were easily accessible and safe, and there was a common currency, a common language, and a well-established legal system. Where these conditions exist, people will be encouraged to travel.

At a similar time period in China, roadways and marine routes were developed to move silk from the emperor's central region to the more western edges of the Chinese territory. Silk had great value and was in high demand. Over time, the silk trade grew throughout Central Asia, into Northern India, along the Mediterranean, and finally into Europe. The land and maritime routes combined equalled over 10 000 km in distance, and, eventually, the silk routes connected with the Roman roads, linking trade between the Han Dynasty and the Roman Empire.

As Roman society began to break down and the central government became unable to keep up with the demands of its extensive empire, the peace and prosperity that made travel easy crumbled. By 400 CE, the Roman Empire had fragmented, and the officials and soldiers who maintained the Roman peace had been recalled to Rome. As a consequence, few people risked travel. The collapse of the Roman Empire ushered in unrest and destabilized the region for close to a thousand years, a period referred to as the Dark Ages.

By the turn of the millennium, the Roman Catholic Church had gained political and social control in many areas of Europe. The growth of towns and a class of people with disposable income combined with the church's support of pilgrimages to religious sites. Inns and hostels grew up along pilgrimage routes to support these medieval travellers. Feudal society had also created a class of wealthy warriors without any lands to govern. So when the Byzantine emperor asked for help pushing back the advance of Muslim Seljuk Turks, the church organized these warriors and sent them on crusades—large-scale military pilgrimages focused on returning Christian access to holy places in and around Jerusalem. The Crusades, nine in total, had a profound influence on medieval culture. One effect was the return of knights and their retinues with stories and souvenirs from faraway lands and cultures. Another was the growth of industries to serve travellers—inns, blacksmiths, traders, and others—along the routes that the Crusaders followed.

Over the course of the Middle Ages, much of the known world was being carved up into kingdoms, with strong families uniting their lands under one rule of law. Towns and cities became larger and stronger. Noblemen moved throughout their lands in caravans, continually checking in on all the towns within their fiefdoms. Merchants began to venture farther into the countryside in search of luxury goods for the wealthy classes. One of the best-known travelling merchants of this period is Marco Polo, whose voyages took him from Europe to the Far East. The spices, silks, and merchandise with which he returned created great interest in foreign lands and cultures.

The Crusades lasted for nearly three centuries. They were closely followed by the largest pandemic in human history, often referred to simply as the Black Death, a disease that is estimated to have cut Europe's populace in half and reduced the world's population by 100 million in just fifty years. A great deal of fear came with each wave of this pandemic, and with each wave, many people who had the means and ability to leave highly populated cities fled to the seclusion of the countryside.

The fourteenth century brought happier and healthier times. Military action was controlled and peace was more prevalent, making room for a renewed focus on art, philosophy, and culture. This was the time of the Renaissance, a period lasting nearly three centuries, a time full of curiosity, intellectual expansion, and humanism, in which the roles of reason and science held a prominent place side-by-side with religion.

In the seventeenth and eighteenth centuries, England's nobility, recognizing the lack of educational opportunities at home, and valuing the cultural opportunities available in France, Italy, and Greece, began to send their sons to the European continent to be educated. This strategy, dubbed **le grand tour**, prepared young nobles for their futures by immersing them in various languages and cultures. They were educated in financial matters, honed their diplomatic skills, and developed a thorough knowledge of religious and legal institutions. The early format of *le grand tour* focused specifically on males in their early to mid-twenties and was rigid in design with expected outcomes. It often lasted multiple years, and included stays in Paris, Florence, Rome, Zurich, and Vienna. Later in the eighteenth century, the tour became less of a formal education and more of a life experience; the length of the tour shortened to less than a year and the age of the travellers included people in their thirties and forties, perhaps revealing some early forms of repeat tourism. *Le grand tour* still plays a part in modern tourism, but modern tourists complete it in days, not years.

The Growth of Tourism over the Last 200 Years

Between 1800 and 1939, there were many changes in modes of travel. Steamships and steam-powered trains made crossing the oceans and continents both easy and available. The invention of the automobile accelerated the travel industry by providing a way for people to travel independently, choosing their own time of travel, routes, and destinations. These characteristics still exist today, maintaining the automobile's dominance as the vehicle of choice in modern times. In 1903, the era of air travel was born when the Wright brothers took their first powered flight in Kitty Hawk, North Carolina. In mere decades, air routes had been established in major cities in North America and Europe. Due to powered flight, the time it took to travel across the oceans had been reduced from weeks and months to days and hours. With fast and accessible modes of travel available, tourism grew.

The outbreak of World War I in 1914 stifled pleasure tourism. Safety concerns rose, along with the reduction of both time and money that people could dedicate to travel. However, investments made by governments in military infrastructure, including substantial advancements in land- and air-based travel, served as a springboard for tourism growth after the end of the war. Overseas transportation was available at more reasonable rates and became more accessible to ordinary people. Beyond the development of better infrastructure, there was also an increase in people's interest in travel. Military personnel returning home often held back any stories of battle but shared experiences about the cities, countryside, and people of Europe. The curiosity of family and friends to see these places expanded as people desired tactile connections to historic events.

The Roaring Twenties ended abruptly on "Black Tuesday," October 29, 1929, with the financial collapse that resulted in the Great Depression. The impact was felt around the world; in a six-month period, unemployment in Canada moved from just over 2% to 21%; one in five Canadians who were actively seeking work could not find paid employment. For the next ten years, people suffered the largest economic crisis on record. Obviously, for the average family, this removed both the financial ability and the free time for pleasure travel. Many people, specifically men, did travel for business reasons, moving from town to town, picking up jobs as they could. However, little of their money was spent on tourist-related activities.

The Great Depression came to an end with the beginning of World War II in 1939. Safe travel once again became difficult and free time was still rare, therefore very few people travelled for pleasure. But once again, governments invested large amounts of resources to push technology forward to gain military superiority. Advancements in flight design, aerodynamics, and speed were made quickly; ships were built stronger, larger, and faster; engines to push land-based vehicles continued to evolve. All of these developments were made to support the movement of troops, supplies, and weapons during battle. After the war, these modern machines fuelled a new growth in tourism. Industrialized nations became prosperous, and with that prosperity came more discretionary income and time. Time, money, peace, safe and accessible transportation systems, and common currency—all of these things have helped build today's tourism sector.

After World War II, many nations also demanded that lasting world peace be a united goal. To this end, the United Nations was formed. At the heart of the United Nations charter is the belief that understanding the identities and beliefs of other cultures would lead to greater mutual understanding and a peaceful co-existence. Peace and an absence of conflict are the cornerstones of tourism, and peace has allowed tourism to reach global heights, providing jobs and revenue to nations of all sizes.

Conditions Necessary for Tourism Development[3]

Ability

1. Destinations need to be accessible.
2. Infrastructure must exist to transport people to and from destinations, as well as to accommodate and nourish them.
3. People must have sufficient discretionary, or "extra," income to travel.
4. People must have available and sufficient time to travel.

Willingness

1. All components of travel, including transportation, accommodation, and food service, need to be perceived as reasonably safe.
2. The destination must be sufficiently interesting and attractive.

Issues for Today and Tomorrow

No history of tourism will ever be complete without mentioning the modern risks posed by terrorist attacks. In the attacks on the World Trade Center (WTC) and the Pentagon on September 11, 2001, more than 2800 people from eighty-six countries, including twenty-four Canadians, were killed. The advances in modern communication magnified the impact as millions of people watched in real time as two jumbo jets exploded into the twin towers and the World Trade Center collapsed. It was the first large-scale terrorist attack on U.S. soil, and it made use of a common mode of transportation as a weapon. The world was stunned. Commercial airlines have been hijacked in the past, and bombs have been placed on commercial airliners causing midair explosions (as with Pan Am's Flight 101 over Lockerbie, Scotland, in 1992). However, the use of fully fuelled jumbo jets as guided bombs to attack a specific target shocked the world and brought the insecurity of travel home to many.

Tourists can also be caught in the violent struggles of warring factions in a foreign destination. Some regions of the world, although attractive to travellers, remain unstable and volatile. Two Canadian travellers enjoying a night out in Indonesia were killed in October 2002, when terrorists bombed the nightclub they were in. London, England, has experienced a series of bombings, and in July 2005, terrorists bombed the Egyptian luxury resort Sharm El-Shaikh, killing eighty-three people and wounding 200. In the last few years, pirating has seen a dramatic increase in many regions, from the coasts of Somalia, where pirates have been attacking both transport ships and personal yachts, to the waters around northern Mexico, where drug cartels have been attacking and robbing tourists. Unfortunately, tourism has become a target for terrorists. Tourists and tourism destinations are considered "soft" targets of opportunity as operators, government, and travellers strive to find a balance between security and openness.

Despite these events, the United Nations' World Tourism Organization still holds to the belief that one of the ways to build a peaceful world is for people from different nations to meet and learn more about one another. Tourism can provide a formula for friendship that no amount of government legislation can match. There is no better umbrella under which to foster such friendships.

Current State of the Tourism Industry

According to the World Tourism Organization (UNWTO), tourism reached an all-time high in 2010, with 935 million international travellers,[4] up 6.7% or 58 million travellers from the declines experienced throughout 2009. International travel in 2010 set a new record, exceeding the levels of the former peak year, 2008, by 22 million travellers or over 2.4%.[5] In 2010, all regions of the world showed an increase in the number of visitors over the preceding year despite continued concerns over economic uncertainty, the price of fuel, regional conflicts, cross-border security measures, and serious environmental events, including the 2011 earthquake and subsequent tsunami in Japan and the 2010 volcanic eruption in Iceland that resulted in the largest disruption on European air travel since World War II.

How has Canadian tourism fared over the past two years? Security between Canada and its largest international tourism market, the United States, has continued to tighten. Passage of the Western Hemisphere Travel Initiative (WHTI),

The magnificent natural landscapes of Canada, such as the peaks surrounding Moraine Lake in Banff National Park, are a valuable part of our tourism industry.
(Photo courtesy National Capital Commission.)

legislation requiring both U.S. and Canadian citizens to carry valid passports when crossing the border, has created additional barriers of entry. (This legislation was designed as an additional filter to prevent potential terrorists from entering the United States across the Canadian border.)

However, while many U.S. and Canadian citizens still do not hold a passport, and the new procedures have created longer border waits, Canada still enjoys a healthy tourism relationship with its southern neighbour. Over 11.7 million trips were made in 2010 from the United States into Canada, generating $6.3 billion in spending. Yet the largest consumer of the Canadian tourism product remains Canadians, with domestic revenues exceeding $59 billion, just over 80% of the economic impact of tourism in 2010.[6]

THE CANADIAN TOURISM PRODUCT: AN OVERVIEW

Why are these figures important to Canadians? They are important because tourism is a "product" we sell, and the revenues from this product are used to help balance the budget and reduce the deficit. Tourism is referred to as an industry or a **sector**, which is a part of the national economy. For example, you have probably heard the terms *manufacturing sector* or *private sector*.

Tourism, as a sector, is much fractured. The products it produces can vary from an attraction like Disney World to a historical site outside of Red River, Manitoba; from a cute single bedroom at the Savoy Arms Bed & Breakfast to a luxurious eight-bedroom cabin at the Fairmont Jasper Park Lodge; from a gourmet meal at Canoe to a hot dog bought at a local hockey game. The comparisons continue, but one point can be made—tourism products are *integrally connected*, meaning one product does not flourish by itself but needs other, different components to help sell it.

In 1993, the Canadian government took a big step toward better understanding the industry by appointing a committee to review the scope of the industry and its impact on Canadian society. The Buchanan Report, a white paper requested by the Chrétien government to review the tourism industry, was issued in 1994; although the numbers have changed, many of the points it made are valid today. The Buchanan Report[7] stated that:

i.   As an industry, tourism has the ability to create more jobs at a faster pace than any other industry in Canada.

ii. The dollars generated by the tourism industry benefit all levels of government, with nearly 40% of revenues split between federal, provincial, and municipal organizations.

iii. Tourism employs more females, more young adults, more visible minorities, more people re-entering the workforce, and more new immigrants than any other industry in Canada.

iv. The quality of jobs created by the industry range from entry level to highly paid executive positions, many of them requiring a strong set of personal skills and a higher set of work skills than generally understood by the public.

v.   The value of tourism is vastly underrated and misunderstood by all levels of government as well as the Canadian public.

Over the next several years, two steps were taken to ensure the continued growth of this industry: the establishment both of the Canadian Tourism Commission (CTC) and the Canadian Tourism Human Resource Council (CTHRC). The CTC became responsible for promoting all areas of the tourism industry, both at home and on a global basis. The CTHRC was charged with identifying and developing training standards and programs for all areas and levels of the industry. At that time, the tourism sector was identified as having eight interlocking subsectors or components: *transportation, accommodations, food and beverage, attractions, events, adventure tourism and outdoor recreation, travel services,* and *tourism services.*

Many tourists come to Canada to enjoy our climate and recreational activities.
(Photo courtesy Canadian Tourist Commission.)

Early Division of an Industry

The Eight Components of the Tourism Sector

1. **Transportation:** All modes of transportation to and within a destination
2. **Accommodations:** Forms of lodging at all levels of service
3. **Food and Beverage:** The largest sector, encompassing food service and drink
4. **Attractions:** Permanent sites that educate and entertain visitors
5. **Events:** Temporary activities that last a short period of time as single happenings or in some recurring form
6. **Adventure Tourism and Outdoor Recreation (ATOR):** Activities that provide hands-on, physical interaction between visitors and the environment
7. **Travel Services:** Support services that work with customers providing information, packages, and sales services
8. **Tourism Services:** Support services that work with tourism businesses providing funding, research, education, consultancy, and networking opportunities

THE NORTH AMERICAN INDUSTRIAL CLASSIFICATION SYSTEM (NAICS)

Several years ago, Canada and Mexico engaged in discussions with the U.S. Department of Labor to update and refine its Standard Industrial Classification System. This would allow all three countries to produce common statistics. These common groups would use the same terminology and sector information, enabling each to determine the health of its own economy and its projected growth rate, and producing figures that could be compared amongst the three economies.

This review also provided the United States with a chance to update its classification system to reflect the rapid changes that have occurred in the last 40 years. The North American Industrial Classification System (NAICS, pronounced "nakes") has classified all economic activity as either goods-producing sectors or service-producing sectors. It recognizes tourism as one common service-producing sector, further subdivided into five distinct industry groups.[8] These groups are: accommodations, food and beverage, recreation and entertainment, transportation, and travel services (see Figure 1.1). In doing so, NAICS has redistributed tourism industries from the eight components used by Canada in the past (outlined above), to five by combining attractions, events, and ATOR into a single group called "entertainment." These groups focus the classification system to answer five basic questions: Where will I sleep? Where will I eat? What will I do? How will I get there? Who will help me do this? Although the eight-component model was distinctly Canadian, this text will focus on the NAICS classification currently in use by the industry.

Accommodations

This group brings together all forms of lodging, including hotels, motels, inns, campgrounds, and resorts. Services in accommodations range from the most basic, rustic elements found in the backcountry to luxurious amenities provided to upscale

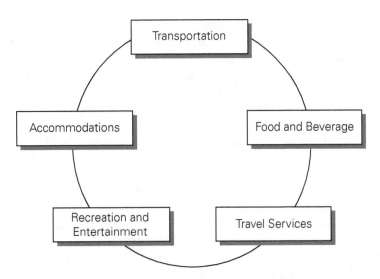

FIGURE 1.1
The five distinct
sectors of the tourism
industry within North
America (NAICS).

travellers. Due to the range in accommodation styles, services also differ greatly. The business traveller in Vancouver requires a comfortable room with full service, a family on vacation may require a room that sleeps four, and the fisherman wants a rustic cabin near a lake that promises good fishing. Over 11% of people working in the tourism sector find employment in the accommodations group,[9] which includes jobs such as front-desk clerk, hostel manager, health club manager, valet, camp counsellor, night auditor, groundskeeper, marketing manager, and room attendant.

Food and Beverage

The food and beverage component is the largest in the tourism sector, employing over 47% of all tourism workers, and provides perhaps the greatest opportunity for the entrepreneur. This industry includes all full-service restaurants (fine dining, family style, specialty, and theme), all limited service eating places (fast food), and drinking establishments (bars, pubs, and taverns). Additionally, contracted food service in lodging facilities, airports, and arenas, plus catering firms and gourmet food shops are included under the umbrella of the food and beverage group. Some of the jobs available in this area include wine steward, banquet chef, baker, bartender, nightclub manager, food service director, catering manager, and food server.

Recreation and Entertainment

Perhaps the most compacted of all the industry groups is the recreation and entertainment group, combining all of the pieces that were once separated into attractions, events, adventure tourism, and outdoor recreation. This new group accounts for over 21% of all employees within the tourism sector. Any activity that provides entertainment, education, or involvement has been brought under one heading. Short-term events such as film festivals, sporting events, and seasonal events like the Calgary Stampede, are available only for limited periods, sometimes annually and other times as a one-time-only gathering.

Attractions remain accessible and open year-round, including parks, certain rivers and waterways, casinos, zoos, and historical sites. Some attractions are completely natural, augmented by operators only to provide safety and access for visitors. Canada's unique and varied geography offers many world-class natural attractions, such as Peggy's Cove in Nova Scotia, Niagara Falls in Ontario, and the Columbia Ice Fields in Alberta. Other attractions are manufactured, providing an even broader choice for tourists. These can include developed sites such as Kingsbrae Garden in New Brunswick, Wild Water Kingdom in Ontario, and the Casino de Montréal in Quebec.

Adventure tourism leans toward more vigorous and involved physical activities. The mountain regions in Canada attract avid skiers, snowboarders, mountain bikers, and climbers each year, while the vast waterways provide ample opportunities for sailing, kayaking, and white water rafting. Less strenuous activities that embrace nature, including hunting, golf, and whale watching, are all activities that attract key niche groups to Canada. Ecotourism, travel that is intended to support the study of earth's biodiversity, also falls into the recreation and entertainment industry. Ecotourism continues to be a growing market, and Canada's geography makes this country a fascinating destination. Polar bears, tidal pools, archaeological sites, tundra, and vast wildernesses put Canada high on the list of places to visit for many. Some jobs in the recreation and entertainment field include heritage interpreter, attraction facility guide, public relations manager, special events supervisor, meeting planner, exhibit designer, ski instructor, lifeguard, golf professional, and recreation director.

Transportation

The transportation industry group includes all of the modes of travel that provide visitors with a way to get to a destination and to get around once the destination is reached. Businesses within this group include airlines, railroads, cruise lines, tour bus companies, and car rental companies. Employment in transportation represents over 16% of the entire sector. More so than any other industry, skills developed in one area of transportation are easily transferred to another. A reservation agent for an airline, for example, could work for a cruise ship or a railroad with little additional training. Jobs in this industry group include pilots, reservations agents, cruise directors, car rental agents, and customer service agents.

Travel Services

The smallest group within the tourism sector is travel services. However, the size of this group hardly reflects its importance to customers and operators. The 2.9% of all tourism workers who make up the travel services group support all four of the other groups, sustaining their interconnective nature. Tour planners and package coordinators bring together transportation, accommodations, food service, and activities into packages based on high levels of product knowledge and a keen understanding of customer needs. Industry operators receive assistance through funding for the development of new small businesses, industry advocates who lobby governments at all levels to create more attractive tourism conditions, and education professionals who continue to train tourism professionals. Most of these people work behind the scenes assisting operators to be more successful. Careers in this field might include tour guides, sales representatives, destination development specialists, travel writers, teachers, accountants, and travel agency owners.

Interestingly, Canadians are often unaware of the magnitude of the tourism sector and its impact on both employment and the economy. Additionally, they do not fully understand how important tourism is to their community, region, province, or country. In fact, many people working in the tourism sector are unaware that they play a crucial role within the industry. For example, if you ask your local bartenders if they work in tourism, many will say "no." Yet they will all agree that they work in food and beverage, which is the largest single industry in the tourism sector. Even though many bartenders serve mostly local customers and very few tourists, because they belong to the food and beverage industry, they are considered to be an integral part of tourism in Canada.

UNDERSTANDING TOURISM TERMINOLOGY

Although the industry groups of the tourism sector have been outlined, what in fact is tourism? **Tourism**, is defined by both the United Nations World Tourism Organization (UNWTO) and the United Nations Statistical Commission as "the activities of persons travelling to and staying in places outside their environment for not more than one consecutive year for leisure, business, and other purposes."[10] Put simply, the tourism sector transports people, provides them with accommodations, food, and beverages, and then entertains or educates them. Tourism continues to expand, and as visitors generate new interests, new tourism product groupings appear. To share a discussion about the tourism industry, it is valuable to understand some of the common terms used within this sector.

Speaking the Same Language

To begin our discussion on tourism, we need some common basic terminology. We have already looked at the new NAICS groups and seen some of the numbers they have produced. To make these figures understandable to any person reading and using them, parameters have been set. Here are some of the key terms used in Canada and other countries around the world when discussing tourism: *trip, foreign tourist, domestic tourist, excursionist, multiplier effect, travel deficit,* and *leakage.*

In Canada, a **trip** is defined as any travel that takes a person 80 km from their place of residence for any reason other than a commute to work or school, travel in an ambulance or to a hospital or clinic, or a trip that is longer than one year.[11] This definition excludes the trip within your own country that is shorter than 80 km.

Canadians love to travel, and they like to travel outside Canada. Here are some of the reasons:

a) Our cold winter weather makes sunny, warm climates popular in winter.

b) Many Canadians have relatives who live outside the country, whom they must travel to visit.

c) Other countries promote their attractions more effectively than Canada does.

d) Canadians are not aware of the tourism treasures within their borders.

In 1937, the Committee of Statistics Experts of the League of Nations defined **foreign tourists** as persons visiting a country, other than that in which they usually reside, for a period of at least 24 hours. Foreign tourists may also be called **inbound tourists** (likewise, Canadians who visit other countries may be described as **outbound tourists**).

Domestic tourists are people travelling within the country in which they reside, staying for at least 24 hours, and travelling at least 80 km from their homes.[12]

According to United Nations guidelines,[13] you are a tourist if

- you are travelling for pleasure, for family reasons, to learn more about the world in general, or for health or religious purposes
- you are travelling for business reasons other than direct remuneration by the country you are visiting
- you are visiting the country as part of a sea cruise or travel package

On the other hand, you *are not* considered a tourist if

- you are actively going to take up an occupation at your destination
- you are establishing residency in the destination country
- you are attending an educational institution and establishing a residence
- you are staying less than 24 hours

Because travel has become both easier and faster, people often travel 80 km from their homes for recreation or entertainment without staying overnight. By definition, they cannot be called tourists because they are not away from home for enough time. The tourism sector calls these travellers **excursionists**, or **same-day visitors**. In Canada, an excursionist is any person who travels at least 80 km from the place of residence, stays less than 24 hours, and is not commuting to work or school, or operating as part of a crew on a train, airplane, truck, bus, or ship.[14]

Tourism is a revenue producer, and much of this revenue goes back into the local economy. The **multiplier effect** of tourism dollars shows the beneficial effect this revenue has on nearly everyone in the community. For example, when tourists stay in a Ramada Hotel, they pay the hotel for their room. The Ramada takes these **tourist dollars** and uses them to pay for salaries, supplies, mortgage payments, electricity, etc.

To follow this money further down the line, let's use an example. Sally Hyung is a front-desk agent at the Ramada. She uses her salary to pay for rent, food, entertainment, transportation, dry cleaning, and so on. The grocer takes the money he receives from Sally and uses it to help pay for his rent, to buy supplies (such as eggs from local farmers), and to pay his employees' salaries. You can see that the ripple effect of tourist dollars in a community benefits just about everyone.

However, every time Canadians leave the country, their tourism dollars are lost to Canada. This loss in tourism revenues is called a **travel deficit**. Simply put, a travel deficit is the difference between the amount of money spent by visitors travelling to Canada and the money spent by Canadian residents travelling abroad, and is referred to as our *international travel account*.[15] It is also considered **leakage** of economic resources, or money, because dollars spent abroad by Canadians do not circulate and grow within our own country.

Leakage also occurs when a community cannot support the influx of tourists and must import workers and goods in order to sustain the industry. For example, the town of Banff does not have enough residents to support the throngs of tourists who arrive each summer. Every year, Banff's hotels, restaurants, and shops must hire workers from outside the community. Banff also needs to purchase supplies from larger centres like Calgary.

To use another example: Bill James, a university student from Vancouver, B.C., is working in a Banff hotel for the summer. The tourist dollars spent in his hotel are used to pay for salaries, supplies, and the mortgage. Bill uses some of his salary to pay for his living expenses in Banff, but he is also saving some of his pay to use for his last year at university. Part of what he makes is being spent in Vancouver, not Banff. This is an example of leakage. When leakage occurs, the community that hosts the tourist does not get the full benefit of the revenue generated. Leakage is particularly harmful in countries such as the Bahamas, an island group with few resources to support its large tourism sector. Most of the products needed to build and sustain its tourism industry must be purchased from other countries. This reduces the amount of tourism revenue the country is able to retain and, therefore, reduces the amount that is shared among its communities.

The Growth of Specialty Tourism

As a modern industry, tourism is still a relatively young sector. The speed of growth in transportation options and communication has opened up regions of the world unfamiliar to many people just fifty years ago. In modern economics, we are now seeing multiple generations of knowledgable travellers who have experienced the tourism product beyond the borders of their own country. With this comes a more discerning traveller, someone interested in a specialized product and service mix that suits their attitudes and interests. To satisfy the wide variety of consumer demands, many niche forms of travel services have been developed and some continue to emerge. Below are a few examples of these niche markets.

Agritourism: Agricultural tourism is a niche area that gives the visitor the chance to work on regional farms and learn more about the production of a specific product. Examples of **agritourism** might include a visit to an organic farm in Ontario's Holland Marsh or the granaries of Saskatchewan, or a vacation on a working ranch in Alberta.

Ecotourism: An expanding area of focused travel that concentrates on the education and protection of the environment. With growing concerns about global warming, often referred to as climate change, there is a distinct group of tourists seeking to increase their understanding of our biosphere—how the varying "pieces" that create the world we live in today work together to produce either positive or damaging results. This might include a vacation that helps them to understand this relationship, to become involved in nature-related experiences, and/or to see a sight that scientists have identified as endangered before it disappears. These vacations are often expensive as well as informative, so you can see why some entrepreneurs have focused on **ecotourism**.

Culinary tourism: There is a growing market of tourists interested in both the production of food and the skilful manipulation of this food into a finished dish. The popularity of **culinary tourism** has been assisted by the explosion of food- and culinary-focused television programs as well as increased interest in local food

FOOTPRINT

The David Suzuki Foundation has been a leader in creating and promoting environmental awareness since 1990. The foundation's main goals include raising awareness about climate change issues, serving as an advocate for climate issues within Canada, pursuing economic growth within the constraints of finite environmental resources, reconnecting people to nature, and building communities around conservation and eco-friendly energy issues. One of the current projects focuses on the proliferation of English ivy in Canadian forests. English ivy invades forest areas and has the ability to choke out native trees within 15 years. Teams of "ivy busters" must physically remove the plants, racing against their continual spread.

At present, over 30% of Stanley Park in Vancouver, B.C. is infested with English ivy.

What does this have to do with tourism? Tourists often visit B.C. to take part in wilderness and wildlife activities. These activities are challenged when a foreign plant species is quickly invading the native trees of the region. As a part of their education strategy, the foundation is trying to educate people about the dangers posed by English ivy to the Canadian landscape, including how they can help. According to the foundation, "what you think is a beautiful wildflower might actually be an invasive weed. Controlling invasive species in your own backyard will go a long way to reducing threats to global biodiversity."[16]

production and consumption. Culinary tourism is a broad topic and might include enjoying the cultural cuisine of Quebec, attending a seminar on growing and using herbs, taking a short course in Chinese cooking techniques at one of Canada's culinary schools, visiting a sugar bush, or touring the vineyards in B.C.'s Okanagan Valley.

LGBT Tourism: LGBT tourism is a niche tourism market focused specifically on gay, lesbian, bisexual, and transgendered people. Operators have realized that this community, defined by sexual orientation, represents a significant proportion of the population. One of the defining characteristics of pleasure travel is that visitors feel safe, comfortable, and welcome. Many tourist businesses have aligned themselves with the LGBT communities, ensuring that their destinations are LGBT-friendly and LGBT family–friendly. In an effort to bring together tourism-related activities that were gay- and lesbian-friendly, the International Gay–and Lesbian Travel Association was founded in 1983; currently, the IGLTA has over 2200 members in 83 different countries. In 2003, R Family Vacations became one of the first companies to provide luxury LGBT-focused family cruises including same-sex marriage ceremonies.

www.rfamilyvacatons.
com

Spa Tourism: Spa tourism focuses on the overall health and well-being of the traveller. Many of the world's resorts have now adopted spa programs for their clients. Guests enjoy spa services like nutrition programs, massages, and facials, while still having access to the resort's other activities like golf or tennis. Dining rooms can cater to appetites for organic, health-oriented dishes as well as to those who prefer a more traditional menu.

Medical Tourism: A branch of spa tourism, in **medical tourism** travellers choose a destination to gain access to a specific medical practice unavailable at home.

TOURISM SECTOR ASSOCIATIONS AND ORGANIZATIONS

There are many tourism associations and organizations responsible for (a) legislation and control of the industry; (b) research, development, and marketing; and (c) professional development of workers. Some of these groups will be highlighted in Chapter 11. Described below are five international organizations and five Canadian organizations that will be referred to throughout the book. You should be able to recognize their names and acronyms. Some will represent one or more industries, and many have more than one role to play. Some are strongly supported by government funding, while others support their activities using funds received from their membership base.

International Organizations

World Tourism Organization (UNWTO): The UNWTO is the official consultative organization to the United Nations on tourism. Its fundamental aim is the promotion and development of tourism, with a view to contributing to economic development, international understanding, world peace, prosperity, and universal respect for and observance of human rights and fundamental freedoms for all, without distinction as to race, sex, language, or religion. Activities of the UNWTO include providing international technical support, education, and training to member states; facilitating tourism by removing obstacles to tourists; providing security and protection to tourists; encouraging environmentally sound planning; and marketing and promoting global tourism.

www.unwto.org

World Travel and Tourism Council (WTTC): Established in 1990 and headquartered in London, England, this private organization works with governments around the world, helping them to realize the full economic impact of tourism. Its members are executives from all branches of the tourism sector. In Canada, the department that focuses on tourism's human resources is located in Vancouver, B.C.

www.wttc.org

Pacific Asia Travel Association (PATA): Founded in 1951, PATA is a good example of countries uniting for the benefit of the tourism sector. Its members come from all components of the tourism sector, and its mandate is excellence in travel and tourism through promotion, research, education, development, and marketing. PATA represents thirty-four countries in the Asia-Pacific area, and it meets annually to present research papers, discuss common problems, and examine and adjust its long-range activities to meet changing needs.

www.pata.org

International Civil Aviation Organization (ICAO): The ICAO is another consultative organization to the United Nations. Its members are governments that have a vested interest in the safe, orderly growth of the world's airline industry. Its mandates include encouraging development of safe airways and airports, discouraging unreasonable competition among airlines, and meeting the needs of the global community by providing safe, regular, efficient, and economical air transport.

www.icao.int

International Air Transport Association (IATA): Established in 1919 and completely reorganized in 1945, this organization has been responsible for

www.iata.int

SNAPSHOT

Newfoundland: Growth of an Industry

One of the most unique provinces in Canada, Newfoundland and Labrador has undergone significant changes over the last sixty years. In 1948, Newfoundland voted for confederation with Canada, becoming the eastern-most province in the nation, an agreement passed in the British North American (BNA) Act of 1949.

From the signing of the BNA Act until recent years, the province of Newfoundland and Labrador has faced a challenging economic situation. The physical separation from the rest of Canada increased the cost of exported goods, and both the weather and landscape limited options for agriculture and development. For decades, the province looked to the sea as a source of economic strength through the fishing industries. The Canadian government assisted the province by providing funds from other regions, called equalization payments. Provinces accepting these payments were often called 'have-not' provinces. After the cod fisheries collapsed in 1992, the province faced a tough situation with growing unemployment, and many Newfoundlanders left the province to find work.

Yet Newfoundland once again looked to the sea for help, not in the form of fish but rather in oil. Many jobs were created in the province thanks to the development of the Hibernia oil fields and royalties earned in oil production that started in 1997. The Terra Nova oil fields were then developed, with production beginning in 2002; although the Terra Nova project encountered many challenges, the government benefited with a stronger royalty agreement. As future projects came on board, the provincial government increased their involvement. A landmark deal was made in 2009 when then-premier Danny Williams signed an agreement to extend the Hibernia oil fields with the province holding a 10% equity stake. That year marked another important milestone: 2009 was the first year since joining confederation that the province of Newfoundland and Labrador did not receive a federal equalization payment, finally becoming a 'have' province.

The growth of the oil industry has also influenced the growth of tourism in Newfoundland and Labrador. From 2003 to 2010, there has been a 22% increase in the volume of non-residential tourists, from 424 400 to 518 500.[17] In this same period, tourism spending increased 36.9%, from $299 million to over $410 million. The growth of the oil industry increased the funds available to the provincial government to invest in facilities, infrastructure, transportation, and marketing. Small businesses first sprouted up to provide services for oil workers, including hotels, restaurants, and entertainment. These same businesses were prepared to celebrate the increased interest in Newfoundland and Labrador, specifically St. John's, and support tourism growth. As the oil industry boomed in the province, it was often said that the streets would be painted black, referring to all the investment and financial strength that came with the oil industry.

Today, tourism is a huge industry in Newfoundland and Labrador. The natural beauty of this region and the culture of warm hospitality create a unique tourism experience for hundreds of thousands of people each year. Yet, the relationships between the tourism industry and other industry successes cannot be overlooked. Tourism is often a symbiotic sector—an appreciation for other industries, as well as our own history, helps us to better understand the tourism business.

1. Discuss some of the issues that have helped Newfoundland and Labrador to develop a strong tourism industry.

2. Why do you think the growth in industries outside of tourism benefit the expansion of, or "piggyback" on, tourism?

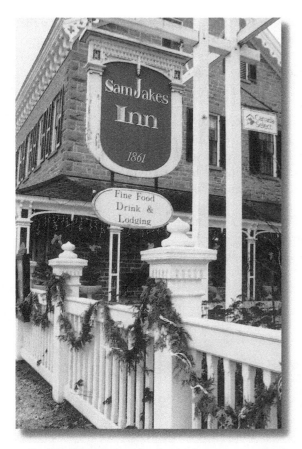

Good food and drink, and a place to sleep are essential parts of a trip. Tourists have a wide variety of accommodation choices, from elegant hotels, through country inns, to local campgrounds.
(Photo: Paula Kerr.)

much of the ease of air travel in the last fifty years. The airlines themselves created and run IATA. IATA is responsible for the one-ticket/one-trip concept and takes an active role in the safety and security of global air travel. Additional information on IATA is also found in Chapter 4.

Canadian Organizations and Associations

There are numerous organizations in Canada that contribute to the smooth operation and the future development of Canada's tourism sector. Some of the key associations include:

Canadian Tourism Commission (CTC): The CTC is a crown corporation of the Government of Canada. Their mandate is "to promote a strong and consistent image of our country to the world through Canada's tourism brand 'Canada. Keep Exploring.'"[18] Established in 1994, it plans, directs, manages, and implements programs to generate and promote Canada as a tourism destination. Additionally, it manages a relationship between industry operators; associations; and various levels of government, federally, provincially, and territorially. The CTC is discussed in Chapter 2.

www.en-corporate.
canada.travel

www.cthrc.ca

Canadian Tourism Human Resource Council (CTHRC): The CTHRC provides a national forum to facilitate human resource development activities that will support a globally competitive and sustainable Canadian tourism sector. This organization brings together the work of the provincial tourism education councils (TECs) under a national framework. You will learn more about these organizations in Chapter 2.

Tourism Industry Association of Canada (TIAC): TIAC was founded in 1931 to encourage tourism in Canada. It is a not-for-profit industry association representing tourism-related businesses, associations, institutions, and individuals. TIAC provides representation at the national level and up-to-date information on tourism-related issues. It works closely with the CTC and in 1996 was given the responsibility for running Canada's largest tourism trade show, Rendez-Vous Canada. It also works with the Canadian Border Services Agency ("Customs") to improve reception of all travellers, is a member of the CTHRC board of directors, lobbies the federal government on tourism issues, and supports research in co-operation with the Canada Tourism Research Institute (CTRI). TIAC will be discussed again in Chapter 11.

www.tiac.travel

Association of Canadian Travel Agents (ACTA): ACTA is the not-for-profit trade association for much of the travel sector in Canada. ACTA's name was changed from the Alliance of Canadian Travel Associations in June 1997. Retail travel agencies and tour operators, as well as any travel or tourism-related companies, provide a broad cross-section of tourism-related member groups.

www.acta.ca

Canadian Tourism Research Institute (CTRI): The CTRI is an integral part of Canada's foremost research institute, the Conference Board of Canada. It is privately funded. It engages in extensive research on the tourism sector, which culminates in reports that inform other tourism organizations, the industry, and the public on tourism's past performance and its anticipated future.

www.conferenceboard.
ca/topics/economics/
CTRI

In addition, each province and territory of Canada has an organization comprising government workers and sometimes private industry members. The focus of their work is the development, growth, and promotion of tourism at the provincial level with one main goal: to make that province the number one destination in Canada. For example, Tourism Saskatchewan is a partnership that is industry-led, market-driven, and dedicated to all aspects of tourism in the province.

CASE STUDY

The Inns and Outs of a New Business

Nestled within the quaint community of Stratford, Ontario, Sophie and Lukas Koch had finally found the perfect location to construct their dream inn. Both were eager to leave their jobs; Sophie was a sales manager for a large IT firm and Lukas was the head chef of a small bistro in downtown Toronto. They were excited to find a piece of land large enough to fit the custom-designed, six-bedroom lodging facility that they had commissioned nearly ten years earlier. It was easy to imagine the future views from the rear terrace that would provide guests with access to the beautiful vista of the Avon River as well as the Stratford Festival's main theatre just over the hill. At last, they could begin building their own business. However, they still needed to secure financing from their bank and had a presentation at the local branch in two weeks. They realized that, at present, their own first-hand knowledge of the industry was not strong enough to justify their business vision.

1. What information about tourism in Stratford, Ontario, do you think their banker would like to know?
2. What resources (for example, surveys, government data, comments cards, and so forth) might the Koch's use to collect timely information about their business? Where could they find this information?
3. Discuss how you think the Koch's inn might become interconnected with the other tourism businesses in the region.
4. Do you think building relationships with other organizations is important to the success of the Koch's business? Which relationships would you advise them to begin building right away?

Municipal Organizations

The smallest, but perhaps the most active tourism organization in your own community will be your local convention and visitors bureau (CVB). Much of the support the local tourist industry receives is from the city's chamber of commerce or its CVB. These groups are responsible for developing and promoting local events, bringing large tours or conferences to the city, and marketing a community's tourism products to a broader regional audience. Municipal organizations are part of tourism services (see Chapter 11).

Reasons for the Growth of Tourism

Tourism has experienced phenomenal growth over the past century. Much of this growth has taken place during the past fifty years for the following reasons:

1. **Advancements in transportation systems.** Clearly, today's travel is very different from that at the beginning of the twentieth century. Humans had not taken their first flight in 1900; by 1971, the first British/French supersonic passenger jet, the Concorde, travelled from London, England, to New York City in just under 2.5 hours. Currently, the Reaction Engine Limited A2 (or A2 for short) is under design for hypersonic flight, potentially travelling five times the speed of sound and carrying 300-plus people from Brussels to Sydney in just over 4.5 hours.[19] Planes are bigger, faster, safer, and more comfortable than ever before. Cruise ships are larger, designed with more entertainment and amenities for customers. Cars are faster, safer, and more spacious. European and Japanese trains can travel at speeds of more than 350 kph. Continued improvements to modes of transportation will make travel less expensive and more accessible to tourists, adding to the growth of tourism around the world.

2. **Advancements in media coverage.** Media outlets have become global and access to them is virtually instantaneous through the use of satellite technology and fibre optic connections. Now, as events happen around the world, we watch them unfold live on networks like CNN, stream them on our computers and mobile devices, and interact with them instantly via microblogging social media tools like Twitter. High-definition television allows millions of people to intensely experience sporting events such as the Olympics and the Super Bowl. The excitement generated on the screen helps create a desire to experience the event in person. Tragic events can also be experienced in real time; when the tsunami hit Japan on March 11, 2011, over 177 million tweets were sent in a single day on Twitter.

3. **The introduction of computer systems.** The introduction of the computer in the 1960s heralded a whole new way of doing business throughout the world. Tourism has benefited enormously from this technology. In activities that range from how guests are checked in and out of a hotel to how meals are prepared, and from how airline tickets are purchased to how air traffic controllers track the flights landing at airports, computers have aided the traveller. It would take an entire textbook to describe the ways in which computers have changed world business practices. In today's world, computer literacy is imperative for all businesses that wish to remain competitive, making the concept of lifelong learning more relevant than ever.

4. **The internet and e-commerce.** The World Wide Web stands as one of the most significant advancements in computer technology. Tourism operators and consumers exchange information, experiences, and money over the internet. Today, having an up-to-date and interactive website is a basic requirement for most industries; increasingly, businesses need to be mobile-friendly, interactive, and highly responsive to retain customers. Using the web, tourists can virtually "visit" a destination in advance, exploring hotel options and styles of restaurants, as well as the range of entertainment and recreation facilities. Making reservations and purchasing services can all be done online. Tourism operators can offer last-minute sales and communicate this incredibly quickly to customers, allowing them to sell space that would otherwise have been empty. Websites have been developed for many museums, attractions, and other tourist facilities in Canada and around the world, making the dispersal of information fast, efficient, and inexpensive.

   Currently, this technology is *enhancing* the way traditional information has been distributed in the past, not replacing it. There remains a solid segment of travellers who are less comfortable navigating the information highway and prefer handling glossy travel brochures and magazines. Yet, the speed with which travellers are adapting to electronic information, and the flexibility that it provides operators to keep data fresh is fundamentally changing the industry. It is clear that tourism companies lacking in web presence, including dynamic webpages and responsible social media interaction, will be left behind.

5. **Better educational systems.** Higher education has become the norm for many young adults. The value of continuing lifelong learning in today's technologically oriented workplace cannot be ignored. Research shows that the more education people have, the more willing they are to travel. Learning broadens a person's perspective and often creates the curiosity that will motivate that person to travel in search of new personal experiences.

6. **More disposable income.** The amount of disposable income (money left over after bills are paid) available for travel has increased because of the rising number of two-income families. The last decade ended with a serious economic downturn, limiting the available income for discretionary spending, including large trips. Yet, for many two-income households, even during recessionary times, vacation still means travel.

   The emerging market of retirees is important in any discussion about disposable income. The baby boom generation (many of whom have chosen early retirement), as well as the generation that precedes the boomers, are having a dramatic effect on tourism sales. These two generations are in good health, have money to spend, and have already travelled more extensively than any other seniors in history. With their mortgages paid off and their children educated, they are ready to continue their travel adventures. These two generations have plenty of time and disposable income to spend on tourism.

   What are they looking for? David K. Foot, a professor at the University of Toronto and lead author of *Boom, Bust & Echo*, has this to say about the "other" generation:

   > These young seniors, born in the 1930s, they really had a rough beginning. They were pre-teens in the Second World War … [they] really did pay their dues up front but they didn't have to serve.

Then they entered the job market in the post-war reconstruction of the 1950s. Did they ever have to worry about getting a job? No. They had their choice of jobs ... [and] did better than they ever expected to do...The richest people in Canada today are in their late 50s and 60s, and these are people who are now retiring.[20]

7. **More stressful lifestyles.** Stress, a by-product of the pace of modern life, creates the physical and emotional need to get away. At the same time, as companies attempt to keep costs down, benefit packages often include longer vacation periods, and overtime work may be repaid not with dollars but with additional time off. So, although the extended vacation seems to be disappearing, the long weekend and the ten-day holiday provide vacationers with the opportunity to travel more often.

8. **Declining cost of travel.** The cost of travel has declined, making it more accessible to everyone. Modes of transportation vary from the least expensive (private vehicle or bus) to the most expensive (air). Deregulation has allowed new transportation companies to compete for business, and as a result, low-cost carriers have given the consumer an alternative to the major airlines. This, in combination with the Open Skies Agreement, has provided North Americans with a wider choice of flights and destinations as well as lower-cost tickets. Frequent-traveller plans and the partnerships that have developed between destinations and the airlines have resulted in better packaging, which reduces the overall cost of travel.

9. **Better marketing and promotion.** Products sell better when they have strong marketing programs, and the tourism sector, with its many industries, has become more active and creative in this area. New tourism advertising campaigns tend to focus on fun, education, and activity, as well as provide substantial information. Electronic marketplaces bring up-to-date information not only to agents and operators but also to clients. From the federal government's perspective, lack of promotion has hurt tourism in the past, giving the Canadian Tourism Commission its primary mandate of promoting the Canadian experience. Across Canada, all levels of government are forming partnerships with local tourism operators to produce proactive marketing plans that feature state-of-the-art promotional materials.

10. **Common worldwide currency.** Travel also flourishes when a **common currency** exists. Since World War II, the introduction of credit cards, travellers' cheques, automated banking, and currency exchange machines has created easy access to money and credit while on vacation. Nowadays, currency can be easily obtained using the Interac banking machines located in just about every major destination around the world. American Express, Visa, and MasterCard all focus on the pleasures of tourism as they promote the use of their cards.

11. **Easing of government travel restrictions.** The fewer regulations a country places on international travellers, the stronger the prospect for a sound international tourism market. The European Union, where unification started in the late 1980s with the destruction of the Berlin Wall, has eased tough border requirements for documentation, and tourism has flourished. Since the implementation of the Bush government's Western Hemisphere

The seasonality of Canada has led to a wide range of exciting activities regardless of the weather.
(Photo: Horseshoe Resort.)

Travel Initiative (WHTI) legislation, which for the first time required Canadians and Americans to carry valid passports when crossing the border, Canada has seen a loss of 4.2% of its largest international tourist market—citizens of the United States. In dollar terms, that translates into $5.7 billion for the year 2006. Few Americans have valid passports and the long waits at border crossings are discouraging U.S. tourists from visiting Canada. With harsh weather a constant factor in Canadian winters, and many Canadians seeking the pleasures of Florida, the United States has not seen as dramatic a decline, but U.S. border towns are feeling the pinch of fewer Canadian spenders, despite the rising value of our dollar.

12. **Political stability. Peace and tourism go hand in hand.** The world has been, for the most part, peaceful over the past 50 years, but in countries where terrorism, civil unrest, or war is a daily threat, tourism seldom plays an important economic role. Countries such as Israel, for which tourism is a significant revenue generator, have seen tourism revenues drop significantly. Terrorist attacks in the past several years have had a negative impact on tourism, with events on September 11, 2001, being the most harmful. Analysts predicted and tourism statistics showed that the fear of terrorism, coupled with SARS and a weakened world economy, had driven down international tourism spending in Canada, with significant increases only in the past few years. On the bright side, economists now believe that tourism is much more resilient than expected.

We are fortunate that Canada has earned a reputation as a safe and peaceful country. Although we felt the backlash of the terrorist attack on the World Trade Center with falling tourism revenues, Canada remains a country that inspires traveller confidence.

The tourism sector itself has become user-friendly, providing travellers with access to many components with a single email or phone call. Transportation systems are linked with accommodations, accommodations are linked with the food and beverage industry, and the food and beverage industry is linked to all aspects of tourism. The sector is beginning to see the benefits of working together as a single tourism unit.

Summary

- In Canada, the tourism industry is one of the largest providers of employment and a massive revenue generator. In 2010, the economic impact from tourism in Canada exceeded $70 billion dollars.
- Tourism has seen many changes over the past 100 years, from the methods and speed with which we travel, to the wide variety of new destinations and activities available to the average citizen.
- The most important factors for tourists are: i) discretionary time, and ii) discretionary money to travel. Tourism destinations are dependent upon accessibility and sufficient infrastructure.
- The tourism industry is divided into five sectors: transportation, accommodations, food and beverage, recreation and entertainment, and tourism services. These sectors are common between Canada, the United States, and Mexico through the North American Industrial Classification System.
- There are two fundamental reasons for travel: business and pleasure.
- The tourism industry has faced many challenges over the last decade, including increased terrorism, border security, and weather events. Shifts in how the tourism industry operates are continuing to unfold.
- In 1994, Canada created a new agency, the Canadian Tourism Commission, to market and promote tourism industries to Canada's many tourist markets.
- Many other diverse organizations help tourism grow, including the UNWTO, IATA, ICAO, PATA, WTTC, CTHRC, TIAC, ACTA, and the CTRI.

Questions

1. a) Define the terms *industry group* and *sector*.
   b) Why is tourism considered to be an important industry for Canada?
   c) List the five sectors of tourism. What is the role each one plays in tourism? Provide two examples of businesses in each sector.
2. Explain how the five sectors of tourism satisfy all of a tourist's needs while on vacation.
3. a) Identify and discuss eight reasons for the growth of tourism.
   b) In your opinion, explain how any four of the growth factors you listed above will affect tourism over the next twenty years. Defend your answer, using examples.
4. What do you believe are some of the current barriers that keep travellers from visiting some of their preferred destinations? Provide examples.

5. Define, in your own words, the following tourism terms: *tourism, trip, domestic tourist, foreign tourist, excursionist, leakage, multiplier effect, cuisine tourism, agritourism, LGBT tourism.*

6. Canada's travel deficit has fluctuated over the past five years.

    a) Conduct some research and provide a clear definition of the term *travel deficit.*

    b) Identify the reasons for this fluctuation.

    c) Suggest one measure that you think should be taken by the CTC in order to help reduce the travel deficit.

7. a) Discuss four global tourism organizations and four Canadian tourism organizations that you feel have a significant impact on Canadian tourism products, explaining why you have chosen them.

    b) Looking at the five sectors of tourism, or NAICS, identify which sector(s) each of the organizations identified in 7a) is associated with.

Notes

1. http://cthrc.ca/en/research_publications/fast_facts.

2. www.virgingalactic.com.

3. Adapted from Biederman, Laitamaki, Lai, Messerli, Nyheim, and Plog, *Travel and tourism: An industry primer.* (Upper Saddle River, NJ: Prentice Hall, 2007).

4. UNWTO World Tourism Barometer, Advanced Release, January 2011, page 3.

5. Ibid.

6. Canadian Tourism Commission, Facts & Figures 2010 Year in Review, www.canada.travel/corporate.

7. The Buchanan report of 1994, *Snapshots*, 2nd edition.

8. http://discovertourism.ca/en/about_tourism/industry_information.

9. Canadian Tourism Human Resource Council, Canadian Census data 2006.

10. www.statcan.gc.ca/nea-cen/gloss/tourism-tourisme-eng.htm.

11. Statistics Canada, Cat. No. 87-4023, p. 140.

12. Statistics Canada, Cat. No. 87–4023, p. 141.

13. Robert W. McIntosh, Charles R. Goeldner, and J.R. Brent Ritchie, *Tourism principles, practices, philosophies,* 7th ed. (New York, NY: John Wiley & Sons, 1995), p. 9.

14. Statistics Canada. Cat. No. 87-4023, p. 141.

15. www.corporate.canada.travel/en/ca/glossary.

16. "Stop the spread of invasive plants," www.davidsuzuki.org/blog.

17. Department of Tourism, Culture and Recreation, www.tcr.gov.nl.ca/tcr/stats.

18. http://en-corporate.canada.travel/Corporate.

19. http://news.bbc.co.uk/2/hi/uk_news/england/oxfordshire/7228341.stm.

20. Tourism Industry Association of Canada conference proceedings, 1996 National Conference on Tourism, Jasper, Alberta.

Tourism Guests and Hosts

Key terms

allocentric
business guest
certification
code of ethics
cultural motivators
demographics
discretionary income
discretionary time
emerit
empty nest
ethics

external locus of control
extrovert
family life stage
guests
hosts
internal locus of control
interpersonal motivators
introvert
midcentric
motivator
occupational standards

physical motivators
psychocentric
psychographics
pull factors
push factors
status and prestige
tourism education
    councils (TECs)
tourism illiteracy

Learning objectives

Having read this chapter you will be able to

1. Identify the fundamental differences between business and pleasure tourists.

2. Explain how motivators, demographics, and psychographics influence travel choices.

3. Discuss the barriers to travel and why they are difficult to overcome.

4. Define the term *tourism illiteracy* and discuss its effect on a community.

5. Identify and evaluate both the positive and negative impacts of tourism on a community.

6. Explain the roles of the six federal government departments that interact with the tourism sector.

7. Discuss the roles played by the Canadian Tourism Commission (CTC), National Capital Commission (NCC), and the Canadian Tourism Human Resource Council (CTHRC).

8. Identify ten human resource issues currently faced by the tourism sector.

In the study of tourism, it is important to understand the psychological and sociological composition of guests and hosts. **Guests** are the outside visitors who have come to be entertained by the people of a community or region. **Hosts** are individuals, communities, or regions who entertain the visiting guests. The correlation between host and guest is an interesting one. When we are guests, we expect to be treated with dignity, respect, fairness, and honesty. We generally will not accept anything but considerate treatment. However, when we are hosts, we sometimes forget how a guest should be treated, especially if our role as a member of a host community or region is passive.

GUESTS: CUSTOMERS OF TOURISM PRODUCTS AND SERVICES

The first half of this chapter will focus on tourism customers, often referred to simply as "guests." As customers, we enjoy being treated as guests. Part of that enjoyment comes from the care and service that we are given during our stay. Tourism operators need to appreciate the diverse range of needs and motives that drive guests to choose particular tourism products and services. This can be quite challenging; trying to define and understand the characteristics of guests can be like trying to put together a giant jigsaw puzzle with pieces missing. Fortunately, there is a great deal of information available that helps us to understand, classify, and organize various groups of guests.

To create better focus on guests, they are commonly grouped into three large categories:

- by the purpose of their trip (business or pleasure)
- by their demographic characteristics (age, occupation, education, income level, and marital status)
- by their psychographic characteristics (personality, behaviours, likes, and dislikes)

Each of these categories will be explored in the following section to provide some clear differences as to why guests travel and what their expectations might be. Through an increased understanding of tourism guests, the efforts to align our products and services to them will be vastly improved.

Purpose of Trip

There are two reasons that people travel: for recreation or for work. You might fly to Vancouver for a series of business meetings or drive to Algonquin Park with your family on a five-day camping trip. The reason for each of these trips carries with it a unique set of circumstances that influence the decision-making process. Let's explore each of these in turn.

The Business Guest

Business travel is most often non-discretionary in nature, in that the guest has few choices of where, when, how, and how long to travel. Business guests travel based on the needs of their employer or company and their times are most heavily dictated by time and location, not price. Business guests fill nearly 35% of all airline seats and are usually members of one or more frequent customer programs. Meetings and conventions continue to be the two main reasons for business travel, as they have been for many years. Other reasons for business travel include consulting, sales, operations, physical functions (maintenance), and management.

Four major types of traveller make up the business market:

1. **Frequent business traveller.** These guests travel regularly and often become faithful to specific hotels and transportation companies that offer loyalty benefits such as instant check-in, customized amenities, and complimentary upgrades. Staff members are encouraged to build relationships with these guests, remember their likes and dislikes, and to address them by name whenever possible.

2. **Luxury business traveller.** These guests desire the best travel experience, often to satisfy both internal needs as well as project an external image of success. Cost is of significantly less concern with these guests; they are more interested in high quality and superior service attitude.

3. **Female business traveller.** In 1970, only 1% of business guests were female. In the twenty-first century, women travelling on business make up over 50% of the business tourism market. Female business guests who are travelling alone have specific needs. They are concerned with safety issues, demonstrate greater interest in quality exercise facilities, and appreciate appropriate room amenities such as properly sized robes and hangers.

4. **International business traveller.** International business travellers come from outside Canada to conduct business, attend conferences, or engage in meetings. They may or may not be frequent business travellers; the fundamental characteristic is that they inject foreign currency into the Canadian marketplace, reflected as tourism export revenues. Travel in this segment is down due to the increased costs of travel, fuel surcharges, a weakened global economy, and the continued risks involved with travel. Many international companies are using internet conferencing as a viable alternative to travel, to meet some of the demand for face-to-face meetings.

An interesting trend that appears to reflect the state of the economy is that business travel is being consolidated—that is, travellers tend to stay on the road a little longer to maximize accomplishments while minimizing cost. Many hotels go to great lengths to ensure the needs and expectations of business guests are met. Some will provide services like a full on-site business office to take care of incidental needs, or give the eco-conscious client the opportunity to purchase carbon credits, helping offset some of the damage to the global environment any trip incurs.

The Leisure Guest

Pleasure travel is very different from business travel; it is heavily influenced by discretionary time and discretionary income, as well as family life stage.

Discretionary time is time people have away from work and other obligations. Vacations obviously involve discretionary time. **Discretionary income** is the extra money people may spend as they please after all necessary household spending and savings have occurred. The relative value of personal income has grown sluggishly in the last decade. Although we have seen a 2.8% increase in U.S. tourism to Canada in 2010 over 2009, in each of the earlier four years, tourism revenue from the U.S. dropped.

From 2006 to 2010, Canada saw a drop of approximately 15% in U.S. tourism revenues, likely due to American concerns about a recession, their mortgage crisis, and the rising price of gas. This drop has only recently begun changing direction. On the positive side, these factors have encouraged more Canadians to vacation at home, in Canada. One trend seen by the industry is the rise of the "mini-vacation." Experts believe our more hectic lifestyles have left us with less discretionary time, and guests must be satisfied with three- to five-day vacations taken several times a year rather than the extended fourteen-day trip.

Family life stage is an important factor in determining when, where, and how a person takes a vacation. Different life stages also affect the amount of discretionary income. Figure 2.1 illustrates the different stages in life. Generally speaking, people

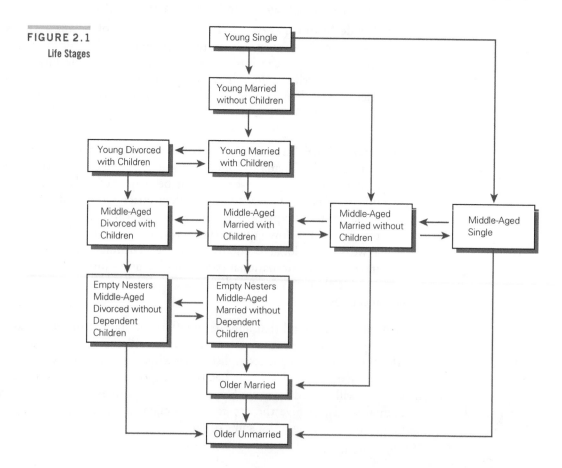

FIGURE 2.1
Life Stages

In Practice

Example 1: *Jon is in his early twenties and has just graduated from university. He and three friends are planning a trip to Nova Scotia to see the sites and visit family. What types of activities, food service options, accommodations, and activities/sites do you think they will prefer? Explain your choice.*

Example 2: *Jon is in his early thirties and is married with two children, ages two and four. He and his family are going to Nova Scotia to visit relatives and take a short vacation. How does this life stage affect his choices for accommodations, food service options, and activities and sites? Explain your answer.*

Example 3: *Jon and his wife have just retired. They have paid off their mortgage and own two cars. With the money they have saved for this trip, they will return to Nova Scotia to visit family and do some sightseeing. What type of accommodations, food service options, and sites/activities do you think will meet the needs of Jon and his wife now?*

who are young and single, and those with an **empty nest** (children have left home) have more discretionary income. They may not have a mortgage to pay or children to support, and may also have greater amounts of discretionary time and fewer family obligations than people in other life stages. In addition, empty nesters who are still working have more vacation days than do younger workers. Families spend their time and money differently than single guests travelling for pleasure. Children have different needs than adults; if the children are happy, the happiness of the parents also increases while on vacation. Therefore, family vacations are normally child-oriented.

The amount of discretionary income and time available will dictate *how much* each guest can spend. However, it is the family life stage that is the best predictor of *what* guests will do on particular pleasure trips.

How do you think Jon's vacation choices will differ as he ages and moves up the lifestyle ladder? (See In Practice box above.)

Demographics

Another method of classifying clients is through demographical information. Demographics are the characteristics of human groups or populations and are useful when exploring distinct segments of the population. In groups, people can be segmented in many ways. Some of the most typical characteristics include age, gender, ethnicity, income, educational level, and location. Frequently, multiple-segment categories are used to refine and sharpen our knowledge of a particular group. Studying these groups increases our ability to generalize about how certain people might behave under various conditions. This, in turn, assists a business to determine the type of facilities and services that might best suit a guest's particular needs.

Knowledge of where guests come from, and where they focus their time and frequently spend their money can also increase our understanding of how to most effectively communicate with customers. This information influences our strategic choices of targeting customers; for example, in deciding whether a business should advertise in the home regions of current guests to continue to attract these visitors, or if it should expand its communication into regions that contain potential new guests in an attempt to expand their market areas.

FIGURE 2.2
Plog's Psychocentric–
Allocentric Continuum

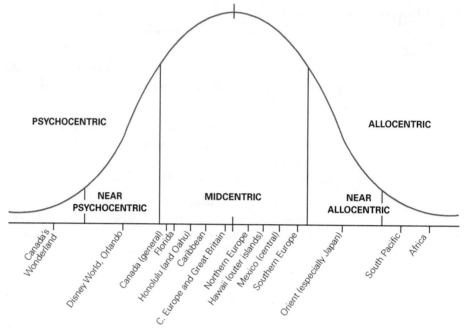

Source: Stanley C. Plog, *Leisure Travel: Making It a Growth Market Again* (New York: John Wiley & Sons, 1991), p. 83. Reprinted by permission of John Wiley & Sons Inc.

Psychographics

Using motives or behaviour to categorize travellers is also useful. Psychographic information helps hosts to understand the activities, interests, opinions, personalities, and likes and dislikes of guests. It is clear that guests at golf and tennis resorts come because of the activity provided. What is not as clear are the reasons guests come to a particular city with many different activities available to them. **Psychographic** data help cities or regions determine the categories into which their guests may be grouped.

The use of personality as psychographic data was first introduced by Stanley Plog.[1] Plog designed a generalized scale outlining the risk tolerance level of travellers. Extremely risk-tolerant travellers are **allocentric**, while extremely risk-averse travellers are labelled **psychocentric**; the majority of travellers are classified as **midcentric** and fall somewhere in the centre of this scale (see Figure 2.2). Allocentrics prefer to move far outside of their normal experiences and are willing to go without the usual conveniences of life in order to gain a fuller travel experience. They are the first to try a new travel destination; once a destination has been established with a broad market base, they move on to a site yet to be "discovered" by the average tourist.

At the other end of Plog's spectrum is the psychocentric traveller. Psychocentrics are "armchair travellers" who prefer high comfort activities and are often reluctant to travel at all. When they do travel, they prefer places that feel like home, where people speak the same language, eat familiar food, and share cultural norms. The mode of travel they choose will be one with which they are comfortable (e.g., their own cars).

For a Canadian psychocentric, learning about "French culture" may mean a trip to Montreal, yet while there, these people will often choose to eat at recognizable chain restaurants and sleep at brand-name hotels like Marriott. Visiting friends and relatives (VFR) is a common motivation for them. Travelling psychocentrics make great repeat customers, because once they have visited an area and enjoyed themselves, they are comfortable returning. Between these two ends of the continuum, midcentrics travel to seek a break in their routine. They enjoy a change of pace and novel experiences, yet they are not likely to choose a vacation that deprives them of the basic comforts of life. Although not a rule, Plog's continuum has shown that, as we age, we are more likely to fall nearer the centre of his continuum.

Do your choices for activities and sites change if you know both Jon and his wife are allocentrics? Explain how this personality type will affect their choices. Which life stages do you think will be interested in the most risky activity and the safest activity?

In Practice

Identify yourself in the following terms:
- psychocentric, midcentric, or allocentric
- high or low activation (level of energy)
- seeker or avoider of change
- introvert or extrovert
- internal or external locus of control

Based on how you identify yourself on each of these personality dimensions, choose your dream vacation and justify your choice.

Fiske and Maddi[2] have extended the personality theory by adding the two personality dimensions—extroversion or introversion—as well as perceptions about locus of control. An **extrovert** is an individual who is outgoing and less inhibited in interpersonal situations. They enjoy external stimulation and are not shy about interacting with locals. An introvert is more concerned with internal thoughts and personal feelings. They may take in the culture of a destination by observing people on the streets or visiting national museums instead of actively engaging with people. While this factor may not influence how a destination is chosen, it will determine how they react once there.

Additionally, people hold quite different beliefs about who controls outcomes. People with an **internal locus of control** believe that they are in charge of what happens in their lives and that they control their own destiny. With an **external locus of control**, people believe that events are predetermined by other powerful individuals, fate, or chance, and accept that what will be, will be. This personality trait helps determine travel choices such as destinations and activities.

The Emerging Modern Traveller So much in life has changed over the past fifty years—how we communicate with each other, how we source information, and how we buy things—so it stands to reason that attitudes are changing, too. Figure 2.3 highlights some of the ways in which new consumers have changed, according to Poon.

Finally, Epperson[4] has identified two factors that are also important in helping travellers choose a destination—push and pull factors.

FIGURE 2.3 **The New Consumers**

1. They are more experienced travellers; more discerning purchasers; and willing to seek novel, adventurous, and niche-related activities.

2. They have changed values reflected in a desire for authenticity, a concern for environmental quality, and a search for personal fulfillment.

3. They have changed lifestyles manifested in healthy living, flexible work hours, higher household incomes, and travel as a way of life.

4. They are products of changing population demographics with an aging population, smaller households, couples without children, and those whose children have left home.

5. They are more flexible and are characterized by spontaneous and more frequent travel purchases, less planning, less rigidity, and markedly changed booking behaviours and specialized or niche product purchases.

6. They are more independent, need to be in control of their travel decisions, and want to embrace their own identity.[3]

The **pull factors**—external things such as scenic beauty—draw guests to a destination and continue to be an important reason for travel. Pull factors include people, places, and activities such as:

friends	scenic areas	cultural events
relatives	historic areas	sports events
celebrities	educational events	
public figures	recreational events	

Push factors are those forces, needs, motivations, and ways of thinking that come from within us. Push factors are generated from our inner selves and include such factors as:

adventure	kinship	rest and relaxation
challenge	novelty	self-discovery
escape	prestige	

WHY TRAVEL?

Demographics and personality have a great influence on where people travel and their activities when they get there. But what actually gets a person travelling? A **motivator** is something strong enough to cause a person to take action. Motivation is rooted in need satisfaction; a need exists when something general is missing, such as food, relationships, or status. When people decide what exactly will satisfy their existing need, they express this with a specific request, or want.

The terms *needs* and *wants* are often used incorrectly. A want is a specific choice made from all available options that could satisfy a need. If your stomach grumbles, you become aware that you are hungry and need food. From all the food choices you could made, you decide that you really want a hamburger, which then becomes the specific satisfier of your food need. Once that hunger (need) has been satisfied by the hamburger (want), the need no longer exists; thus, a need only exists when is remains unsatisfied. Once a need has been satisfied, it disappears.

What then motivates a person to travel? Physical motivators to travel, such as the need to escape a particularly cold winter, are easier to identify than psychological needs. Psychological needs are often theoretical and may be difficult to pinpoint in an individual. Understanding psychological needs, however, leads to a better understanding of the superficial reasons for travelling.

www.statscan.gc.ca

Motivational Theories

Abraham Maslow is one of the pioneers of early motivational theory, categorizing human needs into five overall groupings. These are commonly presented in an order from physiological (physical) needs through relationship requirements to psychological development (see Figure 2.4). Most often, an individual will attempt to satisfy the lowest motivational level (that is, physiological needs) first. Once those have been satisfied, a higher-order need emerges to influence behaviour. Again, it is the unsatisfied need that leads to action.

To apply these principles to tourism, let's look at each step and how it might affect the traveller. *Physiological needs* may generate motivations such as escape from a cold climate or the release of the stress of work through physical relaxation. To the traveller, these needs also include knowledge of how to satisfy basic physical requirements at a destination.

Safety needs must be met in order for travel to take place. Few tourists would knowingly make a travel choice that would endanger their lives. Safety requirements are most frequently monitored by governments who provide police, medical, and infrastructure services as well as consistent regulations on service providers. Bad news—such as of a plane crash, fatal food poisoning in a restaurant, a fire in a hotel, or a theme park ride that has malfunctioned—has an immediate negative impact on a business. In the last decade, the threat of terrorism has created barriers as tourists weigh their safety concerns. Governments have reacted by increasing visible security, monitoring systems, and documentation requirements to increase both safety and the perception of safety.

Social needs are by far the most common motivators, and VFR is the most common pleasure motivator. The need for companionship and belonging may be identified by the choice of a trip. For example, a tour package offers group activities with other people who share similar interests, and a sense of belonging may be fulfilled by a trip to trace a person's ancestral roots. *Ego/self-esteem* deals with a person's need to feel important and special. Included in these motivators might be a trip to see special events such as an elite sporting event or popular concert, or the need for special services such as gold memberships or first-class service. The specialized market of incentive travel (awards for high performance) is built upon this need category.

FIGURE 2.4 Maslow's Hierarchy of Needs

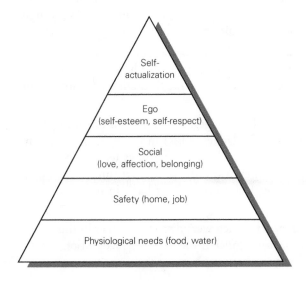

The Citadel, one of Nova Scotia's national historic sites, sits near the centre of the city, making it easily accessible for tourists.
(Photo courtesy Parks Canada/R. Garnett.)

Finally, *self-actualization needs* focus on achieving one's full potential as a human being. These motivators might see a tourist choosing a self-guided walking tour through the vineyards of Bordeaux to learn the language and discover more about French wine, travelling to Toronto to help build homes for Habitat for Humanity, or climbing Mount Everest. This travel is focused around personal growth and development.

McIntosh and Goeldner have looked at motivators from a different perspective.[5] They have divided motivation into four basic categories: physical motivators, cultural motivators, interpersonal motivators, and status and prestige motivators.

1. **Physical motivators** are directly related to health. Sports participation, relaxation, and recreation are preventive health maintenance motivators, whereas medical exams, health treatments, or "fat farm" attendance are curative health motivators. Both types are seen as tension releasers through physical activity or attention to a health problem.

2. **Cultural motivators** are a desire to learn more about the music, architecture, food, art, folklore, or religion of other people. These motivators stem from a curiosity to experience another way of life through travel rather than just through books or television.

3. **Interpersonal motivators** are the strongest motivators of all and include two extremes: visiting friends and relatives (VFR) and escaping from family and friends. People who live close to family sometimes feel a need to get away from the family influence, even if only for a short time. Those who live far from family sometimes feel a need to get back in touch through vacation time.

4. **Status and prestige motivators**, which were discussed earlier in this chapter as ego and self-esteem factors, concern the need for recognition, attention, appreciation, and good reputation.

TABLE 2.1   *Top Activities Participated in* by International Tourists to Canada in 2011*

Activity	U.S. Residents %	All Other International Residents %
Go shopping	19	19.5
Go sightseeing	16.4	16.9
Visit friends or relatives	13.3	11.8
Visit a historical site	9.1	9.4
Visit a national or provincial nature park	8.5	8.7
Participate in sports/outdoor activities	8.4	8.1
Going to a bar or night club	7.4	7.4
Visit a museum or art gallery	7.2	7.3
Visit a zoo, aquarium/botanical garden	4.3	4.4
Attend cultural events	3.7	3.6
Attend a festival or fair	2.9	2.9

* *more than one activity may be participated in while on a trip*

Courtesy: Canadian Tourism Commission and the Government of Canada

www.pc.gc.ca/Banff

Table 2.1 shows what tourists actually do in Canada. For a variety of reasons, people do want to travel. They look forward to their next trip and talk about previous trips. Reasons for travelling always exist and often lead to actual experience.

THE BARRIERS TO TRAVEL

Guests certainly have a wide variety of reasons for choosing to travel, but what *stops* them from travelling? Seven common barriers to travelling are very difficult to overcome. Many of these factors are interrelated and affect other barriers. For example, time, cost, and distance are often interrelated. If you live in Halifax, a trip to Agra, India, to see the Taj Mahal is not only costly, but also consumes a great deal of trip in transit. In a typical two-week vacation, you could spend over 20% of your vacation on a plane.

Cost. The average traveller cannot avoid considering the cost of a trip. In times of economic difficulty, destination, length of stay, and travel method will all be modified by the amount of discretionary income people have available to spend on their vacations. Demographic characteristics, such as occupation and education, influence whether someone can afford the trip as these factors relate to wage levels and discretionary time away from work. Two other factors that affect cost are the number of people travelling in the party and the price structure at the destination. A family of four interested in learning more about French culture may find a trip to Paris too expensive, while a trip to Quebec City provides them with a similar cultural experience at a fraction of the cost.

Lack of Time. The amount of discretionary time you have available for travel greatly impacts or restricts your travel possibilities. If you have only a three-day

Tourists travel to Canada from around the globe to experience the awesome natural beauty of such destinations as the Athabasca Glacier, Banff National Park.
(Photo: © Robert Bush/Alamy.)

weekend available and you live in Halifax, you may go to Sydney, Nova Scotia, to see family, but will not be able to visit family in Sydney, Australia. Available time limits the choice of destination and, often, the mode of travel. The farther the destination is from home, the more likely you are to travel by plane rather than by car. This allows you maximum time to spend *at* the destination rather than travelling *to* it.

Accessibility, Distance, or Ease of Travel. Although travellers may want to reach a particular location, there is always the question of whether or not they can. Do you have to fly? Can you drive? Does infrastructure exist to allow for transportation? This is an especially salient point for Canadian tourism. For example, tourists may come to Canada for sport fishing; they are looking for pristine lakes like those found in our northern regions. These lakes are exactly what the fisher wants, but they are inaccessible by car and must be reached by float plane.

Health and Disabilities. Health issues impact both the ability of guests to travel and may inhibit people from visiting particular regions. One example is the SARS epidemic that peaked between late 2002 and the middle of 2003, and spread over thirty-seven countries around the world. Cities with reported cases of SARS infections were publically identified and suffered an immediate and dramatic drop in tourism. Disabilities, on the other hand, are not communicable diseases but may be caused by an injury, a non-communicable disease, or simple aging. Currently, obesity is a major issue in North America, resulting in travellers being unable to participate in physically active travel. Physical size also affects service delivery. In 2007, the Supreme Court of Canada ruled that an airline could not charge for a second seat if needed by a particularly large person; body mass must be considered as one entity when selling space on an airline. Large people may now travel using two seats for the price of a single fare.

Travel Tastes and Experience. Personality and age affect this barrier to travel. For instance, psychocentrics are not fond of travel at all. In fact, if they take a trip, it will likely be within their own province. Border crossings, a foreign language, and strange food are not on the agenda.

Education. Education levels serve as a strong influence on the decision to travel. Generally speaking, the more education you have, the greater your knowledge of the world and the more likely you are to seek out new experiences.

Age. When we are younger, travel is an exciting adventure. Novel experiences and cultures can be experienced, and better health allows for greater exploration. As we age, it becomes more difficult to handle change; eventually, travel stops altogether due to the inconvenience around health and comfort issues. A ninety-six-year-old woman in a wheelchair will likely travel very little. If she does, it is with great preparation and usually with a younger travelling companion.

Fear. The most difficult barrier to overcome is fear—fear of new places, fear of water, fear of flying, fear of terrorism. Fears do not need to be based on concrete experiences; they can be real or perceived, but either can paralyze activity. For example, the beautiful beaches in Israel have fewer vacationers because of continued terrorist activities in that region. As for flying, the vast majority of flights safely carry passengers to their destinations; in fact, flying is still considered to be the safest mode of transportation. Unfortunately, knowledge does not always overcome fear. In 2008, the Canadian government issued a warning to tourists travelling to Mexico due to an increase in crime against Canadian tourists, even though the regions of volatility in Mexico were not locations where the overwhelming majority of travellers visit. Guests travelling to a foreign country should be aware that the country's rule of law governs not only the citizens, but tourists as well.

THE TOURISM HOST

What is the role of a host? Think of inviting guests for an overnight stay. You want to be sure they are warmly greeted and made to feel comfortable and at home. You want your dwelling to be clean and tidy, and you may add fresh flowers to enhance its beauty. The food will be prepared specially, the beds will be made with clean sheets and pillows, and the towels will be freshly washed. Your conversation will be friendly and polite and you will likely not try to engage in an argument that leaves bad feelings between you and your guests. In other words, you treat your guests as you would like to be treated.

The tourist "host" is often seen as the direct tourism service provider: the restaurateur or hotel team, the transportation company, or the activities personnel. Yet, the host actually encompasses the entire community of providers, and destination communities use a similar strategy for greeting tourists. Streets are kept clean, and flower boxes, gardens, and parks make the destination pretty. Hotels endeavour to provide first-class service and restaurants to provide safe, wholesome food. Travellers also hope to receive a warm welcome from the people in a community. But do they? Have you ever driven behind a car that is obviously searching for a street name or the proper turn, and grumbled, "Learn how to drive"? Have you overheard foreign tourists trying to explain what they need when they do not speak French or English? How helpful has the listener been?

A positive attitude toward guests is crucial if they are to enjoy their stay. Negative attitudes are often caused by **tourism illiteracy**. The major cause of tourism illiteracy is a lack of understanding of the benefits tourism brings to a community. For example, people are often unhappy when tax dollars are used to fund new tourist attractions or events instead of health, educational, or social programs. People and communities can also be "illiterate" in the sense that they don't see tourism as an economic benefit—they don't see the large number of full-time and part-time jobs tourism creates, and they don't realize how the economic multiplier spreads tourist dollars to nearly every member of the community.

Many people are unaware of the volume of tourists in their country, whether domestic or international (Table 2.2), and they don't see the amount of revenue generated both directly from services consumed and the additional tax dollars that tourists generate. What they do see is that tourists intrude on their way of life. Sadly, even governments can show signs of tourism illiteracy when they fail to speak up in defence of tourism in the face of policies that damage the tourism industry. For example, did the Bush administration consider the impact on the tourism industry when it put into place strict border and visa requirements? Northern American states that depend on Canadian tourism spoke out against the proposed legislation, but their words were unheeded. Today, the United States continues to feel the impact of these changes.

TABLE 2.2   *Canada–U.S.A. International Travel Competitive Review 2011*

Trips from	Canada number (#)	Canada 10/09 % change	U.S.A. number (#)	U.S.A. 10/09 % change
Total International	15 576	−2	62 325	4
Americas				
United States	11 471	−2	n/a	n/a
Mexico	124	7	13 414	0
Canada	n/a	n/a	21 043	5
Overseas Key Markets				
France	422	3	1 504	12
Germany	290	−8	1 824	6
United Kingdom	623	−6	3 835	0
China	237	22	1 089	36
Japan	187	−13	3 250	−4
South Korea	140	−11	1 145	3
Australia	216	7	1 038	15
Brazil	74	4	1 508	26
India	163	9	663	2
Total Key Markets	**13 946**	**−2**	**29 271**	**3**

Tourism Snapshot Year-in-Review 2011

Courtesy: Canadian Tourism Commission and the Government of Canada

Throughout the summer, tourists flock to Ottawa's Parliament Hill to see the Changing of the Guard, a ceremony similar to the one held daily at Buckingham Palace in London, England.
(Photo courtesy National Capital Commission.)

Tourism illiteracy is hard to overcome. People who are illiterate about tourism may have developed this attitude because of a bad experience with tourists and may, as a result, label all tourism bad. By expressing their negative feelings to others in the community or directly to tourists, these people encourage further anti-tourist sentiment. How can we deal with this negativity? The best way to overcome tourism illiteracy is for tourism professionals to educate their community about the great value and benefits of this sector. Table 2.2 illustrates the positive gains made by the United States and Canada in regard to the number of visits (not the dollar revenue).

Benefits of Tourism

www.hcareers.ca

Here is a short list of some of the more important benefits tourism brings to a country and a community:

1. **Economic diversification.** The tourism sector provides a community with a wider variety of both full-time and part-time jobs than any other sector, including the hiring and promotion of minorities as well as people with different levels of education. Tourism also provides part-time work for those who cannot accept a full-time job.

2. **Cultural preservation.** One motivation to travel is the chance to learn about other countries and ways of life. Canadian culture has been influenced by many different cultures, and this diversity gives tourists a mosaic of cultural experiences to enjoy while on vacation here. Canadian Heritage oversees the protection and development of many of Canada's cultural and historic sites.

3. **Better choices in entertainment, shopping, and food service.**

4. **Enhanced travel.** Roads, airports, ports, and public transportation are built or improved to better facilitate travel and appeal to travellers.

5. **Area beautification.** Tourists choose Canada as a destination because of its image as a clean, natural, and healthy environment. Destination communities take care to ensure that their region is planted with trees, flowers, and lawns; that towns and roadways are cleared of waste; and that, through municipal legislation, the area maintains its beauty and uniqueness.

6. **Tax revenues.** For every billion dollars of tourism income earned in Canada, $230 million goes to the federal government, $160 million to provincial governments, and $60 million to municipal governments. This money helps reduce our taxes. In the last five years, many municipalities have introduced a lodging/room tax. For example, hotels in the Halifax Regional Municipality (HRM) are required to collect an additional 2% Municipal Hotel Room Tax from all room revenue. The revenues that are generated pay for additional advertising for the area, bringing in more tourists without using local tax dollars.

7. **Foreign capital.** When an international company invests in Canada, those foreign dollars help to build the Canadian product. Jobs are created and revenue is produced for Canadian tourism workers, with less investment needed from the region or municipalities.

8. **Recreational and educational facilities.** Many public universities and colleges would have financial difficulty were it not for government support, and most hospitality schools have some form of government financing. National and provincial parks, historic sites, and some attractions are also funded in part by tourism dollars.

9. **Modernization.** A strong tourism market means roadways must be maintained, new airports built, and other infrastructure regularly upgraded. Local residents as well as tourists enjoy the benefits of these upgrades. Better infrastructure also helps public services such as the police and sanitation crews do their jobs.

10. **A favourable world image.** The value of hosting a large international event cannot be underestimated. For example, Canada has benefited greatly in its involvement in world class sporting events. The 1988 Winter Olympics in Calgary, Alberta, brought incredible coverage to an iconic Canadian winter landscape, and the 2010 Winter Olympics attracted similar attention to Vancouver and Whistler, British Columbia. Since 2000, the International Ice Hockey Federation (IIHF) World U20 Championship, often referred to as the World Junior Hockey Championship, has been held five times in Canada and is scheduled for another four tournaments by 2021. Events like these keep Canada in the forefront of attractive destinations in the world's eye.

www.otec.org

Barriers to Tourism Acceptance

The fact is that tourists can have a negative impact on a community. Some barriers to the acceptance of tourism discussed here are based on fact; others are based on suspicion. All of them are concerns that a community, region, or country might voice against becoming more actively involved in the tourism sector.

1. **Crime and unwanted behaviour.** Tourists come to a destination with money, credit cards, and other valuable belongings. In any host society,

FOOTPRINT

As a way of protecting culturally and historically rich environments, the United Nations Educational, Scientific and Cultural Organization (UNESCO) has been recognizing valuable sites throughout the world, designating them as UNESCO biosphere reserves. Recently, an area of 430 000 hectares in the upper Bay of Fundy in New Brunswick has received full designation as a biosphere reserve. Under this title, it is managed via community-based involvement. Stakeholders, including local businesses and community groups, work as a collective in an effort to promote sustainable development in the region. Additionally, this collective explores research and innovative practices to best preserve and enhance their region.

Ecosystems such as the Bay of Fundy, which include the world's highest tidal systems, are unique attractors for tourists to visit and experience. As a biosphere reserve, this region is not isolated as much as it is protected for a sustainable future. Visit the Fundy Biosphere Reserve website to learn more about this reserve, or the UNESCO website to explore the biosphere program.

there are those who wish to take advantage of people who are unfamiliar with the customs, the area, or potential dangers. Crime against tourists has no national boundaries. Protection of the tourist is an important part of maintaining a safe image to show to the rest of the world. Also disturbing to the host community are unwanted behaviours such as prostitution and drunkenness, which often become more prevalent in a town that focuses on tourism as its main source of revenue.

2. **Air, water, land, and noise pollution.** Adding a million additional people to a region during a short tourism season puts a strain on the ecosystem. Banff is one of the best examples of the problem. To minimize this damage, tighter controls have been established that limit new development and the number of visitors, and reinforce regulations to ensure that the ecosystem is safe.

3. **Congestion of roadways, parks, shopping areas, recreational centres, attractions, and restaurants.** Although a region may benefit greatly from tourism revenues, negative impressions can be created when locals are forced to compete for a seat in their favourite restaurant or deal with the crowds and disruption of daily life brought about by a large event.

4. **Local resentment.** Tension may also develop when large cultural or economic differences exist between guests and their hosts. Visitors with large sums of disposable income and higher visible spending patterns may create resentment from those in the host community who exist on less. Bitterness may also develop if tourists do not follow the social or cultural norms of the host country.

5. **Inflation.** Inflation increases when tourists come to town. During high season, hotels charge full rates, shops are less inclined to offer bargains, and the general cost of living tends to rise. Locals see these changes in pricing strategies and can begin to feel animosity.

6. **Seasonality.** Regions that experience a seasonal tourist influx, such as Cape Breton and Prince Edward Island, will also experience high unemployment once the season is over.

7. **Leakage.** When demand for the tourism product is greater than the destination's local resources, leakage occurs (Chapter 1), and the community does not get the full benefit of tourism dollars.

8. **Increases in the cost of services.** Most tourism events require additional police service and may require on-site paramedics. During annual summer events such as the Pride Parade in Toronto, the hot weather means that additional staff are needed to hand out bottles of water, more paramedics are required to deal with incidents of sunstroke, and more police are needed to ensure the event happens in a safe and orderly fashion.

9. **Diversion of government funds.** Tourism may divert government money and attention from needed projects in order to build and renew a country's tourism products. In 2003, forest fires destroyed some of the historic train trestles that attracted hikers to the Kelowna area. Much to the dismay of many living in that area, Canadian Heritage provided a one-time grant of $50 million to repair them. The tsunami that struck Southeast Asia in 2004 resulted in the rapid rebuilding of resorts, compared with a slower move to rebuild homes and local lifestyles.

TOURISM'S IMPACT ON CULTURES AND SOCIETIES

Many studies have been done on the impact of tourism on the host nation and its people. The impact tourism has on a community is largely based on the community's ability to absorb tourists as well as the community's carrying capacity. The World Tourism Organization defines carrying capacity as "the maximum number of people that may visit a tourist destination at the same time, without causing destruction of the physical, economic, socio-cultural environment and an unacceptable decrease in the quality of visitors' satisfaction."[6]

Larger, modern communities found in countries with looser cultural regulations adjust better to a sudden influx of foreigners. For this reason, while tourists do affect the societies of New York and Paris, the population handles the inconvenience more easily. Smaller towns such as Banff or Niagara-on-the-Lake—or where the living environment of the destination is very different from Canada's such as in Nairobi, Kenya, or Kingston, Jamaica—have a great deal more difficulty. Edward Inskeep suggests that the following differences determine the depth of the difficulties:

- basic values and logic system—what facets of life are deemed important? Education? Finances? Family lifestyle?

- religious beliefs—does religion play an active or a passive role in the society?

- traditions—traditions are often an important part of the lure for tourists, but are they compatible with foreign ideas and traditions (e.g., alcohol consumption, physical contact)?

- customs—do customs meet the norms of the visiting population or do the differences cause conflict (e.g., bargaining at the local market or shops)?

- lifestyles—can tourists adjust easily to the local lifestyle and vice versa (e.g., siesta time interferes with the tourists' need for activity)?

- behavioural patterns (e.g., women are not allowed the same freedoms as men)

- dress codes—can women show their bodies without being considered immoral?

- sense of time budget—a "don't worry, be happy" attitude; tomorrow is soon enough

- attitudes toward strangers—can visitors move freely, comfortably among the local population?

Colouring these differences is the simple fact that when people travel, their own customs change, including spending and dining habits. Researchers have also concluded that the faster a tourism industry develops, the more difficulty local residents have in adjusting to the changes.

A second approach to looking at the cultural effects of tourism has been developed by G. V. Doxey. His "Index of Tourist Irritation" identifies five stages that smaller destinations are likely to experience even if cultural norms are similar.[7]

Stage 1: *Level of euphoria* Positive vibrations occur as tourist dollars begin to flow, the additional jobs and financial resources have a positive impact on the community, and there is an enthusiasm for the development of the tourism industry. Visitors are greeted happily and both tourist and resident enjoy mutual satisfaction.

Stage 2: *Level of apathy* As the industry grows, residents begin to take advantage of the tourist, inflation may have a negative impact on locals, or a two-tier system of pricing develops. Tourists and their financial resources are taken for granted. The warmth first experienced between tourist and local becomes more formal.

Stage 3: *Level of irritation* This stage is reached when the industry is nearing the saturation point and local residents begin to be annoyed by the number of tourists taking advantage of their town and its facilities. As long as the number of tourists is kept at a tolerable level, dealing with the irritation factor is simpler.

Tourists prefer their souvenirs to be authentic, and this often provides income for local artists.
(Photo: Canadian Tourism Commission.)

In Practice

If you were placed in a leadership role in your hometown and were trying to persuade residents of the benefits of tourism, who would be your strongest allies and who would be your toughest opponents? How would you try to sway the opinion of those opposed to tourism?

Stage 4: *Level of antagonism* Irritation becomes more vocal and tourists are blamed for all of the negative occurrences such as increase in crime and bad behaviours, disrespect of property, and a feeling that the townsfolk are being taken advantage of. At this stage, there may be irreversible changes in local culture and moral attitudes.

Stage 5: *The final level* The local residents forget that the way they lived was what first attracted the tourist, they are unable to deal with the changes brought about by the increase in tourism and its trappings, and they must live with the fact that their life has changed, never to be the same again. If the destination is able to make the adjustments and can cope with mass tourism, it will continue to thrive.

If tourism experiences both a high season and a low season, locals can often tolerate the change as they realize there is a predictable break at the end of the high season. However, if seasonality has little impact on tourist flows, this is not a benefit locals can count on. Once tourism has a foothold in a town or a country, its progress is difficult to stop without some sort of government interference, however, if the tourist is made to feel uncomfortable or threatened, the industry flounders. It is in the hands of the government to control the direction tourism takes, and its decisions determine the positive and negative impacts dealt with by the local residents and their environment.

THE FEDERAL GOVERNMENT AND TOURISM

The major host in any country is its national government, which plays an extremely important role in tourism. If the tourism sector does not have the support of the government, it cannot flourish. For instance, when the Shah of Iran was overthrown in 1979, the new government closed the borders of Iran to foreigners. The streets of Tehran, once bustling with tourists eager to spend their money in the city known as the "Paris of the East," suddenly had no visitors. Many of its beautiful shops, hotels, and restaurants went bankrupt, and those that survived had great difficulty and were forced to make major changes in how they did business. Tourism, once a very profitable industry in Iran, became virtually nonexistent.

Japan provides another example of the impact of government regulations. Until the 1960s, travel to and from Japan was tightly controlled. The Japanese were seldom allowed to vacation outside the country, and foreigners were not encouraged to visit Japan. When the ban on travel was lifted, tourism began to flourish, opening Japan to the world and providing new revenues for the Japanese government and its people.

www.tourismhrc.com

Governments not only hold power over their own tourism industry, but also can have a major impact on other nations' tourism. The new Western Hemisphere

Friendly, helpful staff provide a positive experience for tourists.
(Photo courtesy Canadian Tourism Commission.)

Travel Initiative (WHTI) security measures passed by the U.S. government have had a strong negative effect not only on their own tourism industry but also on tourism in foreign countries, especially Canada. In order to gain the ear of decision makers in Parliament, organizations like the Tourism Industry Association of Canada (TIAC) and the Hotel Association of Canada (HAC) constantly examine pieces of legislation that could have a negative impact on the industry. As industry advocates, they lobby "on the Hill," pushing for legislation beneficial to the tourism industry and attempting to alter potentially damaging changes.

Here are the federal government departments that have the most impact on the Canadian tourism sector:

- **Industry Canada** is responsible for the overall well-being of the tourism sector. The Canadian Tourism Commission operates as a Crown corporation under the auspices of this department.

- **Foreign Affairs Canada (FAC)** is responsible for issuing Canadian passports and Canadian entrance visas. Passports are official documents that allow holders to travel from and return to their own countries. The federal government has redesigned Canadian passports to make forgery more difficult by digitally printing the bearer's picture on a secure page and adding a hologram. Children used to travel on their parents' passports, but must now carry their own. Background checks on new applicants are more vigorous and tighter security measures at all border crossings are now in place. The United States and Canada have implemented the NEXUS system to speed up border crossing. Travellers may apply to be classified as low-risk, at which point they then become pre-approved for expedited clearance across the border. Businesses conducting a high volume of trade across the Canada–U.S. border can also apply to the FAST program (Free and Secure Trade) to be deemed low-risk.

    Visas are official documents that give travellers permission to enter a country for a specified period of time. For example, a Hungarian who wishes to visit Canada must now go to the Canadian embassy in Budapest to obtain a visitor's visa. FAC has imposed new, tighter restrictions on all visas issued and have added eight countries to the "visa required" list. The easiest visas have typically been those granted to students enrolling in a school or university; applicants for student visas now face a more stringent vetting process, as most of the terrorists involved in the attacks on the World Trade Center and the Pentagon entered the United States on student visas.

On October 4, 2005, new regulations were instituted at borders and airports. These new regulations require Canadian travellers heading to the United States to give additional specific information to U.S. Immigration prior to their departure. Now, Canadians visiting the United States must also provide U.S. authorities with the full address of their destination, including telephone number and zip code. Simply providing the name of a hotel is no longer sufficient. As of June 1, 2009, Canadians travelling into the US require either a valid passport or NEXUS card; when crossing by land, travellers require a passport, NEXUS card, FAST card, an enhanced driver's licence, or an enhanced identification card.

Because of growing tensions throughout much of the world, the Government of Canada has created a website covering recent developments in 220 foreign countries (Voyage.gc.ca). The information provided on this website includes developments that might put the Canadian traveller in jeopardy—from current conflicts to weather problems or health concerns.

www.voyage.gc.ca

- **Canada Border Services Agency** The first Canadians that a foreign tourist meets are employees of the CBSA, who in turn report to Citizenship and Immigration Canada. These employees are responsible for checking the travel documents of every person arriving in Canada—including Canadians. Prior to September 11, 2001, this office's computer system was not linked to any other law enforcement agency. In recent years, several terrorists have entered Canada first, and then crossed the border into the United States. To try to stop this human traffic, immigration officials are now linked to the RCMP system, which will in turn link to U.S. law enforcement agencies.

    Beyond personal travel documents and security, every country requires arriving travellers to pass through customs control, where purchases being brought into the country must be declared. The CBSA is responsible for customs services. Airline passengers who reside in a foreign country must complete declaration forms and immigration forms upon entering Canada. For returning Canadians, proof of citizenship and the declaration form serve as both entry and customs declaration documents. At airports, Canadians must list on their declaration form all items purchased abroad. Canadians entering the country by private vehicle may be able to make a verbal declaration.

- **Parks Canada Agency** is an independent agency reporting to Environment Canada. It is responsible for overseeing all Canadian national parks; managing 167 of the 950 national historic sites; overseeing operation of the country's seven historic canal systems; coordinating the federal–provincial co-operative program for the Canadian Heritage River Systems; directing and implementing heritage tourism opportunities and programs; and providing services to the more than 20 million visitors who use the national parks system every year. More detail on its role is given in Chapter 9.

- **Transport Canada** oversees the regulation of our transportation systems and helps with the building and maintenance of the transportation infrastructure. It is responsible for investigating all accidents involving death where any form of transportation has been used. In 2002, a tour bus from Ottawa called the *Lady Duck* sank just offshore from the city of Hull in the Ottawa River. Four people were killed in this incident; the Transportation Safety Board investigated and determined that the vehicle had been unsafe for water transportation and charged the tour company. For information on Transport Canada's role in air traffic, see Chapter 4.

A Crown Corporation: The Canadian Tourism Commission (CTC)

The most significant development for Canada's tourism sector was the establishment of the Canadian Tourism Commission (CTC) in 1994. Now a Crown corporation, its headquarters are in Vancouver, B.C. The CTC provides a good example of how the federal and provincial governments can partner with an industry to ensure its growth and success. This partnership provides a unique opportunity to develop and coordinate programs that benefit the industry and the country as a whole. The tourism sector matches government promotional funding dollar for dollar. In 2010, the CTC spent over $105 million dollars on marketing and sales opportunities for the tourism industry. Some of the activities that the CTC supports include gathering and maintaining data on potential markets, analyzing international and domestic marketplace opportunities and issues, market research and analysis, advertising, public relations, promotional projects, and travel trade activities.

There are several activities in which the CTC does not engage. It does not lobby the government or provide direct subsidies or grants to the industry. Those activities are performed by tourism associations, organizations, and provincial and municipal governments. An interested Canadian may judge the performance of the CTC by looking at the yearly results in five areas: overall tourism revenue increases, growth in visitor volumes, reduction in the travel deficit, market share changes, and job creation. Certainly the five-year results shown in Table 2.2 are encouraging.

www.canadatourism.ca

Mandate and Mission Statement for the Canadian Tourism Commission

Vision
Canada will be the premier four-season destination to connect with nature and to experience diverse cultures and communities.

Mission
Canada's tourism industry will deliver world-class cultural and leisure experiences year-round, while preserving and sharing Canada's clean, safe, and natural environments. The industry will be guided by the values of respect, integrity, and empathy.

Strategic Objectives
The main thrusts of the commission are to market Canada as a desirable travel destination and to provide timely and accurate information to the industry to assist decision-making.

A Crown Corporation: The National Capital Commission (NCC)

The capital of a nation always holds a special position, for it is the heart of a country. As such, it hosts the central government and is the site of many historic events that helped to shape a country's culture and heritage. A capital city is the showcase of a country's vitality, talent, creativity, and accomplishments. There were many reasons for Queen Victoria's choice of Ottawa as Canada's capital: the natural beauty of the region with its rolling hills and waterways, its inherently bilingual nature due to its closeness to Quebec, and its distance from the U.S. border, which provided the new capital with military security.

The National Capital Commission (NCC) is an independent legal entity created by Parliament to ensure that public policies pursued on behalf of the National Capital Region benefit all Canadians. The NCC has the broad goal of maintaining the integrity and beauty of the capital region, which extends over a large area of western Quebec and the Ottawa area. It has the following mandates:

- to use the capital to communicate Canada to Canadians and to assist in developing and highlighting the Canadian national identity
- to safeguard and preserve the capital's physical assets and natural setting for future generations

To preserve the natural beauty of the area, an aggressive plan for parks and green space was developed. A wide band of undeveloped land circling the capital was designated to ensure that the city maintained its sense of beauty. Gatineau Park, located on the Quebec side of the Ottawa River, provides the area with the largest wilderness park

Canada's National War Memorial is located in the heart of Ottawa.
(Photo courtesy National Capital Commission.)

In Practice

Why should a country's capital city be a showpiece? List the capital cities of five foreign countries. What sites do they have that create a cultural/historical ambience or a positive world image? Are Ottawa's pull factors competitive with the foreign capitals you have chosen? Why or why not? Should the NCC continue to make decisions for the city of Ottawa, or should the citizens of Ottawa be given the sole power to shape the city's future tourism development? Justify your opinion.

SNAPSHOT

Bruce MacNaughton—PEI Preserve Company

When you first think about jams and preserves, the spreads that grace your breakfast table every morning, you might not make a connection with tourism. Thoughts about your childhood, of picking berries with your family might come to mind. Remembering, the smells wafting in from the kitchen on Sunday afternoons as those berries were transformed into fresh jam are powerful memories for some.

For Bruce MacNaughton, preserving was simply a necessary task when he needed to deal with the remaining stock of his first unsuccessful restaurant: hundreds of pounds of strawberries. Borrowing a friend's kitchen one evening, Bruce processed that jam, adding in the flavour of the liqueur he had in his glass, creating his first flavoured preserve, Strawberry and Grand Marnier. He sold 450 jars of that preserve in his first year and knew that he had found his passion.

After years of building his preserve company, with product selling in over 400 stores throughout North America, Bruce decided to fundamentally change his business model. Instead of chasing around the world with his jams in hand, he decided to "invite the world to our place, instead." The company purchased the old butter factory in New Glasgow, PEI, a location in a rural setting at the corner of a major travel hub on the island. Quality and transparency were fundamental building blocks of the PEI Preserve Company; they constructed a production kitchen with viewing space for all visitors right from the preserve shop.

The PEI Preserve Company and Bruce himself became icons of PEI culture, service, and hospitality. The location began a major attraction, encouraging bus tours on the island to stop, experience PEI warmth, purchase local product, and even enjoy the daily ceilidh, a traditional Gaelic gathering with folk music and dancing. Bruce has received numerous awards as an entrepreneur and retailer; he has also been repeatedly honoured as a tourism operator. The Tourism Industry Association of PEI has recognized Bruce and his company with the Tourism Operator of the Year award and he recently received the Lieutenant Governor's Award, recognizing his powerful contribution to the strength of the tourism industry on Prince Edward Island.

1. Describe the connection between the PEI Preserve Company and the tourism industry.

2. Explore the push and pull factors that are at play with Bruce MacNaughton's operation.

in the capital region. It offers visitors paths and nature trails for biking and walking, downhill ski areas and cross-country ski trails, and beaches for swimming and picnics. One of the capital region's largest tourist attractions is the Fall Rhapsody, a celebration of autumn's colours in Gatineau Park. The NCC is also responsible for maintaining the portion of the Rideau Canal that lies within the city. This historic canal is one of the longest artificial waterways in the world. The NCC donates the land on which many new museums and cultural centres are located and acts as a guardian for heritage treasures such as the Aberdeen Pavilion at Lansdowne Park. It is impossible to walk through the older neighbourhoods of Ottawa without stumbling across unique buildings or sites designated by the NCC as part of Canada's history. The NCC also helps sponsor events in the region such as the Canadian Tulip Festival and Winterlude.

www.canadascapital.
gc.ca

The board of directors for the NCC has fifteen members. The chairperson and the CEO are both appointed by the Governor in Council while the remaining thirteen members are appointed by the minister of transport: five represent the National Capital Region and eight represent the interests of all other Canadians. The board meets several times a year, but in the past has come under criticism for a lack of openness. NCC meetings are now open to the public.

www.preservecompany.
com/about/history

TRAINING THE TOURISM HOST

Over the past twenty years, the tourism industry has become a major revenue producer for Canada. The fact that there is such a variety of small, independently owned and operated businesses creates problems that are not faced when an industry produces just one product—such as the auto industry. This fragmentation hinders united efforts at improving the quality of the product; however, this same diversity allows the industry to offer a broad-based market appeal.

Measuring the dollar value of tourism is easy, but the real economic importance of tourism to Canada also includes the number of jobs it creates. Tourism is a very labour-intensive industry. Tourists do not drive home in the product; when they purchase a trip to Prince Edward Island, they are purchasing experiences and services. Returning home, they must leave behind the island's beautiful beaches, historic sites, and entertainment. So what *do* they get for their money? They get memories. These memories may be warm and friendly—or they may not.

No machine or technological advancement will ever replace the warm and caring interpersonal communication that takes place between a tourist and a professional tourism host. For this reason, when Canada began a review of its tourism industry product, its focus was on people resources. Listed below are 10 of the major problems this review identified.

Human Resource Challenges, Issues, and Concerns

1. **Industry image.** Most Canadians have never viewed tourism as a true profession, instead perceiving tourism workers negatively, as just "hamburger flippers" or "bed makers" working long hours in dead-end jobs with low wages and few benefits.

2. **Unskilled labour.** In some areas of Canada, the shortage of trained workers is so great that employers are forced to hire applicants who have little or no training. Formal education in the tourism industry continues to lag behind national averages.

3. **Poor training practices.** Since training is sometimes regarded as an expense, employers often do not invest in their new employees to make sure they have the skills needed to accomplish the job. Although training does take time and money, professionals know that not only will trained staff be more productive, but they will also provide customers with a more positive experience that, in turn, increases revenues.

4. **Poor attitudes/self-image.** Workers who have not been trained not only lack the skills to perform their jobs well, but also are often unsure about what they are supposed to do. This leads to two outcomes: frustration and negative responses from customers and management, and feelings that range from increased stress and burnout to apathy from employees.

5. **High turnover.** The poor attitudes described above lead to discontent, causing workers to quit. Turnover rates are often 35% or higher, with some businesses experiencing well over a 100% change in staff on a yearly basis.

6. **Shrinking labour pool.** Tourism has always depended on the labour pool that is less than thirty-five years of age. The demand for labour is increasing; however, the number of younger workers and unskilled immigrants is declining, forcing operators to rethink their human resource strategies.

7. **Demand for qualified workers.** As the industry grows, so does the demand for skilled workers. The CTHRC forecasted that 2012 will show an industry labour shortage in Canada equal to 9500 full-time workers; the labour shortage is forecasted to increase to over 219 000 by 2025.[8]

8. **Poorly trained managers.** Many managers have been placed into their positions without benefit of training themselves. They have not developed the skills to deal with personnel problems and do not understand the value of training.

9. **Language barriers.** Tourism is a business that deals with many cultures and languages, both in the marketplace and in the workforce. Language problems will always require additional attention from businesses wishing to maintain a competitive advantage in tourism.

10. **Lack of recognition for institutional training.** Business operators, who themselves may lack formal training, often do not recognize the importance of institutional training.

How will tourism continue to grow if it is unable to find qualified workers? How does an industry that undervalues training and education and yet requires long hours from a dedicated workforce stay in business? How does it attract and keep the best staff? The answer is, it doesn't. Many businesses within this sector, especially in the food and beverage industry, face bankruptcy within a few years.

For today's managers and for those training to be tomorrow's managers, understanding the problems just discussed is essential. The federal and provincial governments are doing their share to help solve these problems by developing industry-based training programs and national **certification** for employees who have demonstrated their competence in specific tourism occupations. Now, owners and managers must take a proactive stance and put real solutions in place for tourism workers. It is up to the industry to make use of these inexpensive training programs, and to develop and use reasonable work hours, appropriate pay scales, and advancement opportunities for their staff. Without these changes, growth in the tourism industry faces what may be an unbeatable challenge.

Tourism Education Councils (TECs)

Between 1983 and 1990, a series of studies were undertaken, focusing on human resource needs and challenges for the tourism sector. Many of these studies recommended that government, industry, and education co-operate to restructure the current education and training practices in the industry. In addition, several of the studies advocated identifying all the occupations found within the tourism sector, developing occupational standards for each one, training programs to ensure each standard was taught, and a system for certifying qualified tourism professionals who successfully passed the training. The task was originally taken on by **tourism education councils (TECs)** established in each province and territory.

In 1993, the CTHRC was established to serve as a national forum, bringing together all the TECs in order to facilitate the development of national occupational standards and training programs. The CTHRC is not responsible for development of these programs, but instead, with the help of Human Resources and Skills Development Canada (HRSDC, now Human Resources and Social Development Canada), provides leadership and support for the TECs. The federal and provincial governments, along with the tourism sector, believe that a trained workforce is the best way to ensure that the Canadian tourism product is both sustainable and globally competitive. See the Appendix for contact information on TECs.)

Occupational Standards

Occupational standards are documents outlining the skills, knowledge, and attitudes (SKAs) that an individual must demonstrate and practise to be deemed competent in a given occupation. The process of developing occupational standards ensures that industry members from across the country identify and validate the SKA components they believe are most relevant to performance. TECs then ensure these SKAs form the critical mass of each occupational standard document. This satisfies employers who have had some disdain for the term *certificate-based training*, which in the past has attached less importance to actual credentials. The current term, *competency-based training*, focuses on experiential learning as well as knowledge.

The *Emerit* Program

In order to make certification accessible to every tourism worker, the CTHRC has developed the *emerit* tourism training brand, an online training program that teaches participants occupation-specific skills. Currently, *emerit* offers close to thirty different industry certifications. This training is interactive and reasonably priced. To be certified, students need to have both industry training and hands-on experience in the occupation of choice.

Students who graduate from a tourism-based college or university program and wish to certify immediately will likely have the required knowledge base; to become certified, they need to either demonstrate where they gained sufficient hands-on experience or accumulate a block of work hours before they qualify. To make the transition to becoming a certified professional easier, *emerit* has created three levels of certification: tourism essentials certification, occupational knowledge certification, and professional certification. These various levels allow members of the tourism workforce to jump directly into the level of certification that they are best prepared for, and then move up, step by step.

The value of certification is its portability and its national recognition. A certified food and beverage server from Winnipeg has met the criteria established by the industry and accepted in all other provinces and territories. As a manager, a certified applicant will have the skill sets needed to immediately provide quality service for customers, saving both time and money by reducing or eliminating training costs. Certified individuals gain an edge in an increasingly competitive job market. Having successfully completed the CTHRC program of choice, the student is then permitted to place a designation after his or her name that signifies the level achieved. For example, a student who completes the tourism certified supervisor level may use the designation TCS. These new designations will soon be recognized by employers both across Canada and globally.[9]

Standards serve the industry in many ways: they help with the development of job descriptions; they streamline the recruitment and selection process; they result in a well-trained workforce that is committed to the industry; they provide recognition of the value of tourism occupations; they increase service levels, thereby meeting or exceeding client expectations; they serve as a basis for training programs; and they address some of the issues identified by HRSDC as challenges for the future.

Ethics and the Host

Ethics are an important part of how we view the world and conduct our lives. As tourism professionals, we need to know what the term *ethics* means, as well as why we should have a code of conduct and how to put it into action. We sell a product that is purchased unseen and untried, our customers pay a great deal of money for the product, and they place their lives in our hands.

Before beginning a discussion on ethics, we must first understand two key words: *morals* and *ethics*. According to *Webster's New World Dictionary*, morals are "the ability to make a distinction between right and wrong conduct." **Ethics**, on the other hand, involves "a system or code of morals of a particular person, religion, culture, group, or profession." It sounds simple, but we all view the world from different standpoints. Your concept of right and wrong may differ dramatically from your parents' or friends' ideas of right and wrong. What one culture views as wrong, another may view as right.

Cultures today may be based on religion, race, or even business. Many corporations have a specific culture created by company founders and executives who set the ground rules or **code of ethics** by putting into words their beliefs on how the business should operate and on the proper treatment of guests and employees.

A business code of ethics should be printed and prominently displayed, and everyone, including the president/CEO, must understand it and live by its tenets. Often this means a training session or two for employees, but the easiest way to teach ethics is to live by them. When you research the different companies you would like to work for, find out if they have and live by a code of ethics. It is also important that employers have faith in their workers' abilities to put the corporation's code of conduct into action, even if some instances require an unexpected expense.

One of the positive impacts the UNWTO hopes will arise out of tourism is the development of a better understanding between cultural groups, a lofty dream at best. While on vacation, tourists hope to slip from the bonds of their life at home and live vicariously in a place where no one knows them. Big problems can arise when the differences between the cultural norms of the visitor and host are very

Training your staff is essential if you wish to develop a reputation for excellent service. Staff at the Canadian Museum of Immigration at Pier 21 in Halifax must be knowledgable and enthusiastic.
(Photo: SteveKaiser Photography.ca.)

great. This was pointed out when we looked at the negative effects of tourism, but because of the rise in concerns and problems associated with differing codes of conduct, a closer look should be taken.

The two areas of wide concern are sex tourism and crime rates. For a Third World country, with high poverty and poor job prospects for women in particular, prostitution can be a way to make money—money that provides for their families the necessities of life. Some destinations, like Thailand and the Philippines, have gained a reputation for their sex trades, which can mean interaction not only with consenting women, but also with children. Where prostitution is illegal, some countries, such as Pakistan, have allowed "red light districts" to form. This type of destination may be chosen by participants for the very reason that what is unacceptable in their home community is more easily attained and less likely to bring about legal action at their vacation spot.

In Thailand, half a million women work in this trade, most of them based in Bangkok. It has such a significant financial impact on the woman and her family that the risks are ignored. Rising rates of sexually transmitted diseases and HIV have been documented. What is not clear, however, is the role tourism plays, as records of the activity are not kept. This also brings about a variety of sociological and religious issues. Forced prostitution is a human rights concern, and sex tourism is seen as one of the ways traditional family structures in these countries are breaking down. Enforcing legal issues or banning prostitution can cause tremendous hardship for families who depend on that form of income, and suggestions that legislation protect prostitutes could improve both the health and welfare of those earning money in this, one of the world's oldest jobs.

The other side of this negative coin is crime. Tourists are easy prey in a foreign land where customs are not understood and visitors on vacation often participate in such activities as excessive drinking, gambling, and using drugs or prostitutes, and this opens the door to crimes such as theft, credit card fraud, beatings, and death. There is no destination in the world that can guarantee that crime against tourists never occurs. Mexico has recently been in the Canadian spotlight, as two sets of brutal murders have taken place and remain unsolved. In Aruba, a young girl enjoying spring break with classmates disappeared and is presumed dead, but the perpetrators remain free.

Cruise ships are also targets for criminals. Most of the sailing a ship undertakes is in open water, under no specified legal authority, so rapes, robberies, and murders continue to go unsolved. In the past, cruise lines have merely fired the perpetrator or requested they disembark at the next stop, and while local police may be brought in, they have no jurisdiction over a crime that took place in international waters.

Tourists are also targeted by terrorists—they are considered easy targets for abduction or other harm and the event receives worldwide attention. All of these problems are costly for a destination and require that it increase its expenditures on law enforcement, security systems, and fire and emergency personnel.

CASE STUDY

Determining the Boundaries between Staff and Guests

As the human resource manager of a resort hotel in Jasper, Alberta, Chantelle was familiar with the influx of new seasonal staff every year. Each April, hundreds of new employees from across Canada would begin arriving for a busy summer of work, staying until the end of August when they returned to college or university.

During their orientation, Chantelle always took the time to explain that as staff members, employees represented the hotel. Guests travelling into Jasper explored not just the hotel but the community and surrounding areas; it was quite common for staff members to repeatedly run into hotel guests in town during non-work hours. In Chantelle's experience, guests rarely distinguished employees based on context; when they recognized staff in town, they immediately connected them back to the hotel. As guests often did things they would not normally do at home, the hotel had a standing policy that hotel employees were not allowed in guest areas and rooms unless on hotel-related business.

During her regular round of room inspections, Roberta, the housekeeping manager, noticed François entering a guest room. François was a new employee working at the front desk that summer, completing a mandatory work term assigned by his college in Quebec. François had always received compliments on his service, as he treated guests like family. However, when Roberta saw him enter the guest room, he was dressed in street clothes and clearly was not on duty. When she returned to her office, she quickly looked up the guest information for the room François had entered; the last name on file for the guest was the same as François's last name.

Company policy was clear; hotel employees were not allowed to mingle with guests. As she sat back in her chair, Roberta knew that François was an outstanding worker, making her next call to Chantelle that much more difficult.

1. Explain the ethical dilemma that Roberta is facing.
2. From François's position, is this breach of rules an ethical issue or a cultural one? What facts are you basing your judgment on?
3. As a manager, how might you avoid facing a similar problem?

Summary

- Guests and hosts comprise the "people" factor in the tourism sector. Guests are the entertained and hosts are the entertainers.
- There are two types of guests. Pleasure guests visit an area by choice using their discretionary time and money; business guests travel for meetings, conventions, or to earn revenue, and their travel is non-discretionary.
- Tourists can be categorized by demographics and psychographics. Demographics provide basic information about where the guest is from, family income, age, occupation, and education level. Psychographic profiles provide insight into the motives, behaviours, interests, and personalities of the guests. Understanding why people travel and the barriers they face when they choose to travel can help the host provide a satisfactory travel experience.
- Hosts must understand the unique characteristics of the tourism product. They must have a good knowledge of the marketing mix and how to use it effectively to attract an increasing number of tourists. Hosts must also be able to identify target markets and provide these groups with the products and services that best suit their needs.
- Some groups, including members of the host community or political leaders, suffer from tourism illiteracy. They might not understand their role as hosts or the important financial role that tourism plays in their community; they rarely support tourism development initiatives. It is important that education is available about the benefits of tourism, including more employment opportunities, an influx of revenue from outside regions, as well as additional sources of tax revenue.
- Industry and government have identified ten problems in the human resource component of the industry. There is a strong need for trained professionals. Industry and the tourism education councils (TECs) have created certification programs that are gaining international respect for both their thoroughness and relevance.

Questions

1. Plan a trip to your hometown for a) a business guest and b) a pleasure guest. Explain how their motivations, needs, and expectations (MNEs) differ.

2. Define the following terms in your own words: *demographics, psychographics, motivators, external locus of control, push and pull factors, discretionary income, discretionary time.*

3. Explain how your tourism region can best fulfill the needs of

   a) a psychocentric

   b) an allocentric

   c) Compare the needs and expectations of each. Justify your answer by defining the terms and choosing an activity that would match the individual personalities.

4. List five different disabilities you might encounter in customers in a restaurant. As a server, what might you do to help make their stay more comfortable?

5. Is your local (municipal/provincial) government "tourism illiterate"? Define the term and justify your answer using local examples.

6. Tourism has both negative and positive effects on a region/country.

    a) List nine negative effects of the tourism industry and ten positive effects.

    b) From each list, choose the three effects (for a total of six) that you believe are most important in your region, and explain why you have chosen them.

7. What is the NCC and why was it established? Should Canadians from across the continent have input regarding the development of the city of Ottawa (National Capital Region)? Justify.

8. List and explain each of the ten issues and concerns identified by the tourism sector regarding its human resources.

9. a) What are "occupational standards" and how were they developed?

    b) Log on to the *emerit* website (www.emerit.ca). On the left side of the homepage, click on the "Get Training" link. Then select the "Frontline Training" option. From this page, select one of the available certification and training options listed, watch the video, and identify the critical skills, knowledge, and abilities needed to be successful in that particular job.

10. What is a code of ethics? List eight items you would include in your code of ethics (conduct) if you were opening a small hotel or restaurant.

11. a) Why are tourists so vulnerable at destinations, frequently considered a prime target for criminals? What might tourists do to better prepare themselves?

    b) Identify three types of crime you believe you might encounter on a trip to a foreign country. What is the best way to avoid getting into trouble with local criminals?

Notes

1. Stanley C. Plog, "Why destination areas rise and fall in popularity." Paper presented to the Travel Research Association, Southern California Chapter, Los Angeles, CA, October, 1972.

2. D. Fiske and S. Maddi, *Functions of Varied Experience* (Homewood, IL: Dorsey, 1961).

3. Poon, cited in Geoffrey Wall and Alister Mathieson, *Tourism Changes, Impacts and Opportunities* (Essex, UK: Pearson Education Limited), p. 32.

4. Arlin Epperson, "Why people travel," *Journal of Physical Education, Recreation and Dance,* 31 (April 1983), pp. 53–54.

5. Robert W. McIntosh and Charles R. Goeldner, *Tourism Principles, Practices, Philosophies,* 6th ed. (New York: John Wiley & Sons, 1990), p. 131.

6. www.unwto.org.

7. G.V. Doxey, "When enough's enough: The natives are restless in Old Niagara," Heritage Canada, 2(2) (1976), pp. 26–27.

8. Canadian Tourism Human Resource Council, Total Tourism Sector Employment in Canada: 2004 Update, March 2005, p. 28.

9. www.emerit.ca.

Planning, Developing, and Marketing a Destination

Key terms

balanced development
catalytic development
centralized development
channel of distribution
clustering
coattail development
demand
destination life cycle
elastic demand
environmental
    protection
forecasting
functional form
hospitality of host
inelastic demand
infrastructure

intangible
integrated development
interdependency
isolation
marketing plan
market match
market segmentation
natural resources
niche market
partnerships
perceived value
place
planning
price
product
product capacity

promotion
qualitative forecasting
quantitative forecasting
rapid development
secondary developers
sense of place
suprastructure
surplus
target marketing
tourist destination area
    (TDA)
transportation systems
trend
trend analysis
unique selling
    proposition (USP)

Learning objectives

Having read this chapter you will be able to

1. Describe the five essential components of a tourist destination.

2. Explain how the life cycle of a product affects tourism destinations.

3. Identify the five priorities the Canadian government uses to help plan future tourism growth.

4. Describe the role of communities and regions in tourism planning and development.

5. Identify the eight steps of the planning process.

6. Explain the differences between the three types of development.

7. Identify seven constraints on the future growth of Canada's tourism industry.

A tourism facility, site, or event does not become a **tourist destination area (TDA)** overnight. An abundance of formal and informal planning, developing, and marketing is required before an area is known well enough that enough people choose a TDA to make it profitable. A century ago, tourism simply "developed," with little or no knowledge of how it was happening. If the TDA already had a home base of residents, tourism was simply another way to make money. If, on the other hand, few people lived in the area but some natural (or ancient cultural) aspect intrigued visitors enough for them to want to visit, then development meant a huge change in lifestyle for locals.

Planning the tourism experience, ensuring that you provide your market base with the facilities and activities they want, and presenting an exciting marketing program that describes your TDA well will help ensure the desired marketplace segment(s) will hear about it and decide to visit.

This chapter looks first at what good planning is and why planning is essential; three basic methods of development are discussed, as well as the characteristics that inhibit the growth of your tourist destination area. Six factors that help create a tourist-friendly TDA are considered, with the understanding that even in a fully developed city like Victoria, Edmonton, Winnipeg, or Halifax, positive changes can be made that will make your TDA more enjoyable. Finally, we examine the odd "product" that we call tourism and how it is really a blend of tangible products and intangible services that combine to form an overall experience.

Planning is an essential component of profitable tourism. It is here that you decide where and how to develop a new TDA or add to an existing one. The planning stage tells you whether or not the community is ready to embark on a "tourism venture" with you. This is the stage where you determine what your customers want now and what they might be looking for in the future. Ignoring proper planning may doom a project to failure. However, the same process can be applicable whether a group is looking to add a whole new level of industry to a TDA, to simply add a new activity or site, or to create a totally new product from scratch. The concepts that follow in this chapter may be used by any business or region—from a small entrepreneurial tourism business to an entire country. In this chapter, for simplicity's sake, a tourism destination area (TDA) may be that single unit or it may refer to a more diverse product.

THE FIVE COMPONENTS OF A TOURIST DESTINATION

Right from the start, five essential components must be in place if the TDA is to host travellers. These components work together, moving from the raw physical resources and opportunities through to the attitudes and characteristics demonstrated by the community within the destination area.

1. **Natural resources.** A destination must be physically able to support tourists. It needs land, a habitable climate, a water supply, and natural beauty. Hawaii is an example of a destination that has many **natural resources** available— soft sands, beautiful waters, and flora and fauna that have intrigued people from early times. The Jasper and Banff valleys are good examples of spectacular Canadian scenery, and although they lack the warm temperatures of Hawaii, their majestic snow-capped mountains, unique wildlife, and changing seasons have helped create a huge tourist market. Not all destinations need such a dramatic backdrop to entice the tourist, but they must all have the natural resources available to support life and the tourist's needs.

2. **Infrastructure.** Often called the "guts of the city," **infrastructure** is the first component put in place in any area that is being developed for habitation. Components include roads, telephone service, electricity, sewage and drainage, docks, railroad tracks, airport runways—all the essential services that are both seen or unseen. Infrastructure sets up the conditions of flow: flow of power, water, utilities, communication, and people.

3. **Suprastructure.** A community's **suprastructure** consists of all the buildings found at the destination. Lodging facilities, restaurants, terminals, sport complexes, stores—these are all examples of the suprastructure of a site. Suprastructure is connected directly to infrastructure. Should a destination encourage rapid growth in demand and development of suprastructure components, such as additional buildings, then the infrastructure must also be reviewed to ensure it can handle the additional capacity.

4. **Transportation system.** A **transportation system** incudes the actual vehicles that use the infrastructure. What good are railroad tracks if there are no trains? Transportation systems are completely dependent on infrastructure; together, they provide the guest (and host) with access to the destination and a way or ways to get around it.

5. **Hospitality of host.** The **hospitality of the host** destination includes the social and political climate, but involves much more than laws and culture; it is the genuine warmth shown by the local population—the smiles and greetings, and the willingness to tolerate the changes that tourism brings. The host city may have the finest hotels, the best restaurants, and the most modern methods of transportation and yet not attract the tourist market because of a less-than-welcoming attitude.

A TDA that is already developed will have these components, so the processes move forward at a faster pace. In the case of a TDA that has not been developed, these components must be in place if the TDA is to entice the midcentric and psychocentric traveller. The allocentric, however, ready to give up some of life's comforts just to be one of the first, may visit before a site is even considered a TDA.

As an example of how these components fit into an area that has already seen some development, consider Newfoundland and Labrador. After benefiting significantly from oil revenues and increased demand, there has been substantial investment in tourism and new tourism growth. This province has an abundance of natural beauty to attract the tourist. Gros Morne National Park on the west coast of Newfoundland is a UNESCO (United Nations Educational, Scientific, and Cultural Organization) World Heritage Site. With over 200 member countries,

UNESCO is an agency within the United Nations specializing in international co-operation around scientific and cultural matters. Gros Morne National Park, nicknamed "the Galapagos of geology," has an abundance of wildlife, spectacular mountains, and fiords carved by glaciers from a distant time. Infrastructure and transportation systems are already in place—Newfoundland has many beautiful scenic roads to travel, and airplanes and ferries connect cities on the island to one another and to the mainland. Gros Morne National Park also offers the tourist a unique infrastructure—more than 65 km of hiking trails! Newfoundland's suprastructure intermingles the modern hotel with bed and breakfast inns, historical forts with state-of-the-art museums, craft stores with shopping centres, and ski lodges with golf courses. But it is the outgoing, warm hospitality offered by Newfoundlanders that makes this province a great, exciting tourist destination.[1]

www.unesco.org

FOOTPRINT

The "Greening" of Fairmont Hotels

Canadians should have tremendous pride for one of its "own"—Fairmont Hotels. In the early 1990s, Fairmont began to establish a green program unlike any other in the world. With many of their hotels placed in ecosystems such as the Banff and Jasper valleys, they decided to do something about the environment long before other hotels were even thinking about it and published a booklet called *The Green Partnership Guide*. In it, they listed publicized programs they were embarking on to reduce waste and to reuse and recycle products when possible. Here are some of the objectives they have met over the past decade.

Name of hotel	Overview	Example of one measure implemented	Total savings per year
Delta Toronto	296 rooms $700 000 in upgrades	Centralized energy management system	$80 000
Fairmont Château Laurier	429 rooms Over $3 million in energy retrofits	Installation of high-efficiency incremental units in all guest rooms	$575 000
Fairmont Banff Springs	770 rooms $600 000 in retrofits	Retrofit of all guest room lighting and heating systems	$315 000
Fairmont The Queen Elizabeth	1000+ rooms $3 million in upgrades	Lighting retrofit of all guest areas and installation of ventilation waste-heat recovery system	$500 000

Fairmont hotels recycle just about everything possible from food service leftovers (sent to soup kitchens or to become fertilizer); unused guestroom soaps (melted down and reformed into bars that are donated to agencies working in developing countries); and pamphlets that encourage guests to think wisely about water conservation during their stay (fewer hot baths, reusing towels, and sleeping on sheets for more than one night).[2]

Planning for tourism means providing wide, clean walkways, and streets with accessible local transportation.
(Photo: John B. Kerr.)

THE LIFE CYCLE OF A DESTINATION

Every product, service, and business moves through its own cycle of life, in much the same way a person does. Although the life cycle of a product or service might vary—some only last a short period of time while others last many decades and beyond—the cycle itself it fairly consistent, typically with four stages.

In a **destination life cycle**, the first stage is called *conception*. This is when the creative entrepreneur comes up with a new concept that is different and exciting. Ideas flow, plans are made, and research is done to ensure that there is a demand for the new product or service. The second stage of the life cycle is the actual *building* of the product or service. If done well, it is built to meet the needs of a specific set of targeted groups: a local establishment that offers traditional experiences might be interesting to a psychocentric traveller, but an allocentric traveller might be attracted to a destination that is newly discovered and remains unique. The further along development moves, the more tourists the product may attract. The third phase is *maturity*. During this phase, all components of the destination are fully developed, the product is being marketed successfully, and visitor use is high.

Once a site has enjoyed several years of high activity, it begins to lose visitors as they move on to newer destinations they have not yet experienced. This phase is called *decline*. The product itself may be well used and beginning to look a little rundown. At this point in its life cycle, the destination can choose to close, to become a second- or third-rate activity, or to rethink the product—returning to the conception stage, and reinventing and renewing the destination to attract a new set of visitors and to bring past visitors back again.

The Canada's Wonderland theme park (located just north of Toronto) provides good examples of how tourism products avoid the decline phase. Every few years, new attractions are added, such as a steel hypercoaster in 2008, called Behemoth, and the new giga-coaster Leviathan, measuring over 300 feet in height, which opened in 2012. The park has changed ownership multiple times in its thirty-year history, but

Urban centres are increasing their appeal to adventurous risk takers. The "Edge Walk" at the CN Tower in Toronto gives brave souls a unique perspective of the city.
(Photo courtesy Canadian Tourism Commission.)

has remained focused on continual growth, with new rides and attractions, and this has made it one of the most-visited seasonal theme parks in North America.

In an effort to revitalize the CN Tower in Toronto, this attraction has added lights at night for visitors and a new glass elevator so they can enjoy the entire ascent/descent—from floor to ceiling. Realizing they had a unique opportunity to provide a rare experience, the CN Tower launched the EdgeWalk in 2011. People can now walk hands-free around the main pod of the tower, over 116 stories, or 356 metres, above street level.

No product is free from its life cycle. Tourism professionals must be constantly looking for ways to improve and renew their products and excite their target markets if they wish to stay competitive in the global world of tourism.

PLANNING FOR TOURISM

Planning is an activity all businesses must do, whether it is on a daily basis, by the month or year, or even years into the future. Government plans usually focus on long-term activities five to ten years away. When they focus on the future, they usually identify the important goals they wish to achieve and how they intend to achieve them. With this in mind, the Canadian government developed a tourism direction in their report, "Building a National Tourism Strategy."[3] It established six national priorities for tourism development:

1. Ensure the efficient flow of tourists to and from Canada at border crossings.

2. Emphasize the need to implement transportation policies and programs that take into consideration national, provincial/territorial, and regional tourism economic benefits.

3. Ensure that existing products are enhanced and new products developed to take advantage of new and emerging opportunities.

4. Ensure that the supply of tourism/hospitality labour is consistent with the demand.

5. Improve access by governments, businesses, and stakeholders to relevant information and analysis for decision making, and improve measurement of tourism's performance and impact on the economy.

6. Better harmonize and coordinate marketing activities between the CTC and provinces/territories (P/T) to better position Canadian destinations and optimize existing resources through increased government collaboration.

Most tourism professionals never deal with tourism planning on a national level, but if you decide to become an owner, you will likely get involved at a provincial, regional, or local level of planning. You do not have to be an owner to become involved at these levels; you simply need to be concerned about the direction in which tourism in your area is moving. Involvement may be as simple as planning some form of regional fundraiser or small event, or it may mean getting involved at the political end of the spectrum to help focus your region on positive, achievable tourism goals. Although each community should develop goals specific to its own strengths and interests, the following goals should be part of a community's tourism plan:

1. A framework for improving residents' quality of life by developing infrastructure and suprastructure for residents and visitors alike

2. Improvement of residents' standard of living through the economic benefit of tourism

3. Guidelines for appropriate development within the city limits and within a certain radius of the city

4. A tourism program designed to fit residents' economic, cultural, and social views and attitudes

5. A yearly evaluation policy for the tourism plan

As seen in Figure 3.1, the planning model is cyclical. Once the original cycle is completed, it starts over again. The eight steps in tourism planning are basic to

FIGURE 3.1
The Planning Process

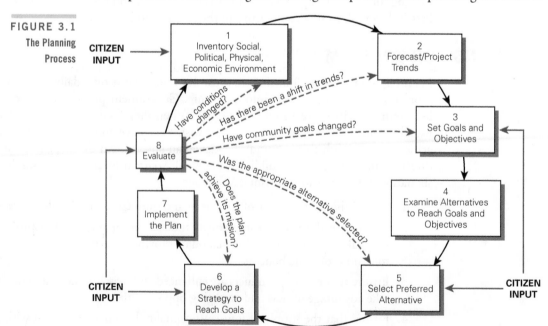

Source: USTTA, *Tourism USA* (Washington, DC: Department of Commerce, 1986), p. 20.

almost any planning process. The process begins with an inventory of what already exists and ends with an evaluation of what has been accomplished. The intermediate steps identify the specifics required in good tourism planning.

PUTTING PLANS INTO ACTION: REFLECTING BACK ON THE 2010 VANCOUVER WINTER OLYMPICS

In July 2003, the International Olympic Committee (IOC) announced that British Columbia had been chosen to host the 2010 Winter Olympics and Paralympics. Winning the right to host the Games is an expensive process, requiring a lot of preparation and commitment, but British Columbia has always led the way in Canada in developing its tourism industry. The province has had strong tourism leadership for many years, and, as always, a plan. The following discussion attempts to illustrate how the eight steps of the planning process might have been used by the Vancouver Organizing Committee (VANOC) for the 2010 Olympic Games to help ensure their ability to create a strong and profitable event.

Step 1—Inventory

The first step is to conduct a thorough inventory of the community's social and political atmosphere and its physical and economic environment.

a) **Political atmosphere.** Assess the political atmosphere of the community, including attitudes of local politicians and community leaders toward tourism. Some attitudes might require positive support while others may need to be changed or reinforced. How does the community feel about the tourism industry, and do they understand the benefits it will bring to residents? These are all political areas that need to be navigated.

b) **Social atmosphere.** Outline the political and cultural history of the region. Note festivals and special cultural events. Assess community awareness of the value and benefits of tourism. If the region is found to be tourism illiterate, it is important to inform residents of the tourism planning process and the value of the industry to their region. This can be done in a variety of ways: town meetings, television or radio talk shows, newspaper articles or editorials, and a general education campaign. It is also important to identify the "people resources" in the area: individuals with artistic abilities, those with knowledge of local cultures, and those with training in the industry who are willing to get involved. Using local talents during the development process helps to eliminate opposition and encourages a sense of pride and commitment in the community as the plan proceeds.

c) **Physical environment.** Consider the region's geography: its location, natural resources, climate, and natural history. Every region has unique beauty and characteristics that can be highlighted as tourism opportunities.

d) **Infrastructure and suprastructure.** The **product capacity**, such as the number of guests your infrastructure and suprastructure can accommodate, must be examined. This is often called *carrying capacity*. Will transportation systems to and around your destination support an influx of visitors? What improvements are needed? Will additional infrastructure be required and who will be responsible for its development and cost?

List the accommodations, restaurants, attractions, and conference facilities available for the tourist. Can a tourist play a round of golf? Take a swim? Go canoeing or biking? Are any facilities geared toward the adventure tourist?

e) **Economic environment.** If a community has a strong economy, then it may not see a need for tourism development. If this is the case, it might be useful to focus on the fact that tourism diversifies the economy by providing employment for students, those returning to the workforce, and new immigrants. If a community is economically depressed, then it may lack the financial resources to invest in tourism. Finding the capital to help fund tourism development can provide a much-needed infusion of money and jobs and can help solve a region's economic woes.

Before beginning the process of putting together a bid, British Columbia had to assess its readiness to go after the Olympics. Politically speaking, the province has long recognized the value of the tourism sector to the overall well-being of the province. Their tourism workforce is large and they have good training programs in place. They have the economic base to actually build the new facilities that were required to run the Games—and who could ask for a more beautiful spot than our westernmost province? Vancouver already had a good urban transportation system, a wide variety of hotels and restaurants, and good shopping areas. While the snow-sport competitions were held in the mountains, indoor sports like ice and speed skating were staged in urban areas to facilitate access for the many visitors who love to watch these events.

Step 2—Forecast Trends

Forecasting trends is important in our industry because it identifies opportunities for regions or developers and helps keep a destination and its tourist activities on the cutting edge of what is popular. A **trend** is "a current style or preference." However, people are fickle, and what is trendy one year may not be so the next year. Quick change is difficult for tourism because most infrastructure and suprastructure is expensive to build—and permanent. Tourism entrepreneurs must be able to recognize trends that will have a longer shelf life and avoid investing substantially in brief fads.

Forecasting means looking to the future. Edward Inskeep states that planning, in the broad sense of the word, is simply "organizing the future to achieve certain goals."[4] While no one can predict the future with certainty, there are two general methods that provide information to increase our ability to make best guesses. They allow us to look at the potential growth of the community and the surrounding region, and to see how that growth will enhance or hinder tourism in the future. The two basic methods used in forecasting are:

1. **Qualitative methods.** Qualitative information collects data surrounding experiences, perspectives, feelings and understandings using non-statistical information. Common techniques include interviews, open-ended surveys, focus groups, and observation. When studying people and the social environment, qualitative methods have exploded in the last thirty years.[5]

One form of **qualitative forecasting** is the Delphi technique, a systematic survey of tourism industry experts who are asked a series of questions developed by a panel of community members. The experts' collective opinions are sent back to the panel, which reviews the answers until a consensus on the timing of future events is reached. This structured method is particularly useful for analyzing medium- and long-term changes in demand and in weighing less tangible factors such as motivation. Qualitative approaches usually require less data and money than quantitative approaches.

2. **Quantitative methods.** Quantitative techniques draw on current and historical data, and through the use of various statistical methods of analysis, seek to generalize actions and predict future activities.[6] Quite often, industry places greater value on numerical data as a tool to base decisions on; what quantitative data might lack in richness of experience, they make up for in predictive confidence.

Quantitative forecasting requires an adequate database to which a range of numerical techniques can be applied. **Trend analysis** plots historical data over a number of cycles. For example, tourist arrivals at some future date are estimated by analyzing past arrivals and projecting these numbers into the future.

One difficulty is the scarcity of reliable data. Although hotels and restaurants have for some time been collecting and using information such as occupancy percentages and average guest cheques, only recently has the tourism industry as a whole been concerned with such data. Timely and reliable data are needed to make tourism strategies more effective and less risky.

Looking at the past, it is clear that the value of hosting the Olympic Games has increased. For example, between 1972 and 1985, the growth rate of international visitors to Alberta was 0.25% annually. However, by the time the 1988 Olympics were held in Calgary, international tourism had jumped 15%. Of course, this growth was due to the huge draw of the Olympics, but in the years following, the province maintained a steady annual growth rate of 3.25%—a nice increase from 1985. In 1994, Norway hosted the Games in the small town of Lillehammer. Tourism to Norway during 1994 jumped by 43%, and the Olympics put Lillehammer on the map. It is estimated that more than two billion people watched the Salt Lake City Olympics on television in 2002. These numbers show that interest in the Olympic Games is big and that international awareness of a region and country grows when it hosts such a global event. B.C. experts forecasted that the Games would generate $10 billion in tourism revenues, provide over 228 000 jobs, and bring in an additional $2.5 billion in tax revenues.[7]

Step 3—Develop a Vision, Mission Statement, Objectives, and Goals

Each development should have a clear vision of where it is heading, who it is serving, and why it has value. Without a clear vision and direction, the entire development can lack purpose. A mission statement should articulate the overall vision for the destination, site, or activity. A good mission statement not only reflects the purpose of the development, but also provides specific objectives on how the project will improve the quality of life in the region. Care needs to be taken here as many mission statements lack direction, content, or clarity. If the vision is unclear, the mission statement cannot help but also be so. Often, mission statements become the home of overly positive phrases and industry jargon without actually providing an understandable direction.

Objectives are then crafted as markers, set out along the path to achieve the vision. After the mission statement and objectives have been written, specific goals should be identified. Goals should be clearly stated and measurable, helping to determine if the plan was a success. Most important of all, goals must be realistic and achievable.

VANOC developed a vision, a mission statement, and a set of objectives with goals. These reflected the International Olympic Committee's three pillars of Olympism: sport, culture, and the recently added third pillar—environmental conservation.

The vision: A stronger Canada whose spirit is raised by its passion for sport, culture, and sustainability.

The mission: To touch the soul of the nation and inspire the world by creating and delivering an extraordinary Olympic and Paralympic experience with lasting legacies.[8]

These objectives aimed to ensure they considered the needs of citizens, today and tomorrow, as well as integrating and optimizing sport, environmental, social, and economic considerations. They worked to help build community, domestic, and international support. Overall, they wanted to ensure sustainable legacies and enable the Games to showcase sustainability to the citizens of Canada and the world through the Olympic medium.

www.olympic.org/
vancouver-2010-winter-
olympics

Step 4—Study Alternative Plans of Action

Good plans prepare multiple methods of achieving a set of goals rather than identifying only one method. This provides options and alternatives on the route of meeting those goals. To develop different methods, it is important to brainstorm as many alternatives as possible. During idea generation, a particular suggestion may seem outrageous; however, a different idea might be manipulated into an innovation that has not been used before. At this point, public discussion or the use of experts may again become important. Each alternative should be looked at from both a positive and negative point of view.

The development of the Vancouver Olympics required that many different venues be developed, including additional infrastructure and suprastructure. As a result, the building of Olympic sites was handled by a wide variety of businesses. For each of the Olympic development sites, VANOC considered all bids, carefully examining each for the specifics that the committee identified as essential to the process.

Step 5—Select Preferred Alternative

Once all possible ways of building or achieving goals have been thoroughly examined, decisions must be made. Alternative plans of action need to be arranged in an order that best fits your outcomes and costs, and a primary plan must be chosen. Secondary plans can remain as back-up if, during future evelutions, the primary plan is shown to be achieving appropriate goals.

VANOC chose companies that best reflected and would be able to achieve quality and sustainability in the final product, and considered each business's ability to create the product in an environmentally sound way.

Gatineau Park in Canada's Capital Region is one of many examples in spectacular natural settings available close to major urban centres.
(Photo: Raymond Chan, Photomedia.)

Step 6—Develop a Strategy to Reach Goals

At this point, an outline is needed of specific objectives that must be met in order to reach the goal, as well as a detailed plan that allows community members to see exactly how the goals will be achieved. Plans should consider all community components, address the varying levels of services provided, and identify when, where, and how each objective will be met. A timeline showing deadlines for each objective helps individuals focus.

From the beginning, VANOC had a timeline in place, and most of the target dates were met.

Step 7—Implement Plan

When business plans are executed, they rarely unfold without changes. Field Marshall Moltke wrote that "no plan survives contact with the enemy,"[9] a military sentiment that transfers well from the battlefield to the boardroom. During the construction stage of development, setbacks will likely occur; unexpected developments and changing circumstances, including weather and political movements, can interfere. A multitude of influences may alter plans, and a change in thinking and possibly revised plans may be required.

Community support through local chambers of commerce, city councils, and other businesses is a prerequisite for success in a community-planned business. The grand opening of an event or attraction should be a gala affair with many community members present.

The development of competition sites and the expansion of the Sea to Sky Highway leading from Vancouver to Whistler were completed. In April 2005, VANOC unveiled the 2010 Olympic emblem Ilanaaq (the Inuit word for "friend").[10] The emblem was based on the traditional inuksuk, a navigational landmark used by the Inuit. Over the years, the inuksuk has come to characterize friendship, hope, and hospitality. As part of the Olympic promotions, a soft, cuddly Ilanaaq was released for the 2007 Christmas season and the biggest problem it created was that demand far outweighed supply! Many different Canadian corporations became sponsors of the Games, and stores carried numerous articles bearing the Games' official emblem.

Step 8—Review, Evaluate, Revise, and Continue with Plans

Everything in tourism needs to be evaluated continually, from Step 1 right through Step 7. Operators need to appreciate the achieved successes and acknowledge factors that are blocking success. Plans need to be evaluated against budgets and time-lines, as well as the established visions. Ongoing evaluation is essential because early detection of problems allows for changes to be implemented while they are still feasible.

VANOC was able to meet their goals set forth to the International Olympic Committee. Construction and operations spending, according to PricewaterhouseCoopers, reached $604 million and $1.84 billion, respectively, meeting budgetary projections. Were these Olympics profitable? Some estimations put the financial contribution of the Vancouver Olympics to the B.C. GDP at over $2.5 billion; how long the Olympics will continue to affect the B.C. economy remains to be seen.

In Practice

Choose a community in your area that could benefit from a tourism plan. Write a brief description of the social, political, physical, and economic environment in that community. Based on this information and your knowledge of the area, design a mission statement with corresponding objectives for tourism planning for the community. Craft goals for each objective, then write out specific strategies to achieve two of these goals.

TOURISM DEVELOPMENT

Tourism development ranges from well organized (areas that are ultimately pleasant to visit) to haphazard (areas where past and current upheaval in the community is obvious).

One classification of tourist development, defined by Douglas Pearce,[11] is based on the division of responsibility in the development process. **Integrated development** comprises development by a single promoter or developer. **Catalytic development** occurs when a major promoter encourages complementary development by other companies or individuals. **Coattail development** occurs when visitors are enticed to an area of natural or unique qualities, and development takes place to provide the facilities and amenities they desire.

Integrated Development

Walt Disney World is a classic example of *integrated development*, which occurs when an individual or company acquires a large parcel of land and develops the property to the exclusion of all other developers. The resort can usually stand alone, with all the necessary amenities.

The following factors are characteristic of integrated development:

1. **One developer.** The entire resort is built by a single developer who has all the financial and technical resources. As a result, local participation is largely excluded from the development process.

2. **Balanced development.** Because the entire property is under the same ownership, one portion of the resort can operate at a deficit that is offset by a more lucrative portion. For example, at a ski resort, the sale of ski tickets and the operation of chairlifts may not be very profitable, but these low margins may be offset by large margins from condominium sales and rentals, creating a **balanced development**.

3. **Rapid development.** Once approvals are given to build, a single developer generally will not encounter roadblocks caused by other groups or the community. Because it is private, the company can move quickly in the building phase, resulting in rapid **development**.

4. **Functional form.** An individual developer has the power to build an entire resort community based on a cohesive theme. This theme requires all buildings to adhere to a **functional form**: to look a certain way, to be located in the most convenient spot, and to enhance the recreational activities of the tourists.

5. **Isolation.** Complete freedom is necessary to develop such resorts. As a result, these resorts are commonly located away from existing settlements. Eventually, community development may occur nearby, but generally this type of development remains in **isolation**.

6. **High prices.** This type of resort is generally first class in all respects and attracts those who can afford the high prices. The increased costs of developing an integrated resort are usually offset by the high cost of staying at the resort. In fact, the isolation of the resort may enhance its status.

Catalytic Development

Whistler, British Columbia; Banff, Alberta; and Mont Tremblant, Quebec, are examples of *catalytic development*, in which initial development stimulates other projects. The catalytic development process is characterized by the following steps:

1. **Centralized development.** Initiating **centralized development** is a single, large promoter who provides the basic facilities such as ski lifts, major accommodation units, and promotion. Again, the developer usually has a large parcel of land to develop, but is basing the success of the resort on the added facilities others can provide. In a general sense, the developer is providing the infrastructure for the other facilities.

2. **Secondary developers.** Based on success in the initial years of the resort, **secondary** developers build complementary facilities such as nightclubs, movie theatres, restaurants, shops, accommodations, and additional recreational activities such as miniature golf or swimming. These developments require less capital investment, which permits active participation by local companies and individuals.

3. **Interdependency.** The success and increased expansion of this type of resort depend on the entrepreneurial activities of others, creating a condition of **interdependency**. If the initial resort development does not succeed, other developers will not proceed with their projects. Conversely, if the other developers do not succeed, it could lead to the demise of the primary resort. In some cases, the principal promoter will pressure municipalities to block secondary developments considered incompatible. Additionally, the local government may intervene to control growth.

Coattail Development

Niagara Falls is a good example of *coattail development*, which tends to occur around national parks, historic sites, and unique natural attractions. People are so drawn to these areas that entrepreneurs jump at the opportunity to ride on the coattails of the original site. Some of the characteristics of coattail development are:

1. **No common theme.** Without a central organizer, there is no effort to have a common theme. Businesses develop because tourists are readily available in the area. Initially, the nearby community sees little or no reason for a common theme. As tourism evolves, however, a community may develop a theme to fill a demand from a particular group of customers, or **niche market**, in order to create a sense of uniqueness that will compete with other coattail communities in the area.

2. **Duplication and redundancy.** Because no single promoter dominates this area, no guidelines or regulations are established stating what type of business is needed. Many entrepreneurs build similar businesses. Consequently, the variety of motels, restaurants, and shops is limited.

3. **Greater competition.** An offshoot of duplicated effort is increased competition in the area. If tourists have four T-shirt shops from which to choose, they are more likely to compare prices and variety before making a purchase. This competition among retailers produces a healthier business atmosphere.

4. **Late community involvement.** Most coattail development is piecemeal, which means development occurs as the need arises, without an organized plan. Many communities are now seeing the need to create consistency in the look and atmosphere of the town. But, because most of the tourism businesses were established years ago, it is difficult to convince the business leaders of the need for change. Communities are starting with business improvement district (BID) approval, which encourages the improvement of downtown areas. Through a BID or other form of regulatory process, the community can influence the types and appearances of new businesses and promote the area as a unified group of shops, restaurants, and accommodations. The Niagara Region of Ontario, for example, has worked hard to redevelop the destination, and today Niagara serves as a model of tourism planning.

Natural attractions like Niagara Falls are an important part of Canada's tourism product.
(Photo courtesy Canadian Tourism Commission.)

SIX KEY FACTORS TO A TOURISM DESTINATION AREA'S SUCCESS

What makes a destination "tourist friendly"? Why is one destination so much easier to navigate for a tourist than another? Why is one attraction in the centre of town and another in the suburbs? Smith and Reid[12] have identified six factors that are key to helping a destination provide tourists with the least amount of discomfort and the maximum amount of enjoyment during their stay:

1. Identifying a sense of place
2. Ensuring the product/market match fits
3. Clustering facilities (e.g., sites, restaurants, accommodations)
4. Creating good transportation systems
5. Creating positive partnerships within the community
6. Maintaining/restoring the environment

Identifying a Sense of Place The first selling point of a TDA is its ability to define itself, to identify something that is unique about the city, something no other city can claim. This **sense of place** may arise from a natural resource or may be created by people through historical perspectives or design. A destination marketing organization (DMO) would call sense of place the destination's **unique selling proposition** (**USP**), the unique characteristic that sets one offering or experience apart from all others. For Niagara Falls, of course, it is their magnificent waterfalls. For Edmonton, it is likely the West Edmonton Mall. For smaller towns, deciding on a USP can be difficult. A USP for Brantford, Ontario, could be that it is the birthplace of Wayne Gretzky. Another element that impresses visitors to a TDA

Unique towns and villages, such as Saint-Jean-Port-Joli, Quebec, provide tourists with the opportunity to purchase local crafts and to snap a few photographs.
(Photo: Paula Kerr.)

right from the start is the effective use of a grand, welcoming entrance—an access point that signals to visitors that they have arrived. An effective entrance creation may simply be noticeable and attractive signage, or it may include regional symbolism and important information for tourists.

The capital city of a country should be one of the best examples of a tourist-friendly destination, but are they? Washington, D.C., is an excellent example of the use of the six key factors. Is London, England? Nairobi, Kenya? Melbourne, Australia? Is it possible for a city, already defined by growth factors, to create a friendlier, more accessible tourist experience? Using Ottawa, Canada's capital, as our example, you will be able to see that a well-developed city can still, if it decides to do so, become more tourist-friendly by adjusting a number of these factors.

Ottawa is a good example of how these six key factors can make a stay more (or less) enjoyable. Ottawa was a logging town with no apparent destiny until Queen Victoria chose the city to be the capital of Canada. Other cities were unhappy because their positions were far better—they were bigger, had more money, and already had a presence in the country. However, as mentioned in Chapter 2, Ottawa was a distance from the U.S. border, making it harder for the Americans to invade, and the possibility of a safe water route to the large port of Kingston (Toronto was just another short sail away) were two factors that influenced the monarch's decision. Of course, the rapids on the connecting Rideau River meant that a canal and a series of locks would have to be built between Ottawa and Kingston. This incredible feat was accomplished in just six years. Queen Victoria handed Ottawa, the once wild logging town in eastern Ontario, its most valuable unique selling proposition, that of capital of Canada. Ottawa has transformed over the last century into one of Canada's key tourism destinations and the Rideau Canal has been recognized by UNESCO as a World Heritage Site.

Product/Market Match When the product that a destination is selling meets the target market's needs and expectations, a **market match** is made. For example, if you are targeting the family market, then your destination will feature reasonably priced accommodations, family-style restaurants, and activities that focus on family fun or education.

If you are targeting the mature market, you must understand that it has very different needs. Here, your product will probably reflect the higher income of this market, as well as its desire for cultural and learning experiences, and provide upscale accommodation and dining facilities. Targeting the group market, on the other hand, might require special check-in and check-out procedures at a hotel. Since destinations usually attract more than one market, a variety of facilities are needed.

Because of its position as capital of Canada, Ottawa provides for a wide variety of tourist markets, ranging from high-tech business visitors to groups of students from all age categories, from "empty nesters" and "boomers" to young families with small children, and including foreign visitors to Canada. The one market the city continues to struggle with is that of large conventions and conferences. Many hotels have nice facilities for smaller conferences and there are a few external locations for midsized gatherings, such as the Ottawa Convention Centre; however, space is limited for handling large numbers of conventioneers or international-level trade shows. Hosting conventions and conferences can have significant financial rewards. The city simply rents the space, perhaps helps find volunteers and the necessary equipment, and the organization looks after most of the other details. Convention delegates also tend to spend a great deal of money on recreational activities after the sessions. They may bring along their families for a "mini-vacation" or may decide the city is so attractive, they will return with friends and family in the future.

Clustering Clustering is also important to a visitor, especially one with a limited budget and no personal transportation available. **Clustering** keeps sites, food services, accommodations, and events in one area, allowing easy walking access to all.

Tourism planning in most Canadian cities has been in the *coattail* category; in other words, it has developed without much forethought. Clustering sites can be difficult once the city has developed.

Clusters can often be created through zoning bylaws. In the historic area of Niagara-on-the-Lake, Ontario, facilities focus on an upscale market and adhere to historical designs. The well-known Shaw Festival (featuring the works of the great playwright George Bernard Shaw and his contemporaries) is held here annually, and accommodations include many smaller inns and bed and breakfasts, in addition to a few large, modern hotels.

In Vancouver, on the other hand, some of the sites are spread among different communities, and while they are not within walking distance of each other, the hosting community can share in the tourist dollars. Clustering does appear in the downtown area with a wide variety of hotels, eateries, and shops available to the visitor, along with some sites such as the Vancouver Aquarium and Crab Park at Portside.

Ottawa has recently begun clustering its sites, and now most major national museums are within a thirty-minute walk of each other. Many events held in Ottawa take place in the large parks that complete the city centre.

Transportation System Even when clustering does occur, the importance of a good transportation system cannot be overstated. How do tourists get to, and around, their tourism destination areas? Are signs for sights and attractions clear and are they placed so that the driving tourist has time to move into the correct turning lane? Is the traffic flow simple, or are there many one-way streets, confusing signs, and poor parking facilities? Good, clear, visible road signs accomplish three things: they allow tourist traffic to flow more smoothly through the area, they reduce the risk of accidents, and they make it easier for tourists to find sites, accommodations, or destinations.

Niagara has highly visible directional signs. Parking facilities are located at the edge of the city, and a special bus service moves tourists from one cluster to another. Tourists are encouraged to use this system, minimizing traffic congestion and pollution. Ontario's Highway 401 alerts visitors to the Niagara exit as far ahead as 5 km, giving them time to get into the right exit lane. Vancouver has the SkyTrain, SeaBus, and other standard methods of transportation. In some cities, one of the "must do" experiences is using one of their transit systems: San Francisco's cable cars, London's double-decker buses, the TGV in Tokyo, and the Paris Métro, to mention only a few.

Ottawa was a city in crisis when it came to transportation. For twenty years, the city had been trying to establish a source of transportation that would provide an alternative to its aging, polluting, transportation system, OC Transpo, with little success. Tourists without cars had to use taxis at a high cost to get to some of the outlying attractions. However, in the last six years, Ottawa's transportation system has grown dramatically, including extensions on their dedicated roadway system, called the Transitway, as well as the new O-Train, an 8 km light rail that runs from the downtown core, through Carleton University, to the major transit artery near the airport.

While most of the sites are clustered, seasonal bus service, such as the one provided in London, England, would give tourists without cars the chance to see some of the unique attractions located outside the cluster area. But even if you have a car, there are still problems. A new highway does link tourists coming from the Toronto area to downtown Ottawa, but the highway that crosses Ottawa gives little advance warning for exits (unlike in Toronto and Vancouver), and once a tourist is in the downtown area, the city is a poor mix of one-way and dead-end streets and infrastructure projects.

All cities need to do road maintenance during the summer, but Ottawa provides little in the way of alternate routes. Added to that mix is the fact that each street has a confusing "bus lane" reserved for buses only, with large signs warning drivers of the fines for using them, as well as a lack of parking. You begin to see the difficulties a visitor experiences trying to navigate Ottawa in a car.

Community Partnerships The fifth key to success lies in **partnerships**. In Chapter 2, we discussed the successful partnership between the Canadian Tourism Commission (CTC) and the tourism sector. Partnering with government is essential, because governments provide not only the infrastructure for tourism, but also many social and support services.

Historically, tourist regions have vied against one another for customers. The tourism marketplace has changed, however; competition comes not just from our neighbours but also from businesses around the world. Destinations need the strength that is found in alliances and partnerships. Tourism businesses want the same thing—a healthy, economically stable tourist product. Partnerships are hard to forge and can be difficult to maintain. Once created, however, they improve each product's chance of success by linking resources. Partnering also means that the visitor can be supplied with a full, diverse package using one-stop shopping.

As an example, a tour to Niagara-on-the-Lake might combine the services of the Prince of Wales hotel, dinners at local restaurants, promotional discounts for local shops, tickets to the Shaw Festival, lunch and a tour of Inniskillin Winery, and admissions to local attractions like Fort George. Partnerships are also an integral part of any public festival or event, and without the support of local businesses, some events have been forced to cancel their activities.

Ottawa is a city of festivals. Over 150 festivals, from the Canadian Tulip Festival held in late May to the Labour Day Gatineau Hot Air Balloon Festival, the city celebrates music and heritage from around the world. Finding sponsors/partners can be difficult, with even the widely popular Tulip Festival facing elimination, from time to time, for lack of support. Providing an event with financial or other forms of support is good both for the company (advertising) and for the economy. Without willing partners, tourism businesses face even harder times.

Environmental Protection The final key to successful tourism is environmental protection. The World Tourism Organization has stated that the protection and enhancement of the environment is fundamental to balanced and harmonious tourism. Sustainable tourism development is a primary goal in tourism planning, and it means that a destination fulfills the needs of the tourist with as little damage to the environment as possible. It is unrealistic to expect tourism to bring in revenue and yet cause no added pollution or damage to the environment.

Politicians must not allow indiscriminate or poorly designed construction to destroy the natural environment. Niagara is now struggling with this problem. In the past ten years, local politicians have been loath to deny building permits for large hotels along the embankment of the Niagara River. There is no question that a view of the falls is a **unique selling proposition**, but tall buildings have blocked not only the natural light needed by the ecosystem in that region, but also the spray that has for centuries kept the area's soil moist. As a result, the dry soil cannot sustain plant life, which in turn endangers the local species that live on the banks of the river. The dry soil itself is eroding, as well. Perhaps the most important impact has been the lack of cooling spray given off by the falls, making the air less comfortable for visitors. Several more high-rise hotels are being considered, and there has been an outcry from local citizens to stop all new development along the riverbank.

Every city should take responsibility for the environment, but as the capital, Ottawa should have the environment as one of its first concerns. Partnerships are extremely important here, as funding for environmental projects is one area that politicians tend to cut first. Ottawa has two groups that oversee maintenance and renewal of the local environment—the National Capital Commission (federal dollars) and the city of Ottawa (municipal tax dollars).

Looking after the environment is not only the city's job, but it is also an individual responsibility. For example, as a result of a ban on smoking in public buildings in place, in many cities people will find cigarette butts (non-biodegradable) carelessly thrown on the ground when a "butt out" container is just fifteen feet away. Tourists also tend to be less concerned about littering on vacation, but this is one area that can rapidly earn a negative reputation for a TDA. "Dirty cities" are more difficult to sell and seldom bring a tourist back for a second visit.

In Practice

Do a quick SWOT analysis of one of your regional attractions by identifying its **S**trengths, **W**eaknesses, an **O**pportunity it could take advantage of, and a **T**hreat to its continued success.

WHAT SLOWS TOURISM GROWTH?

The Canadian and provincial governments understand that while growth potential for tourism in Canada is excellent, factors hindering that growth also exist. Some are grounded in costs, others in training and knowledge. Throughout this book, you will find references to many of these concerns:

1. **Concern for the ecosystem.** Demand for sustainable tourism and concern for the environment continue to grow, while the availability of new tourism land and resources are declining. Future tourism development must plan to protect the ecosystem upon which it is built, and existing tourism operations must change to become more environmentally conscious.

2. **Financial concerns.** Developing new projects is expensive, and negotiating who should pay for new developments is a challenge. Although financial institutions may lend money to major city-regions, they are often reluctant to provide capital to outlying regions. In addition, financial institutions often have a negative perception of the tourism sector, often basing their decisions on the poor performance of old products without acknowledging the tremendous success of modern tourism products, such as cruise lines.

3. **Tourism illiteracy.** Not all communities see tourism as beneficial. For some, increased tourism negatively affects their daily lives and their communities. Communication, information, and education may all be needed before a community starts any tourism projects.

4. **Seasonality.** Mentioned throughout the text, seasonality will continue to be a concern for Canada. The tourism sector is focusing on making Canada a four-season destination by developing events and activities that can take place year-round.

5. **Lack of trained personnel.** Strong training programs must be readily accessible to tourism workers at a reasonable cost. Tourism remains, as a sector, an undertrained workforce.

6. **Transportation costs.** Many things affect transportation, from the quality of our aging infrastructure (roads, rails, harbours, and runways) to the cost of fuel (including prices at the pump and fuel surcharges).

7. **Poor product packaging and the lack of an integrated market plan.** Both packaging and marketing must be emphasized in any new tourism plan. Many books have been written on marketing, and most Canadian colleges and universities offer diplomas or degrees in this subject.

What is marketing and how can Canada change the way in which we package and market our tourism products? This responsibility actually lies with the Canadian Tourism Commission, our destination marketing organization (DMO), but what problems does it face when setting up a marketing plan? What problems are faced by *any* marketing company you hire to lay out a marketing plan? To create a successful marketing plan, you should first understand the uniqueness of our products.

UNDERSTANDING AND MARKETING THE UNIQUE TOURISM PRODUCT

According to Morrison, "marketing is a continuous, sequential process through which management plans, researches, implements, controls, and evaluates activities designed to satisfy both customers' needs and wants and their own organization's objectives."[13] Marketing is the bringing together of products, the seller, and the purchaser. However, tourism is not like manufactured products—we sell service, experiences, and time.

When you purchase a car, you begin by researching different car manufacturers. Then you go to a dealer who sells the kind of car you want and you look at the different types and styles available. You sit in the car, kick the tires, and take it for a test drive. If the product suits you, then you make your purchase. If the colour you desire is not available on the lot, the dealer will get it for you. That car is your property and sits in your driveway until you decide to get a new one.

Compare that procedure to the process you might go through to purchase a two-week holiday in Barbados. Although you do research on your destination, you are unable to physically see or handle any of the components you are purchasing. You must rely on second-hand information, available data, and the experiences of others. No one can package it and send it to you—you must physically go somewhere to use it. Your vacation doesn't actually exist until you are a part of it. Finally, when you finish using the product, you must leave it behind, coming home with only memories and a scrapbook. The "product" you purchased—Barbados—is still available to be sold to the next customer!

Obviously, the tourism product has some unique characteristics that need to be explored. To be able to sell a product well, salespeople must first understand it. The tourism product is complicated, not only from the standpoint of its diversity, but also from a marketing perspective. Here are some of the characteristics of tourism, a unique collection of products, services, and experiences:

1. **Tourism is intangible.** The tourism product is intangible in that it cannot be touched or perceived by the senses. It does not sit on a shelf. It cannot be handled, examined, or tried prior to purchase because tourism sells "time," which becomes experiences and memories. Although most consumers would not purchase a sound system without first testing it out, they willingly spend $1500 on a cruise package without ever having stepped on a ship. Therefore, the person who is marketing the product has been granted a high level of trust by the consumer and must represent the product accurately.

2. **Tourism products are highly perishable.** Tourism professionals sell time, and time is fleeting. Every day hotel rooms sit vacant, planes leave with empty seats, and attractions are not filled to capacity. Each one of those empty "units" means lost revenue, revenue that can never be recovered. An airline cannot sell a seat on an aircraft that departed ten minutes ago. The seat is still there, but the customer with the money is waiting at the airport

for the next flight. The tourism industry must sell its products daily or lose the revenue it can generate. Marketers have helped control this situation by putting together seat sales and last-minute discounts, but last-minute purchases of our products are not common. People like to plan their vacations in advance.

3. **The tourism product is heterogeneous.** The delivery of the tourism product is often crafted at the time of the transaction by a specific provider for a specific customer. Each side, both the provider and the customer, continuously change, creating variations in the created product or outcome. Different customers and different operators all have unique styles and characteristics that influence the developed product/service/ experience.

4. **The tourism product cannot be stored.** In a product-only industry, a business that understands the demands of the marketplace can often take advantage of periods when demand for its product is high. For example, if Christmas is a time when many people purchase television sets, then the manufacturer can produce and store enough televisions for the Christmas rush. However, "time" cannot be stored to be used at a later date. Even though demand for a product may be high during the summer, businesses cannot store up unused "units" from February to sell in July—so some people who wish to purchase your product may have to go elsewhere.

5. **There is a fixed supply of the product and it cannot be easily altered.** Because of the immense cost of building hotels, aircrafts, cruise ships, and resorts, and because of the length of time construction takes, tourism cannot quickly add to its size. Adding 100 rooms to a 250-room hotel is a long construction process. Even if the hotel increases the number of rooms to 350 in order to handle the high demand in July, it must bear the loss of revenue from those empty rooms in January. Airplanes that seat 200 passengers cannot suddenly increase their capacity to 300 during spring break. The demand is there; the capacity is not.

6. **The tourism product is highly seasonal.** Tourism experiences periods of great demand (peak demand) and periods of very low demand. Many Canadian resorts close during their slow season, which is often the winter. During the tourist season they are full to capacity, but the cost of carrying empty rooms over an extended period of time reduces profit margins. By closing during low season, a company reduces wages, electricity costs, etc. Other businesses prefer to reduce their rates during the off-season in order to attraction additional customers. Beautiful Canadian resorts that offer summer golfing packages also look at providing winter activities that focus on cross-country skiing; many are developing spas that operate no matter what the season, and they court the lucrative convention business market. Creative marketing minds continue to create packages and products that can help build business during the low season.

7. **Travel is a costly product.** Vacations are something that many of the working public saves for all year and must pay for with their extra or disposable income. People do not mind spending money on their vacations, but they do expect value for their dollar.

8. **The use of the product is curbed by time constraints.** Few people have endless vacations; they only have a few weeks available every year for pleasure travel. If time is constrained, then planning a trip to Australia for a Canada Day long weekend may be possible, but quite impractical. A two-week tour of the Cabot Trail is not possible if a tourist has only one week of vacation.

9. **The quality of the individual product often depends on factors beyond the control of the producer or seller.** Tourism consists of many components, all separate entities run by different businesses. A delayed aircraft could mean that an important business negotiation cannot be completed. A hotel may be wonderful, but a rude reception by a customs official or taxi driver may overshadow the entire stay. A bout of food poisoning from a local restaurant may ruin the memories of the perfect resort.

Weather is perhaps the most influential factor determining enjoyment of a vacation. The tsunami in Southeast Asia was an enormous natural disaster. In Austria and Germany, floods have ravaged ancient towns, destroying buildings that have stood there for hundreds of years. Travellers depend greatly on the generosity of the host country during such disasters, but when real trouble sets in, like the hurricanes that have pounded the Caribbean, Mexican, and southern U.S. coastlines, they demand help from their homelands. However, Canadian tourists have learned that if you are stuck in a foreign country due to weather disasters, you will need to be patient and prepared for many changes in travel plans when finding your way home.

A good tourism experience depends on so many factors that marketing the product becomes a real challenge. When working with a marketing firm, professionals need to know the marketing process, understand the tourism product, and have an honest and creative approach in order to succeed with this unique product.

Tourism's Elasticity of Demand

Another constraint on the tourism product that marketing agencies must consider is high elasticity of demand. What is *elasticity of demand*? To understand that, it is necessary to understand the term **demand**. Demand (in the marketplace) is created by the need or desire for goods and services—that is, the number of purchasers wanting to buy a product. Elasticity of demand refers to the reactive nature of purchasers to the price of a good or service. If a product has **inelastic demand**, people will continue to purchase a similar amount regardless of large changes in price, either up or down. Gasoline is a good example of a product with an inelastic demand. Car owners must buy gasoline regardless of the cost per litre. When gas prices rise, there is little change in the consumption of gasoline. On the other hand, when the demand for a product is very sensitive to price changes, it is described as having **elastic demand**. With every price change, there is a proportionally larger change in demand: the lower the price, the higher the demand and vice versa.

Why do most tourism products have an elastic demand? Travel is a luxury, not a life-sustaining product. It is bought only when the purchaser has the discretionary income needed. As a luxury purchase for most people, as the price of the vacation rises, the demand for that vacation drops. There are a few tourism products that have created inelastic demand, but they usually appeal to an elite clientele and offer a product or service that is unique or unmatched. A destination that is in vogue, and is popular with movie stars, royalty, and millionaires, may enjoy a period when people will pay any price for the chance to mingle with the rich and famous!

The First Four Ps of the Marketing Mix

All products are made up of a marketing mix—controllable factors that may help satisfy customer needs or wants. Here we will discuss the basic four: product, place, promotion, and price.

1. **Product: What do you sell?** We have already discussed the generic tourism product and its unique characteristics, but *products* also have a physical and service component. Each of these components is developed based on specific market needs—for example, the type of hotel, its rooms and amenities, and the level of services it provides for guests. From a marketing standpoint, these qualities are the most important. How does the location and physical layout of a hotel differ from other hotels in the area? What services does a hotel offer that set it apart from similar hotels?

2. **Place: Where are you going to sell your product?** *Place* is also called the **channel of distribution**. The travel services industry is the packaging and sales force for the tourism sector and can be effectively used by the smart business owner. Many businesses have sales departments that handle marketing and sales.

   The most important channel of distribution today is the internet. Many hotels, restaurants, and attractions have websites that provide clients with pictures or short videos of the location. These websites show package deals and pricing, and make it easy for the client to book. Larger sites such as Expedia.ca or Travelocity.ca offer many destinations, different types of hotels, meal packages, attractions, and airline reservations that can be bundled into a self-made tour package at a reduced price.

   The travel agency is another venue for selling the tourism product. When the Cruise Lines International Association (CLIA) first organized the modern cruise industry in 1960, they used travel agencies as their sales force. It was a system that was already in place and it brought the cruise lines immediate success. Ninety-five percent of all cruises are still sold through travel agencies.

3. **Promotion: How will you advertise your product?** What is your advertising budget and how can those dollars be most effectively used? Which media format is most likely to be seen or heard by your target market? The choices are vast and the cost of advertising varies widely. Businesses must know who their clients are and how best to reach them. Large international businesses might opt for national newspapers or TV promotions, but the small business must focus on using community news, radio, brochures, mail-outs, or their own website. (In today's world, a business that does not have a website may be losing customers.) Tourism makes use of two important methods of *promotion*.

   The first is the internet. Tourism is made up of a variety of small, often unrelated businesses at a given destination. Historically, these businesses

VANCOUVER · OTTAWA · ST. JOHN'S · LONDON · SINGAPORE

Colourful brochures with beautiful views of destinations help give substance to the intangible tourism product, prior to purchase.
(Photo: Paula Kerr.)

have had very little ability to market themselves effectively before tourists actually arrive. However, for a very low cost, websites can now be created to introduce a product to travellers long before they even anticipate their trip. As people become more comfortable with using the internet, this method of promotion will become essential to business survival.

The second important method of promotion in our industry is packaging. With less discretionary time, consumers are looking for one-stop shopping opportunities. Linking tourism products in tour packages, whether these packages are designed for individuals or groups, means that each product enjoys the strength of joint marketing initiatives.

4. **Price: How much do you charge for your product?** Many factors influence the *price* of a product, including location, time of year, and quality of service. Of course, pricing strategy must cover basic costs and expenses and include a profit margin. The elasticity of demand for a tourism product must be considered as well as the competition's pricing structure. Knowledge of clients and their purchasing power is also important.

Customer-Oriented Marketing

In order to effectively sell tourism products, businesses must create and implement marketing plans. A **marketing plan** is simply a written short-term plan that details how a product will use its marketing mix to achieve a goal (financial or other) over a specified period.

How does a business develop a customer-oriented marketing plan? First, the business must understand its products and services. It must also have a clear understanding of the needs and expectations of its customers.

CASE STUDY

Confusion in Kelowna

It had been eight years since Amar and Laksha Dutta's youngest child was born. As parents of two teenage boys and a young daughter, they had spent the majority of their time creating a stable home environment in Calgary, Alberta. Vacations were focused on the children and remained close to their home city. In the summer of 2011, Laksha's parents arranged an extended two-month vacation in order to connect with their grandchildren. Taking the opportunity for a small break, Amar and Laksha arranged for a five-day couple's vacation in the Okanagan Valley in British Columbia. They had been told by friends that the wine region was breathtaking and would allow them to reconnect as a couple.

Upon arrival at the airport in Kelowna, they had a difficult time finding the car rental agency that they had booked with, as their plan was to drive around the scenic valley. To speed up the process, Laksha asked at the information counter for directions. The agent on duty appeared agitated at having to end a personal call and provided accurate but curt directions. Amar experienced a series of mix-ups in their car reservation; although it was finally resolved, they ended up with a larger car than they needed, and they both found it particularly difficult to drive. Three separate times, they found themselves lost on the drive to their first resort, mostly due to confusing road signage in the mountains. By the time they finally reached the resort, it was quite late. As the front desk agent checked them in, they were told that the restaurants had just closed, but had they arrived earlier there would have been lots of space. As they took their bags up to their room, neither were in a vacation frame of mind any longer; both were ready to return to the airport and go back to the comfort of their family.

1. Identify some of the problems that the Duttas experienced.
2. What do you believe are some of the root issues of these problems? Relate them to the themes already covered in this chapter.
3. Present some clear solutions to these problems. How would you go about implementing your suggested solutions?
4. What do you think the Duttas might do differently with future vacation plans? How will this experience change their travel behaviours?

Customers come to a business with specific expectations. They have preconceived ideas about what a product is and how well it will fulfill their expectations. A good marketing plan identifies these expectations and is able to provide value for the customer's dollar. Perceived **value** is the customer's mental estimate of the worth of a product. For some, value is price-sensitive, but for others the total experience is what matters—the friendliness of service and the quality of the experience. The key aspect of perceived value is that it needs to be greater than the price of the product in the opinion of the customer. The gap between the value point they set and the price they pay is extra value—customers actually feel they have received more than they paid for from the exchange. As long as this **surplus** exists, customers will be satisfied.

Can one product fulfill everyone's needs? Will a tourism product that satisfies one traveller's need for hard adventure also satisfy the traveller who wants the comforts of home life? Obviously not. **Market segmentation** is one way to deal with the wide variety of personalities, life stages, and motivations that travel products must satisfy. Market segmentation is simply the division of the overall possible market into smaller groups of people who share common characteristics or have similar needs. Disneyland in Anaheim, California, provides a good example of how one company handles a diverse marketplace.

When it opened in 1955, Disneyland's original market was families with young children, a very healthy audience group, since the theme park opened right in the middle of the baby boom. This market served Disney well for the next few decades. However, two developments occurred to force Disney to revisit their audience. First, as the baby boomers grew into adulthood, they no longer vacationed with their parents. Second, the lower cost for international travel allowed vacationers to expand potential destinations. In response, Disneyland continued to target families with children; however, they also opened up to a new market of older travellers. Older couples, the original parents, are now invited back to the theme park for a more adult-focused trip.

This kind of niche or **target marketing** is essential to our industry because of the diversity of clientele and their needs and expectations. The wide variety of tourism products available makes this kind of marketing strategy easy. A career in tourism marketing (see Chapter 11) could be an exciting option. As each destination creates additional attractions, the role of the marketing consultant will be even more important.

Summary

- Although planning and development are separate endeavours, they must occur together for tourism to succeed on a local, regional, or national level.
- Canada has developed a series of guidelines for developing and maintaining its tourism product.
- Planning is a cyclical, eight-step process:
  - The cycle begins by taking an inventory of the social, political, physical, and economic environment of the community or business. This inventory gives direction on what is needed, what can be accomplished, and what should not be attempted.
  - The second step is to look at trends. Forecasting provides a basis for deciding whether to proceed with certain plans.
  - The third step is to develop a mission statement, goals, and objectives, which together creates guidelines for action.
  - Steps four, five, and six require the community or business to study alternative plans, to select the preferred plan, and to design strategies to reach the goals.
  - The seventh step is implementation.
  - The final step includes reviewing, evaluating, and revising the original plan.
  - Without planning, tourism development is a hit-or-miss operation.

- Integrated development is achieved by a single company or individual, but most communities do not develop tourism this way.
- Catalytic development occurs when a developer brings a major attraction to an area and encourages other businesses to build nearby, giving local and regional businesses the opportunity to participate and become successful.
- Coattail development occurs when visitors are drawn to an area because of its scenic beauty or natural qualities.
- A USP, or unique selling proposition, separates you from other destinations.
- Marketing tourism products can be challenging; as well, tourism has unique characteristics:
  - Tourism products are intangible and cannot be tried before purchase.
  - They are expensive.
  - They are highly perishable and cannot be stored for future consumption.
  - They normally have a fixed available supply.
  - They are frequently are seasonal, and must be used within time constraints.
  - The quality of tourism products often depends on factors beyond our control.
- Tourism is an elastic product; the volume of sales is very sensitive to price changes.
- A marketing plan is a written, short-term plan that details how a product will use product, price, promotion, and place to achieve its financial goals.

Questions

1. Illustrate how your city is effective as a tourism destination by exploring how it meets the five essential components of a generic destination.

2. Describe the four stages in the life cycle of a destination. Can you provide an example of the destination for each of the four stages?

3. Outline five goals that a viable tourism destination should meet in order to enhance the community.

4. a) Briefly explain in your own words the eight steps in tourism planning.
   b) Which of these steps do you feel is most important? Explain.
   c) Identify two factors or situations that VANOC might have encountered that could have slowed the building process of the 2010 Winter Olympic and Paralympic Games. How might these situations have been handled to return the process to its original timeline?

5. Define the following terms as they relate to tourism planning: *planning, functional form, product capacity, qualitative forecasting,* and *quantitative forecasting.*

6. a) Illustrate the differences between integrated, catalytic, and coattail development of a tourism destination area.
   b) Which style of development do you feel is best? Explain your answer.

7. Identify what you believe are the five most important constraints on tourism growth identified by the Canadian and provincial governments.

8. a) List the six key factors of a TDA as described in this chapter.
   b) Looking at your city, which of these factors does it handle best? Why did you make this choice? Which key factor should your city be working to improve?

9. You are working in the marketing department of a large luxury hotel. Define the following marketing terms and provide an example of how you are trying to control or minimize the impact of these situations:

   a) The room you are selling is "intangible."

   b) The room you are selling is very "perishable."

   c) You cannot store leftover rooms to be used next week.

   d) You cannot add twenty-five rooms to be used for a large conference.

   e) The quality of your room depends on factors that you cannot control.

   f) The room you are selling has a high "seasonal" demand.

10. If a product has an elastic demand, what does that mean? If it is inelastic, how does it differ?

Notes

1. *Newfoundland-Labrador* (St. John's: Tourism Newfoundland–Labrador, 1995).

2. www.oee.nrcan.gc.ca/publications.

3. www.ic.gc.ca/eic/site/dsib-tour.nsf/eng/h_qq00141.html.

4. Edward Inskeep, *Tourism Planning: An Integrated and Sustainable Approach* (New York: John Wiley & Sons, 1991), p. 25.

5. Prasad. *Crafting Qualitative Research* (M.E. Sharpe, Inc., 2005).

6. Robert W. McIntosh and Charles R. Goeldner, *Tourism Principles, Practices, Philosophies*, 6th ed. (New York: John Wiley & Sons, 1990), pp. 265–267.

7. www.vancouver2010.com.

8. http://torc.linkbc.ca/torc/downs1/2010_Olympics.pdf.

9. English translation: in Daniel J. Hughes (ed.), *Moltke on the Art of War: Selected Writings*. (1993)

10. www.vancouver2010.com.

11. Douglas Pearce, *Tourism development*, 2nd ed. (New York: John Wiley & Sons, 1989), pp. 67–70.

12. Smith and Laurel Reid, *Six Key Factors to a Destination's Success* (video available from University of Western Ontario bookstore).

13. Alistair M. Morrison *Hospitality and Tourism Marketing* (Albany, NY: Delmar Publishers Inc., 1998), p. 4.

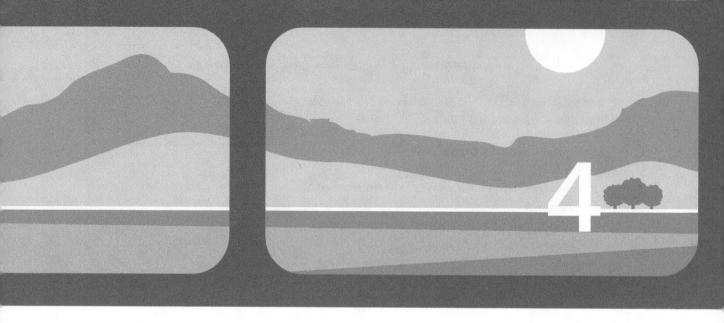

Transportation

Key terms

airfares
bilateral agreement
BritRail pass
bullet train
bumped
charter
circle trip
corporate rates
direct flight
e-ticket
Eurail Pass
fly/coach tours
Freedoms of the Air

gateway airport
hub and spoke
interline connection
International
    Air Transport
    Association (IATA)
International
    Civil Aviation
    Organization
    (ICAO)
landing fee
load factor
Maglev

motor coach package
non-stop flight
online connection
open-jaw trip
Open Skies Agreement
Orient Express
overnight/short tours
round trip
scheduled air carrier
sightseeing/day tours
special interest cruise
unlimited kilometres
VIA Rail Canada

Learning objectives

Having read this chapter you will be able to

1. Discuss the emergence of modern transportation systems.

2. Explain why travellers choose one mode over another.

3. Summarize the effects of deregulation in Canada on transportation systems.

4. Describe the Canadian air transportation system, and the impact of global and bilateral air agreements.

5. Identify the core characteristics of automobile-based transportation systems.

6. Discuss products and services that exist in railway travel.

7. Describe the cruise options currently available and outline the advantages of cruising.

The transportation system, along with the infrastructure that supports it, plays a significant role in tourism: if visitors cannot reach their destinations, then the other tourism components suffer. Transporting a visitor to a chosen destination begins the tourism experience.

Part of the joy of travelling is getting to use transportation modes unavailable at home: England's double-decker buses, motor scooters in Rome, camels in the Sahara, the maglev monorail in China, jeepneys in the Philippines. If it is unique, travels fast, or does something unusual, you can be sure tourists will want a ride.

While it is important that a travel destination be able to provide methods to carry passengers from one site to another, more important are the modes of transportation travellers use to get to their destinations. The choices serve different purposes: to get tourists to their destinations quickly, to give tourists the chance to see the countryside, or for older travellers, to step back in time and enjoy a method of travel used when they were young. The many different modes of transportation, and why tourists choose one mode over another, is an interesting area of research. How important is transportation to the tourism sector? The sector would not exist without it, and this chapter looks briefly to the past, present, and future of this important industry.

Until the Industrial Revolution, in the early nineteenth century, people had little choice in the speed or method of transportation. Horses, camels, and donkeys carried you from one place to another, perhaps pulling a cart or caravan in which you stored your goods. Travel by water was faster if the prevailing wind was in your favour, but travel by ship was difficult, uncomfortable for most passengers, and dangerous. Still, the desire to see the world and trade with other nations has existed through all of our history, and adventurers like Marco Polo and Christopher Columbus brought back stories and goods that helped change global perspectives on life. With the invention of the steam engine, transportation suddenly became easier, safer, and more accessible to ordinary folk. Ships and trains were the first to get the "amazing steam engine," and they became major systems of early modern transportation. Now you did not have to be wealthy to travel, and many immigrants to the New World travelled in pest-ridden and filthy ships across the Atlantic Ocean.

However, it was Henry Ford's invention of the automobile that had the most powerful impact on transportation. It changed not only travel methods, but also travel's accessibility. Cars were not only within the financial reach of the middle class, but they travelled with a minimum of infrastructure—a pitted track and you were off on an adventure! Cars gave people the ability to reach areas of the country that were not accessible by trains or boats. So you could say that it was the invention of the automobile that gave birth to the modern tourism sector, because it made travel fun and open to all who wished to try the travel experience. For future travellers, the latest frontier of transportation is within our grasp—space travel.

SELECTING A MODE OF TRANSPORTATION

The availability of the right infrastructure and suprastructure determines the choices a traveller has–harbours and ports, train tracks, roads, and runways must be in place for most methods of transportation. What else helps travellers decide on their mode of travel? Here are some of the obvious factors:

Cost is often one of the first factors an aspiring tourist considers. Transportation is a large portion of a travel budget, so knowing your needs and your financial situation may be the most important consideration. Obviously, the more family members you have travelling together, the more cost affects your choice.

Service will always be a consideration when choosing a mode of transportation. Perceptions or knowledge of the quality of service will affect a traveller's decision. Customers want to be treated well, and service is a way that a transportation company can differentiate itself from its competitors. Service can include additional components or amenities, such as food and beverage service. However, service is often measured by how well you are treated and the level of attention provided by the people you encounter, including porters, ticket agents, and flight attendants. Customers share their experiences with others, and current technology allows every customer to magnify their opinions and expressions.

Time is the third factor you are likely to consider. A business traveller will usually choose the fastest method available to allow maximum time for business. Pleasure travellers will often try to condense as much vacation time as possible into their one-week or two-week vacations. However, if travellers live in Halifax and want to visit family in Calgary with only one week of vacation time, travelling by bus, train, or car gives them little time for family reunions. Flying, the most expensive option, becomes necessary.

Convenience of the travel mode is another consideration. Obviously, if you have a car and are transporting your family, it is the most convenient mode of transportation available to you. Other things to consider regarding convenience are the location of the departure/arrival terminals, the check-in procedures, the ability to travel with equipment you will need at your destination, and how the mode of transportation handles travelling with babies or family pets.

Safety issues continue to be a concern. Customers want to feel safe moving from destination to destination. Safety works on multiple levels: a person can arrive at their destination without incident, but they may feel unsafe during the process. Continuous effort must be shown in keeping people safe.

Yet, the industry needs to communicate their engagement with safety issues through visual signs, symbols, and operations. We must manage perceptions as well as outcomes. For example, some customers remain hesitant about flying after the events of September 11, 2001. However, in 2007, the airline industry held the title of the "safest mode" of transportation. The number of accidents that have occurred over the last ten years have been between 1.74 per million flights to just 0.75 accidents per million flights.[1] Checkpoints at security, increased presence of Transportation Security Administration (TSA) agents in the United States and agents from the Canadian Border Services Agency (CBSA), as well as more thorough examinations of both people and baggage have gone a long way to visibly demonstrate additional safety efforts.

Route structure is another concern. In 1976, train travel in Canada changed with the creation of a single passenger line, **VIA Rail Canada**. Many smaller towns with track accessibility were no longer serviced by the train. During the winter, some areas of Canada have no air service. Keeping a global perspective, smaller countries may have only one airport and the balance of transportation must be done by car or bus. The longer it takes you to reach your destination and the more complicated the route structure you are using, the less time you will have for fun and relaxation.

Frequency of departures is also a major consideration. Travelling from Vancouver to Vancouver Island forces tourists to adhere to a limited schedule with ferry crossings that take several hours. Although more expensive, going to and from the island in the same day is more easily achieved when travelling by plane as there are many more planes departing and the speed of the commute is much shorter. Some major city centres have frequent arrival and departure times, providing flexibility to travellers. Yet, many smaller towns in our north may have air service only one or two days a week.

Personality and psychology issues also factor into choosing a mode of transportation. In his research, Dr. Jagdish Sheth has identified several *psychological factors* that influence the decision-making process.

1. *Fears and prejudices* formed during childhood will affect a person's choice of transportation. A child who grew up with a fear of water will likely not choose to travel by ship as an adult. Fear of flying for a business person may make travel so difficult it impairs his or her ability to perform effectively on the job.

2. *Stereotypes and perceptions* are also difficult to overcome. Perceptions are often based on a lack of knowledge, and similar to fears, perceptions may impede our ability to make informed choices.

3. Finally, our *self-image* and our *desire for status* may eliminate a method of travel that would otherwise serve us well. A person wishing to travel from Calgary to Vancouver may choose an airline over a bus, despite cost factors, simply because travel by air reinforces a personal image of success.

Transportation operators are aware of these many emotions, needs, and constraints, and their marketing programs address each in detail. Tour bus companies focus on the quality of their equipment, the ease of seeing the countryside without having to drive, and the friendliness and knowledge of their staff. Airlines promote fast, friendly, and safe travel, using images of qualified pilots and crewmembers, and caring, concerned mechanics and ground personnel. Providing high-quality service is an integral part of any transportation promotion. In the end, the choice of how we travel is a personal one. We use all of our experiences and knowledge to choose the mode best suited to our needs at a given time.

TRAVEL BY AIR

The airline industry has the most significant impact on international business development of any industry. From a financial aspect, it provides over 33 million jobs globally that range from airline distribution personnel, pilots, flight attendants, and ground support personnel to sales and marketing forces.[2] Air is the major carrier of goods: in 2011, the industry handled 46 million tonnes of freight. There were 29.6 million scheduled departures of the over 27 000 commercial aircraft that moved 2.7 billion passengers. But more important are the actual economic and social benefits the industry brings to people around the world:

- Transportation is the major force behind the growth of international tourism and trade.

- It connects people, countries, and cultures in a fast, safe, and mostly convenient manner.

- It provides access to global markets.

- It is a force that encourages both economic and social progress.

- It forges links between developed nations and those struggling to improve their economic standing globally.[3]

Air Travel from a Historical Point of View

How quickly this industry has developed from the brief first flight in Kitty Hawk, North Carolina, in 1903. Sixty-six years later, the first men walked on the moon! The SST *Concorde*, which flew in the 1970s–1990s, travelled faster than the speed of sound, picking passengers up in London at 11:30 A.M. and depositing them in Miami by 8:30 A.M. of the same day! And now people are booking seats for space travel with Richard Branson's Virgin Galactic.

www.aircanada.com

Air service did not arrive in Canada until twenty-seven years after the initial flight, but in the 1930s, the federal government began Trans Canada Airlines (TCA—now Air Canada). Canadian Pacific Airways (CP Airways), privately owned, was granted permission to fly international routes to Pacific Rim countries and struggled for many years to gain equality with the government-owned TCA. In 1967, the *National Transportation Act* was passed, and while it also dealt with other forms of transportation in Canada, it finally gave CP Airways rights to 25% of Canada's domestic air routes.

In the 1970s, "regulated competition" was introduced, which liberalized the strict rules of charter regulations. This change saw the emergence and growth of new, small charter airlines. While Wardair, a charter airline based in Edmonton, Alberta, had been fighting for scheduled routes, regulations were opened further allowing privately owned companies like Wardair and Pacific Western, based in Vancouver, to enter the tough air marketplace.

In 1978, the United States government made a daring move and deregulated the U.S. airline industry. Prior to deregulation, travel by air had been viewed as a service industry, which should provide fast, efficient transportation to all parts of the States. The politicians who opposed the strict government regulations sought to free the airlines—they felt market forces and competition should determine the price of a ticket, not the government. It was a challenging time for airlines south of the border with many smaller and several larger airlines going bankrupt or being bought out.

Also recognizing the need for change in the airline industry, Canada passed a new *National Transportation Act* in 1987, which replaced the *Passenger Ticket Act* and the *Government Railways Act*, and this new legislation was far-reaching. It affirmed that a safe, economic, efficient transportation network was necessary to meet the needs of Canadian businesses and travellers. It replaced the Canadian Transportation Commission with a new agency, the National Transportation Agency (NTA), and privatized Air Canada. Pricing regulations were eliminated and entrance into the scheduled airline business was opened to all Canadian airlines.

Canada's *National Transportation Act* did not go as far as the U.S. legislation in deregulating the airline industry. Recognizing the difficulties of serving vast, thinly populated areas, especially in the north, the government continued to regulate northern routes. However, it soon became clear that the same chaos the United States was living through was now at our door. Smaller airlines attempting to compete with larger ones failed, and many airlines merged rather than leave the business entirely. For example, Pacific Western Airlines (PWA) and Wardair merged with Canadian Pacific Airways to become Canadian Airlines International (CAI). Entering the difficult years of the late 1990s, Canadian Airlines International was forced to seek bankruptcy protection. In 1999, with a foreign company in the bidding, the federal government stepped in and gave purchase rights to Air Canada, leaving the country with only one major carrier.

Small airline companies—like Bearskin Airlines and Calm Air—lived through the turmoil by not expanding into the larger markets and continuing to operate as regional or "feeder" airlines, servicing destinations like London and Sudbury in Ontario, and Yellowknife, Northwest Territories. These small airlines have been able to survive because they use smaller, more fuel-efficient aircraft, carry fewer passengers, and require fewer personnel.

One benefit of deregulation has been the emergence of no-frills or discount airlines, which focus on shorter flights with limited services or charters. Discount airlines can be strong competition for the major carriers because they control their costs so efficiently. WestJet, established in 1996 and based in Calgary, has been one of the most successfully cost-focused by keeping its eye on service and lower fares. Clive Beddoe, WestJet's CEO, acknowledges that it has been difficult with the rising cost of fuel, but says "you succeed in business because you provide quality service for a good price."[4] WestJet's simplified fare structure, with low ticket pricing based on the day of the week or time of the year, does just that.

Route structures also changed with deregulation. During the early years of the airlines, routes were linear. In other words, they flew in "straight lines" on one flight, such as from Toronto to Vancouver. They returned via the same route. Linear routes are still common in international flight structures. However, with deregulation, the **hub and spoke** system emerged. Airlines concentrated their services at major airports, reducing costs by consolidating staff in one or two major centres. The larger aircraft (Airbuses and Boeing 747s), which are more expensive to operate, carry passengers between major cities, then transfer them to smaller planes (more cost-efficient) for the flight to their final destination. Feeder or regional airlines are the link between the hub city and the smaller, final destination. In Canada, our major hub cities are Montreal, Toronto, and Vancouver. Some regional or feeder airlines, such as Air Nova, Air BC, and Air Ontario, are affiliated with Air Canada.

Safe transportation has always been a concern for the airline system as well as other modes of travel. In the late 1960s and 1970s, airlines had been forced to deal with a rising number of hijackers who used passengers and planes as bargaining chips for their causes. The events of September 11, 2001, created a completely new picture of terrorism, as jumbo jets were used as moving incendiary bombs. Four planes were hijacked. Two were crashed into the two towers of the World Trade Center in New York City, and one crashed into the Pentagon in Washington, D.C. Passengers on the fourth plane fought back against their hijackers, and the plane eventually crashed into a field near Shanksville, Pennsylvania.

When officials determined this was a terrorist operation, the Federal Aviation Administration (FAA) closed U.S. airspace. In two-and-a-half hours, over 4500 aircraft nationwide were forced to land or were diverted. International flights destined for the U.S. landed in Canada, flooding small and large airports with stranded, frightened passengers. U.S. airspace stayed closed for three days, and by the time operations began again, faith in the security of the airline system had been badly shaken.

Airline companies suffered extreme financial losses. United Airlines, the world's second largest carrier, lost over $5 million daily. Some governments provided one-time bailout grants: Air Canada received $5 million. Several airlines declared bankruptcy, including Scandinavian Airlines (SAS) in Europe, and Canada 3000 in Canada. Air travel has never recovered fully.

In January of 2003, the Canadian Air Transport Security Authority (CATSA) began operations at most Canadian airports. CATSA's mandate is to ensure the safety of passengers, with improved screening processes for both airport workers and airline passengers, thus decreasing the risk of terrorist acts. This increase in security has meant an additional security surcharge added to each airline ticket to cover costs. Critics maintain that airport security is still too lax, as airport workers and their access areas do not undergo the same screening procedures as passengers.

By April 1, 2003, Air Canada was financially troubled and forced to file for bankruptcy protection. The company emerged from bankruptcy protection in 2004 through a combination of external financing and reducing costs through lay-offs, restructured union contracts, minimized services, and changes to the customer baggage allowances.[5]

On March 11, 2005, one of Canada's deep discount airlines, Jetsgo, grounded its fleet and declared bankruptcy. In June of 2008, Zoom airlines did the same thing. Passengers in both cases were stranded across Canada and in resort destinations, inconveniencing them and costing them money. Although British Columbia, Quebec, and Ontario already had protective legislation in place, this event prompted those provinces without legislation to investigate the implementation of consumer protection laws.

The Travel Industry Council of Ontario (TICO) takes an aggressive stand to ensure that travel agencies and tour operators meet higher standards of performance. TICO has fought Bill C-44 (legislation tabled in Parliament in 2005, aimed at creating a more efficient transportation system), asking that the legislation provide more protection for the travelling public and that the position of airline travel commissioner (ombudsman for the airline industry) be retained, not eliminated.

In a speech delivered at the Aviation Forecasting Conference in October of 2005, James May of the Air Transport Association of America identified five major issues facing airlines today:

- Airlines are being heavily taxed by governments, often adding as much as 50% to the cost of a ticket.

- Politicians and airline executives must rethink the structure and operation of airlines.

- Resources must be provided to allow the antiquated air traffic management systems around the world to move to a satellite-based system.

- Current soaring fuel prices make profitability a continued challenge.

- Bankruptcy of one major airline has a direct impact on feeder airlines, companies that depend on the transfer of passengers from major airlines.[6]

Understanding Canada's Air System

The federal department responsible for all of Canada's transportation systems is Transport Canada. It sets the rules and regulations for licensing pilots, flight engineers, and airplane mechanics. It provides licences for each commercial aircraft and determines the number of hours a plane can fly between maintenance checks. It sets the appropriate weight loads allowable for each type of aircraft. It also sets the maximum number of hours a pilot may remain on duty. Many airlines choose to set pilot hours at eight hours of flight time with an additional four hours "on ground." Many flights that extend beyond 6.5 hours, called long-haul flights, will operate with a "double cockpit" that includes a second captain and second co-pilot to relieve the fatique of the first team.

For more than sixty years, Transport Canada also operated the country's air navigation system. In November of 1996, NAV CANADA (NAVCAN), a non-share, capital, private-sector corporation was given ownership and control over the country's air navigation system. By putting the safety of airline passengers under one private corporation, the government hoped to save money and provide Canadians with a more efficient, safer air system. NAVCAN currently provides aircraft with air navigation, air traffic control, flight information, weather briefings, airport advisory services, electronics, and services such as training and electronic maintenance. NAVCAN charges users (primarily commercial airlines) service fees, which are, of course, passed on to the consumer.

www.tc.gc.ca

Understanding Air Terminology

Air travel is best described in terms of *scheduled* and *non-scheduled service*. In addition to scheduled commercial flights, air travel includes fleets for use by private corporations, small private planes for business and pleasure, and planes for special services such as fire prevention and law enforcement.

Scheduled air carriers operate with published timetables on defined domestic or international routes for which licences have been granted by the government or governments. Air Canada and WestJet are both scheduled carriers.

Charter airlines or charter air services arrange to fly wherever and whenever a group plans to travel. A group of travellers may charter any form of transportation, usually at lower rates than those of regularly scheduled service.

Charter operators have much more flexibility than operators of scheduled flights; they can fly on their own time, even cancelling the flight if necessary. Using cheaper chartered service does have its problems from a passenger standpoint, as these aircraft fly only on the dates, times, and departure points pre-set by the charter company. Tour operators with large groups often choose to charter an aircraft to help keep costs lower.

Some of our finest wilderness experiences can be reached only with float planes.
(Photo courtesy Canadian Tourism Commission.)

Airports

Airports fall into two major categories: *air carrier* airports and *general aviation* airports. Most of Canada's major airports are now leased by the government to a private company or airport authority. Since these companies are in business for profit, service charges have gone up. Increased landing fees, which of course must be passed on to passengers, have been a major concern to airlines. Cities with airports currently under private management include Halifax, Montreal, Ottawa, Toronto, Winnipeg, Calgary, Edmonton, and Vancouver. Some airports are owned and operated by provincial authorities, and a few remain under the control of Transport Canada.

Many of our airports require extensive remodelling, new and longer runways, and improved services to stay competitive and handle expected higher passenger volume. To cover these costs, most airports charge passengers departure taxes called air improvement fees (AIFs), which may be added to the ticket at the time of purchase or collected when passengers go through security. Airports also make additional revenue from rental spaces, parking facilities, and other services. The year 2007 was one of the worst travel years for customers in the United States, with major airports so badly congested that heavy delays and flight cancellations became the status quo. As a result, the United States proposed adding a "congestion fee" to encourage passengers to use other airports—this fee in the U.S. has since been withdrawn.

Airport Components Airports consist of many different components: passenger terminals, parking lots, control towers, hangars, runways, taxiways, loading aprons, chapels, customs and immigration facilities, restaurants and bars, lounges reserved for first-class travellers, souvenir shops, car rental agencies, banks or money exchange services, administration offices, and any other service that the airport feels is needed by a traveller. Some airports have hotels as an integral part of the terminal, and others have direct access to subways or a train station. Many major airports around the world can provide passengers with a unique experience and enjoyable stopover. One such experience attempted was the Common-Use Self-Service (CUSS) kiosks being set up in all major airports.[7] They allowed passengers to check themselves in, no matter which airline they were flying on. Although approximately 100 airports adopted this technology, the program was formally closed in 2008.[8]

Another change bound to decrease boarding time is the introduction of bar-coded tickets. This means passengers may check in at home and print a computerized document valid for their entire round trip. When travellers are boarding with this document, computers will scan and check in each traveller. Over one hundred airlines around the world now offer this convenience.[9] Although some initial concern was raised by airlines and passengers, by 2012 this self-service had not only become readily adopted but was extended to mobile devices. Passengers can now use the high-quality screens on their mobile devices to bring up a mobile-friendly e-ticket, one that can be scanned by many ticket readers.[10]

Airline Terminology You Should Know

landing fee	fee charged to an aircraft each time it lands at an airport; passed on to the consumer in the ticket price
gateway airport	an airport that receives a high volume of international flights
e-ticket	ticketless travel where a code is your check-in document. Since May 2008, all IATA airlines should be using only the e-ticket.
bumped	term used when a flight is oversold and confirmed passengers are denied boarding
round trip	trip that originates in one city, takes passengers to their destination, and returns them to the originating city using the same airline
circle trip	a type of round trip in which the route taken to the destination differs from the route taken from the destination
open-jaw trip	trip that takes passengers to one destination, allows them to use another mode of travel to a second destination, and flies them home from there
non-stop flight	a flight that travels from one destination to another without a stop
direct flight	a flight that travels from one destination to another, making at least one stop, then continuing on the same plane
online connection	a flight that requires travellers to change aircraft to get to their destination
interline connection	a flight that requires travellers to change airlines to get to their destination

Airfares and Reservations

Deregulation and more efficient operations have dramatically reduced **airfares**, and as suggested earlier, when airfares drop, more people take to the skies. The airline industry is, however, greatly affected by changes in oil prices. The dramatic rise of gas prices since 2004 has caused hardship for the already struggling airlines. Most airlines have now added a fuel surcharge, allowing them to quickly adjust ticket prices to cover these rising costs.

Airfares are set according to two very broad markets: the business traveller and the discretionary traveller. Business travellers usually want to adhere to a relatively strict schedule, so they have fewer options on flight times. Because of this inflexibility, they pay the standard fare or even the higher business or first-class fare. Discretionary travellers, who can shop around for more convenient flights at the best price, are usually able to get discount fares because they are not locked into a specific schedule.

Airline strategies in discount fares have led to multi-tiered pricing, with as many as 100 different prices for the same route. The difference in price between a standard fare, a discount fare, and the last-minute sale price made over the internet can be considerable, but selling these unoccupied seats at the last minute can bring the airlines at least a minimal fare to cover costs. (In Chapter 3, we looked at the perishability of the tourism product—and here is an example of how an industry tries to sell its products in a timely fashion.) For passengers able to travel at the last minute, these fares can be an added bonus to a trip. This arrangement also allows airlines to increase their load factor—the average percentage of seats filled by paying (revenue-producing) passengers. Generally, the major costs of the flight, such as crew salaries, aircraft depreciation, and maintenance, are fixed, and incremental costs to carry one more passenger are minimal. Therefore, revenue is maximized by pricing some seats at a lower rate to encourage additional passenger travel.

The International Air Transport System: How It Works

Bilateral agreements are international agreements made between two countries. Every country with air service will have signed bilateral agreements. These agreements cover a number of issues, including the number of flights permitted from each country into a specific airport, the size and capacity of the airplanes, and special fares. The **Open Skies Agreement** of 1995 is an example of a bilateral agreement between Canada and the United States. It has "opened the skies" above North America, providing tourists with more options for carrier, destination, and type of flight. This agreement has benefited cross-border tourism, allowing Air Canada to serve many new U.S. destinations, and U.S. airlines to provide some cross-border competition for Air Canada. In 2005, Canada and the United States updated this agreement, giving greater access for Canadian and U.S. passenger and cargo flights and providing more flexibility in pricing structures, which should bring lower prices for consumers.[11]

Most countries claim ownership not only of their land but also of their shorelines, waters, and skies. In the early years of aviation, this ownership caused some concern for aviators. To ensure the right of safe flight, the nations of the world sat down to write some very basic rules. Rules regulating air activity have been developed at worldwide conferences, through bilateral agreements, and by organizations like the International Civil Aviation Organization (ICAO) and the International Air Transport Association (IATA).

Airline Associations

IATA The **International Air Transport Association (IATA)** was formed in 1919 and reorganized in 1945. Its members currently include more than 200 of the world's scheduled airlines, with major flag carriers taking a leadership role. The principal function of IATA is to facilitate the movement of persons and goods from and to any point on the world air network by any combination of routes. Some of IATA's mandates are to:

- provide a forum for airlines to meet and discuss mutual concerns
- promote air safety
- represent the airlines in travel agency affairs
- encourage global air travel

www.iata.org

Each country has absolute right to its airspace and can set any conditions it likes with regard to air travel, so to be effective, rules or tariffs formulated by IATA must also receive approval from the appropriate government.

By 1940, IATA had overseen a series of world conferences that set up parameters for controlling a variety of flight issues, including aircraft registry, issuing airline tickets, setting liability of the airline with regard to lost luggage, and setting liability in the event of passenger injury or death.

One of the more important accomplishments of these world conferences has been the development of rights called **Freedoms of the Air**. The first two freedoms deal with the rights of passage for an airplane. After the Bay of Pigs incident in 1963, in which the United States encouraged an unsuccessful invasion of Cuba by Cuban expatriates, Fidel Castro rescinded all Freedoms of the Air for U.S. airlines. Because Canada still has these rights, Canadian airlines may fly across the island, but U.S. airlines are forced to fly around it.

FOOTPRINT

IATA is stepping forward to urge both airlines and countries to invest in critical areas concerning global warming. Their aim is to get companies to reinvest in modern, fuel-efficient aircraft that eliminate most of the carbon waste currently emitted by those in use such as the B747, A310, and the B737. It asked that stop-gap measures, such as fuel surcharges and new charges being levied to offset the rising cost of fuel (like checked baggage charges), be eliminated; that management and unions recognize the need to control labour costs (reducing salaries and management bonuses) so that investment in newer aircraft is possible; and that airlines be freed from national ties and bilateral agreements that strip the companies of the ability to create route structures that benefit the needs of passengers.

CEO Giovanni Bisignani stated that "governments must drive progress by taking the politics out of air traffic management, acting globally on emissions trading, and supporting positive economic measures to drive innovation." In 2007, IATA Green Teams created savings of 10.5 million tonnes of CO_2 and shortened 395 routes, but governments still think punishment for emissions rather than investment in carbon-neutral flights is the answer. Fuel efficiency in the past decade has improved by 19% and non-fuel costs have dropped by 18%. However, average air margins for the industry are just 0.3%. Fuel-efficient aircraft, better equipped airports, and more efficient route structures would be a big step toward eliminating most of the negative impact of aircraft emissions.

(*Canadian Travel Press*, June 9, 2008, p. 3)

The next four freedoms are called *traffic rights*. They deal with the dropping off and picking up of passengers. The last two freedoms are the newest. They give special rights to certain airlines under specific circumstances. The eighth freedom, called *cabotage,* gives a foreign airline the right to carry passengers from one destination within a country to another, allowing Delta Airlines, for example, to pick up passengers in Toronto and let them disembark in Vancouver. Canada does not currently give U.S. airlines the right of cabotage. Some believe that granting this right to foreign airlines would prevent Canada's flight system from becoming monopolistic. However, this proposal has not been met with much support because our Open Skies Agreement already gives considerable freedom to North American airlines to form partnerships and to share routes and fare structures. All freedoms can be found on the ICAO webpage[12] and a few core freedoms include:

First Freedom: right of transit (e.g., Air Canada departs Toronto and flies over the United States to reach Mexico City)

Second Freedom: right of technical stop (e.g., Cathay Pacific departs Toronto and lands in Anchorage to refuel en route to Hong Kong)

Third Freedom: right to discharge passengers in a foreign country (e.g., Air Canada boards passengers in Halifax and they disembark in London, England)

Fourth Freedom: right to pick up foreign passengers in another country and transport them to the airline's country of registration (e.g., Air Canada boards passengers in Miami, Florida, and allows them to disembark in Montreal)

Eighth Freedom: right of an airline registered in one country to fly passengers between two points within another country (e.g., United Airlines picks up passengers in Montreal and flies them to Calgary; this is an example of *cabotage*)

If Canada were to lose one of its airlines and Canadians had just one choice of carrier, the impact such a monopoly might have on the price of a ticket could be high. As an alternative, the Canadian government could give a U.S. airline (e.g., American Airlines) cabotage rights in Canada, providing some competition and taking away monopoly rights.

In Practice

Canada has one large airline in Air Canada, along with two strong competitors, WestJet and Porter Airlines. The United States is one of the only countries to have more than one major airline. Australia, Great Britain, France, and Germany are examples of countries with just one national airline.

In groups of four to six, take a piece of paper and divide it into two sections. On one side, list the advantages of having just one major airline. On the other side of the paper, list the problems you see arising from one major airline possessing a monopoly on air travel. Now, make a decision: Should the Canadian government protect airlines like WestJet to ensure competition? Or should Canada follow other nations and move toward a single air carrier? Perhaps Canada should look at giving cabotage rights (the eighth freedom) to one U.S. airline? Create a position paper and be prepared to defend your choice.

SNAPSHOT

Maxwell William Ward

Maxwell William Ward was born to fly. "Max," as he is affectionately known in the tourism sector, lived and slept with dreams of flying throughout his childhood. Those dreams became a reality in 1940 when, at the age of eighteen, he enlisted in the Royal Canadian Air Force (RCAF) as a pilot. His first flight was marked by "poise, courage, and breakfast," as Max quickly found out that he was prone to airsickness! But dreams overcome many of our weaknesses, and Max went on to get his wings and graduate at the top of his class. As did many young fighter pilots, Max itched to get into World War II. It was not to be, and instead he spent his years in the RCAF training other pilots for action.

At the end of the war, Max left the air force to work for Northern Flights Limited, but he soon discovered that he was not interested in flying for someone else—he wanted to be his own boss. The trials and tribulations Max Ward faced over the next forty-three years clearly reflect how the federal government "hog-tied" Canada's commercial airline industry until deregulation. In June of 1946, Max began his first airline, called Polaris Charter Company Limited, and with the help of family and friends, he bought his first aircraft, a single-engine biplane called a Fox Moth. His career as an airline owner/operator did not start auspiciously as his first commercial flight ended with a crash. Then his company was forced to fold when the Air Transport Board (ATB) discovered Max had not applied for a commercial licence.

By 1949, after a series of mishaps and a broken partnership, Max decided to give up his airline dream, and he returned to Alberta to build houses. Within three years, he realized that life without flight would be no life at all, and he applied to the ATB for a commercial charter licence. He was turned down the first time, but his persistence finally paid off, and Wardair was officially launched. He chose a de Havilland Otter as the company's first aircraft, and he flew gold miners and equipment into the northern territories. It was tough going for the little airline, as the purchase of every new plane required that Max cut through the mass of red tape needed for government approval to fly commercially. Every new route Wardair applied for was initially turned down. However, despite the negative, restrictive government climate, Wardair beat the odds and survived. By 1961, Wardair was making a profit and Max changed the name to Wardair Canada Ltd. Within a year, Wardair had flown its first passenger charter from Calgary to Ottawa and its first international charter to Denmark. In 1966, Wardair took delivery of its first jet, a Boeing 727, the first one of its kind in Canada. It looked as if the little airline that Max had built finally had its wings.

Trouble followed hard on the heels of his first success. In the early days of charter flights, only groups or associations could charter an aircraft, and the rules defining a group were very restrictive. Max tended to define his clients in the loosest sense of the word *association,* and soon the Air Transport Board of Canada had expelled him for breaking the rules of charter flights. To add to his difficulties, the government set new, tougher guidelines for charter companies, called the "charter affinity rule." This made it even harder for private airline companies to compete with the newly renamed national carrier, Air Canada. Max refused to give up. Lobbying Ottawa against its restrictive, unfair air

continued…

transport policies, Max succeeded in having the affinity rule abolished. Max was invited back into the Air Transport Association of Canada, given a lifetime membership, and named Transport Man of the Year.

By 1975, Max Ward had been awarded the Order of Canada and was running Canada's third-largest airline. In 1978, after the United States deregulated their airline industry, Max went back to Ottawa to demand more freedom in the charter airlines business. He was successful, and Wardair was finally given permission to fly domestic charters. He booked his first advance-booking charter. Wardair International expanded aggressively, and its high-quality service earned it the title of "world's best charter airline." As the Canadian government began to consider deregulation, Wardair was granted its first scheduled route between Canada and the United Kingdom. Max had achieved the success he had striven so hard for, and his little airline entered the big leagues.

In 1988, deregulation in Canada went into effect; to meet the demands of the marketplace, Ward bought twelve Airbuses and sixteen McDonnell Douglas MD-88s. Not only was Wardair recognized as one of the best airlines in the world, but its aggressive, creative marketing also placed the airline in a favourable position against the two big carriers—Air Canada and Canadian International.

In the real world, however, Jack seldom beats the giant, and so it was with Wardair. Max Ward had not invested wisely in computer reservation systems, and he had over-extended the company in purchasing new equipment. Unable to compete effectively with Canada's two major carriers, Max sold his beloved company to Pacific Western Airlines Corporation, and Wardair merged with Canadian Airlines International.

Max Ward is one of tourism's most beloved pioneers: he created a fine airline, he fought to reduce government red tape and overregulation, and, in the end, rather than see his employees out of work, he made the hard decision to sell his company before its competition, Air Canada, bankrupted it. "I don't think he would consider himself totally a success in business," his son, Blake, once said. "He didn't beat them." Those who knew Max saw him for what he was—a giant in the Canadian airline industry, a fighter who never quit, and a man who stood for excellence in service and helped create the Canadian air system as it exists today.

Space Travel Becoming Reality

Deep in the Mojave Desert, Richard Branson's Virgin Galactic[13] is finalizing plans to make private suborbital space travel a reality, allowing travellers the same magnificent view of the earth that astronauts have had for decades. At sixty feet in length, SpaceShipTwo will have the capacity to carry two pilots and six passengers into space, orbiting the earth at 2500 kph, just over three times the speed of sound. SpaceShipTwo will be carried close to its orbit height by the transport ship WhiteKnightTwo, named Virgin Mothership (VMS) Eve after Richard Branson's mother. This experience will be based out of the state of New Mexico at the newly constructed Spaceport America. Reservations can be made with a deposit of US$20 000, 10% of the total US$200 000 ticket price.

ICAO The **International Civil Aviation Organization (ICAO)** is an agency of the United Nations, and its members are representatives from UN member countries. ICAO was formed to ensure that the development of the airline system is both safe and orderly. ICAO is responsible for organizing world conferences, mediating disputes between members, and setting standards for aviation equipment and operations. Canada has played an active role in ICAO and promoted an international no-smoking policy.

Air rage—when passengers abuse cabin crew or other passengers—has become another security problem that airlines must deal with. In the United States, stiff penalties and jail terms can be given to any person disturbing the normal activities of the cabin crew. Canadian law is not as tough; however, crews today are more cognizant of their passengers, and pilots are quick to respond when given an alert by the flight attendants. If trouble begins in the cabin, the aircraft will land at the nearest airport and the perpetrator will be turned over to local police. Despite the problems air travel has experienced over the past decade, it remains the safest and most viable method of transportation for the long-distance traveller.

TRAVEL BY LAND

AUTOMOBILE AND RECREATIONAL VEHICLE TRAVEL

Transportation's transition from horse-drawn carriage to private automobile changed domestic travel habits, and more than any other factor in tourism, gave the average family more freedom of movement. Before the automobile, travel patterns were very predictable. Resorts and hotels were built along rail lines and in ports. The automobile introduced a more random, unstructured pattern of travel movements. Hotels, motels, and attractions sprang up along the highways and enjoyed success.

The automobile continues to be the most popular mode of travel for the tourist. People choose to travel by car for the following reasons:

1. Low cost, especially for three or more people
2. Convenience of having the car at your doorstep
3. Flexibility in departure and arrival times, routes, and stops
4. Enhanced trip experience
5. Easier luggage transport with fewer restrictions
6. Assured transportation on arrival at the destination
7. The enjoyment of having your "own space" with your own comforts

Recreational vehicle (RV) travel, of course, has all the advantages of the automobile plus the convenience of carrying one's home along on the trip. RV travel eliminates the hassles and the expense of hotels and restaurants. The traveller can experience the great outdoors without really leaving the comforts of modern-day life, thus enjoying the best of both worlds. The style of an RV varies dramatically from simple pop-up tents to luxurious rolling homes, fully equipped with every convenience including big living rooms, fireplaces, and full bathrooms with Jacuzzi tubs. Upscale RVs may be bigger than your house and often are not used for travelling vacations, but are pulled to a specific RV park and placed semi-permanently on their own pads. Nearly 13% of all Canadian households own some type of RV. It is interesting to note that when travelling in their RVs, most people tend to stay in their home province, 8% say they prefer to travel to other provinces, and 7% choose to go south, into the United States or Mexico.[14]

The family vacation market accounts for about 80% of all vacation travel in both the United States and Canada, and much of this travel is done using the family's car or RV. Concerns about the rise in fuel costs and about the impact the price will have on tourism have been raised across North America. RVers are hit the hardest as their vehicles demand more fuel, but it is interesting to note that 48% of RV owners say they are unconcerned about the price of gas. Fifty-two percent show concern for oil prices, but they will deal with it by shortening their trips, staying in their own provinces to vacation, and looking at spending longer in one spot. Owners agree that travelling by RV is such a cost-saving way to vacation, they will be able to offset the price of gas by changing spending habits on the road. Some RVs are now winterized, allowing travel to continue throughout the year. Those who do choose to travel during the winter say the campsites are very quiet and the outdoor experience is healthy for their children.

Why RVers love their RVs[15]

- They can experience the outdoors in greater comfort
- Easy to get to events and activities
- Can bring the conveniences of home on the road

- RV travel can be 50–70% less expensive than other forms of vacation travel
- Ability to visit friends and family while bringing their own accommodations

---

The Car Rental Industry

www.hertz.com

The car rental business can be traced back to the early twentieth century. Recognizing that not everyone could afford a car but might need one for a day or two, a wise entrepreneur decided to offer them for rent. Hertz started renting cars in 1918, and his company is now the largest and oldest car rental agency in the world. Car rental agencies did not see a real boom in business until the age of jet travel. Expansion was rapid once business travellers found that, although they could travel long distances by air in a short period of time, they needed a car at their destination.

Business travellers still make up the greatest percentage of renters, but in recent years the leisure market has expanded dramatically. Combining a car rental with another mode of transportation provides a leisure traveller with the freedom to get around at the destination, a convenience that is becoming increasingly more popular. Fly/drive packages are a good example of how the industry has learned to package products.

Some car rental agencies provide customers with a wide variety of cars and SUVs, others choose one brand name, like Ford, while still others may go for

With rising concern for global ecosystems, some tourists choose their mode of transportation based on its carbon footprint.
(Photo courtesy Canadian Tourism Commission.)

niche markets—low-cost rentals or high-end car rentals with vehicles from Cadillac, Porsche, and Mercedes Benz. As in any tourism business, you must know your market's needs and be able to fulfill them if you are to be successful.

Car rental companies glean additional revenues from a variety of sources besides the rental fee. Add-on charges can include insurance, gas tank filling, customer drop-off and pickup, and lost key charges. Although these extra fees may be irksome to consumers, they do represent costs incurred by the car rental business. One reason add-on fees are itemized apart from the standard rental fee is so companies can advertise more competitive prices. To remain competitive with larger firms, small agencies may not charge some of these fees.

Marketing Strategies Car rental agencies do not often provide information on fleet size or structure because these components change frequently based on levels of demand. However, basic product, price, and location strategies are visible to everyone. Pricing in car rentals remains very competitive. Value programs have become quite popular, such as arranging for a contract with **unlimited kilometres** that allows the traveller to drive as many kilometres as desired for a flat fee. **Corporate rates** are reduced rates given to companies with a high rental volume. In addition to the corporate rate, some rental companies have separate check-in areas for their corporate customers. The major car companies have frequent-driver programs (similar to airlines' frequent-flyer programs) to encourage customers to stay with the same company each time they rent a car.

RAIL TRAVEL

Travel by rail in Canada has a long history, binding our country together, coast to coast, with steel rails and wooden ties. So important was a national rail line that it was included as a condition of Confederation. Yet it is also the mode of transportation that captures the majesty of the Canadian landscape, a romantic and classic mode of travel from a period in our history that focused on style and experiences. Whether you are crossing the Siberian landscape or seeing the beauty of South Africa or the Canadian Rockies, train travel has always had a comfortable image in the eyes of many travellers and is often the chosen method of transportation.

History of Train Travel in Canada

For baby boomers and others, the words "All aboard!" evoke the romantic thrill of travel by train. In 1836, when Canada's first train roared over the tracks between La Prairie and Saint-Jean-sur-Richelieu at a breathtaking speed of up to 48 kph, a love affair began between Canadians and the train. Not only was the new form of transportation fast (a trip of 23 km could be made in just forty-three minutes), but it also soon became the most convenient form of transportation for Canadian travellers. By 1856, all the major centres in Upper and Lower Canada were connected by this new mode of transportation.

As the United States promoted settlement of its western territories with the offer of free land, British politicians worried about maintaining control over their North American colony and construction of the Canadian Pacific Railway from Montreal to Vancouver began. The line was completed in November 1885, and with the last spike driven into the ground at Craigellachie in British Columbia, Canada was united from sea to sea. In June 1886, the first transcontinental train, the Pacific Express, left Montreal and arrived in Port Moody, just east of Vancouver, a remarkable six days later. Canada had moved into the golden age of rail.

Over the next twenty years, many small entrepreneurial railroad companies emerged and prospered. Trains not only linked the Canadian provinces, but also extended their services into the United States. Two of the more famous international routes were the Allouette (Montreal to Boston) and the Maple Leaf (Toronto to New York). Because this method of travel was safe, efficient, and comfortable, it continued to be the major form of land travel until the 1930s.[16]

The first glimpse of trouble for Canadian railroads emerged as immigration and settlement of Canada slowed during World War I. By 1923, many of the smaller railroads were financially unable to continue operations, so their companies were united under the government-owned Canadian National Railways, providing direct competition for Canadian Pacific Railway. The Great Depression of the early 1930s caused financial ruin for many, and the railways suffered along with the rest of North America. There was a brief resurgence of popularity for rail transportation during the war efforts of the 1940s, but the golden age of rail was over.

www.viarail.ca

In 1976, the Canadian government reviewed the future of rail transportation. It concluded that Canada could not support two passenger railroad companies and called for the merging of the passenger services of Canadian National Railways and Canadian Pacific Railway. This new Crown corporation, VIA Rail Canada, was to be responsible for all passenger traffic. At first, there were few changes to the system, but in 1981, VIA Rail downsized, eliminating 20% of Canada's rail system.

By 1990, VIA Rail operated only one transcontinental train, The Canadian, from Toronto to Vancouver, through Edmonton and Jasper, and it abandoned the southern route through Calgary and Banff. Seizing the opportunity, a team led by former motor coach operator Peter Armstrong established a luxury rail company, Rocky Mountaineer Vacations, allowing rail travellers to experience the best of the Rockies in complete luxury. By 2002, the Rocky Mountaineer had welcomed half a million passengers; today, it is the largest privately owned passenger rail service in North America.[17]

Three factors have contributed to the decline of rail travel in Canada. First, the automobile provided travellers with more freedom to choose time and place, so as more people bought cars, the need for train travel diminished. Second, the convenience and speed of airline travel, its relatively low cost, and the easy connections between cities have made flying a desirable way to travel long distances. Finally, the cost of maintenance, equipment, and labour is high for train travel compared with other types of surface travel.

Over the past few years, VIA Rail service has focused on the Quebec–Montreal–Toronto–Windsor corridor. Both VIA first-class service and economy service are provided on these routes, giving travellers a choice of service level and price. For very simple reasons, many business travellers choose the train over the plane when travelling in this corridor. First, the train from Ottawa to Toronto takes only four hours, and passengers arrive at Union Station, right in the heart of Toronto. Seats on the train are comfortable, meals are available, and there is time to get some work done. Weather has little effect on the trip or the arrival time.

At first glance, a four-hour train ride seems long compared to a one-hour flight. However, passenger check-in is now required one hour prior to departure at the Ottawa airport, and the trip from Pearson International Airport to a downtown Toronto destination will often take an additional 60 minutes. Those three hours of travel time easily increase with traffic or weather delays. The price of the trip by train has no surcharges and is competitive with the cost of air. With new, faster locomotives coming on line, it seems that the train may be a good option after all.

In 2000, the transport minister persuaded the federal government to earmark $400 million over the next five years to rebuild, refurbish, and renew VIA Rail. By the end of 2003, VIA Rail was expected to have 139 plush new cars and twenty-one new locomotives. In 2007, the federal government recommitted to transforming VIA Rail with a five-year $516 million investment in passenger rail service; this was followed in 2009 with another $409 million capital investment through Canada's Economic Action Plan. Significant portions of these investment dollars have been spent improving the rail corridor between Toronto, Ottawa, and Montreal.

VIA Rail Accommodations Each standard coach on VIA Rail trains has up to seventy-six reclining, turn-around seats with with adjustable footrests, overhead luggage racks, and tables. There are washroom facilities located in each car. VIA's The Canadian offers dome cars that feature skylights for better viewing, dining cars with table service and gourmet meals, and four types of sleeping accommodations: double berths, single bedrooms, double bedrooms, and drawing rooms.

Double berths have both upper and lower berths, and privacy is obtained by simply pulling a curtain around the bed. Washroom facilities are found at the end of the car. Single bedrooms or roomettes accommodate one passenger and

VIA Rail's The Canadian provides tourists with a spectacular transcontinental ride from Vancouver through the Rockies, across the Prairies, and around the top of Lake Superior to Toronto.

(Photo courtesy Canadian Tourism Commission.)

contain a fixed seat, private toilet, and folding bed. Double bedrooms sleep two and have a variety of seating and sleeping layouts. Two bedrooms can easily be combined to sleep a family of four by removing the partition between them. Each room has its own set of controls for air conditioning and lighting, and can be adapted in the day to a private living space with large, comfortable armchairs that swivel to face a picture window. Drawing rooms are approximately 25% larger than the bedroom layout and can sleep three passengers. Bedrooms and drawings rooms are provided with the appropriate amenities and have private bathroom facilities. Not all trains have these sleeping configurations available, and surcharges are added to the larger bedroom/living quarters.[18]

Foreign Railways

Although travel by train in North America has declined, it is one of the most widely used modes of travel in Europe. Here are some of the reasons travel by rail is so popular there:

1. Rails crisscross most of Europe. As countries built their own railroads, they also connected their systems to neighbouring countries. This network of railroads is now called the international intercity network.

2. Train terminals are usually conveniently located in the heart of the city.

3. While many Europeans own cars, the cost of gasoline has made driving an expensive way to travel.

4. The proximity of one country to another and the short distances between major towns and capitals make travel by train an efficient way to move from one destination to another.

5. Trains in Europe are noted for their on-time arrivals and departures.

6. Many railroads are still owned and operated by European governments.

7. European countries co-operate by marketing their trains as one rail system.

The **Eurail Pass** is a good example of a marketing strategy that has proved highly successful. This pass is available only to inbound European tourists and cannot be purchased in Europe. It provides unlimited first-class travel in seventeen countries and is also valid on some ferries, intercity bus routes, and rental cars. The pass has a range of validity periods, from fifteen days to three months.

Although Great Britain does not participate in the European network, it is linked to the rest of the European rail system by the Channel Tunnel (Chunnel). They also offer similar discounted fares for the British Isles through the **BritRail pass**. Many tourists travelling in Europe feel that the train is the only way to go. It is a relaxing, comfortable travel experience that allows the tourist to fully enjoy the scenery while mingling with local residents.

Trains of the World

Bullet Train Japan, on the leading edge of train technology, has one of the most advanced rail systems in the world. The Japanese created the high-speed train and built the first **bullet train** in 1964. This train, known as the Shinkansen, connects major Japanese cities at speeds of up to 200 kph. Russia lays claim to the longest train ride in the world with the Siberian Express, which travels from Moscow to

Mongolia during a leisurely nineteen-day trip. The Blue Train of South Africa provides a luxurious trip from Cape Town to Pretoria. The Royal Scotsman, staffed by servers in kilts, gives tourists a slow, comfortable trip through the Scottish Highlands in the true elegance of days long past.

Orient Express   The grande dame of the rails is the famous **Orient Express**. In 1833, the Orient Express began service from Paris to Istanbul, carrying queens and kings, political leaders, the very rich, and the very powerful. The route was spectacular and the service fit for royalty. The train was also the setting for many famous stories, including Agatha Christie's *Murder on the Orient Express*. Fame, in the end, could not save it: in 1977, tired, worn, and forgotten, the Orient Express made its last run.

However, one of the values of the tourism sector is its vision, which often leads to the restoration and renewal of disappearing cultures and history. Five years later, under the direction of James Sherwood, founder of Orient-Express Hotels, many 1920 vintage railcars were restored to their original splendour and a shorter version of the Orient Express was inaugurated. The Venice–Simplon–Orient–Express tour travels from Paris to Venice, passing through some of the most spectacular scenery in Europe. This journey has allowed many tourists a chance to travel back in time and ride the magnificent Orient Express. Sherwood has since added several luxury vintage train excursions in Asia and Australia, as well as a luxury train in the Andes Mountains, to complement his three new Peruvian luxury hotels.[19]

The Maglev   Fifteen years ago it was just a dream and now it is reality. But what is its future in the business of tourism? The superconducting **mag**netic **lev**itating vehicle (**maglev**) is a train that runs on a monorail using highly powerful magnets that allow the train to run on an air pocket between the rail and the body of the train. In 2001, the Chinese government signed a contract for the first-ever commercial maglev system. Produced in Germany, the train has undergone intensive mechanical trials and checks. Two concerns were what the top speed attainable would be, and whether two trains could pass each other at top speed without incident. In November of 2003, one train travelling at 501 kph (a world record) passed a second train travelling at 430 kph without incident. With the last obstacles set to rest, the Shanghai train began commercial operation in 2004, running on 30 km of track between Shanghai International Airport and the Shanghai Luijiazui financial district. This trip now takes just under eight minutes.[20]

In Practice

Knowing why people travel by train and why they do not, what methods could VIA Rail use to increase ridership? In light of the aging population of North America, what future do you see for train travel? Why?

MOTOR COACH TRAVEL

Travel by bus has long been an alternative for tourists for whom travel by car was not readily accessible. In 1949, scheduled intercity bus service peaked at 208 million passenger-kilometres. By 1996, a steady decline had reduced that number to just 18 million passenger-kilometres. Buses play an important part in many lives, beginning with the first step onto a yellow school bus. They provide transportation for class trips or to various sporting events, and for those without cars, they provide transportation around cities and regions, and between city centres as well. Most tourists are comfortable using a bus, but surprisingly, people often have a negative perception of bus services. They believe that travel by bus necessarily means riding in an old, uncomfortable, dirty vehicle.

However, the new tour bus design includes more comfort, with a larger, reclining seat, footrests, and more leg space. Wraparound windows now provide a full view for passengers. Services on the bus no longer just include overhead storage bins and modern washroom facilities; today's motor coaches have plugs at every seat for electronic devices, offer free WiFi connection while travelling, and run on engines far more environmentally friendly than their predecessors. Some executive coaches provide refrigerators, microwaves, and lounges with sofa-style seating. Experts predict that travel by bus will be an increasingly popular mode of transportation for baby boomers as they retire.

www.brewster.ca

The Canadian bus industry is still regulated in terms of entry and exit requirements, but both federal and provincial governments have indicated that they intend to deregulate it. As with many other tourism businesses, consolidation of the industry is inevitable. There will be fewer family-owned and -operated bus companies.

Today, the key players in Canada's bus industry are Coach USA (which operates in twenty-five states and two Canadian provinces), Greyhound, Laidlaw, Brewster, and Trailways. Most of these larger companies focus on the lucrative tour market rather than on scheduled, intercity services.

The Advantages of Motor Coach Travel

People choose to travel by bus for many reasons. It is the least expensive of the travel modes, except for personal automobiles, so cost is often cited as a prime factor. Scheduled intercity bus service is particularly price-sensitive. However, for small towns that have no infrastructure to handle rail and air, bus service is the only commercial transportation that links them to larger cities. Someone who chooses to travel by car must concentrate on driving and may miss most of the sights along the route. A driver must also know the route, where parking is available at the destination, and if moving from province to province, how traffic laws differ.

Charters versus Tours

With most charter services, a pre-existing group secures the services of the bus at a reduced price. Group members may belong to a particular club or organization, or may simply form as the result of a common interest in travelling to a destination at a reduced cost. A bus tour, on the other hand, has very specific components. Depending on the duration of the tour and the level of service the operator wishes to provide, bus tours will contain one or more of these components: (a) transportation, (b) accommodations, (c) attractions, (d) sightseeing, and (e) meals. These factors help determine the price and the grade of the tour. The higher the quality of the components, the higher the grade of tour. Bus tours are currently graded as budget, first class, and deluxe.

Categories of Tours

Bus tours are categorized as sightseeing/day tours, overnight/short tours, longer tours, and fly/coach. **Sightseeing/day tours** may focus on an urban area, such as Vancouver, or they may be a day excursion to a special event or festival. With day tours, the price of admission is usually included in the tour price. **Overnight/short tours** include accommodations. Longer tours can vary from three to thirty days and are usually referred to as a **motor coach package**. In this type of tour, a tour director accompanies the group to ensure all goes well.

Longer tours normally include several major city destinations and may include some interesting off-the-beaten-track local sights. Tours normally focus on regions: perhaps Calgary and Vancouver, Nova Scotia and Cape Breton; or the wine region of Niagara. **Fly/coach tours** combine airfare with an escorted bus tour. This type of tour is essential for visitors travelling a long distance, and is particularly popular with Japanese tourists who often fly into Vancouver, travel by motor coach through Banff and Jasper national parks, and then fly out of Calgary.

Marketing Bus Tours

Marketing a bus tour is similar to marketing any other tourism product. Product, price, place, and promotion all play an important role. Niche, or target, marketing is becoming increasingly important. The Ontario Motor Coach Association (OMCA) has identified several special markets. Focusing on education and learning experiences, the *youth market* provides an important and growing opportunity for tour bus operators. During the school year, school groups may travel to historic sites such as the forts of the Niagara Peninsula, or special museums to gain knowledge about a specific branch of science. In the winter, they might participate in outdoor activities such as skiing, while during the summer, exchange tours allow students to visit and learn about new cultures.

Most destinations have some form of unique transportation. In Banff, gondolas carry tourists to the top of Sulphur Mountain.
(Photo: Canadian Tourism Commission.)

The *mature market* (age fifty-five and over) has been a cornerstone for the bus industry in the past and it will continue to be a big market now that baby boomers have begun to retire. How will boomers change the tour product? They are looking for a more active tour, for soft adventure and learning activities that allow them hands-on experience. They are more sophisticated than their predecessors, have a higher level of education and more disposable income, and demand good service. These characteristics will influence their choice of accommodations and food services included in a tour package. This market enjoys the companionship of a touring experience, likes a mix of ages—and prefers not to be called the "seniors market."

Finally, the growth of specialty markets over the past ten years has been strong. Special-interest tours may include trips to see live theatre in Stratford, Ontario, attend special events such as the World Junior Hockey Championship, or visit Native Canadian artists.

In Practice

Assume that you want to start your own tour bus company in your hometown. To be successful, you will need to identify the potential markets in your region. List local clubs, groups, associations, businesses, and churches that might be interested in a group tour. How would you increase your likelihood of success? What marketing strategies would you use to gain business?

TRAVEL BY WATER

CRUISE INDUSTRY

The History of Cruising

Although people have travelled by water from earliest times, it was not until the invention of the steam engine that travel for pleasure began in earnest. Ships in those days carried passengers from one destination to another and were called ocean liners or passenger ships, not cruise ships. Ocean liners in the early 1900s focused on wealthy patrons who enjoyed travelling in high style and living in luxurious surroundings. However, hidden beneath the luxury on the lower decks was another, very different cargo—immigrants trying to reach America to start a new life. This below-decks class of service was called "steerage," and the conditions were squalid. In 1907, the Cunard Line developed and installed improved engines on their two newest ships—*Mauritania* and *Lusitania*. These ships still had luxurious interiors, but more important, they provided passengers with a faster, smoother ride, reducing the Atlantic crossing from ten days to four and a half.

Not to be outdone, the rival White Star Line launched its new ships in 1911 and 1912. *Olympic* and *Titanic* were slower than Cunard's ships, but what they lacked in speed they made up for in grandeur. The builders of *Titanic* had provided the ship with new, innovative safety features and claimed that it was "practically unsinkable." Looking for a marketing edge, however, White Star eliminated the word "practically" from its advertising and proclaimed the ship "unsinkable." Although they followed the regulations of the day, *Titanic* did not provide enough life jackets or lifeboats to accommodate the passenger load. On April 14, 1912,

Titanic struck an iceberg and did sink, losing 1495 passengers and crew.[21] The sinking of *Titanic* was the single worst disaster in the history of the industry. Despite the tragedy, ocean liners thrived until the end of World War I.

With the outbreak of World War II, ocean travel became dangerous and many ocean liners were refitted as troop carriers. At the end of the war, tourism entered a boom era and so did the ocean liner business. People wanted to experience foreign destinations; with increased disposable time and wages to spend, they flocked to the passenger ships.

In October 1958, the world of tourism changed forever. Pan American World Airways flew the first non-stop passenger flight from New York to Paris in just seven-and-a-half hours. Within six months, ocean liners had lost two-thirds of their business, and by 1960, they carried a mere 5% of the trans-atlantic traffic. To survive, passenger lines were forced to redesign their product. Cunard's slogan changed from "Getting there is half the fun" to "Being here is all the fun." Cruise lines repositioned themselves as "resorts on water," not as a mode of travel.

In 1971, cruise lines carried half a million passengers; by 1990, this number had increased to over 3.7 million passengers. Nineteen years later in 2009, the number of passengers worldwide had risen to an all-time high of 13.4 million![22] The growth trend in cruises is a positive sign for the tourism sector. When cruise-line passenger volumes increase, revenues also increase for complementary tourism products including airlines, hotels, and restaurants. This positive correlation has encouraged co-operative arrangements between cruise lines and airlines, railways, resorts, and attractions.

In Canada, the port of Vancouver has seen dramatic growth over the past ten years. It is now ranked as one of the busiest ports in the world, serving more than 500 000 passengers a year. Most cruise companies are based in the United States, but an increasing demand for small-vessel cruising favours the Canadian cruise industry. Canadian cruise ships carry between fifteen and 250 passengers on short trips ranging from three to ten days. The Canadian cruising experience often focuses on historical sites, wilderness themes, or adventure, and pampers the tourist with gourmet food and a professional, knowledgable crew.

Cruise Types

The image of sailing on a large luxury liner like the Love Boat characterizes only one aspect of the cruise line industry. Cruise lines are certainly the largest component of the industry, but smaller cruises on rivers, coastal areas, and lakes are also common.

Sea Cruises Sea cruises range from one-day "see nothing" trips to three-month, around-the-world trips. One-day trips may cost as little as $70 per person, whereas a three-month world trip may cost more than $24 000 for two people. The typical sea cruise is three to seven days with stops at various ports.

A sea cruise is now promoted as a vacation in itself. The stops are an added luxury to an aboard-ship vacation of sun and relaxation, whether cruising in the Caribbean or Mediterranean, or viewing mountains and glaciers along the Alaskan and Canadian coasts.

In the last decade, Saint John, NB, has transformed itself into a major port of call for many international cruise lines, servicing hundreds of ships each season.
(Photo: Saint John Port Authority.)

The Caribbean and Mediterranean are the most popular destinations for warm-weather cruises. Other warm-weather destinations are Mexico and the Mexican Riviera, the Bahamas, Hawaii, and the Pacific Rim islands. North American trips include cruises along the Pacific coast from Los Angeles to Vancouver, or from Vancouver to Skagway or Prince William Sound, Alaska. Northern Europe is also popular for its scenery in and around Norway and Sweden, and Mediterranean cruises provide travellers with a sense of history enjoyed in the comfort of a cruise ship.

Cruise lines have been very creative in marketing their product to new target groups. Theme and **special interest cruises** are gaining in popularity—for example, country and western cruises, which book top country and western singers to perform nightly. The entire cruise offers a unique opportunity for fans to enjoy their favourite performers. Special-interest cruises fall into six distinct categories:

- recreation (sports, bridge, backgammon)
- culture (opera, theatre, music)
- education (conferencing, history, religion, wildlife, financial planning)
- health (diet and exercise)
- hobbies (stamp collecting, gourmet cuisine, murder mystery)
- adventure (a trip up the Amazon, to the Galapagos, to Alaska)

The final type of sea cruise available to tourists is called the *repositioning* cruise. Ships that cruise the Alaskan routes or sail northern European waters have a limited season in those areas. As the weather grows colder and ice becomes a threat, these ships must relocate—change their home ports and destinations. For a tourist who loves to cruise, this kind of trip offers an interesting set of ports, perhaps combined with an ocean crossing, often at a reduced cost.

Why take a sea cruise? One of the most important factors is the level of satisfaction cruisers have with the product. Forty-five percent of all passengers rate the experience as "extremely satisfying." The top five reasons a person decides on a cruise over another type of vacation are:

- multiple destinations visited (with no packing and unpacking)
- all-inclusive price and service levels
- best opportunity to relax and unwind
- convenient booking (one-stop shopping) and having all activities close at hand
- sightseeing and activities off the ship

River Cruises The river cruise, like the sea cruise, can be short or long. A short trip may be two to three hours, whereas longer river cruises may last twelve days. One of the most historic and romantic cruises is down the Rhine River in Germany. Many sizes of boats with differing service levels are available, and passengers may often get on and off the ship at any point in the trip to view the historical areas they are passing. In North America, the Delta Queen Steamboat Company carries passengers on luxurious paddlewheel boats back in time to relive life on the mighty Mississippi in the 1880s with its riverboat gamblers and lush living.

Many riverboats are used for company retreats, wedding receptions, and other group parties. The seasonal aspect of the business is a disadvantage, as many northern rivers freeze during winter months. Unlike a cruise ship that can head south to another season of tourist traffic, the riverboat must close down for the season.

In Canada, many rivers have short cruises available, and each province has its own cruise experience. Winnipeg offers a variety of cruise options along both the Red River and the Assiniboine, including the MS *Paddlewheel Queen*, Canada's largest riverboat, which sails through the heart of the city offering an afternoon of sightseeing or an evening of dinner and dancing. The St. Lawrence Seaway offers cruises that have gained worldwide recognition, such as the whale-watching cruise that departs from Tadoussac, Quebec, and sails up the Saguenay River. In the Northwest Territories, tourists cruise Great Slave Lake, live on board the MS *Norweta*, and hike the rugged terrain to learn about the wildlife habitat of this beautiful region.

Lake Cruises and Ferries Lake cruises are common in some of the Great Lakes. Combined as a ferry and a cruise, the ship travels to a destination across the lake, then turns around for the return trip. Many vacationers take their vehicles across Lake Superior on these ferries to experience the cruising life, as well as to avoid the long journey around the lake, through Chicago. Ferries travel day or night across the lakes.

Ferries that carry passengers, and often their vehicles, onboard are common around Seattle and New York, between Alaskan and Canadian islands and the mainland, across the English Channel, and around other spots where people need to get across a body of water with their cars to work or play on the opposite shore. Ferries have managed to maintain ridership throughout the increased popularity of the plane and automobile because they go to areas where plane service is expensive or non-existent and automobile access is limited or non-existent. Ferries that travel short distances usually have informal seating and deck space. Long-distance ferries may have cabins, food service, and even recreation rooms.

Most ferry service in Canada is found along the coasts. On the east coast, ferry routes connect Saint John, NB, to Digby, NS; North Sydney, NS, and Port aux Basques, NL; and various points in PEI to both Nova Scotia and New Brunswick.

Tourists and B.C. residents may opt to use the high-speed catamaran that connects Victoria and Vancouver.
(Photo: John Kerr.)

In British Columbia, ferries connect Vancouver Island to the mainland and Victoria to Seattle, Washington.

Charter Yachts, Sailboats, and Houseboats   In the past, chartering a yacht, sailboat, or houseboat was an activity for the very rich. Now it is within the reach of people with middle incomes. Charters can be arranged for a few hours or an entire vacation. A charter can be rented with the crew included, or without a crew to people experienced enough to sail on their own. Many private owners are willing to charter their boats to keep up with maintenance costs. Houseboats provide family-style living on the water, and the chance to get away from the hassles of travel while still enjoying different ports of call.

Cruise Line Marketing Strategies

The cruise industry knows it has a great untapped market and is using a variety of strategies to win potential cruisers. Creative marketing is required to secure the business of the return passenger and to encourage new passengers.

Product   The product a ship has to sell depends on the target market it has chosen. Many ships will look at both families and singles, like the Carnival Fun Ships. Others are developed for the mature market and some ships do not allow children at all. Ships try to reach their markets with specific products like the amenities and services on board, and the route. Each part of the product is provided with quality and service in mind. A big sea cruise liner is physically laid out to accommodate a large number of passengers without feeling crowded. Accommodations may come with or without balconies or may be inside cabins with no view of the sea. If you are claustrophobic, you will need an outside cabin and porthole.

The rest of the ship is the resort centre for the vacationing guest. The cruise liner may be equipped with large multi-purpose rooms for meetings, conferences, or dancing. Most ships have health spas, fully equipped gyms, and swimming pools. Newer ships have ice rinks, rock climbing walls, and wedding chapels. The deck is laid out so that passengers can sunbathe next to the swimming pool, play board games in the sun, or simply lie back on a lounge chair and read a book.

Since the price of a cruise includes meals, food becomes a major source of entertainment. Elegant dining rooms serve a wide variety of North American and ethnic foods. Some dinners have a theme—for example, an Italian night with fine Italian dishes and wines and perhaps strolling musicians. Some cruise ships have ventured beyond the more formal dining setting and are providing specialty restaurants like pizza and burger parlours, salad bars, and Italian bistros for customers wishing more casual dining. The midnight buffet and the captain's cocktail party are two favourite events. Food is available twenty-four hours a day and passengers can indulge in their favourite foods at no extra cost. Beverages, both alcoholic and non-alcoholic, are not included in the cost of a cruise and are an important method of increasing onboard revenues while keeping the cost of a ticket low.

To maintain quality service, cruises need a high ratio of crew to passengers. Labour costs are offset by the onboard revenues generated from a ship's casino, souvenir and clothing sales, duty-free shops, and added services that help make the ship a total resort experience. These services usually include a spa facility, an exercise room with all the latest equipment, virtual reality centres, and special sports opportunities such as golfing and skeet shooting.

Shore tours also add to the expense of a cruise. A number of free activities often complement these fee-based services. For example, a seminar on how perfume is made may encourage passengers to pick up a new scent at the duty-free shop; a seminar on skin care may encourage passengers to try the spa. The conference and meeting market is the latest target for cruise ships; the *Allure of the Seas* has meeting space that can accommodate up to 1400 attendees! The actual route and stops en route are also part of a key marketing strategy. These cruises usually stop for several hours in one or more ports to allow passengers to shop and to experience another culture.

The price of each cruise, just as with resorts and hotels, varies according to cruise and is affected by the season and length of the trip. Other considerations used when calculating price are the ship's age or profile, and cabin choices. A ship's profile includes factors such as the number of outside cabins with balconies, the variety of recreational activities, the number and quality of restaurants and lounges, the size and placement of the cabins, and the ports and entertainment during the cruise. Most cruises are popular because the passenger pays one price and receives the same service as everyone else on board. There is a cruise that will satisfy even the most unusual interests or hobbies and prices to suit any wallet.

Promotion directly to the consumer is usually through newspaper advertisements, individual mass mailings, or through trade shows that focus on vacation choices. Some of the larger cruise lines, such as Royal Caribbean, advertise extensively on television.

In Practice

The number of travel agents working in the tourism industry continues to decrease. Yet they are still in demand for certain products and services. Are travel agents the best means of selling cruise vacations to the consumer? Why or why not? Explore how selling a cruise line ticket may be quite different from selling an airline ticket through a travel agent? In groups of four, try to design a new method of ticket selling for a cruise line.

TRAVEL AT DESTINATION

PUBLIC TRANSPORTATION

Once you get to your destination, you need to know how to get around. Having a car and a good map is great, but many tourists don't have cars at their disposal. Public transportation is any organized passenger service available to the general public within a small geographic area. Visitors commonly use these transportation systems to see the city sights.

Most cities have some form of bus transit system; some cities have created iconic transit images that are a particularly popular choice among tourists, such as the bright red double-decker buses that operate in London, England. These red buses have gained popularity in other cities as well. London and Edinburgh, Scotland, have special inexpensive and easy-to-use buses that carry passengers from one site to another with onboard guides who provide a description of the route. These services run all day long, and for the cost of a day pass, passengers may make as many stops as they want. Yet public transportation is quite varied. In the Philippines, visitors can ride the brightly decorated jeepneys. The modern subway systems of Washington, D.C., and Paris have gained worldwide reputations for their user-friendliness. In San Francisco, the cable cars are not to be missed. The list of public transportation methods is as varied as the number of cities a tourist can visit.

Travellers need to understand how an individual public transportation system works. For example, if you ride the GO Train in the Toronto region, you are responsible for validating your own ticket; if you fail to do so, you may be fined. In Tokyo, *white glove pushers* will literally push you onboard the transit trains during rush hour. They are not being rude—simply doing their job by putting as many people on the train as possible. Calgary has light rail transit (LRT) systems that run on their own tracks, circumventing traffic. LRT systems are not only quick, but also relatively environmentally friendly. Cab drivers in Halifax have all had special training developed by the CTHRC and the Tourism Industry Association of Nova Scotia.

Airports offer limousines, buses, and taxis as options for the traveller. At John F. Kennedy Airport in New York City, an alternative to the bus service is the Air-Train JFK, or "train to the plane." This special subway takes passengers into the heart of the city, thus avoiding traffic delays on the expressways.

CASE STUDY

An Untimely Death

Marc had been working with Cool Travel as a counsellor for four years. He had developed good profiles on all his regular clients, which had helped make him successful. One day in late March, one of his regular business clients paid a surprising visit—surprising because for the first time, the client wanted a vacation trip. Mr. Bennett stated plainly that he wanted lots of sun, good margaritas, to gamble into the night—and he wanted the total package to be inexpensive. Marc had just received a promotional brochure for a new resort casino in the Caribbean. Together they looked at the brochure, read the fine points, and discussed the problems sometimes encountered when booking a resort right after it opens. But the price was right, the time was available, and Marc booked the trip. Wednesday evening, just before the Easter holidays,

a very happy Mr. Bennett headed to the Caribbean. As Marc closed shop on Saturday of the long weekend, he got a call from the distraught casino manager. Mr. Bennett had been found dead on his bed, a half-finished beer on the bedside table.

The police were summoned, but the only contact information they could find in the room was for Cool Travel. The resort doctor confirmed that the guest had died of a heart attack.

The manager had called Marc to ask how to get in touch with Mr. Bennett's family. On his travel forms, Mr. Bennett had indicated to Marc that in the case of an emergency, he should contact Mr. Bennett's secretary. Mr. Bennett's office was closed, his secretary was gone for the Easter weekend, and Marc had no idea where to start.

1. If you were Marc, would you feel responsible for the care of Mr. Bennett? Why or why not?

2. If you were the casino manager, and the police left, saying the situation was not within their jurisdiction, what would you do?

3. What steps should you take in trying to get Mr. Bennett's body home? Which step would be the hardest to accomplish? Why did you choose this step?

4. Does Cool Travel have any liability in this case? Does the resort? Why?

5. If you owned a travel agency and had profiles on all of your clients, list six items you would be sure to include in each profile.

Summary

- The mode of transportation chosen by a traveller depends on a multitude of factors, both practical and psychological, including time, cost, route structure, frequency, and ease of access.
- Deregulation in the airline industry has opened the doors to more carriers, increasing both the volume of traffic and the choice of destinations.

- Increased competition and a more open system brought about a hub-and-spoke airport system in North America, and produced price wars and other marketing strategies beneficial to consumers.
- The airline industry is divided into two groups: scheduled air carriers and charter air services.
- Airfares for flights change daily. Computerized reservation systems allow airlines to respond immediately to a competitor's fare change. Discount tickets with restrictions have become a standard pricing technique to increase the load factor on the plane.
- Car and RV users represent the largest group of travellers. More kilometres are logged by private automobiles than by airlines, and family vacations by car account for 80% of all vacation travel in the United States.
- The car rental industry is volatile and competitive because of its ability to rapidly change fleet size and structure.
- Marketing strategies in the car rental industry include specialized vehicles, fly-and-drive programs, and pricing strategies such as unlimited kilometres for a flat fee.
- Car rentals from airport locations make up nearly 80% of all the rental business, making location a prime concern in the industry.
- The passenger rail industry has suffered with the advancement of alternative modes of transportation. Although VIA Rail nearly collapsed financially, government support has helped them slowly rebuild. They now provide more comfortable seating and sleeping arrangements, convenient stops, speed, and package vacations at prices competitive with other means of transportation.
- The bus industry comprises scheduled bus service, charter service, and tour service, and also uses a hub-and-spoke model. Convenience and price are often cited as reasons people travel by bus.
- Charter service is provided by bus companies that simply rent the bus, and sometimes the driver, to an interested group. The popularity of the charter business is growing with student, church, and social groups because it provides an opportunity for members of a club or organization to travel with friends and acquaintances with common interests.
- The cruise line industry is the fastest-growing segment of the travel industry. Passenger numbers have increased 7% annually for the past few years and are expected to continue at that rate of growth.
- Themed cruises as well as business and convention cruises are the latest trends. Other methods of water transportation include ferries, lake cruises, freight liners, riverboats, and charter yachts and sailboats.
- Public transportation is an important means of moving tourists from one site in a city to another.
- Many cities have transportation systems that provide the tourist with a unique cultural experience.

Questions

1. Many factors help determine the mode of transportation a traveller chooses.
   a) What three factors would most likely influence a business traveller?
   b) What three factors influence your choice of transportation? Explain your answers.

2. Briefly summarize the impact of deregulation on Canada's transportation systems.

3. a) How does the role of IATA differ from the role of ICAO? Explain your answer.
   b) Why were the Freedoms of the Air developed and how do they affect Canada's air industry?
   c) What is the name of Canada's latest bilateral agreement regarding air travel, who is the agreement with, and how has it affected our air transportation system? What does the new article, added in 2005, do to change this agreement?
   d) Why has Canada privatized its air transportation system? Who runs it? How has privatization affected airlines?

4. Compare and contrast three advantages and three disadvantages of travel by automobile and travel by motor coach.

5. a) Using the four Ps of the marketing mix discussed in Chapter 2, discuss the following tourism products: motor coaches, railways, and cruise lines.
   b) What is the greatest challenge faced by each of these tourism products? Explain how you, as a marketing consultant, might deal with each challenge.

6. Compare and contrast the following terms as they relate to the transportation industry (use examples where possible): *direct/non-stop flight, online/interline connection, scheduled/charter trip, open-jaw trip* and *circle trip, theme/special interest cruise, day/overnight tour.*

Notes

1. "Industry sees fewer fatalities," www.iata.org/pressroom, May 8, 2008.

2. www.iata.org/pressroom/facts_figures.

3. Ibid.

4. *Maclean's*, interview with Clive Beddoe of WestJet, October 3, 2005.

5. "Changes to checked baggage allowance," www.aircanada.com, August 23, 2005.

6. "James C. May at the annual Aviation Forecasting Conference, October 5, 2005," www.airlines.org/news, December 7, 2005.

7. www.iata.org/pressroom/facts_figures.

8. www.iata.org/whatwedo/stb/cuss/Pages/index.aspx.

9. www.iata.org/pressroom/facts_figures.

10. www.laptopmag.com/business/travel/your-next-e-ticket.aspx.

11. "Skies Set to Open, Maybe," News and Events, www.canadatourism.com, November 25, 2005.

12. legacy.icao.int/icao/en/trivia/freedoms_air.htm.

13. www.virgingalactic.com.

14. www.gorving.ca/media.

15. www.gorving.ca/why.asp.

16. David Wright, *Professional Travel Counselling*, 2nd ed. (Toronto: Canadian Institute of Travel Counsellors of Ontario, 1994), p. 208.

17. www.rockymountaineer.com/en_CA/about_us.

18. www.viarail.ca/planner.

19. www.orient-expresstrains.com.

20. www.maglev.com.

21. www.encyclopedia-titanica.org.

22. Cruise Line International Association, "2010 CLIA Cruise Market Overview."

Accommodations

Key terms

affiliation
American Plan (AP)
back of house
bed and breakfast
    (B & B)
Bermuda Plan (BP)
boutique hotels
campgrounds
cannibalization
cash bar
chain ownership
condominium
conference hotel
confirmed reservation
Continental Plan (CP)
corporate rate
day rate
double
double double

dude or guest ranch
European Plan (EP)
Family Plan (FP)
franchise
franchise advisory
    councils (FACs)
franchisee
franchisor
front of house
guaranteed reservation
heart of house
hospitality suite
hostel
hotel
inn
joint venture
management contract
Modified American
    Plan (MAP)

motel
niche
open bar
overbook
rack rate
referral system
real estate investment
    trusts (REITs)
resort
run-of-the-house rate
single
spa
suite
time-sharing
tourist courts
turn-down service
twin
walking
weekend rate

Learning objectives

Having read this chapter you will be able to

1. Discuss the scope of the accommodations industry.

2. List and discuss the interactions between the nine major departments in a large hotel.

3. Identify ten different types of lodging facilities available for tourists.

4. Compare and contrast the four basic management systems within the lodging industry.

5. Explain eight factors that affect the pricing structure of a hotel room.

6. Explain trends in the lodging industry.

7. Discuss the growing niche market of disabled travellers and their needs.

8. Analyze the Green Key rating system and its advantages for the owner of a lodging facility.

Accommodation is one of the oldest components of the tourism sector, with the earliest rules for innkeepers appearing in the Code of Hammurabi, the oldest set of inscribed laws known to exist.[1] Providing lodging and offering other services with the room evolved as a way to enhance the experience of guests began as soon as people began to travel. There are a wide variety of hotels and experiences to be had in Canada, and the lodging industry has remained in a slow but steady growth pattern.

Canada provides guests with more than 456 689 rooms found in over 8486 hotels[2] and other types of accommodations. These rooms offer a variety of living experiences ranging from deluxe accommodations to classical, heritage inns or rustic cabins with no indoor facilities. In 2010, all of the accommodation facilities in Canada collectively earned over $12 billion directly from room rentals and an additional $4.37 billion from a combination of food and beverage sales and other related activities. During this same period, 283 760 people were employed in the Canadian accommodations industry.

This chapter discusses history and trends in accommodation, lodging management systems, the departments within a hotel and their responsibilities, the variety of lodging choices available in today's market, factors that affect the pricing of this product, and career opportunities within this industry.

LODGING HISTORY AND TRENDS

For as long as people have travelled, they have needed lodging and food along the way. The history of the accommodation component of tourism began long ago, and the earliest known "hotel" system belonged to the Roman Empire. The early Romans were great road builders, and along their roads they built lodgings to house travellers—Roman soldiers who journeyed to distant provinces to keep peace and order in the empire, as well as Roman citizens who travelled for business purposes, education, or relaxation. The different needs of these Roman travellers required the lodging system to provide a variety of accommodations ranging from simple huts to more elaborate dwellings with all the amenities of the day. In the city of Pompeii, frozen in time by the eruption of Mt. Vesuvius, two examples of ancient hotels—the *hospitium* (full-service inn) and *caupona* (budget inn)—are still visible. With the breakdown of the Roman Empire, around 400 CE, travel became a rare and dangerous undertaking and this early system of lodging disappeared.

By the year 1000 CE, the Crusades into the Holy Lands had begun. Religion, for a brief period, was the cornerstone of the accommodations industry. Monasteries and other religious institutions provided lodging, believing it was their holy duty to offer shelter to weary travellers. Soon, however, the flow of soldiers and pilgrims to Jerusalem became greater than these religious institutions could handle. To meet the growing demand for lodging, people along the routes began to offer rooms and meals in their homes. In 1282, in order to protect their interests, the merchants of Florence, Italy, formed a guild that controlled the licensing of the city's innkeepers and ensured that each inn received its fair share of business. During this period of time in Europe, travellers would find beds in rustic inns, local homes, and sometimes in castles. Luxury was a bug-free bed and a pint of ale.

With the influx of immigrants and trade industry in North America, the growth of the lodging business became an imperative; inns and support services were established, specifically along water routes and in seaport towns. The first inn was built in Jamestown on the Virginia coast in 1607.[3] These inns typically provided family-style meals, a large common room (known today as a lobby), a number of private bedrooms, and a stable for guests' horses. The inn also became a meeting place for politicians, clergy, and other local groups.

Roadside inns began to appear throughout the eastern seaboard, as horse-drawn coaches became a familiar sight. Early city hotels were much grander than the inns of the day and had many more amenities for guests, including single and double rooms, locks on doors, soap, towels, bellhops, and room service.

In Canada, the first building specifically designed as a hotel opened in 1831 in Aylmer, Quebec. Upper Canada Village, a living-history museum located near Morrisburg, Ontario, invites tourists to wander through an exhibit of two of Canada's earliest inns.

The hotel era boomed in the days of railroad expansion as trains became the dominant mode of transportation. Towns sprang up along the railroad routes, with hotels to accommodate the rail passengers. With the completion of Canadian Pacific's trans-Canada railroad, tourists began flocking to the Banff region to enjoy the hot sulphur baths. The hotel now known as the Fairmont Banff Springs is Canada's first and best-known example of lodging built in a national park specifically for the pleasure tourist market.

www.fairmont.com

The Great Depression of the 1930s saw a collapse of the travel industry, with money as scarce as travellers, but tourism rebounded after World War II. In the 1950s, there was a period of rapid expansion, as automobiles became part of family life and the ability to travel became easier. Helping the industry to grow was a new method for financing properties—a method called *franchising*.

Technological advancements have had the greatest impact on the development of the hotel industry, beginning with those that emerged from the Industrial Revolution in the early nineteenth century. Besides providing accommodations with modern innovations, such as the elevator, the Industrial Revolution dramatically changed the modes of travel, as discussed in Chapter 4.

Accommodations have evolved over the years, based on the needs of both the transportation system and the traveller. For example, prior to the early nineteenth century, courtyards with stables for guests' horses were an integral part of any inn or hotel. When railroads became a major form of transportation, hotels were built along the rail routes. Many hotels were constructed directly beside or over the train station. The Fairmont Château Laurier in Ottawa and the Fairmont Royal York in Toronto, each linked to train stations by underground tunnels, are excellent examples of historic railroad hotels.

With the emergence of the automobile as a major form of transportation, the design of hotels changed. Mom-and-pop **tourist courts** provided the customer with a small cabin and a parking space. Soon the tourist court evolved into the motel. Motels differ from hotels in that they provide not only free parking, but also access to a guest's room directly from the parking lot, eliminating the need for large lobbies.

In the 1960s, the jet age of travel saw new hotel development clustered around local airports. Airport hotels have evolved into highly specialized facilities that provide unique services to fulfill the needs of their transient guests. As these hotels are not located in the heart of a city's business district, they must be able to provide many services that might otherwise be supplied by merchants in the downtown core.

No new modes of transportation have evolved since the jet age, but hotels have continued to evolve, moulded not by new transportation systems but by new technology, global economies, and changing consumer needs. In the 1970s, when economic difficulties arose because of a gas shortage, hotels focused on an inexpensive, no-frills product. In the 1980s, as global business boomed, new city hotels were built in downtown cores, and older hotels in these areas underwent massive restorations. In the 1990s, convention and conference facilities became the focus of new hotel product offerings. This decade also saw the emergence of the all-suite hotel. Rooms in these facilities resemble an apartment, allowing guests to cook their own meals if they wish.

In the first decade of the twenty-first century, the focus shifted to consider the total person; for example, spas developed for the wellness of both body and spirit. Depending on the property, spas may be simple or they may have all of the latest equipment. Even smaller hotels began providing spa experiences by hiring a masseuse or renting space to therapeutic practitioners.

New technology has significantly altered the way most properties do business. Travellers who once depended on knowledgable travel agents for information now use the internet to determine which hotel might best suit their needs. Formerly, conference attendees usually booked reservations at a negotiated "conference rate"; they can now easily conduct their own research to find the most economical room rates in the area. Customer reservations, files, check-ins, and check-outs are streamlined with the use of computer systems and specially designed property management systems (PMS). These systems quickly produce daily reports for managers that summarize the day's activities, as well as clearly showing patterns for all future bookings.

Automated heating and cooling systems streamline these internal functions, ensuring operations when a guest is actually registered in the room. Even the keys used in many major hotels have changed—the big, old brass keys of the past are collectors' items now, replaced by electronic cards that open the door. Today, a high-speed internet connection in the guest room and public areas, preferably wireless, is a "must have," not just an added advantage.

The accommodations industry experienced steady growth to the end of the twentieth century, and the tourism sector appeared to be full of promise. However, 2001 opened the next century in a series of economic challenges; sales in the high-tech industry slowed down, the North American economies shifted in a recessionary direction, and lower-than-expected profits negatively affected stock markets around the world. Businesses had less money to spend on their operations and unemployment began to grow, both factors serving to reduce the number of people travelling.

Just as the Canadian economy was technically entering into a recession, the United States fell victim to terrorist attacks on September 11, 2001. In the wake of these events, business travel fell by almost 60% as firms struggled to deal with both the existing economic downturn in the high-tech industry and heightened fear over additional terrorist attacks.

MAKING GUESTS WITH DISABILITIES COMFORTABLE

For disabled persons, travelling is often a challenge; facilities and services that are available to able-bodied people are not always extended to those who are less mobile. To accommodate various disabilities, rooms need to be large enough to accommodate a wheelchair; they should have levers instead of doorknobs and doors that open outward, which are crucial for easy manoeuvring. Wheelchair-accessible bathrooms with roll-in shower stalls or tubs are scarce in Canadian hotels, and grab bars should be available not only in bathrooms, but also in areas of the room where guests cannot navigate a wheelchair. For example, a grab bar near the bed makes getting in and out much easier. In addition, entrances to buildings need ramps and wider doorways in order to accommodate wheelchairs.

For the visually impaired, good lighting is essential, and important information should be provided in a large, bold print. Instructions in Braille are a very basic feature that should be available in all hotels today. For the hearing impaired, a bed shaker for wake-up calls and alarms, closed-captioned television, and lights that flicker when the phone rings or someone is at the door are all important features. Making guests with disabilities feel comfortable and welcome makes good economic sense for the hotel business.[4] The United States has developed strong legislation that forces business establishments to provide adequate facilities for the disabled traveller. Unfortunately, Canada has been slower to follow suit.

Beautiful, historic hotels like the Fairmont Chateau Montebello in rural Quebec are one of the area's pull factors.
(Photo: Fairmont Le Château Montebello.)

OWNERSHIP AND ORGANIZATION

When the accommodations industry was in its infancy, how the operation was organized was fairly simple and the ownership was straightforward. In today's market, however, operations and control have become more complicated. The terms *owner* and *manager* do not necessarily refer to the same person; these two roles are often separated and specialized. In smaller, independently owned properties, the owner often acts as the manager; in larger hotels and within chains, different people normally carry these titles.

Up to the time when chain motels became prevalent, ownership by individuals was common. Today, with the diversity of the lodging industry, ownership can be organized and structured in four different ways: by an individual (private ownership), by a corporate chain, by a franchise chain, or by a management contract. A description of each of these methods follows, along with a brief discussion of referral systems and hotel real estate investment trusts (REITs) in the lodging industry.

Private Ownership

Nearly half of all lodging establishments in North America are privately owned and operated as independent businesses. They tend to be smaller accommodations, including mom-and-pop hotels and motels, inns, and bed and breakfasts; these are important components of the accommodations industry.

The primary advantage of individual ownership is that the owner has full control over policies and operating procedures. Owners are free of bureaucratic red tape and are able to make their own decisions regarding the operation. Additionally, individual operators do not need to share profits with other owners. The major disadvantage is that the owner/manager assumes full risk for the property. In bad times, independent owners can lack the financial resources of a larger, multi-property company. Furthermore, the individual owner lacks the advantage of national advertising and a centralized reservation system—both serious shortcomings when competing with national chains and franchises. Finally, independents can face challenges raising capital to expand, especially during difficult economic times.

www.hotelsmag.com

Sometimes hoteliers may opt to form partnerships with investors instead of assuming all of the risk alone. These joint ventures often work because one partner supplies the expertise in lodging operations while the other partner provides the financial investment needed for a new property. By combining these two specific skill sets, both are better able to leverage each other's strengths to develop a successful business.

Affiliations To compete with larger and better-known hotel brands, independent hotels often become affiliated with organizations such as the American Automobile Association (AAA), the Canadian Automobile Association (CAA), Independent Motel Association (IMA), or the Hotel Association of Canada (HAC). An **affiliation** increases the credibility of small businesses; travellers generally feel more comfortable staying in a lodging facility that has been officially recognized as having met certain quality and service standards. In addition, both the CAA and the AAA will recommend their approved hotels and motels when designing itineraries for members; this type of recommendation can be very powerful for driving additional business.

Referral Systems There are other ways that an independently owned property can compete with the large franchise chains, including the branding strategy called a **referral system**. The largest hotel chain in the world is, in fact, a system of independently owned hotels represented by a referral company called Best Western. The most valuable aspect of becoming a member of Best Western is the use of their brand name. Travellers often look for a brand name facility because they are more confident about the quality of the product. Remember that a unique characteristic of the tourism industry is the inability of a customer to test the product or service before purchase; a brand name reduces potential anxiety about staying at unknown hotels.

In addition to the brand name, the independent owner also has immediate access to a worldwide reservation system, as well as national and global advertising campaigns. As an example, when a family-owned hotel in Ottawa wanted to expand its clientele, its owners chose to join Best Western. The move allowed them to operate their hotel as they liked, while instantly linking them to a larger global market. A large percentage of their market had been people visiting friends and relatives (VFR), but within a year of joining a referral system, the owners saw an increase in their business of more than 15%, directly attributable to their new affiliation. Service fees charged by companies such as Best Western are similar to those charged by a franchise operation, and the quality of the hotel is monitored.

www.hotels.com

Corporate Chains

The term *chain* is used to describe a group of facilities that use the same name. Four Seasons is a good example of **chain ownership**. The company owns and operates a number of properties, all reporting to corporate headquarters. All major organizational decisions are generated from headquarters, so changes to management procedures, available services, and decor are much simpler to implement. Four Seasons has created a **niche** in luxury accommodation, yet—although the level of service does not vary—each Four Seasons hotel has its own unique ambiance, capturing the local culture. For example, the property in Bali is not a hotel building but cottages with private pools, porches, and ceiling fans. Although ownership is centralized, hotels in a chain have more operational independence than franchises; while customers are seldom aware of ownership structures, they can sense the distinctive feel of a hotel.

Franchise Chains

The third type of operation is the **franchise**. The franchise relationship consists of two parties: a name brand company, called a **franchisor**, and the property owner, called the **franchisee**. Those who opt to purchase a franchised business are usually buying a proven business formula and access to brand systems. Franchising offers the advantages of a brand name product; although more of the operational systems and procedures are dictated by the franchisor, ownership and personnel management control normally remains in the hands of the owner (franchisee). The franchisee agrees to follow all of the franchisor's management policies, to pay an initial development fee, and to pay a monthly franchise fee, usually between 3% and 6% of the total gross room sales. All the hotels in a franchise have the same decor and image; unlike the varied Four Seasons properties, a Holiday Inn Express in Halifax is very similar to a Holiday Inn Express in Regina. Franchise companies often agree to keep all their properties far enough apart to avoid **cannibalization**, or competition within the franchise.

The advantages of the franchise system include the following:

1. Use of a nationally known brand name and a known product
2. National and international advertising and reservation systems
3. Lower borrowing costs because lending institutions are more willing to lend to a mortgagee affiliated with a nationally recognized franchise organization
4. Professional managerial assistance provided by the franchisor
5. Group buying power and a central purchasing office that provides supplies at much lower costs (franchisors provide architectural plans, layout, decoration, and other critical development components at substantial savings)
6. Employee training available at little or no cost to the franchisee
7. Common decor and a familiar atmosphere for travellers

However, a franchise does come with a number of disadvantages:

1. Initial franchise fees that are generally quite high
2. Franchise fees that usually include a percentage of the monthly gross revenues
3. Adverse effects when other franchise owners do not live up to customers' expectations
4. Financial consequences for the franchisee if the franchisor becomes financially insolvent or does not provide the management assistance required
5. Little or no flexibility for the individual owner regarding policies and procedures that are set by the main office and require strict adherence
6. A clause in the franchise agreement that allows the franchisor to buy back or cancel the franchise if the franchisee does not follow the rules set by the franchisor

Franchising does not always result in a happy partnership. It is important to research the company with which you are investing to ensure that they manage a quality product in an ethical manner. In the 1950s and 1960s, when hotel franchising mushroomed, many disputes about interpretation of franchise agreements arose between franchisors and franchisees. To create a better working relationship, **franchise advisory councils (FACs)** were started. These bodies represent the franchisee and provide a forum in which to address concerns and solve problems. Individuals thinking about investing in a franchise must find out whether the company has a working FAC. Most large franchise companies work well with their FACs, recognizing that their success is dependent on the success of their franchisees.

Management Contract

The fourth type of management system is the **management contract**, which separates hotel ownership and the operations of the property. Management contracts can be arranged with both individual properties or with hotel chains. The owners (the investors in this relationship) contract with a professional management team to operate the property (the investment) for a fee or a percentage of gross revenue.

Fairmont Hotels and Resorts is a good example of a management contract company that currently services over sixty properties worldwide. It is a preferred method of management when the property owners and/or investors have limited knowledge of the hospitality business. Lending institutions are more likely to step forward with financing if they know a professional, experienced team is managing the investment. International hotel chains use the management contract system to establish hotels in foreign countries, especially if the country does not permit outside ownership or is politically unstable.

When a chain takes on the role of the manager, it often places its name on the property, allowing the hotel to access the brand name, international reservations system, and professional marketing plans. However, the contract chain may also operate as a silent management team, with only employees aware of who pays their salaries; in this case, the property could have outside ownership and a silent management contract team running the operations while branded under a completely separate name.

The disadvantages of a management contract are similar to those of being part of any large company, especially if communication between owners, investors, and management is not good. Some owners believe that they are not kept adequately informed about the managers' business activities. Owners may disagree with some of the operational decisions made by the property's management, but owners generally do not have control over those decisions. Owners must agree to pay a guaranteed management fee of between 1% and 3.5% of gross revenues, regardless of hotel profitability. Although hiring operational expertise has many advantages, sometimes management contract companies lack an understanding of the local culture when operating a foreign property. To be successful, any business must have a good knowledge of and working relationship with local cultural traditions.

These are the four basic styles of ownership and operation of lodging properties. It should be noted that variations are common; today, most major hotel chains are associated with other chains through franchises and management contracts. Employees need a clear understanding of their property's ownership and management structure to follow company policies.

Hotel Real Estate Investment Trusts (REITs)

Many traditional hotel companies, such as Fairmont, are using **real estate investment trusts (REITs)** as a new form of property ownership. REITs emerged at a time when hotel companies searched for new ways to raise funds for development, using sources other than financial institutions. Hotel REITs are separate companies that buy hotels and hotel resort properties, essentially becoming real estate investment groups. They then sell shares in their company to investors, allowing these shares to be traded on the stock market. From an ownership perspective, REITs are used to gain funding for acquisitions, new construction, and renovations. From an operations viewpoint, they have allowed hotel operators to focus on their expertise in managing lodging establishments, rather than real estate. The remarkable success of REITs is generally attributed to their excellent performance for investors. They provide hotels with liquidity in the capital marketplace and the financial support they need to expand in this growing industry.

Organization and Functions

The organization of a hotel or motel depends on its size and ownership. Owners of small, individually owned motels might hire only maids, performing most of the other work themselves. They do not usually have any kind of food service, with the exception of vending machines. Most hotels, however, require a fairly large staff to function properly. The hotel staff is divided into those who work in the **front of house** and have direct contact with customers: front office, food and beverage, housekeeping, and customer services; and those who have little contact with the guests and work in the **back of house**: administration, sales and marketing, accounting, engineering, and security.

Administration The administrative staff includes the general manager, assistant manager, and all the department heads. The general and assistant managers are responsible for the overall operation of the hotel. They assist and direct the other managers and keep all departments informed about the day-to-day business of the hotel. The department managers are responsible for their departments' success and the direct supervision of their employees. They must all work together, meeting regularly to report on their progress and share information. For example, all managers need to be aware of the needs of any arriving group that has been booked by the sales managers, as well as specific promises made by the sales managers.

Sales and Marketing This department is responsible for four different areas: sales, advertising, research, and public relations. Sales include both group and convention sales—promotions, rate setting, and travel trade sales (group bookings from travel agencies and tour operators). The sales staff spends most of its time bidding for conventions, corporate meetings, and other multiple room reservation contracts.

Public relations involves creating a favourable image for the property by cultivating contacts with travel writers and editors or becoming involved as a sponsor with a major event such as the Festival of Fire, held each summer in Victoria. News releases, press kits, and promotions are part of public relations.

Marketing, as a discipline, is a relatively young field of study. As a holistic concept, marketing is part of every aspect of a business, especially when that business focuses directly on customer service. There are specific tactics used by marketers, including understanding customers, designing products and services that satisfy those customers, and maintaining up-to-date knowledge about competitors and the current industry environment. Marketing functions include communications, personal sales, and promotions. Often, and quite incorrectly, marketing and sales are used synonymously. However, the process of selling is just one skill set within the larger overall function of marketing. A company that seeks first to satisfy the wants and needs of its clientele is one that has a marketing management style.

Front Office and Guest Services These are the people who have direct contact with guests. They are normally both the first and the last people to be in touch with the guest. The image, attitude, and professional standards they convey set the tone for the guest's total experience. The responsibilities of front-office personnel include check-in and check-out, providing information, answering telephones, and cashiering. The service staff includes the concierge, bellhops, bell captain, lobby porter, and doorperson. Although most of these positions are entry level, the guest will judge the hotel through encounters with these people.

Accounting The accounting staff is responsible for tracking all financial information. In some instances, the control function is separated from other management functions by having the comptroller or financial officer report directly to the home office rather than to the general manager of the hotel. This method decreases the possibility of perpetuating ineffective accounting procedures and allows the general manager to concentrate on guest relations rather than on financial issues. Under this arrangement, the comptroller becomes a key financial advisor for the hotel. Other positions within this department may include auditors, accounts receivable supervisor, payroll supervisor, cashier, and purchasing agent.

Food and Beverage (F&B) Most hotel food service areas are owned and operated by the hotel, although some hotels opt to rent out space to franchised companies or independent restaurant owners, with a percentage of gross food and beverage sales going to the hotel. Hotel food and beverage service comes in many forms: fine dining, fast food, coffee shop service, room service, buffets, banquets, poolside bars, snack bars, and lounges, and can provide up to half of the hotel's overall revenue. Food preparation may be part of the food and beverage department, or it may be a department on its own. The executive chef and assistants are responsible for maintaining an enticing menu. The food and beverage department needs to be aware of hotel reservations in order to forecast food and beverage and staff requirements. For example, a large conference will require extra servers for banquets and socials; a full house of independent travellers will require extra workers in the restaurant and lounge. Open communication with other departments ensures effective cost management, resulting in increased profitability. In addition to serving guests, many hotel restaurants and lounges offer incentives for community residents to eat and relax at their property. This service requires knowledge of the community and good marketing or promotional incentives to encourage local use.

Room Service Room service is a travel luxury that pampers the guest by delivering meals directly to the room. Many people get this type of pampering only on vacation. All first-class hotels are expected to provide this service to their guests

Many Canadian hotels are known for their superb cuisine, but the Fairmont Jasper Park Lodge goes one step further with outstanding views.
(Source: Canadian Tourism Commission.)

even if it is not a profit-making venture. Room service is expensive to operate and requires a great deal of organization to be successful. Equipment must keep hot food hot and cold food cold, and meals must be delivered as quickly as possible to satisfy the guest. Breakfasts account for 70–90% of room service orders, with continental breakfasts topping the list.[5] Some hotels have special service elevators that help staff provide fast service without disrupting guests.

Banquets and Catering Banquets and catering are the responsibility of the catering director or banquet manager. Catering is usually set up as a separate function within a hotel's food and beverage department because it requires different services and meals from a hotel restaurant. Although banquets can be hosted by other restaurants, most do not have the capacity to compete with the hotel's banquet capabilities. Banquets range in size from small business meetings of perhaps fifteen people to groups of more than a thousand convention-goers. Weddings, conventions, bar and bat mitzvahs, anniversary dinners, reunions, and business meetings account for the majority of banquets. All convention hotels have catering services.

Catering services can be profitable if well organized; the group holding the event must provide the catering manager with the total number of guests expected and agrees ahead of time on a set menu at a set price. Even if some people do not show up for the meal, the group must pay for the number it guaranteed. Revenue from the sale of alcohol, either through a **cash bar** or an **open bar** (where the host pays for the alcohol), makes banquets even more profitable. In addition, events are staffed with servers only for the time needed, food quantities are known ahead of time, and the speed with which a banquet can be served ensures economies of time and expense.

Housekeeping This department ensures guests' comfort by keeping individual rooms and public areas clean and neat. In larger hotels, a head or executive housekeeper is responsible for supervising all room attendants, floor supervisors, and housekeepers. When a guest needs an extra towel or an iron and ironing board, housekeeping delivers. This one-on-one interaction with the guest requires well-trained and pleasant employees. Hotels are constantly challenged to hire and keep good employees for the housekeeping department.

Engineering This department, sometimes called maintenance and operations, focuses on the physical structure of the hotel. All problems with air conditioning, plumbing, electricity, functional equipment, and outside maintenance are sent to the engineering department. A director of engineering must have considerable knowledge of building maintenance and equipment. Although guests have little contact with them, the importance of engineering personnel cannot be overemphasized; any problems with the physical structure of the hotel will mean inconvenienced or uncomfortable guests.

Security In many larger hotels, especially in downtown areas, a security department is essential. This department is responsible for protecting guests and property. Some, but not all, security officer positions may require police training. Generally, the presence of a security officer at the entrance to a hotel makes a statement that the property is safe for the guest. Hotels usually prefer to have security personnel in street dress rather than uniforms because the presence of uniformed security guards can upset guests, who wonder whether there are security issues of which they are not aware. Because security officers need an understanding of law enforcement rather than of hotel operations, these positions are not usually stepping stones to hotel management.

In Practice

How do a Comfort Inn, an independent motel, and a Sheraton hotel differ in terms of management and ownership? Which would you prefer to work with, and why?

CLASSIFICATIONS WITHIN THE ACCOMMODATIONS INDUSTRY

The two main categories in the accommodation industry are the hotel and the motel, and the two differ in several ways. A **hotel** has a central lobby, its rooms are accessible from the hotel lobby, and guest parking may or may not be provided. Hotels can also be classified by their location, the purpose and duration of guest visits, and the room rates and level of service provided. Table 5.1 shows the world's largest hotels.

Location

Hotels may be classified as downtown, suburban, airport, town, highway, or resort (located in a natural setting such as near the seaside, a mountain, or a lake).

Downtown Travellers who choose to stay in a *downtown* location are willing to pay for the convenience of being near attractions or their place of business. These visitors often fly into a city and prefer to use public transportation rather than rent a car. An example of a niche hotel in this area would be the boutique hotel, specifically designed for the upscale business traveller. The atmosphere at a boutique hotel is one of old-world wealth, with a quiet, understated but lavish luxury. Guests receive highly personalized treatment, from the greeting at the door to individualized amenities.

www.hiltonhotels.ca

TABLE 5.1   *World's Largest Hotels*[6]

First World Hotel	Genting Highlands of Malaysia	10 000+ rooms
Venetian/Palazzon "Megacenter"	Las Vegas	7 128 rooms
MGM Grand	Las Vegas	5 044 rooms
Wynn Las Vegas/Encore	Las Vegas	4 750 rooms
Luxor	Las Vegas	4 408 rooms
Mandalay Bay/THEHotel	Las Vegas	4 332 rooms
Ambassador City Jomtien	Thailand	4 210 rooms
Excalibur	Las Vegas	4 008 rooms
ARIA	Las Vegas	4 004 rooms
Bellagio	Las Vegas	3 993 rooms

Conference Hotels Conference-goers stay at **conference hotels**, usually found in larger cities with strong pull power or in resort-like settings. These hotels must provide large meeting spaces and smaller meeting rooms, and have portable food service available. It is expected that modern conference centres can provide equipment such as slide projectors, overhead LCD projection units, portable computer systems, and internet connections; some even have in-house audio and video recording facilities as well as online conferencing capabilities. Group meetings can be arranged in special audio-visual rooms designed to record the meeting from a variety of angles, with up to ten different video cameras. Large convention hotels may have audio-visual staff on hand and subcontract these services out as demanded. All these services are needed for hotels to succeed in the very competitive convention market.

Suburban A family taking a touring vacation could very well prefer a *suburban* location. They might want to be near family who live in the suburbs, or they may be concerned with cost. These visitors often drive their own cars and look for inexpensive lodging with free parking. It does not matter how far they are from the attractions, because they have the convenience of their own transportation.

Airport These hotels generally target the air traveller. Stays are short, often only overnight, and many hotels offer day rates for travellers forced to spend a full day waiting for a specific airline connection. Many airport hotels offer 24-hour valet and food service. Quick check-in and check-out are particularly important for weary travellers who must catch a plane.

Guests staying in Num-Ti-Jah Lodge, located on the Icefields Parkway, enjoy a quiet drink after exploring the Columbia Icefield in the Canadian Rockies.

(Source: Canadian Tourism Commission.)

Small Town/Country Hotels Even small towns require some type of accommodation for the traveller. Many of the smaller towns located near major tourist destinations provide lodging at a reasonable cost and accept the tourist who has been unable to book a hotel room near an attraction or event. Some towns have converted historic buildings into inns or hotels, providing the opportunity for entrepreneurs to use the local culture and history to their advantage.

Highway Highway motels provide convenient lodging to travellers. Many are located on the edges of towns so as to connect them with additional services (food, fuel, supplies). Due to the expansive Canadian geography, many mom-and-pop motels exist outside of towns and become a welcome stopping place for the long-distance driver.

Hotel Terminology You Should Know

single	one person staying in the room, no matter how many beds
twin	room with two twin beds
double	two people staying in one room
double double	double room with two double beds
suite	accommodation with two or more rooms—one set up as a living room
hospitality suite	room that has a bar and sitting area, often provided to the executive of a conference to be used for informal meetings
rack rate	standard daily rate
weekend rate	discount rate charged for weekend stays
run-of-the-house rate	discount rate for block bookings
corporate rate	discount rate given to members of an organization, usually negotiated ahead of time, based on anticipated volume of business
family plan	special family rate that allows children to stay with parents at no additional charge
day rate	rate charged for short stays during the day, often at airport hotel locations—usually 9:00 A.M. to 9:00 P.M.

Resort Finally, **resort hotels** usually promote a specific destination, and as a vacation destination, provide an escape for travellers from their normal routines. Even in ancient times people needed to escape the cities, the summer heat, or the winter blues, and they travelled to the seaside, health spas, or mountain resorts for relaxation, recreation, and entertainment. Summer **resorts** can offer golf, tennis, swimming, horseback riding, boating, fishing, or canoeing. Winter resorts might include skiing, snowboarding, snowmobiling, skating, or sleigh rides.

Thanks to Canada's many beautiful natural sites and destinations, our resorts have gained fame around the world, including the Fairmont Banff Springs, Deerhurst Resort, and Fox Harb'r Golf Resort & Spa. Over the past thirty years, resort hotels have emerged—multi-purpose lodgings built with a wilderness setting are good at changing with the times. Because of the variety of entertainment and recreation offered at a resort, total vacation packages meet the needs of a wide variety of target markets. Resorts are particularly popular with families as facilities are geared toward different age groups.

A resort may stand alone as a destination or, like the Fairmont Château Whistler in British Columbia, it may support additional businesses. Nestled in the coastal mountains of British Columbia, this carefully planned resort community offers shopping, a variety of dining options and evening entertainment, as well as other amenities such as babysitting and daycare, church services, fitness centres, laundry and dry cleaning, medical and dental clinics, a public library and museum, video rentals, and movie theatres.

Every province has a variety of resorts to fulfill the needs of vacationers—from luxury travellers to those seeking a more rustic vacation. However, in today's world of tourism, seasonal resorts are having a difficult time remaining profitable and are looking to expand their businesses throughout Canada's four seasons.

Purpose of Visit

Another way we classify hotels is based on the *motivation* or *purpose* of a visitor's trip. *Business guests* stay at business hotels, usually found in downtown areas or near major airports, which provide specific services for the business traveller, such as airport limousine service, computer hook-ups with working space, room service and mini-bars, valet services, and easy check-in and check-out. Many business hotels provide a check-out system that may be accessed from the room using the TV screen. Business travellers are important because they use committed business dollars, or non-discretionary money, as a way to earn business revenue. As customers, they are less concerned with cost of travel and more concerned with the provided service. A strong business clientele provides revenue for a hotel even during the off-season and recessions.

The final grouping by motivation or purpose is the *pleasure/vacation guest*. As pleasure travellers can use only money for travel that is left over after the necessities of the home are taken care of (in other words, their discretionary income) they are frequently more concerned with price above extra service offerings. In order to meet the pricing needs of the pleasure traveller, hotels might lower their rates during periods not in use by business travellers. These lower rates become attractive to the pleasure guest while serving to fill slower periods for the hotel.

Level of Service

Hotels may also be classified by *level of service,* which is determined by the needs of the hotel's target market (Figure 5.1). *Budget hotels* are designed to provide clean, safe, low-cost rooms. They offer very few services and may not have in-house food service. Instead, budget hotels may choose a location near a restaurant strip or provide a menu in each room from a local restaurant that is willing to deliver. A Comfort Inn is a good example of a budget hotel.

A *mid-scale hotel* will have a coffee shop on its premises, may have a swimming pool or exercise room, and may or may not provide airport service. A Ramada Inn is a good example of a mid-scale hotel.

Upscale hotels are far more service-oriented, providing a wide variety of benefits such as room service, concierge, dining and lounge areas, pool and exercise areas,

FIGURE 5.1
Marriott Corporation's
Hotel Operations

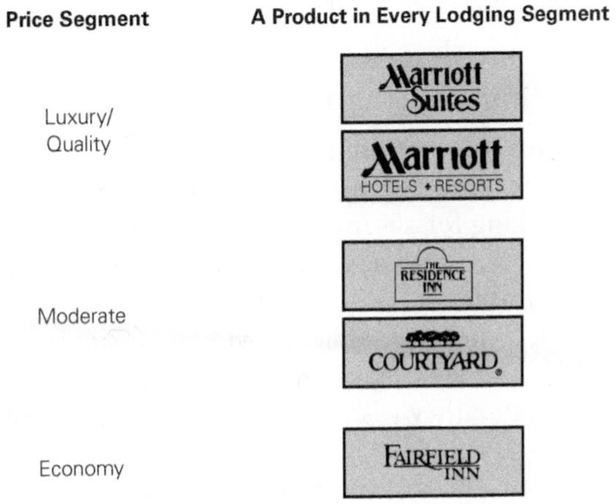

Price Segment	A Product in Every Lodging Segment
Luxury/ Quality	Marriott Suites
	Marriott HOTELS · RESORTS
Moderate	The RESIDENCE INN
	COURTYARD
Economy	FAIRFIELD INN

Source: Marriott Corporation.

and gift shop or mini-mall. *Luxury properties* take service to an even higher level. Located in a prestigious area of the city or countryside, a luxury hotel's lobby is often large and spectacular (for example, it might include a waterfall or an indoor garden), with elegant furniture and lighting. Service is discreet and efficient. Luxury hotel chains such as the Four Seasons cater to travellers who can afford the expense and expect their every want and need to be fulfilled.

Duration of Visit

Length of stay is the final category for classifying hotels. Not all hotels cater to *transient guests*—that is, those who spend only a short period of time at the hotel. *Residential hotels* provide guests with long-term accommodations, sometimes for a year or more. Most of these hotels are mid- to upscale, and all their services are available to the resident guest. A transient hotel may also opt to provide residential rates. In Ottawa, where a great many politicians spend six months of the year representing their riding constituents, hotels providing residential rates are more common than in Halifax, for example.

Clearly, hotels can fit into several classifications. For example, an upscale hotel might be located downtown and cater to business clientele and the conference market.

Motels As previously mentioned, motels and motel chains first appeared in the 1950s with the establishment of interstate and interprovincial highway systems. A **motel** is a lodging property that is typically one or two stories in height and the main door into each hotel room is located outside. These properties have little use for large lobby areas beyond basic front desk services, perhaps a guest computer station, regional information, and possibly a breakfast area. Motels generally offer free parking to travellers, as they are a drive-up style of lodging. Although some motels can still be found in city centres, most are located on highways and offer simple, clean, and inexpensive accommodations to tourists travelling by car.

Chains and franchises choose simple room plans that translate into savings in design and construction costs. Rooms are usually limited to one or two double beds. Many motels cater to the family or seniors market, both of which look for a clean, safe, and comfortable room with few amenities. A traveller usually chooses a motel over a hotel based on two factors: cost and location. Canada's largest motel chain, Choice Hotels Canada, owns Comfort Inns, Sleep Inns, Econo Lodges, Quality Inns, Rodeway Inns, and Clarion Hotels.

Other Lodging Options

Inns Modern inns are usually found in smaller towns that have a tourist base. Often the building is historic, renovated to meet the expectations of travellers looking for an upscale but quiet vacation. Most **inns** have excellent dining rooms that attract local patrons as well as guests. They create a "homey" feel by providing fireplaces in guest rooms or small libraries for guest use. Many inns now cater to their clients by either providing on-site spas or partnering with a nearby spa service. Some hotel chains, such as Holiday Inn, deliberately take on the term "inn" because they wish to create the perception of a homey, intimate lodging facility.

Spas The ancient Romans knew the value of rejuvenation. Their **spas**, which were frequently located by the sea, offered many of the services that modern spas offer: mud baths, massage, exercise programs, and healthy food. In fact, spas have thrived in many cultures throughout the ages. Focusing on the body and mind as one, spas pamper and work the human body back to health.

Spas are found all across the accommodations industry. Resorts and hotels may offer a spa weekend; inns have joined the trend, and even cruise ships promote spa cruises. Their staffs include certified professionals who deliver the spa program, and chefs with a solid knowledge of nutrition who prepare healthy gourmet food. Facilities allow the client to achieve complete relaxation. Hydrotherapy tubs, massages, and exercise rooms become a necessary component of the lodging facilities, as have hot rock massages, mineral pools, yoga, Pilates, and many forms of beauty treatments. The price tag for a week at a spa may be higher than for other vacations, but for those who want to feel rejuvenated, spa vacations provide a healthful alternative. Most spas also have beautiful, relaxing restaurants that serve the spa-goer with healthy, inviting, calorie-reduced meals.

Boutique Hotels These belong to the upscale/luxury market. **Boutique hotels** have all of the convenience of a modern hotel, but bring back an era of luxury and uniqueness. Each room has its own décor, its own subtle luxury. They are smaller, more intimate hotels where the doorman actually does remember your name and housekeeping puts the type of bottled water that you prefer in your room along with a plate of home-baked cookies. These hotels appeal to the business traveller who spends a great deal of time on the road and is looking for a more familial, less sterile setting.

Condominiums and Time-Shares Condominium and time-share units are also resort accommodations. The word **condominium** means "joint domain" in Latin. Condominiums allow an individual to have full ownership over one unit in a complex. In many cases, the owner uses the condominium for only a few weeks each year and rents it out through an independent management agency for the remainder of the year. The management agency maintains the grounds, roads, and recreational facilities, and provides security and cleaning services for a percentage of the rental fee. Resort condominiums in places like Florida, Hawaii, and Colorado allow the traveller to have apartment-style accommodations in an area filled with recreational amenities. The baby boomer market has begun to retire, pushing this type of investment and holiday back into vogue.

Time-sharing involves buying a vacation segment for a specific period of time, usually two weeks, in a condominium unit. The purchaser owns only the two-week segment, not the entire unit. The segment is

Memorable vacations do not need a five-star hotel.
Some visitors are happy with just a tent for two with a view.
(Photo: Canadian Tourism Commission.)

scheduled so that only one owner may use it at a time. Some time-share companies encourage their owners to swap segments, allowing them to go to a new resort each year.

Dude Ranches Another type of resort is the **dude or guest ranch**, which is usually family-owned and -operated and offers the guest a ranch-style experience. The dude ranch is becoming an alternative choice for city dwellers with a desire to experience true rustic living and "rough it" while getting away from some of the creature comforts of modern society.

A dude ranch experience can vary widely; it may be a working ranch where guests assist the owners in day-to-day operations, or it may be a luxury resort with swimming pools, horseback-riding lessons, and rodeo shows. Dude ranches include guest ranches, resort ranches, working cattle ranches, fly-fishing ranches, hunting ranches, and cross-country skiing ranches. Many ranches are located in the western United States, British Columbia, and Alberta. Foreign and domestic tourists are also opting to spend a week working on a farm in rural Ontario, helping out egg farmers in Nova Scotia, or joining the harvest on a wheat farm in Saskatchewan. Guests pay for their lodging and meals, and enjoy some of Canada's agricultural tourism products.

www.bbcanada.com

Bed and Breakfasts (B & Bs) Nearly every city and country around the world is home to **bed and breakfasts**. B & Bs provide foreign travellers with a cultural experience and the opportunity to live with a family in a new city or town, enjoying the daily life of the local people. Domestic travellers may decide to explore their own backyards and hidden communities by searching out B & Bs. Guests are usually pampered by owners who enjoy sharing local folklore and recommending points of interest and good places to eat. B & Bs are often unique buildings, such as restored older homes in rural settings, scenic waterfront estates, cozy Gothic cottages, train stations, converted schoolhouses, or old mills or plantations.

Because these lodgings have been converted from single-family homes, former train stations, or old school houses, many do not have private washroom facilities for each guest, so the communal bathroom down the hall must be an acceptable alternative for vacation and business travellers. Guests can mingle and meet new people in the parlour. Most B & Bs serve family-style breakfasts; some offer dinner as well.

At the Train Station Inn at Tatamagouche, Nova Scotia, old railroad cars have been renovated as bedrooms, providing unique sleeping accommodations.
(Photo: Paula Kerr.)

A B & B is usually family owned and operated. In a small B & B, the staff may be strictly family members; larger properties may hire extra help. Checking in guests, cooking, baking snacks, cleaning, accounting, designing advertising campaigns, and acting as tour guide could all become part of a daily routine at a B & B. Owning and running a B & B is a unique and fun way to learn about the accommodations business on a small but comprehensive scale.

Hostels   Generally known as a youth hostel, a **hostel** is a lodge with communal washrooms and bedrooms designed for four to twenty people. Hostels may be found in specially constructed buildings or in older homes, YMCAs, and even churches. In most cases, guests prepare their own meals or assist in meal preparation and cleanup. The low cost makes travel feasible for students and others on limited budgets. The hostel has been popular in Europe and many other countries for decades.

www.hihostels.ca

Hostelling International-Canada (HI-Canada) provides services such as discounts on already inexpensive accommodations and on different types of organized tours, including hiking, bicycling, canoeing, and skiing. HI-Canada represents more than eighty different hostels across the country. At a hostel, the guest reserves a bed rather than a room.

One of the more interesting hostels in Canada is the Ottawa Jail Hostel. This historic stone building, located on Nicholas Street in downtown Ottawa, served as the Carleton County Gaol from 1862 to 1971. In 1972, it opened its doors to the public as a youth hostel called Nicholas Gaol. The colourful history of this building attracts many travellers. The prison was the site of Canada's last public hanging and—allegedly—of many evil deeds. During the building's renovation, a mass grave was discovered in the courtyard. A few visitors have claimed over the years that they hear ghostly voices moan stories of cruelty and mistreatment. Today, the cozy surroundings show few traces of the past, and the hostel has been renamed the Ottawa Jail Hostel.

Campgrounds   As a form of accommodation, **campgrounds** have always been popular with cost-conscious travellers, outdoor enthusiasts, and RV owners who simply want to enjoy an area surrounded by the comforts of their own belongings. In the past, campgrounds offered a piece of grass to set up a tent, and possibly a lake for fishing and swimming. Such campgrounds still exist in North America, but many people are demanding more than a spot to set up camp. Camping has increasingly become a sophisticated art, with first-class RV hook-ups and campground programs for all ages. Many campgrounds have hot showers, coin-operated laundries, electrical and sewer systems to accommodate RVs, playgrounds, swimming pools, and recreation rooms. Campgrounds may also have small grocery stores, and some even have gift shops.

In Practice

How do campgrounds and dude ranches fit into the hospitality industry? What differentiates an economy hotel from a luxury hotel? Name three different hotels for each service level: economy, moderate, upscale, and luxury.

MARKETING THE ACCOMMODATIONS INDUSTRY

Using marketing techniques to communicate and promote a nationally known chain or franchised hotel differs greatly from the techniques and approaches used for a small, family-owned inn or bed and breakfast. Larger hotels have more resources with which to create higher-profile advertisement campaigns across a full range of media: television, radio, newspapers, and magazines.

Smaller properties and independently owned operations are limited in resources and must focus their communication efforts on specific areas. For both the major hotel chains and the small, privately owned lodgings, skill and knowledge of advertising and promotional techniques are becoming more and more essential. The question for all lodging facilities is how to best utilize the four Ps of marketing: product, place, price, and promotion.

Product

There is often more to a lodging establishment than simply a place to sleep. Some no-frills hotels pride themselves on simply providing an inexpensive, clean, comfortable place to sleep. Luxury properties have a wide variety of facilities, provide special amenities such as **turn-down service** (folding down the bedspread and placing a chocolate on the pillow at night), and take great pride in the friendly expertise of their staff.

Although the hotel room is intangible to the customer at the time of purchase, very tangible elements of a property need to be properly conveyed. Decor, ambience, facilities, and services may be illustrated through colourful pictures and written words. This may be done in a brochure format and mailed to prospective clients. However, current technology allows a lodging establishment to clearly showcase their property and services through a dynamic website. Web presence through both static websites and engaged social media activity develop intangible relationships before the guest ever arrives. There has also been a dramatic increase in mobile devices, such as smartphones, that people can use to access web content. In 2012, there were over 1.2 billion mobile web users throughout the world, and 8.9% of all web content was consumed on a mobile device.[7] Smart lodging companies will ensure that all of their web content is mobile-viewing ready.

How do prospective clients determine the quality of a product? As mentioned earlier in this chapter, organizations such as CAA provide a rating scale for lodging properties, with 90% of Canadian provinces sharing in a common rating system developed by Canada Select Accommodations Rating Program (Table 5.2). In addition, some provinces, such as Alberta, go further and provide information on an accommodation's ability to provide services for people with disabilities. The Green Key program now alerts customers to the quality of a lodging and the concern it has for the ecosystem.

Price

Very few hotels have a single fixed price for a room. Prices depend on a number of factors:

- location (of the hotel and the room)
- the room size and its amenities

TABLE 5.2 *Canada Select Accommodations Rating Program Categories*

★	clean, comfortable accommodations
★★	clean, comfortable accommodations with some amenities
★★★	very comfortable accommodations with a greater range of facilities, guest amenities, and services
★★★★	a very high standard of accommodations with an extensive range of facilities, guest amenities, and services
★★★★★	exceptional properties that are among the best in the country in terms of their outstanding facilities, guest services, and quality provided

Source: Canada Select Accommodations Program.

- the pricing expectations of target markets
- competitors' pricing strategies
- seasonality
- group purchase discounts (e.g., conference, tour, or corporate)
- discounts given to special market segments (e.g., travel agents or seniors)
- available meal plans (Table 5.3)

www.marriott.com

Reservation agents need to be fully aware of all pricing options and should provide the guest with the best possible price available. Price is both a way to influence future purchases and communicate to guests what they should expect at a location. Although business travellers are less influenced by price, it is important to remember that the tourism customer, overall, is price sensitive. In economic terms, we refer to this level of price sensitivity as *elastic*; demand for a product or service will change rapidly when customers are faced with relatively small price fluctuations. At the turn of the millennium, many hotels were surprised to find they had overestimated what the public was willing to pay and were left with empty rooms and lost revenue.

Place

The term *place* for accommodations has multiple meanings. Firstly, it can speak directly to the physical or geographical location of the lodging facility. The Fairmont Empress in Victoria, B.C., would absolutely showcase its beautiful location on Vancouver Island. However, *place* also relates to how customers connect with companies, sometimes called channels of distribution, or how customers and tourism companies are brought together. What are the channels of distribution for the

TABLE 5.3 *Meal Plans*

European Plan (EP)	room only with no meals
Continental Plan (CP)	room rate that includes a continental breakfast: juice, coffee, and roll or pastry
Bermuda Plan (BP)	room rate that includes a full American breakfast: juice, coffee, eggs, sausage/bacon, toast
American Plan (AP)	rate that includes three full meals: breakfast, lunch, dinner
Modified American Plan (MAP)	rate that includes two meals, usually breakfast and dinner

accommodations industry? The internet has become one of the most important sales tools for the industry, allowing travellers to log onto a website to see rooms, facilities, menus and dining room, and other services. Many websites now provide mini-tours of the property. Websites do not have to be very interactive to attract customers, but a good website is a sales tool no lodging should be without. Hotel rooms are also sold through websites, such as Expedia.ca, that provide tourists not only with a broad selection of properties but also with an entire vacation package.

Hotels also sell directly to the public using their own reservation systems. Large chains may use a single toll-free number for all properties, allowing clients to access reservations from anywhere within the country. Individual properties may choose to join a referral system.

One final channel of distribution is the travel agency and its resource materials, such as the Official Hotel Guide. Travel counsellors can often suggest the hotel best suited to the customer's needs, as well as activities to suit the customer's interests.

Promotion

Accommodations are promoted through a series of communication devices, including advertising, personal selling, public relations, and sales promotions. Advertising is important in the industry. Although it may not seem essential during high season, the lower season can prove challenging for any hotelier. Some hotels wisely create packages that suit the needs of a specific target market. For example, a hotel in a downtown location with a large business clientele may be booked during the week but have rooms available on the weekends.

Creating a package that provides local residents with "romantic getaways" or "stress relief weekends" may be part of the answer. Included in this type of package might be an overnight stay, use of the pool and exercise facilities, dinner for two in the hotel's elegant restaurant, and a champagne breakfast. For the higher-value tourist, some hotels provide special floors that offer limited access, open bars in a comfortable lounge, and free breakfasts. Still others may provide frequent-guest cards, airport limousine service, and instant check-in/check-out for corporate guests.

Public relations are also an important part of promotion. Supporting a special festival or event, raising money for local charities, and supporting local town improvements in association with a chamber of commerce or convention and visitors bureau all enhance a hotel's image in a very competitive business. The goal of public relations is to influence the reporting of positive events and the minimization of negative stories in local, national, and international media; the power of public relations is in its reach and its low direct cost, but none of the message creation falls within the hands of the organization. There are high levels of risk and reward involved in public relations. Promotions can be as creative as the promoter, and understanding marketing principles and the needs and wants of the clientele is the best way to ensure that promotions are effective.

Reservation Concepts A **confirmed reservation** means that a hotel has a room waiting for a client—but the hotel can sell the room to a waiting guest if the client does not show up by a specified time (usually 4:00–6:00 P.M.). Disney properties have a special desk that deals solely with confirmed but unclaimed room reservations! A **guaranteed reservation** means the client has supplied a credit card number and must pay for the room whether or not they use it, unless the reservation is cancelled by a certain time and a cancellation number obtained.

Most hotels have a high season and a low season. Because their product is so perishable, it must be sold daily—a room that goes unsold represents lost revenue. Sometimes a hotel will **overbook**, or sell more rooms than it has, anticipating that not all guests will show up. Occasionally, the hotel is then left with too few rooms for the guests holding confirmed or guaranteed reservations. This is an unpleasant position for any hotel to be in, and it is the responsibility of the hotel to find the guests rooms at another property. Doing so is called **walking** or *farming out*. Usually the hotel will cover the guest's room charge and offer some additional compensation.

SNAPSHOT

Cesar Ritz

Ritzy and *putting on the Ritz* are just two phrases that bear witness to the master of graciousness and quality—Cesar Ritz. He was born into a family with no wealth, yet the mere mention of his name conjures up visions of glamour, prestige, and elegance. Who is Cesar Ritz and why is he an important part of tourism's past?

He began work as an apprentice at age fifteen in Brig, Switzerland. At nineteen, he moved to Paris, and by the late 1860s, he had become a restaurant manager—not an easy feat for one so young. Realizing that his education was far from complete, he left his managerial position to become an assistant waiter at the most famous restaurant of the day, Le Voisin. Here, he learned everything he could about service, including the correct and genteel fashion in which the wealthy enjoyed dining. It was not long before he had developed such a knack for pleasing his customers that they insisted on having him as their waiter. He knew their likes and dislikes, their vanities and their habits. Cesar Ritz learned the finer points of service by understanding one of the basic needs of people: to be recognized and made to feel special.

At twenty-seven, he became manager of one of Europe's most elegant hotels, the Grand National in Lucerne, Switzerland. It was here that he partnered with the great Auguste Escoffier, and together they not only returned the hotel to profitability but also continued to work successfully together for many years.

In 1887, Ritz was asked to take over the management of London's grand new hotel, the Savoy London. Barely open six months, it was losing money at an enormous rate. Ritz was given carte blanche to operate the hotel. Soon, he had created a dining room that boasted fine culinary treats and live bands playing Strauss. He designed lighting that would flatter the complexion, and he instituted a dress code, making evening wear mandatory. In 1898, he and Escoffier opened the first Ritz hotel, with Escoffier preparing some of the world's best food while Ritz ensured that each detail in the hotel was perfect and each guest taken care of with equal concern.

While he went on to develop his own chain of hotels, the difficulties of the early 1920s and 30s proved too great, and he sold his share so that his hotels became the Ritz Carleton, long revered as a deluxe hotel chain.

Cesar Ritz was a man who believed in excellence. He felt that his customers' wants, needs, and expectations should be fulfilled in a prompt, courteous, and quiet manner, and that their surroundings should be elegantly comfortable. He believed that service was the key to satisfied, repeat business. It is a testament to his steadfast devotion to beauty and charm that a new word became part of the English language. *Ritzy* means elegant, luxurious, and grand; *putting on the Ritz* means living, behaving, or dressing in a refined and fashionable manner.

At the Inverary Resort, Baddeck, Nova Scotia, guests can choose from bedrooms in the main lodge, in two-room cabins, or in outlying buildings.
(Photo: Paula Kerr.)

Focus on Environmental Issues The Green Key Eco-rating Program is designed to be as all-inclusive as possible, welcoming all lodging facilities. Its simple, online approach makes becoming a partner easy. The graduated **Green Key rating** system helps owners determine how well they are doing when it comes to recycling, reusing, and reducing. The program illustrates how owners can save money by

FOOTPRINT

TABLE 5.4   *Accommodations: The Green Key Program*

♀	A hotel has taken steps to reduce environmental impacts by analyzing its operations and identifying opportunities for improvement. An action plan focusing on resource conservation and waste minimization has been established and is supported by a firm commitment to continual improvement.
♀♀	A hotel has taken considerable strides to identify environmental impacts and implement policies, (i.e., best management programs to minimize ecological footprints). A firm commitment to continual improvement has resulted in programs and actions that have shown effective results.
♀♀♀	A hotel has taken significant steps to protect the environment. Strong environmental programs, best management practices, training programs, and engineering solutions have been implemented that have benefited the environment and the local community.
♀♀♀♀	A hotel has shown national industry leadership and commitment to protecting the environment through a wide range of policies and practices. Hotel has mature programs in place that involve management, employees, guests, and the public that have shown substantial measurable results.
♀♀♀♀ ♀	A hotel exemplifies the highest standards of environmental and social responsibility throughout all areas of operations. The hotel employs cutting edge technologies, policies, and programs that set the international standard for sustainable hotel operations.

reducing operating costs while helping "green" the planet. It includes all major departments of an accommodation and is adjusted for those who do not have full services available.

The multiple choice quiz is done online, and results are given within minutes of finishing the quiz. It covers energy conservation, water conservation, solid waste management, hazardous waste management, indoor air quality, community outreach, building infrastructure, land use, and environmental management. Points are scored based on the impact on the environment and social structure of a community. The Footprint box that includes Table 5.4 shows the level of concern ownership has for our ecosystem based on how they operate their establishment.

In Practice

Write the names of ten hotels or motels in your community. Identify their locations and what else is in the vicinity. Does the location dictate the type of clientele of each motel or hotel? What type of marketing strategies does each use? Why does one facility do better than another in the same community?

CASE STUDY

Killing the Golden Goose

Arnold Jackson owned a large sheep farm in New Zealand. After listening to a presentation by a Canadian trade delegation regarding business possibilities in Canada, he decided to travel there to check out business opportunities for his family's beautiful handmade woollen products and his organically raised lamb. His first stop was in a large Canadian city, and he chose to stay in a large hotel in the downtown area because he was an inexperienced traveller and nervous about being in a foreign country. He quickly discovered that Canada was like home—the Canadians he met were friendly and enjoyed entertaining him. He made some excellent business connections and enough sales to pay for the trip. However, when he checked out of the hotel, he was shocked to find that his total bill was approximately $400 more than the $1720.55 he had anticipated. Fully expecting additional charges for tax, he was still surprised to find a "promotion tax," and surcharges for housekeeping and room service, for restocking the mini-bar (which he had not opened), and for a high-speed internet connection. When he went to the assistant manager to question these items, he was told that every hotel in the city added these charges and nothing could be done to eliminate them. Not wanting to make a scene or miss his flight, Mr. Jackson paid the bill and left, taking with him a very poor memory of what should have been a positive trip.

1. What was the main cause of Arnold's dissatisfaction?
2. Was there any course of action the assistant manager might have taken immediately to reduce Arnold's distress?
3. What might the hotel do to ensure that other customers do not have the same experience?
4. What might be the long-term negative impact of the taxes and surcharges Canadians are adding on to tourism products, especially hotels, restaurants, and air travel? Is there any way the negative spin might be contained?

Summary

- The accommodations sector of tourism has a long history and is wide-ranging in scope. Options in accommodations range from small roadside inns to luxury city-centre hotels, from quaint resorts to time share condominiums.
- Hotels are operated under four basic types of management:
  - The individual owner usually has a small property and single-handedly manages the business, operating it in any manner desired.
  - A company chain operates its own hotels from a single, corporate headquarters.
  - Franchise properties are owned by an individual (or sometimes a company) but operational decisions fall under the guidelines of the franchisor in the franchise relationship.
  - Under a management contract, one company owns the property, but another company (usually a chain) manages it.
- Properties should make good use of the internet and have an easily accessed website with pertinent information for prospective guests. Most importantly, these sites must be accessible on mobile devices, a rapidly growing way for customers to both consume information and conduct business.
- Lodging facilities must also adapt their rooms to suit the growing number of travellers with disabilities.
- Hotels are classified as economy/budget, mid-scale, upscale, or luxury.
- Customers can evaluate how well a lodging establishment adheres to environmental activities, such as recycling programs and energy reduction, through the Green Key rating system.
- Each type of accommodation uses a different strategy for attracting guests; location, price, and service remain crucial components when a traveller is determining where to stay.

Questions

1 a) Explain the differences in the way a hotel or motel is operated based on: i) individual ownership, ii) chains, iii) franchises, iv) referral systems, and v) REITs.

   b) Which types of management are represented in your region? Provide examples.

2 Briefly describe the duties performed by three front-of-house departments within a hotel and three back-of-house departments.

3 Many Canadian lodging establishments have not designed their rooms to suit the growing number of travellers with disabilities.

   a) Why is this market growing?

   b) What types of adjustments should a hotel consider to make the disabled more comfortable?

4 How do the following hotel classifications determine the scope and quality of the hotel product? Back up your answer using examples.

   a) location

   b) room rate

   c) purpose of visitors' trip

d) level of service

e) length of stay

5 The text discusses a wide variety of lodging facilities that might be used by a traveller. Choose five types of accommodation, and briefly describe—then explain why you would like to stay in—each one of your choices.

6 a) What does the term "highly perishable" mean in the context of tourism products?

 (See the section in Chapter 3 entitled "Understanding and Marketing the Unique Tourism Product.")

 b) How does an upscale hotel attempt to handle the highly perishable nature of tourism products?

7 Using a hotel advertisement taken from a newspaper, magazine, or hotel, show how the property has used product, price, and place in its promotion.

8 Define the following terms as they relate to the accommodations industry: *AP, MAP, EP, walking, back of house, cannibalization, guaranteed reservation, time-sharing,* and *hospitality suite.*

Note

1. W.C. Firebaugh, *The Inns of Greece and Rome, and a History of Hospitality from the Dawn of Time to the Middle Ages* (Chicago. Reprint, New York: Benjamin Blom, 1928).

2. Hotel Association of Canada and PKF Consulting, *Canada's Lodging Sector, 2011,* www.hac.ca.

3. David W. Howell, *Passport* (Cincinnati, OH: South Western Publishing Co., 1989), p. 141.

4. *Ask Right Questions When Booking a Hotel,* www.icanonline.net.

5. *Ontario Restaurant News,* May 2002, p. 9.

6. www.vegastodayandtomorrow.com/largesthotels.htm.

7. http://mobithinking.com/mobile-marketing-tools/latest-mobile-stats.

Food and Beverage

Key terms

200 km menu
allergy awareness
bistros
buffet house
cafeteria
coffee houses
commercial food
    service
contract caterers
contract food service
corkage fee

ethnic restaurants
destination restaurant
family-style restaurant
fast food restaurant
fine dining
haute cuisine
menu
multi-unit corporate
    restaurant
non-commercial food
    service

organically grown foods
pub
signature item
social caterers
specialty restaurant
taverns
theme restaurant
upselling

Learning objectives

Having read this chapter you will be able to

1. Discuss the impact the food service industry has on tourism.

2. Explain briefly the history of the food service industry.

3. Differentiate between the two major divisions of food service: commercial and non-commercial.

4. Explain various styles of food service in the commercial division.

5. Explain the importance to the tourism sector of non-commercial food service.

6. Discuss current trends in the food service industry.

Food means life. Without food, even the tiniest organism cannot survive. As human beings, we use food not only for survival but also as part of our recreational life. Early human beings would light the fire, roast the great beast they had just killed, dance, and sing of their great fortune. We celebrate with food the birth of a child, birthdays, graduation ceremonies and other events of success. Food plays a central role in both happy occasions like marriages and solemn events such as wakes. Movies have long used food service as a backdrop for action, such as *Diner* and *The Godfather*. Some even use food as their main focus, including examples like *Babette's Feast, Eat Drink Man Woman, Vatel* (a glimpse into seventeenth-century feasting), *Chocolat,* and *Sideways*, a movie that focuses not only on relationships but also on the wines and wineries of California.

Books that focus on food and eating are highly popular and have been written by chefs and celebrities; some have even been created around fictional characters. These books often focus on diet, entertaining, specific foods or cultures and, sometimes, just simple, old-fashioned home cooking. Actors, in particular, seem to have a strong affiliation with food, creating their own product lines (Paul Newman) or opening restaurants (Robert De Niro). A restaurant associated with a famous person helped to develop the term *destination restaurant*, which will be discussed in more detail later in the chapter.

The food and beverage industry is the largest of all components of tourism and one of the hardest to track for revenues, as not everyone who dines out is a tourist. This sector contains more independently owned businesses than any of the others. According to the Labour Force Survey compiled by Statistics Canada each year, this industry employs over 1 084 500 people[1] and it is the only tourism industry that would likely survive, though in a very different state, the total collapse of the tourism sector. It is also a challenging industry to work in. Due to the high labour and utility expenses, and low profit margins, Statistics Canada states that "new accommodation and foodservice entrants have a 60% chance of surviving beyond their second year and a 22% chance of surviving beyond eight years."[2]

This chapter focuses on the food service industry, including a look at its history, the split between commercial food services and non-commercial food services, ownership options, and current trends in the industry.

HISTORY OF THE FOOD SERVICE INDUSTRY

Food has always been a necessity, but from the early days of civilization it has also been associated with celebration, cultural rituals, and friendship. Dining out has a long history. As early as 1700 BCE, the Egyptians were meeting in public places to share simple meals of fish or fowl, olives, grains, fruits, and vegetables. However, it was the ancient Romans who were the first to create truly lavish banquets with live entertainment and portable food services for their troops. Public eateries were discovered in the ruins of Pompeii, including the remains of *tabernae* (bars), *thermopolia* (snack bars), and *popinae* (the world's first fast-food restaurants).[3]

The Western Roman Empire collapsed around the fifth century CE, bringing in an extended period of regional splintering, decreasing overall safety through the former empire and increasing risk when travelling: the Dark Ages. Historians differ on the exact length of the Dark Ages, but estimate it lasted between 500 and 900 years. The end of the Dark Ages was signalled by safer travel and commerce.

Accommodations, food services, and public entertainment were again part of community living.

Peasants ate simple foods made from grains, but seldom had meat, fish, or fruit to put on their tables. The diet of the aristocracy was slightly more varied and included roast meats; fresh salads made from bitter, leafy greens and onions, accompanied by a strong vinaigrette dressing; and sweet puddings. Utensils for eating were not common, even in the large courts of England and France. The fork was introduced to the French court when Catherine de Medici was betrothed to King Henry II of France in 1533. Desolate at having to leave the comforts of the Italian court for the more barbaric ways of France, she agreed to the marriage only when her father promised to send his chef and kitchen staff with her. (So it was in the roots of Italian cuisine that the world-renowned French culinary tradition arose.)

As travel increased, so did the number and the variety of food service establishments. The tradition of elegant French dining was heavily influenced by the French Revolution in 1789. As the royals rode to the guillotine, the talented chefs who worked directly for the aristocracy suddenly found they were out of jobs. A number of them became entrepreneurs and opened small, fine-dining establishments in Europe that catered to the new upper class. Many, fearing for their safety during the revolution, relocated to North America, taking their talent to a new and growing marketplace.

In the United States, the first true full-service restaurant opened in New York City in 1827. It was called Delmonico's and was operated by three brothers—John, Peter, and Lorenzo. Delmonico's closed during the Great Depression of the 1930s. Tourists visiting New Orleans today often make a point of dining at Antoine's, another historic restaurant that opened its doors in 1840. A restaurant with an excellent reputation for fine dining, Antoine's holds the record for the longest continuous restaurant service in North America. While many other restaurants in New Orleans were destroyed by Hurricane Katrina, Antoine's sits on higher ground in the historic district; it was spared and continued to operate during the recovery.

As North Americans fell in love with the automobile and took to the roads, a new kind of restaurant emerged—the franchised fast food establishment. Companies such as A&W, Kentucky Fried Chicken, and McDonald's sprang up in many neighbourhood corners. Ray Kroc understood the nascent demand for inexpensive and quick food when he purchased the McDonald's chain from the McDonald brothers in 1961. Other quick-service restaurants sprang up with their own unique models for food delivery. A&W developed the "drive-up" restaurant, which allowed the occupants to stay seated while servers on roller skates took their orders and delivered the food to the car window. In the 1970s, fast food operators cashed in on their customers' more mobile, busier lifestyles and began opening for breakfast, thereby taking advantage of a time period during which the restaurant had previously been closed.

In the 1980s, fast food franchises began linking their product with children's television programs like *Sesame Street* or with newly released children's movies—and toys, not food, became a drawing card for kids. In the 1990s, family-style restaurants such as East Side Mario's and Red Lobster flourished as they catered to busy families and parents looking for friendly, quick service and reasonably priced food served in a more relaxing atmosphere than fast food could provide. Yet toys continue to remain a big drawing card. Understanding that children play a strong role in the decision about where to dine, much of today's hype continues to focus on movies or other branding initiatives for children available at major restaurant chains.

During this time, competition in the fast food industry had become extremely fierce, and the era of the elegant and pricey *haute cuisine* restaurants was coming to a close. The profits in these sumptuous restaurants were undermined by the cost of highly skilled servers, equipment and maintenance expenses, higher insurance premiums due to liability for tableside flambées, as well as clientele dealing with both a faster lifestyle and changing needs. As a result, many haute cuisine establishments transformed into fine dining establishments, allowing them to maintain quality of service and gourmet cuisine while reducing both equipment and labour costs.

SNAPSHOT

Portrait of a Pioneer: Georges Escoffier—King of Chefs and Chef to Kings

Did you know that the way we lay out our kitchens, use standardized recipes, work in professionally styled uniforms, and use menus that explain to guests what they are ordering is the legacy of just one man? Georges Auguste Escoffier is perhaps one of the most recognized names in the culinary world. Escoffier was the creator of the modern kitchen. He transformed it from a medieval, cluttered collection of people cooking into a space organized by food products and preparation methods.

Escoffier recognized that cooking is really a science and so created standardized measures to ensure uniformity of his food products. His recorded recipes included descriptions of each ingredient and the method used to create the product. He laid out his kitchen keeping hot and cold preparations separate; he kept food products apart—beef, chicken, vegetables, sauces, etc., giving each product (and chef) a separate workspace (which, of course, reduced the risk of cross-contamination); he made cooks into professionals by giving them the tools they needed and responsibility for their product. Escoffier created the clean, white uniforms, and it is only recently that colours have again been accepted as part of the kitchen uniform.

The position of expediter, so important to smooth service, was another Escoffier advancement. He insisted that his dining room servers carry triplicate order pads—for the kitchen, themselves, and the guest. He created the modern, classical French menu with specific courses served when the taste buds and tongue were ready for a new flavour and texture. He added descriptions on his menus so the guests might know in advance what they were ordering. No single person, at any time before or since, has had the impact that Escoffier had on the culinary world. He lived to be ninety-one and won many honours including France's highest, the Legion of Honour, but nothing fits his achievements better than the title he earned from his peers—that of "king of chefs."

The food service industry in North America has experienced lower revenues as the number of business and pleasure travellers has dropped. The forecast of, at best, a stagnant North American economy over 2012 and 2013 will continue to challenge all restaurants, especially the fast food arena. For restaurants, surviving the current economic downturn means keeping a sharp eye on cost control, being able to implement quick, cost-saving changes, and investing in service initiatives that increase customer retention and loyalty. McDonald's, once a staple in the fast food industry, is now rebranding itself to connect with the baby boomer generation. As "McCafé," they are shifting their focus to higher-quality food, healthier meal options, and gourmet coffee offerings. By 2012, customers were able to enjoy freshly brewed espresso sitting by a fireplace at their nearby McDonald's restaurant.

THE DIVISION IN FOOD SERVICE

The food and beverage industry is divided into two distinct divisions: commercial and non-commercial food service. **Commercial food service** makes up approximately 79% of the food service marketplace[4] and includes restaurants, fast food outlets, private clubs, bars, and pubs. **Non-commercial food service**, often referred to as **contract caterering**, comprises the remaining 21% of the marketplace and includes food services found on airlines and railways, in stadiums, museums, and department stores, and at recreational events and camps. The entire restaurant industry in Canada generated over $60 billion in revenue in 2010.[5]

Commercial food service describes any food service establishment whose primary business is food and beverage service. It includes

a) full-service restaurants: licenced and unlicenced fine dining, and casual and family restaurants, including restaurant-bars

b) limited service restaurants: fast food, cafeterias, food courts, and takeout and delivery systems

c) drinking establishments: bars, taverns, pubs, cocktail lounges, and nightclubs (with limited food service available)

Non-commercial food service establishments are those whose primary business is something other than food and beverage service. (Branded restaurants in any of these settings are considered commercial food services.)

a) social and contract caterers: supplying food to airlines, railways, institutions, recreational facilities, and special events

b) institutional food service: hospitals, residential care facilities, schools, prisons, offices, and factories

c) retail food services: department store cafeterias and restaurants

d) other food services: stadiums, sports and private clubs, movie theatres, special events, vending machines, and other seasonal or entertainment operations.

According to the Canadian Restaurant and Foodservices Association (CRFA), there is still a great deal of economic uncertainty, forcing consumers to be cautious with their spending. Commercial food sales did increase in 2011 by 3.6%

The Midas Touch—Fibre in Your Diet!

A few years ago, a new franchise, called the Magic Oven, entered the Canadian food service market. This high-end takeout pizzeria boasts many qualities not found currently in most pizzas. Called "Pizzaceuticals," each pizza contains a number of antioxidants, and the crusts are made with an ancient, extremely healthy grain called "spelt."

A grain grown by farmers as early as 5000 BCE, spelt is high in fibre and B-complex vitamins, contains significantly more protein than wheat, and has, of course, both simple and complex carbohydrates. Most people dealing with gluten sensitivities have been able to eat products made from spelt, allowing those who have this allergy the opportunity to enjoy a tasty pizza crust. Spelt's heavy husk allows it to be grown without the use of pesticides, which makes it easy to grow organically.

Tony Sabherwal developed the pizzas to meet the needs of a niche market that looks for vegan, dairy free, or organic foods, and he insists all their products be organic and locally grown. That is not the only difference in the Magic Oven's pizza offerings: for $108, you can purchase the "uber-Sustenance" pizza, making the person you are treating feel like a king. It glitters with gold! As gold is inert, providing no nutritional value but also causing no hurt to the human digestive system, the ancients used it to "cure" a wide variety of medical problems including bronchitis and arthritis. Tony is not the first to revitalize interest in gold as a garnish, and you will find it in liquors, on cakes, and in marmalade. But really, who buys a pizza worth $108? Fifteen-plus "uber-Sustenance pizzas" are sold weekly to corporations wishing to honour an employee with a product that is not only healthy but also sparkles with the Midas touch.

and are forecasted to continue growing in 2012 by 2.9%; most of this growth will come from predicted menu price increases of 2.5% and not significant increases in actual sales.[6] Non-commercial food service is predicted to increase by 3.7% in 2012. However, changes in both these categories remain closely tied to both the Canadian and U.S. economies; the direction of overall economic change, whether positive or negative, will directly influence food service revenues.

Commercial Food Service

Commercial food service covers a wide variety of eating establishment styles. A *full-service* restaurant allows customers to sit down and have their orders taken by a server, who then serves the meal. How their food is prepared, presented, and served depends greatly on the style of restaurant and the philosophy of the owners. Full-service restaurants cover a range of styles, although differences may be somewhat blurred, as many restaurants combine aspects of more than one style.

Haute Cuisine This very elegant and expensive style of restaurant is noted for its opulent decor, highly trained staff, exemplary service, beautiful table settings, and exclusive clientele. The **haute cuisine** restaurant has beautiful silverware, crystal goblets, fine linen tablecloths and napkins, and fresh exotic flowers. Wait staff are exceptionally well trained and include positions such as commis (junior waiter), chef de rang (chief server), maître d' (head waiter), and sommelier (wine steward). The food is fresh, cooked daily by the chef and sous-chef, and the menu often includes signature items—dishes that have been created specifically for the restaurant. The food is frequently prepared tableside on a *guéridon* (cart) and may be flambéed in front of the guest by the chef de rang. The wine cellar is stocked with a wide variety of excellent vintage wines. The entire dining experience is elegant, a true adventure into the world of gastronomy. These restaurants were popular at the turn of the century, when those who dined out were wealthy. In order to survive in a very competitive world, many of these restaurants have had to reduce their costs by eliminating the finer touches, such as the sterling silver place settings and the crystal goblets; the quality of service, wine list, and foods have not been changed. The George V Hotel in Paris boasts one of the finest haute cuisine restaurants left in the world.

Fine Dining Many restaurants still provide elegant service, but have dispensed with the many levels of wait staff and the costly table settings. The food remains unique and exciting, and the staff still require a high level of skills. Few of these **fine dining** restaurants continue to flambée food because of high liability costs. Food is prepared from fresh, raw ingredients and is artfully presented on the plate, or plated, in the kitchen. Great care is taken to ensure that presentation is a wonderful collage of exciting colours and tastes. These fine dining restaurants boast extensive wine cellars stocked with wine that is well chosen to suit a variety of clientele tastes and price ranges.

Dining This category includes a wide variety of dining experiences and is the largest group of full-service restaurants. Ranging from a good local eatery to the greasy spoon around the corner, this style of restaurant is distinguished from the fine dining/haute cuisine experience by its more casual approach to the guest, the menu, and the price. (Remember that all restaurateurs bring their own philosophy of food and service to the marketplace, but successful restaurateurs understand their clientele's needs and are able to fulfill expectations.)

Bistros, cafés, and trattorias show how the restaurant industry has responded to the demand for more casual dining combined with the fresh, eclectic food served by fine dining establishments. Although decor in these establishments is simple and the restaurant is usually small, the food from the kitchen may feature unusual pasta dishes; pizza from a wood-burning oven; exotic lettuces, oils and vinegars; homemade desserts; and specialty coffees.

The **family-style restaurant** is often found in the suburbs or near tourist attractions. This type of restaurant designs its service to be fast, its food to be "comfortable," and its decor to be suitable to the younger diner. As customers walk through the door, they will see high chairs and booster seats along the wall. Children's menus are provided, and the decor can handle spills and messes. Servers are not required to handle complicated menu items, but they need to be friendly, fun loving, and ready to serve young customers. These restaurants attract families by using many different marketing techniques, such as activities for children, a "kids eat free" policy, or family specials.

Another style of restaurant that often caters to the family market is the **specialty restaurant**. This restaurant differs from the family-style in that it serves one kind of food. For example, Red Lobster is known for its seafood, St. Hubert and Swiss Chalet for chicken, and Tony Roma's for ribs.

A **destination restaurant** is a restaurant that people will travel a good distance out of their way to visit. Some restaurants gain fame due to architecture, such as the Yellow Treehouse Restaurant in Auckland, New Zealand. Often, it is the lure of a famous chef, a celebrity owner, or simply an outstanding location. The Hillebrand Winery Restaurant is located in Niagara-on-the-Lake, in the heart of Ontario wine country. It has a strong reputation for outstanding cuisine along with wine pairings chosen from house vintages. Other establishments are famous due to geographic location and the popularity of regional personalities. Rita MacNeil's teahouse in Nova Scotia is an example of a celebrity dining spot. It is open only during seasonal months and patrons often line up down the road hoping for, and often getting, a brief conversation with the famous Canadian songstress.

With the tremendous immigration Canada has seen over the past forty years and the numerous cultures that have become part of the Canadian way of life, **ethnic restaurants** specializing in dishes from a variety of cultures have sprung up across the country. French, British, and American foods have always been available in Canada, but today, customers can choose from a global marketplace of restaurants. There are three main reasons for the growing desire for foods with a foreign flair. First, Canadians are travelling to more exotic places or learning more about foreign foods. Second, the population of Canada has become more diverse, and immigrants have brought their own culinary traditions. Finally, grocery chains and frozen-food packagers are responding to these trends with lines such as Memories of … (from Loblaws); dishes like moussaka; and products such as arborio rice, fresh figs, and papayas. More and more Canadians are now willing to try something new, making ethnic restaurants a viable alternative to standard Canadian fare.

With the emergence of theme parks has also come the development of **theme restaurants**. These restaurants transport a customer to a time and place, often providing entertainment before, during, and after the meal. The theme is carried through the choice of foods served and their description—with the theme often becoming more important than the food. Theme restaurants do not have to be big, but because of the expense involved in creating the theme, many are quite large. They are usually located in major cities with good tourist traffic, appealing to the conference and convention market as well as the general public. Medieval Times, located near Toronto's Exhibition Place, is a good example of a theme restaurant. This U.S.-based company opened its first restaurant in Orlando, Florida, and the Toronto site was developed in 1990. During their meal, the audience watches a program that shows how classic Andalusian stallions are trained and then are treated to a spectacular re-creation of a battle between the Knights of the Kingdom and their archrivals, the Visigoths. Servers are dressed in period costumes and serve menu items that are appropriately named. Medieval Times has the capacity to serve 2500 customers at a time, focusing on large groups that come to the Toronto area for conferences and conventions.

During the late 1970s and early 1980s, North America saw the re-emergence of the **buffet house**, a concept that is centuries old. A buffet is a wide assortment of both prepared hot and cold dishes. Customers help themselves to the foods they want in portions they desire. These restaurants provide a customer with limited table service, such as removal of empty dishes and service of drinks, coffee, and tea. They combine the speed of a fast food restaurant with the attention of table service—a nice combination in a busy world.

Canada boasts many fine restaurants and a variety of gourmet eating options thanks to award-winning, world-class chefs.
(Photo courtesy Canadian Tourism Commission.)

Limited Service Restaurants The serving style of the **fast food restaurant** is to let the customer share in the work. Customers order at a common counter, carry their own food and accessories, and even help clean up after the meal is finished. This style is very common in traditional cafeteria service found in schools and institutional settings. This serving style decreases the cost of the meal, since servers and assistants become unnecessary. In the world of fast food restaurants, the drive-through concept has contributed to lower costs by increasing the output of food without adding additional seating.

Fast food franchises include McDonald's, Kentucky Fried Chicken, Harvey's, Pizza Pizza, Taco Bell, Extreme Pita, and Tim Hortons. These outlets have learned the secret of success by locating along busy highways and near resorts, theme parks, recreation areas, and malls—locations that provide convenient stopping places for the traveller. It is very common to see several fast food restaurants located within a few blocks of one another along a major travel route, on the theory that people are more likely to stop if they see a choice of restaurants.

How to Run a Successful Restaurant

- Begin with a strong business plan and enough cash reserves to take you through the first few difficult years.
- Understand and implement tight cost- and portion-control methods, food specifications, and proper receiving and storage of food products.
- Keep labour costs in line.

- Keep up with trends and have a good vision of your customers' likes, dislikes, and needs.
- Hire and train those willing to invest time in your establishment, then treat them as well as you want them to treat your customers.
- Keep everyone's focus on quality foods and on service beyond customer expectations.

Not all fast food restaurants are franchised; many are independently owned. Every country around the world has its own variety of single, often mobile restaurants with fast food menus that serve products popular in their specific region. Many Canadian restaurants will serve the standard hamburger fare, but in Quebec, tourists will also want to try poutine—french fries topped with cheddar cheese curds and smothered in gravy. This dish is so popular in Quebec that some McDonald's restaurants now offer it. Many regions have developed specialty treats, although tourists are sometimes reluctant to try these new foods. In Ottawa, Hooker's Beavertails serves a must-try treat that is popular all year round, but particularly in the winter. A Beavertail is a deep-fried French pastry shaped like a beaver's tail, served with a variety of toppings such as maple syrup, cinnamon sugar, or strawberry jam. Despite the name, tourists soon give in to the desire to sample this tasty treat. In 1996, Hooker's Beavertails made the move south to Walt Disney World and can be found at the Canadian Pavilion at Epcot. Today, they are also available all over Canada as well.

Coffee houses are returned in popularity as a fun, stylish place to gather, serving coffees from faraway places such as Kenya, Jamaica, and Hawaii, and providing a full range of specialty drinks such as cappuccinos and lattes, as well as specialty items like Japanese green tea. Tim Hortons, Second Cup, and Starbucks are the leaders of this trend. Coffee houses traditionally sold snacks like doughnuts and muffins, but due to consumer demand now serve a full meal with soups, sandwiches, wraps, salads, etc.

Drinking Establishments Bars, pubs, taverns, cocktail lounges, and nightclubs comprise the final group in commercial food service. **Pubs** and **taverns** try to recreate the ambience, menu items, and types of beer and whiskey typical of an English, Irish, or Scottish bar. Prime Restaurants, based in Mississauga, has developed not only the Irish pub concept (for example, D'Arcy McGee's and Sláinte) but has also added a new concept with Esplanade Bier Markt in downtown Toronto, which boasts Canada's longest beer list. Cocktail lounges are often found

Schools often contract out their food service. For example, the University of Alberta, is home to well-known fast food chains like Pizza Pizza, Tim Hortons, and Taco Bell.
(Photo Paula Kerr.)

in casinos or upscale hotels, and nightclubs bring in local and name talent for guests' entertainment.

In Practice

Divide a piece of paper into eight columns and put one of the following food service types at the top of each: independent fast food, hotel restaurants, theme restaurants, family style, cafeteria, coffee house, specialty, and ethnic. Write the names of restaurants you have patronized in each of the appropriate categories (no more than five in a column). Compare and contrast the restaurants within each column and among columns on food quality, quantity, service, and price. Do you notice any significant trends in your data?

Non-commercial Food Service

Non-commercial food service includes any food service located in a business whose main reason for existence is not to serve food, for example, in airports and museums and at events.

Social and contract caterers are important to the tourism sector because they are the major suppliers to the airlines and rail systems. They also run the food service at recreational camps, in museums and at historic sites, at sports arenas like the Rogers Centre in Toronto, and at many special events. These host venues choose not to run their own food service because they have no expertise and no desire to be in the food business. Using professional food providers relieves them of many headaches and provides their staff and customers with a better product. The airlines recognized years ago that their business was transportation, not food service. Cara is a major player in both commercial food service and is also the largest provider of non-commercial food service in Canada to both the airline and railway industries.[7]

Train, bus, and air terminals offer meals to their travellers either through contract services or by leasing space to franchises. It is becoming more common for terminals to use nationally known restaurants. Cara Operations, McDonald's, Tim Hortons, and Starbucks are just a few of the big corporations that understand the valuable link between food service and transportation. Restaurants in a terminal have a valuable captive audience. The restaurant's brand name offers travellers comfort from the stress of travel. The terminal avoids worries about feeding the traveller, yet still makes money from the rented space.

www.restaurant.org

Institutional food services are not directly tied to tourism as a sector, but the industry is growing and it happily embraces those students who have hospitality training. Hospitals, retirement homes, schools, and offices make good use of students with hospitality and culinary training, and the working conditions, including the hours, are very different from commercial food service.

Retail food service is often found in department stores. While traditional department stores such as Sears have simple cafeteria-style food and newer big-box budget stores such as Walmart provide space for fast food outlets, eating at Holt Renfrew can be an elegant experience. Many large retailers see the benefits of retaining shoppers who need food or drink. Some have partnered with franchises, such as Indigo books and Starbucks, or Walmart and McDonalds. Other retailers have developed their own offerings; many large grocery stores have converted space for retail food service and consumption.

SNAPSHOT

In Canada, **contract food service** has not yet reached the size and scope of its U.S. counterpart. However, some colleges and universities that offer "board plans" have moved to professional food providers, such as ARAMARK, Sodexo, Compass Group, and Cara Operations. With changing demographics, such as an increase in the number of seniors looking for upscale retirement homes, many new opportunities will arise in this area of food service.

Independent food service operations, such as Honeybeans Coffee, Teas and Treats, have the ability to blend quality products with outstanding service.
(Photo: Matthew Honey.)

Non-commercial food services also include private clubs, festivals and other seasonal events, and stadiums. Scotiabank Place in Ottawa is home to the NHL's Ottawa Senators, and during "dollar dog hockey night," more than 15 000 hot dogs are sold in just three hours. As well as fast food outlets, Scotiabank Place has a fine dining restaurant called the Club Scotiabank, and casual dining experiences like Frank Finnegan's and the Senate Club.

RESTAURANT CONSUMERS

Restaurants can be divided into three types: tourism sales dependent, tourism profit dependent, and resident sales dependent. Determining the number of restaurants dependent on tourism dollars is difficult. In some communities, over 40% of all restaurant sales are to tourists, but the total percentage in Canada and the United States is unknown. However, keen managers work hard to understand what percentage of their customers are tourists.

Tourism Sales Dependent Restaurants Tourism sales dependent restaurants earn more than half of their revenues from the tourism market. In communities that prosper from tourism, nearly all restaurants depend on tourist sales. Ski resorts are a classic example. Without Banff National Park, the town of Banff in Alberta might not exist, nor would all the restaurants located in Banff. Dependence is determined by location, not type of ownership. A McDonald's located across the street from a train depot may be tourism sales dependent, whereas another McDonald's just three miles east may depend on sales to residents.

Tourism Profit Dependent Restaurants These restaurants make 20% to 50% of their sales from tourists. Most restaurants fit into this category. Even though residents make up half or more of their market, these restaurants could not maintain profitability without tourists. Location is paramount. The restaurant must be close enough to a major highway, an attraction, a high-traffic shopping area, or a lodging establishment to attract tourists and yet be easily accessible to the community. When a restaurant starts attracting more tourists than residents, the manager must be careful not to offend local people. Local traffic must be maintained to keep the restaurant open during slow tourism periods, especially when tourism is seasonal. During the National Hockey League lockout of the 2004–05 season, restaurants near professional hockey arenas struggled to make ends meet. Only a small number went bankrupt, but clearly the loss of business from regular ticket holders was devastating to these restaurants.

Resident Sales Dependent Restaurants A restaurant that derives less than 20% of its sales from tourists is in the resident sales dependent category. These restaurants may profit from tourist dollars but could operate without them. In metropolitan areas, resident sales dependent restaurants can succeed easily, but in smaller communities with some tourist traffic they tend to be less successful.

Although the food and beverage industry is not totally dependent on tourist dollars, tourists are dependent on food service. Many commercial operations in the downtown core of a city rely heavily on tourist traffic for their profit margins. For tourists, one of the great pleasures is leaving behind the grunt work in their own kitchen to dine out, trying different restaurants and food service options. Depending on the method of transportation and type of accommodation, tourists will use food service establishments that best suit their needs at the time of a meal. If tourists are staying in a hotel, they can order breakfast in the room (if the hotel offers

---

How to Build a Destination Restaurant[9]

- Create and prepare quality food using fresh local products whenever possible.
- Create an ambience in your establishment that is fresh, unique and always puts the guest first.
- Provide guests with foods and service that go way beyond their expectations.
- Be sure your servers are familiar with your menu and recommend your signature items to guests—those items you do best.
- Keep guests comfortable at all times, especially if you do not take reservations and the wait is long.

- Better yet, take reservations. Know your turnover times and book accordingly. If a customer with a reservation is kept waiting more than fifteen minutes to be seated, give the meal for free or offer some other apology gift, such as a bottle of wine.
- Understand that your guests come a long way to enjoy your food; train your servers to find the time to talk about local sights and events of interest; make guests feel comfortable both with you and your city/town or area.

room service), they can buy muffins from the corner store and make coffee in the room (many hotels now provide coffee makers for guests' convenience), or they can eat in a coffee shop or restaurant in the hotel or local area.

Tourists need information about local eateries and are finding more and more convenient ways to collect information. Each city, through its convention and visitors bureau, may provide an information booklet that includes information on local restaurants. Hotels will often leave this type of information in each room. Many tourists choose to do research on the internet prior to arrival at a destination; restaurateurs not advertising on the internet may be losing customers. Even without spending a lot on advertising, restaurants should at least have a clean, easy-to-find webpage that is connected to key web search engines. Word-of-mouth references have become extremely frequent through social media sites like Twitter, foursquare, and Yelp, where customers can post their uncensored reviews to open, searchable networks.

Restaurants that have good reviews, provide a unique dining experience, or reflect the culture and cuisine of the region are most popular with tourists. Travel packages that are booked using online services such as Expedia.ca often include dining packages that are available for each destination. Visitors might also ask the front-desk attendant or concierge for advice on where to eat, and many restaurants will put menus in their windows to entice customers into their establishments. Zagat.com has, for some time, offered a service for tourists that researches their vacation destination, searching out restaurants that meet their styles and pocket-books. Recently, a small company emerged in Vancouver that will also provide similar information for the allocentric eater (the risk taker), the midcentric eater, and the psychocentric eater, who simply wants food "just like Mom makes."

Canadian restaurants face a particular financial challenge because of legislated wage levels. Canadians working in the food and beverage industry are paid better wages with better benefits than are their counterparts in the United States. In Ontario, minimum wage was increased from $8.00/hour to $10.25/hour in 2010. The wage for students aged eighteen or younger, working under twenty-eight hours per week, increased by $2.10/hour and liquor servers' wages rose from $6.95 to $8.90 in 2010. Alberta has also raised its minimum wage and other provinces are sure to follow. Although this is good for workers, it puts additional financial strain on a fragile industry. With real profits before tax at around 3% of total revenues, to survive, restaurateurs will have to be able to do more with less.[10] That means tighter control of food and labour costs, simplifying menus, being innovative in production methods, training wait staff, and providing customers with the products and services they demand.

MARKETING THE RESTAURANT BUSINESS

Branding has become extremely important for restaurant success over the past few years. How does a single-unit, no-name restaurant survive in the highly competitive marketplace of food and beverage? Many do not, and research shows that 78% of owner-operated businesses go bankrupt in their first five years of operation. Yet the single-unit restaurant continues to exist, and new establishments quickly open in the spaces vacated by failed ventures. The challenge of the restaurant business is often underestimated by new owners, but the dream of success drives them to try to succeed where others have failed.

A restaurant has numerous ways to sell the products it creates. One of the most effective in-house marketing tools is the **menu**. The menu defines a restaurant by theme and style; good menus are designed to capture the customer's attention and create interest as well as help people navigate through their choices easily. Food descriptions must be well written and well designed to intrigue and tantalize customers into ordering that special soup, salad, or dessert—and to come back again to try a different entrée. Pricing should reflect the quality and value of the selections, as well as the customer's pocketbook. Menus may rely on colour, design, material, or shape to create uniqueness. The menu is primarily an internal tool, but it should be displayed so that passing pedestrians can read it and be enticed into stopping to dine. Menus should also be easily found on a restaurant's webpage.

Restaurants advertise and promote their business in a variety of ways, including local radio stations, newspapers and various web-based methods. For a restaurant, the best advertising is word of mouth. With the explosion of social media tools in the last decade, it has never been easier for customers to share their opinions electronically. Customer comments and feedback can enhance or impede a restaurant's reputation and should be continually monitored.

www.crfa.ca

Actively partnering with the local community and with other tourism products is becoming more important in today's competitive world. Local restaurants will sponsor sports teams and take part in community activities such as food drives and charity fundraisers. Restaurants located in the tourist area of a town often partner with accommodations, tourist attractions, festivals, or events, join the convention and visitors bureau, and ensure the restaurant is listed in its local information guide. Providing "order-in" service for a hotel with limited food services adds value to the hotel product and brings more customers to the partnering restaurant. Linking the restaurant product with tour operators reaches an additional source of revenue, as does becoming an active participant in a festival or special event and setting up food booths for the event. This kind of strategy allows both the local resident and the tourist to taste a restaurant's product and experience its hospitality.

Understanding tourism and the needs of the tourist can provide opportunities that other establishments miss, and can mean that a restaurant is one of the 22% that learn how to thrive in this highly competitive industry.

In Practice

Flip through any edition of your local newspaper and list the various promotional techniques used by restaurants. What types of restaurants are advertising? How are they drawing the value-driven customer? What restaurants are not advertising? Do you believe they are doing better, worse, or the same as those that advertise? In your experience, which restaurant in your community has best responded to current trends in dining out?

Getting the Most from the Tourism Sector

Have you given any thought to how your establishment might encourage visitors to drop in for lunch or supper? According to surveys, people are more likely to treat themselves to a mid-scale or upscale restaurant when on vacation. Fourteen percent of all vacationers choose full-service, fine dining restaurants, 32% choose

CASE STUDY

Making Ends Meet

When Dan was hired by the owner of a small bistro, the job sounded like a good deal. Along with his salary as manager, he would receive a 20% incentive pay bonus. Dan was good at inventory control and he worked well with people. He made sure that waste was kept to a minimum, and after the first year, he had received the bonus pay every single month. But the amount kept getting smaller as prices on little things began to increase. The import tax increased on the unique products the bistro bought from Caribbean suppliers. Even the cost of rice had risen.

Dan convinced his owners to buy a proofing oven, and he began making his own bread and hamburger buns. To the owner's satisfaction, the fresh quality of these products brought in new customers and increased sales. Then the value of the loonie began to rise against the U.S. dollar, fuel prices doubled, and the cost of food increased again. For two months, Dan struggled to keep within the budget. His bonus pay disappeared. Finally, he made a decision. He chose three items listed on the menu: a 1 1/4-pound lobster that sold for $39, the 6-ounce hamburger that began at $8, and the 16-ounce sirloin steak that sold for $24. Dan adjusted these products thusly: the lobster went to a pound, the burger dropped to five ounces, and the sirloin dropped to fourteen ounces. He did not reflect these minor changes on the menu. As he expected, his bonus pay was restored and no one was the wiser!

1. What caused Dan's problems?
2. Which of the two solutions that Dan came up with is ethical? Why?
3. "No one was the wiser"—what emotions and thoughts might the owner have when he learns the truth? The customer?
4. If you were the owner, how would you handle this problem? What would be the positive and negative impacts the other staff might feel? The customers?

mid-scale restaurants, and 53% eat at fast food establishments. Compare that to resident choices: 8% of local clientele choose fine dining establishments, 23% opt for family-style/mid-scale restaurants, and 69% choose fast food.

Vacationers tend to choose fast food for breakfast and lunch to get a quick start on the day's activities. At night, they are ready to relax and enjoy their meal and tend to choose a full-service restaurant. Some restaurateurs have discovered the advantages of group tours. Many tours offer meal services, and tour operators are willing to schedule dinner a little earlier than normal if the price is right. Partnering with tour operators by providing quality food and service at a discounted price may mean additional revenue during the early, slower dining period. Since the meal is usually a set menu and the number of guests is known in advance, profit margins should be good. At this point in history, with a growing boomer market, partnering with other tourism businesses may mean the difference between success and failure for the independent restaurateur.

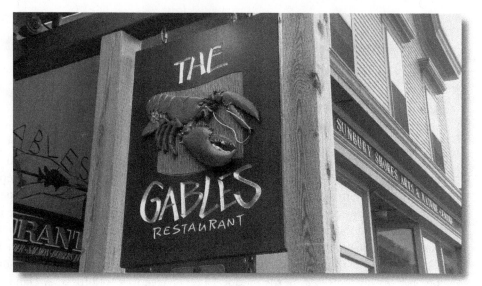

Your town does not have to be big to have fine dining available for the tourist. St. Andrews By-the-Sea, NB, hosts a variety of eating options.
(Photo courtesy Canadian Tourism Commission.)

In Practice

Identify twelve restaurants in your community and classify them as tourism sales dependent, tourism profit dependent, or resident sales dependent. If possible, talk to some of the restaurant managers to confirm your guesses. Next, identify which factor discussed in the previous section has the greatest effect on the sales status of the restaurants.

RESTAURANT OWNERSHIP

Restaurants may be owned or managed in three ways: as independents, under a single corporate structure, or under a franchise agreement. Unlike hotels, the majority of restaurants are owned independently, but brand names from large corporations are gaining ground.

Independents

The majority of restaurants are owned by one or two individuals. These are flexible businesses that allow the owners to change menu items at will, or redecorate to tailor their establishments to the changing needs of the community. However, such independence can be risky because it requires a huge personal investment of time and money. Bankruptcy rates have fallen dramatically over the last ten years, but opening a restaurant is still a very risky business.

Multi-Unit Corporate Restaurants

Just as in the hotel business, a single corporate headquarters often runs a series of restaurants in one city or across Canada. For a **multi-unit corporate restaurant**, corporate headquarters provides the leadership, control, and planning for each restaurant. Managers are trained by the corporation and given the freedom to operate independently—as long as company policies are adhered to and the profit quota is met. Companies may own and operate restaurants that are very similar,

Quality food begins with fresh products. Granville Island, in Vancouver, provides tourists with delicacies prepared in front of them.
(Photo courtesy Canadian Tourism Commission.)

such as Lone Star, based in Ottawa, or Boston Pizza International, a chain from Vancouver. In this case, their expansion will usually be provincial, or perhaps national. Boston Pizza also operates as franchisor.

Still other corporations own and operate restaurants that are very different. These corporations will focus on a region or a city, keeping their locus of operational control small and easily handled. An example of this model is SIR Corp., based in Burlington, Ontario. One of Canada's fastest-growing restaurant companies, SIR Corp. operates Jack Astor's Bar and Grill, Alice Fazooli's Italian Grill, and Canyon Creek Chophouse, then branches out with several specialty restaurants: Reds (an award-winning bistro/wine bar), Four (a high-end bakery and café), the Loose Moose Tap and Grill, and Far Niente (their award-winning, upscale restaurant).

Larger corporations will often purchase a successful corporate chain, adding a new but established product to their business. CARA Operations, which operates Swiss Chalet, Harvey's, and the Cara Airline Solutions group, has added Milestones from the Spectra Group; Kelsey's Inc. of Oakville includes both Kelsey's and Montana's as two of its distinctive brands.

www.cara.com

Franchises

Another form of ownership allows someone to own a restaurant while using the brand and operating formula of an established company. Franchising is one of the major forms of ownership in the commercial food service business. Franchises may fall under a corporate chain or may be held by a parent company. The same pros and cons apply to restaurant franchising as to accommodations franchising (Chapter 5). There are two important benefits to the franchise relationship. First is the association to national advertising and the heft of a brand name such as McDonald's, Boston Pizza, or Tim Hortons. Second, banks and lending institutions are also more willing to lend money to an established brand restaurant with a proven record of success. Other advantages include assistance in finding the right location, a proven layout and design, training procedures for all levels of staff, group purchasing power, food and beverage labour cost control systems, and managerial support.

Of course, there are disadvantages as well. It is costly to purchase a good franchise restaurant, and a given percentage (usually around 15% of gross revenue) must be paid yearly to the franchisor. The franchisee has no say in how the business is run and cannot adapt to serve local needs (for example, to use local food products), or to take advantage of trends in the restaurant business. For tourists, a franchised restaurant means a familiar menu and decor no matter which province, state, or country they are visiting. Brand names and familiar foods in a foreign country provide a level of home-style comfort that is often a treat for a traveller.

TRENDS IN THE FOOD AND BEVERAGE INDUSTRY

New items are always appearing on menus to intrigue and invite customers. It is important to understand the difference between a food fad and a food trend. Fads have a short life. They may be in the marketplace for just six months or they may last as long as a couple of years, but fads come and go. Trends, on the other hand, stay on the menu in one form or another for a period of five to ten years; if they remain popular, they become "mainstream items," those items consistently found on menus. An example of a fad (circa 2000) was the "tasting menu." Started in New York City, customers would come to a well-known restaurant. For a fixed price, the chefs would choose and present samplings of their most exotic, tempting menu items. Instead of one appetizer, the client might receive small portions of carpaccio of fresh sturgeon, a tiny heart-shaped pastry full of wild exotic mushrooms, and a serving of Mexican shrimp with a confit of tomatillo. Although an interesting concept and fun when it first started, it was time-consuming for the kitchen to prepare, the cost was high, and not all guests enjoyed the choices. Wraps, on the other hand, are examples of fads that became trends and are now mainstream items on most menus because their flavour and low carbohydrate/caloric content have kept them popular with clients.

Concern for the environment has meant changes in the food service industry. Coffee cups are now biodegradable, as are the napkins and paper wraps. Newer products made from sugar cane are appearing as takeout/take-home food containers. These new containers are replacing plastic ones, reducing decomposition time from over fifty years to just under a year.[11] Knowing the clientele is even more important today. If you are located in a region that strongly supports recycling of all types, adding a few cents to the cost of a product because you are using new biodegradable containers could be a strategic marketing tool. People in other areas who are less concerned may balk at higher prices even when the item is proven to be "green."

One of the newer trends is purchasing local foods, sometimes called the 200 km menu (the distance can change depending on where you are located). These **200 km menus** use products raised and grown in the local area. Chefs realize the value of having fresh, local food products whenever possible, and a menu item identified as "200 km" indicates that all the major ingredients have been grown within 200 km of the restaurant. Canadian seasonal changes make this more difficult in December, but it is still possible to create some dishes that meet these criteria in the dead of winter by buying from local beef, poultry and dairy farms. Many consumers today are also looking for **organically grown food**—foods raised without the use of chemicals or foreign substances. These customers prefer meat and poultry to be raised "free range" in local pastures with pesticide-free vegetables and fruits. First, it provides customers with the freshest possible foods, and second, it brings the tourist dollar directly into the hands of community farmers. The 200 km menu meets two criteria at once.

With the influx of new Canadians, more and more cultural diversity is being developed beyond the ethnic restaurant. New spices are on the market and there is a growing desire to use pure spices over the blended types found in a grocery store. These "vintage" spices are far superior with truer flavours and scents. Blending these herbs and spices with the wide variety of global cooking methods provides chefs with new ideas with which to design their **signature items**, those menu items that have been carefully created just for that particular restaurant by the chef.

Service The most important reason for consumers to return to a particular restaurant remains service. In the past, there has been a large discrepancy between management's perceptions of customer satisfaction and the actual level of satisfaction customers express. This gap indicates that restaurants need to look more closely at their customers' expectations and satisfaction. Restaurant surveys and customer contact are the easiest ways to appraise customer satisfaction, but these methods require extra time and money and are often overlooked until the restaurant is desperate to find out what is wrong. By that time, it may be too late for the restaurant to recover its losses. Hiring people certified as food and beverage handlers helps to ensure the quality of table service, and giving them the ability to make quick decisions if a customer is dissatisfied allows for smooth handling of situations before they get out of control.

Takeout Delivery and takeout are an important driving force behind the restaurant industry's growth, with takeaway traffic representing nearly 50% of the industry's total. This is expected to increase by 9% over the next several years.[12] As lives become busier and more stressful, with both parents in a household often working, takeout food offers a family the chance to sit and eat together in the comfort of their home. Grocery stores are finding significant portions of the food dollar budgeted by a family for groceries is being spent on takeout or prepared foods.

To recapture this lost revenue, grocery stores are offering more ready-to-eat foods. Fried or roasted chicken, chicken wings, ready-made pastas, salads, and even sushi are all part of their product lines. To meet this challenge from grocery stores, smart restaurateurs have made their own menu items readily available as takeout. For example, delivery is one of Swiss Chalet's meal purchase options and the chain has recently added drive-through windows. While non-traditional for family food service, they serve a growing need—fast meals with no waiting in line.

Casual Dining As more people stretch their financial resources to make ends meet, the luxury of fine dining is being replaced by a more casual dining atmosphere. Plants, natural woods, and earth tones have replaced the formal look of cut-glass chandeliers, crystal goblets, and sterling silverware. Restaurants are becoming smaller and more intimate. Menu choices have an ethnic flair, and unless a restaurant is using frozen food products, there are fewer menu items from which to choose. Value-driven consumers are setting the trend for restaurants to provide lower-priced menu items. Pasta, pizza, and bistro fare are still popular with a focus on whole grains and fresh, lower-fat sauces. Larger franchise restaurants focus on family dining with children's menus and props like crayons (with paper or a picture to colour) or a toy of some sort.

Nutrition For more than a decade, nutrition and health have been national issues, reflecting both governmental and consumer desire to reduce intake of foods high in saturated fat and cholesterol in an effort to stem the quickly rising obesity rate among citizens. Fat-free, low-carb, and low-fat foods are proliferating on grocery store shelves and restaurant menus. Fast-food and family restaurants have responded by using all-vegetable oil or shortening for frying, and have expanded their menus to include pita sandwiches, wraps, and interesting salads. Fast-food establishments are also giving customers choices for side dishes—for example, a salad instead of fries. However, research shows that less than 5% of sales are derived from these nutritionally sound choices. Although good nutrition remains a top concern for diners, it does not entirely translate into menu choices. Many people who watch their diets at home choose to "treat themselves" when dining out. People who are dieting are likely to choose what they want and return to their diet the next day. This behaviour changes, however, if they (for example, business people) eat out on a regular basis.

In Ontario, a private members bill provided little concern in the industry as it passed its first reading in parliament. Bill C-283 would have forced restaurants with annual sales of over $10 million to list, alongside every menu item, its calorie count, sodium level, and sum of saturated and trans fat as a percentage of the recommended daily intake. Bill C-283 was defeated. But other states, provinces, and cities are also looking at methods to trim down their constituents.

New York City passed legislation in July 2008 that bans foods containing trans fat.[13] Trans fats are not highly prevalent in most foods, but they are in the oils commonly used for deep frying. This is an inconvenience for New York restaurateurs (KFC has already eliminated trans fat from its chicken and Taco Bell units), but it is not a devastating decision. Many other cities are watching to see how much success New York has with similar legislation waiting to be passed. Along with this ban, however, comes an addendum that requires restaurants to label foods on menus with their caloric content, sodium, and fat content. The theory behind this legislation follows the labelling of packaged foods in a grocery store. New York politicians note that many consumers now check the information posted on foods purchased in a grocery store, helping them to make healthier choices. Oddly, this information is already available in most restaurants, and fast food units hang a large poster with this information on it, but few people make their restaurant food choices based on this information.

Allergy Awareness The issue of **allergy awareness** continues to concern the food and beverage industry. The growing use of ready-to-cook and ready-to-eat foods means that, because kitchen staff do not prepare these foods from raw ingredients, they often do not know the ingredients. However, consumers have begun asking for a list of the ingredients that have gone into creating the dishes they order, and they have a legal right to know. Monosodium glutamate (MSG), peanuts, nut oils, preservatives—all of these products must be identified for a customer on request, and it is the responsibility of restaurant staff to identify all ingredients in a dish, whether or not that dish has been prepared on the premises. Health Canada requires that all food items sold in Canada have a full listing of their ingredients, which makes the staff's task much easier. Concern for customers may help prevent legal action—and a tragedy.

Legal Issues Legal issues have become a great concern to Canadian restaurateurs. New laws enacted over the past twenty years dealing with alcohol consumption and smoking have changed revenue generation and owner liability. Prior to current drinking-and-driving legislation, many full-service restaurants could expect beverage sales to be at least 50% of the total dinner bill. Today, alcohol consumption accounts for less than 25% of the revenue generated.

Restaurants and alcoholic beverage producers are addressing this problem in a number of ways. Many restaurants sell all wines by the glass and quantities smaller than a full bottle, allowing customers to enjoy their favourite wine with the meal. The cost of the bottle is usually recovered with just two glasses of wine. All servers are then made aware of recently opened wines so they can promote them to other customers. In addition, half bottles of wine are sold whenever they are available. For champagne lovers, Piper-Heidsieck has introduced the Baby Piper, a 200 mL bottle. In British Columbia, patrons who don't finish a bottle of wine are now permitted to carry the open, partial bottle home in a doggie bag. Ontario is allowing restaurants to purchase a licence that allows guests to provide their own bottle of wine. Restaurants can then charge a **corkage fee** for opening the bottle. Patrons in Quebec have been doing this for years.

To make up for the loss of alcohol revenues, restaurants must generate more money from the sale of food. This is difficult because the number of seats is static and cannot easily be changed. Servers are trained to use **upselling** techniques, such as suggesting a soup or salad before the meal, or a dessert with coffee. Upselling should never be aggressive, but should consist of helpful suggestions. Of concern to customers is the amount of tax added to a bill; up to 13% of the total cheque consists of goods and services tax (GST) and some provinces also add food and beverage taxes.

Over the last ten years, indoor smoking and tobacco use has been a large legal issue facing restaurants. Numerous provinces initially allowed restaurants and bars to build costly designated smoking areas (DSR) and restaurants invested in these facilities in good faith that their investment dollars would eventually be retrieved. However, provincial governments continued to pass stricter no-smoking legislation that forced public places to eliminate all smoking. This ban includes any public area, including restaurants, bars, bingo halls, and legion halls. According to Statistics Canada, as of January 2008, British Columbia became the last province in Canada to ban smoking in public areas.[14] A few provinces still allow designated smoking rooms (DSR) in private spaces, long term care facilities, and a few public areas that do not serve food. In these areas, the air must be redirected outside or cleaned through a ventilation system. However, continued legislation is expected to tighten these regulations.

Canada is not the only country to put an end to smoking in public places. Other countries like the United States, Australia, Britain, Sweden, and even France, to mention a few, all have similar legislation in place. Although smoking was for decades common in France, as of January 1, 2008, smoking was banned in all public areas with over 70% public support.[15]

Summary

- The food and beverage industry is the largest of all eight tourism components.
- It has two divisions: commercial and non-commercial food service.
- Commercial food service is further divided into two distinct categories: full service and fast food.
- Non-commercial food service is found in establishments whose primary purpose is not the service of food. Canada's largest contract food server is CARA Operations.
- Non-commercial food service is growing quickly, and is now found in locations such as museums, sports arenas, schools, hospitals and retirement homes, at festivals and special events, and within the transportation system.
- Restaurants can be owned by an individual, as part of a multi-unit corporate group, or as a franchise.
- Trends and concerns in the industry include the 200 km menu, use of organic foods, quality of service, fast food and takeout, nutrition, concern for the environment, allergy awareness, and legislation affecting alcohol consumption and smoking.
- Restaurants that depend on tourist dollars for their existence, such as lodging restaurants, are tourism sales dependent.
- Restaurants that are tourism profit dependent need both the tourist dollar and the local dollar to maintain profits.
- Many restaurants depend almost completely on patronage from local residents; these are called resident sales dependent restaurants.
- The tourism maintains a symbiotic relationship with the food service industry; the financial benefits of this relationship have sometimes been overlooked.

Questions

1. Restaurants, like hotels, may be owned and operated in several different ways. Briefly explain the differences between and the pros and cons of owning i) an independent restaurant unit, ii) a multi-unit restaurant chain, and iii) a franchise.

2. Commercial restaurants are categorized by level of service, style of the restaurant, and menu. Briefly describe eight different types of restaurants found in your area and give at least two examples of each.

3. a) Looking over the trends in food service, list them in the order of importance you feel is most appropriate and provide a brief explanation of each.

   b) Justify your ranking of the top three trends and the bottom trend on your list.

   c) Which of these trends do you feel is most prominent in the industry today? Why?

4. a) Agree or disagree with this statement: "Non-commercial food services will continue to play an increasing role in the tourism sector." Support your answer with examples.

   b) If you were to choose contract food services as your career, design your career ladder and discuss the benefits you would enjoy working in this industry.

5. Differentiate between a tourism sales dependent restaurant, a tourism profit dependent restaurant, and a resident sales dependent restaurant, and provide an example of each from your area.

6. Define the following terms as they relate to the food and beverage industry: *200 km menu, organically grown food, menu, bistro, contract and commercial food services.*

Notes

1. www.crfa.ca/research.

2. Ibid.

3. Harold McGee, *On food and cooking* (New York: Collier Macmillan, 1984), p. 131.

4. www.crfa.ca/research.

5. Ibid.

6. http://restaurantcentral.ca/Canadianrestaurantsales2012.aspx.

7. www.hcareers.ca/seeker/employer-profiles/cara-operations-food-service-canada.

8. Uel Blank, *The Community Tourism Industry Imperative* (State College, PA: Venture Publishing, 1989), p. 17.

9. Eric Hahn, "What makes a destination restaurant?" *Chef 2 Chef News Desk*, no date, http://chef2chef.net/news/foodservice/Editorial-Chefs_Corner/What_Makes_A_ Destination_Restaurant.htm.

10. *Ontario Restaurant News*, May 2002, p. 9.

11. *The New York Times*, September 12, 2001, p. 4.

12. *The New York Times*, September 12, 2001, p. 1.

13. www.yaleruddcenter.org, May 24, 2008.

14. www.statcan.gc.ca/pub/82-003-x/2006008/article/smoking-tabac/t/4060721-eng.htm.

15. "France to ban smoking in public," BBC News, October 8, 2006, http://news.bbc.co.uk/1/hi/world/europe/6032125.stm.

Recreation

Key terms

amusement park
aquarium
art museum
casino gambling
children's museum
heritage or cultural
    tourism

historical museum
historic site
living history museum
mega-mall
museums
oceanarium
parimutuel gambling

scientific museum
site-specific
theme park
UNESCO World
    Heritage Site
zoos

Learning objectives

Having read this chapter you will be able to

1. Explain the importance of attractions to the tourism industry.

2. Define the scope and variety of tourist attractions.

3. Discuss UNESCO's criteria for designating World Heritage Sites, using Canadian examples.

4. Discuss how public, private, and non-profit attractions differ.

5. Provide examples of public attractions and compare them with private or commercial attractions.

Visitors from across Canada and around the world come to Drumheller, Alberta, to visit the Royal Tyrrell Museum, take day trips to dig for dinosaur bones, and gaze at nature's spectacle, the hoodoos.
(Photo: Mervyn Rees/Alamy.)

Tourism organizers understand that visitors require things to do once they arrive at a destination, activities and interests that attract them. Great destinations attach these attractors as part of their tourism brand. When you think of a particular country, what comes to mind? Perhaps you think of a particular iconic building, a mountain or beach landscape, or even a piece of that country's history. Likely, there will be at least one specific attraction that comes to mind. If your interest in that attraction is high enough, you will add the country to a list of destinations you would like to visit. Choosing where to spend your vacation depends on many things, but the entertainment value of a destination is critical in the decision-making process. Ask foreigners what picture the country "Canada" brings to mind, and their answer usually has to do with our spectacular landscapes or our weather. Much of Canada's attraction for tourists lies in its natural resources (mountains, lakes, rivers, oceans, forests, and wildlife); however, tourism also depends on artificial attractions that have been created to entertain and educate visitors and residents alike.

If we look at tourism as a single platform upon which to build an industry, the first three supports would be transportation, accommodations, and food services. A traveller must have all three to survive. The fourth support would be entertainment. The next three chapters focus on tourism activities and the entertainment of visitors, perhaps the main reason people choose to travel in the first place.

When determining our gross domestic product in tourism, the North American Industry Classification System bundles three activities into one grouping called "entertainment." Under this broad heading, there are three separate, important areas of tourist activity: attractions, events, and adventure tourism/outdoor recreation. For a clearer understanding of the components, they are best studied separately, as each component attracts different target markets.

Attractions consist of permanent sites/facilities that are always available to a tourist. Regardless of season, tourists can come and enjoy the Museum of Civilization in Ottawa, shop at the West Edmonton Mall, or visit the Vancouver Aquarium. One of the values of permanent facilities is that tourists do not have to book vacations around specific times. Many travellers prefer to see the Eiffel Tower in October when the weather is still good but the hordes of tourists in Paris have gone home. In contrast, *events* are created by a destination in order to attract specific target markets at specific times. For example, every July the city of Toronto hosts the Scotiabank Toronto Caribbean Carnival (formerly known as Caribana). This festival has been an annual event since 1967 and has become one of the largest festivals to focus on Caribbean culture, attracting those who wish to enjoy "island heritage" without leaving Canada. *Adventure tourism and outdoor recreation* provide a totally different style of vacation for tourists who want to be physically active and enjoy the great Canadian outdoors.

The large grouping of attractions may be further subdivided into *natural attractions, cultural attractions*, and *attractions that entertain*. No matter the type, there are some important criteria to include when designing (or redesigning) an attraction:

- **Determine the sustainability of the attraction.** Areas need to be studied to determine how many people can be brought in on a daily/yearly basis without doing irreparable damage. At a certain point, the number of visitors may simply overwhelm the facility and make it less enjoyable.

- **Identify the target markets.** Facilities must reflect the needs and expectations of visitors, including language, culture, and accessibility. When dealing with foreign visitors it is important to ensure that rest facilities, food service, and welcoming facilities can meet their differing needs. Tourists often look to capture a memory of their visit through souvenirs and mementos; a gift shop may benefit both the attraction and the visitor. The items you choose to sell must also reflect your market—people are willing to pay a great deal more when choosing a souvenir if the item is authentic and handmade.

- **Determine visitor flow patterns.** No matter the size of the attraction, determining where patrons enter and pay (if applicable), identifying the areas where they tend to spend more time, and providing good signage to guide people through your site are extremely important. Strategically placed rest stations and easy access to parking should be provided. Also important are signs on local streets showing how to reach the facility. For example, if parking is set at a distance from the site, there may be need for a transportation system to move people to and from the attraction.

- **Training of workers and management of the facility.** Whether your attraction is natural or cultural in nature, it is valuable to use workers who have an understanding of the site and its background. Operators who have visitors from a wide range of ethnicities need to train workers to be sensitive to the differing needs and customs.

CANADA'S ATTRACTIONS

Natural attractions depend solely on what the country's landscape offers to the visitor. In Canada, people look to our glorious mountains, oceans, rivers, miles of untouched wilderness, and animals that are found in our national and provincial parks. While a tourist would not look forward to meeting a grizzly bear face-to-face, watching and photographing a herd of deer on the mountain slopes or capturing the splash of a whale's tail from the safety of a boat are considered part of Canada's attractions. So it is of utmost importance that areas being developed recognize this and build toward sustaining the natural environment.

Forty years ago, many prospective visitors viewed the history of Canada, at merely 400 years old, as new, and felt that, compared to the incredible, ancient sites in Asia or Europe, we had little culture to promote. Now the world is taking notice of the original inhabitants of this country, our First Nations and Inuit people. This has helped promote a keen interest in their arts, history, and religions. Particularly interested in our Aboriginal cultures are people from Pacific Rim countries, areas from which it is believed the First Nations may have migrated.

In many cases, attractions are the reason people travel. Attractions may be the primary destination or only one component of a larger vacation. The attractions a country has to offer, however, provide increased incentives for foreign travellers to visit.

OWNERSHIP

Attractions differ not only in type but also in ownership; they may be privately owned and operated, non-profit, or publicly owned. Table 7.1 identifies the type of ownership, sources of funding, and the different types of attractions found in each category. Theme parks, museums, zoos, casinos, and Broadway-style theatres are only a few of the different types of attractions found around the world. Attractions come in so many shapes, sizes, and types of ownership that throwing them all into a single category called "attractions" seems incongruous. Comparing Walt Disney World to Niagara Falls, or the CN Tower to the Mayan ruins of Mexico, is inappropriate, yet each is classified as an attraction.

www.attractionscanada.com

In Practice

In groups of four to six people, take ten minutes to brainstorm sites and attractions you have both visited or heard about in Canada. Once your time is up, review your list. Identify attractions you think are most attractive to visitors while eliminating sites you think are least attractive until you have crafted a list of top ten sites. Write your list on a large sheet of paper supplied by your instructor and post it in the classroom. Review your classmates' lists. Have you chosen any similar sites? Using these lists, create a final list with your class's idea of Canada's top ten sites. What criteria do you think were most commonly used to choose these sites? How might these lists change ten years from now? What new attraction do you think will gain in popularity?

TABLE 7.1   *Sources of Funding in the Attractions Industry*

	Public	*Non-profit*	*Private*
Funding	Taxes	Admission Fees	Admission Fees
	Admission Fees	Donations	Food & Beverage
	Donations	Grants	Merchandise
	Grants	Memberships	Entertainment
			Parking
Types	Museums	Museums	Theme Parks
	Zoos/Aquariums	Zoos/Aquariums	Amusement Parks
	Historic Sites	Historic Sites	Carnivals/Circuses
	Casinos		Theatres
			Shopping Malls

CULTURAL ATTRACTIONS: PUBLIC AND NON-PROFIT

As provincial and federal governments cut budgets, money for the upkeep and enhancement of public and non-profit attractions has dwindled. Many Canadians fear that continual funding cuts will undermine institutions that support heritage, culture, and the arts.

Governments own and operate *public attractions.* Taxes often serve as the prime source of funding for these attractions, yet in the face of government cutbacks, public institutions have been forced to become more creative in their fundraising efforts. In addition, some taxpayers are less tolerant of the idea of fully supporting a public attraction. As a result, many public attractions now charge entrance fees, actively encourage donations and are bringing in exciting special events or shows as additional sources of revenues. Income is also generated from parking fees and the sale of souvenirs and gifts.

Many attractions raise additional revenue through non-traditional uses of space as well as offering food and beverage service. After hours, space may be rented for private functions. For example, the Vancouver Aquarium provides a fascinating setting for people attending a conference in the city. Guests gain an opportunity to view the attraction at their leisure and to enjoy a meal away from the hotel setting.

Non-profit attractions are just that—they are not focused on earning returns for owners or shareholders, instead funnelling earned profits directly back into the attraction. The goal is not profit generation, but sustainability. Some non-profit attractions began as public attractions that are no longer funded by government. The Log Farm in the Ottawa region is a perfect example. One of the area's earliest farms, it was used as a living history site, showing tourists and local residents the farming methods of the early nineteenth century. When the federal government ended its funding, a group of concerned citizens took over the operation. It now exists on revenue received from grants, donations, membership fees, and special events such as the Sugar Bush Celebration. In the early spring, visitors come to watch the traditional crafting of maple syrup being made in huge cauldrons. Volunteers boil the maple sap to make fresh syrup and maple taffy, which is then sold to the public.

Admission fees and the sale of souvenir items often bring in revenue for non-profit attractions. Additional revenues are generated from the sale of memberships, donation boxes at the entrance, benefit dinners, and special events. Membership benefits may include free admission, monthly newsletters or event information, plus the satisfaction of knowing they are contributing to a cause in which they believe. Based on where funding for an attraction is coming from, it is sometimes hard to distinguish between a public and non-profit attraction, an issue often of more interest to the attraction operator than the tourists enjoying the attraction.

The Diefenbunker in Carp, Ontario, is another example of how non-profit attractions begin. Between 1959 and 1961, at the height of the Cold War, this huge four-storey bunker was built into the Carp Escarpment to protect government officials in the event of nuclear war. In 1994, the bunker was abandoned. It was later purchased by the citizens of the town of Carp. Prior to sealing its entrance forever, final tours for interested area residents were conducted and it became apparent that this unique site provided a glimpse into the Cold War era in Canada. The bunker has been restored and operates as the only Cold War museum of its kind in the world. Funding comes from a blend of admission fees, donations, and some grants provided by the Ontario government and the regional municipality of Ottawa-Carleton.

Museums

Visiting the museums of an area is an important part of many itineraries and can sometimes be the main focus of a trip. **Museums** are historical, scientific, or artistic and can display just about anything: from paintings to motorcycles, from books to boats, the International Council of Museums (ICOM) defines a museum as "a non-profit, permanent institution in the service of society and its development, open to the public, which acquires, conserves, researches, communicates and exhibits the tangible and intangible heritage of humanity and its environment for the purposes of education, study and enjoyment."[1]

Most museums divide into permanent areas that display the same exhibit at all times and flexible areas that can house a succession of travelling shows. These special events keep local people coming to the museum; changes in artists, new historical displays, or recent scientific discoveries are promoted to local residents as well as tourists. Museums and galleries were once cultural centres in metropolitan areas, attended primarily by society's elite who gathered to express their opinions about the works of a particular artist. However, Canadians have long had the opportunity to visit both nationally and provincially funded art museums.

Art museums can be found in local communities and major city centres. Young artists usually start by displaying their work in smaller galleries, which in turn support the local art museum. The artist may also autograph a limited number of prints during a showing, giving tourists and locals alike a direct connection with the artist. Open houses, social hours with local dignitaries, and other small events are held in these locations so that the work of the artist can reach more people and the museum can showcase itself. Art museums, both large and small, strive for variety, providing all types of artwork, including sculptures, oils, watercolours, and carvings.

www.gallery.ca

Historical museums are more likely than art or scientific museums to be in small communities. These museums usually present relics, along with written explanations of the pieces, and sometimes struggle to maintain an uncluttered look as they receive more and more items that donors expect to see displayed.

Living history, which uses people in period costumes to portray historical figures and times, is a popular trend for historical museums. **Living history museums** are popular among all age groups. Lang Pioneer Village located in Keene, Ontario, and the Fortress of Louisbourg located just outside of Cape Breton, Nova Scotia, both provide visitors with an early Canadian experience. Living history museums are successful because they are both fun and educational; they also provide jobs to local people and bring tourist dollars into the area.

Modern museums have replaced the old "do not touch" mentality with interactive displays, eliminating the need to keep young hands off artifacts. Video presentations and computers are replacing the more expensive museum interpreters and engaging the user with the communication so vital in today's educational style. The designers of the Canadian War Museum, which opened in Ottawa in May 2005, used this strategy to create a "real life" experience for all visitors. The museum is laid out in historical avenues so that visitors may choose to know more about the War of 1812, or move to the corridor that explains the events of World War I. The Canadian War Museum does not glorify war, but instead illustrates its dreadful conditions and pays homage to its casualties. Throughout the museum, various interactive activities bring war to life for visitors by allowing them to hear the control tower clear a bomber heading to Germany; try on a helmet worn by soldiers on the ground; or move into a dark, smelly trench like those used by the soldiers of WWI. In the trench, visitors listen to the silence, and hear the "soldier" next to them whisper, "Here they come."[2] The night sky then lights up, the platform shakes with the explosions, and gunfire is heard all around. Intermingled with these sounds are the cries of frightened and wounded soldiers. Providing a balance of "real life" and simulated experience is vital to the overall mission of educating the visitor.

Perhaps the most memorable element of the new museum is the Memorial Hall, which houses the headstone of the tomb of the Unknown Soldier from World War I. Light from a single window reaches the headstone only once a year—on November 11 at 11:00 A.M. In its first thirty days of operation, the new Canadian War Museum attracted more visitors than the old war museum attracted during an entire year.

With environmental concerns in mind, the designers of this museum made good use of its location. From a distance, the museum almost melts into the landscape with its "green roof," which is planted with native grasses. A green roof helps insulate the museum from both cold and hot weather. The Ottawa River, which flows past the building, provides water for the modern cooling system. With research and innovation, museum designers have created a unique Canadian museum.[3]

Scientific museums showcase items ranging from dinosaur bones to spaceships. These museums tend to show a process, whether it is the existence and extinction of dinosaurs as at the Royal Tyrrell Museum in Drumheller, Alberta, or the history of the space age as at the Kennedy Space Center in Florida. The Royal Tyrrell Museum is located near Dinosaur Provincial Park, one of the world's most extensive dinosaur graveyards. Tourists from all over the world visit the museum, which houses one of the world's largest collections of dinosaur bones. Climbing onto the back of a *Tyrannosaurus rex* could be the highlight of a child's visit to the museum. Interested tourists may also book a daylong tour to help search for dinosaur bones.

Niche market businesses can be very successful at attracting tourist business. The PEI Preserve Co. not only sells unique hand-made jams, but also entertains with a daily ceilidh of Gaelic music and dance.
(Photo: Debbie Brady.)

One of Canada's most respected museums, the Royal British Columbia Museum, is located in Victoria. It is typical of a large museum in that it blends both science and art; the museum houses the best collection of totem poles and Aboriginal art in North America. One floor is dedicated to dioramas of West Coast forests and seashores, and another floor presents the human history of the province. The Royal B.C. Museum is also noted for its programs on ecology.

Scientific museums such as the Ontario Science Centre in Toronto provide hands-on experience for visitors; it is impossible to simply stroll through without getting involved. Many scientific museums, such as the Royal Tyrrell Museum, are **site-specific**—that is, they are located where the scientific event took place. Small communities that claim a scientific history can easily create a museum in honour of the person, animal, or event. The latest trend in scientific museums is the **children's museum**, which allows young children to experiment with various scientific discoveries. In downtown Halifax resides Nova Scotia's only hands-on science centre that is directly targeted toward children. The museum hosts children's birthday parties and child-oriented special science events such as 'Grossology,' where kids get to learn the science of the human body.

www.royalbcmuseum. bc.ca

Overall, museums endeavour to involve the young, understanding that if youngsters become interested, the museum will have their support for life. Museums are becoming more family oriented and more visible in community events and tourist advertisements for the area. In the off-season, museums become classrooms. Local support is increased through school events at the museum—a smart use for a tourist attraction.

Historic Sites

Historic sites are located in every country that has taken the initiative to commemorate them, and Canada has thousands of special-interest sites. Some are commemorated with just a marker that explains the historic importance of the site, but many have interpretive centres or small museums. The United Nations Educational, Scientific, and Cultural Organization (UNESCO) has placed several of Canada's national parks, historic sites, and culturally important sites on their list of World Heritage Sites in recognition of the outstanding universal value of the area. Nominees for UNESCO heritage-site designation are carefully reviewed by an international panel before being given this status (see Table 7.2).

L'Anse aux Meadows, on the northwestern tip of Newfoundland, is a **UNESCO World Heritage Site** that commemorates the arrival of the first Europeans in North America a thousand years ago. This site is

In 2012, the Grand-Pré National Historic Site became the latest Canadian location to receive UNESCO standing as a World Heritage Site.
(Source: Mark Eastman.)

TABLE 7.2   *Canada World Heritage Sites*

Name	Province/Territory	Year Designated	Focus
Nahanni National Park Reserve	Northwest Territories	1978	Natural
L'Anse aux Meadows Archeological Site	Newfoundland and Labrador	1978	Cultural
Kluane National Park • Wrangell—St Elias • Glacier Bay/Tatshenshini-Alsek Park	Canada & USA	1979 added in 1994	Natural
Dinosaur Provincial Park	Alberta	1979	Natural
Head-Smashed-In Buffalo Jump	Alberta	1982	Cultural
SGaang Gwaii	British Columbia	1981	Cultural
Wood Buffalo National Park	Alberta/Northwest Territories	1983	Natural
Canadian Rocky Mountain Parks • Banff National Park • Jasper National Park • Yoho National Park • Mount Robson Provincial Park • Mount Assiniboine Provincial Park • Hamber Provincial Park	Alberta/British Columbia	1984 and 1990	Natural
The Historic District of Old Québec • Fortifications of Quebec • Artillery Park	Quebec	1985	Cultural
Gros Morne National Park	Newfoundland	1987	Natural
Waterton Glacier International Peace Park	Canada & USA	1995	Natural
Old Town Lunenburg	Nova Scotia	1995	Cultural
Miguasha National Park	Quebec	1999	Natural
Rideau Canal	Ontario	2007	Cultural
Joggins Fossil Cliffs	Nova Scotia	2008	Natural
Landscape of Grand Pré	Nova Scotia	2012	Cultural

Source: Courtesy of Parks Canada.

the only authenticated Norse settlement in North America. Nearby at L'Anse-Amour, tourists visit the 7500-year-old burial mound of the first residents of Newfoundland and Labrador, the Maritime Archaic people. In 2012, UNESCO declared Nova Scotia's Landscape of Grand Pré, which includes the Grand-Pré National Historic Park, as Canada's newest World Heritage Site. Grand Pré was a region with Acadie first settled as a French colony in the mid-seventeenth century. As a region rich in natural resources, including farm lands and access to the Bay of Fundy, Grand Pré thrived as a community. In 1755, caught in the ongoing war between the England and France, the Acadian people in the Minas Basin were held prisoner, their villages destroyed and over 6000 Acadians were deported. Today, Grand Pré stands in remembrance of early Acadie and its rich culture that is now celebrated in Eastern Canada over 400 years after a French presence was established in Canada.

Prince Edward Island's Province House is considered the birthplace of Confederation. The first meeting to discuss federal union was held here in 1864. Several rooms, including the Confederation Room, have been restored to their nineteenth-century appearance. This building also houses the provincial legislature. In New Brunswick, tourists may visit the Acadian Historical Village, which chronicles the Acadians' struggle for survival after their expulsion from Nova Scotia in 1755. In Nova Scotia, the town of Lunenburg, which was declared a UNESCO World Heritage Site, can trace its history back to 1753, when the first settlers arrived. Lunenburg is famous for its shipbuilding, and in particular for the *Bluenose*, the sailing ship that was champion of the seas from 1921 to 1946.

Quebec City is Canada's oldest city. The original section is walled, with narrow cobblestone streets and ancient greystone houses, churches, and the old stone fort, still complete with its massive gates and cannons. Montreal, unlike Quebec City, was first established as a mission whose goal was to convert the Iroquois to Christianity. It is not surprising that Montreal has been known for its magnificent churches. Many tourists walk up Mont-Royal, following the path to the summit to see the modern cross, placed on the spot where Maisonneuve placed a cross in 1643.

In Manitoba, tourists visit the site of the last rebellion in Canada, led by Louis Riel and his band of Métis. In Saskatchewan, which has more museums per capita than any other province, the history of Canada's red-coated Royal Canadian Mounted Police comes alive at training headquarters. Alberta is home to another World Heritage Site, Head-Smashed-In Buffalo Jump, where Aboriginal tribes of the northwest killed buffalo by driving them off high cliffs.

The Aboriginal people of British Columbia, working with cultural ecologists, have reconstructed much of their history. Both the Haida and Gitksan peoples are famous for their arts and crafts, especially their magnificent totem poles. The villages of Kitwanga and Kitwancool have some of the finest totem stands in North America.[4] 'Ksan, a Gitksan village designed to teach its history to visitors, has replicas of ancient cedar log houses and a salmon smokehouse. Tourists can watch Gitksan carve their dugout canoes, or may be guided around the museum by Gitksan women who vividly describe their ancient culture. The Frog House of the Stone Age presents Gitksan life before the arrival of Europeans, and presentations of "Breath of our Grandfathers" illustrate the songs and dances of the Gitksan people.

Heritage Tourism

Heritage tourism is to a culture what ecotourism is to nature. Prominent tourism specialists argue that ecology and culture are so intertwined that the term "cultural ecotourism" should be used instead. **Heritage tourism** includes the landscapes, crafted and natural artifacts, and the cultural traditions that have been passed through generations that, together, form a potential tourism product.[5] Heritage is our past—what we have received from our ancestors and what we pass on to future generations. By showing people how and why cultures differ, heritage tourism becomes a strong link to world peace, teaching the value of art, traditions, culture, and history. Because both ecotourism and heritage tourism are part of a learning process, they require experienced, knowledgable guides. The number of visitors and guides involved in these activities continues to grow.

FOOTPRINT

Rebuilding National Heritage

In the 1880s, a small railroad company, the Kettle Valley Railroad (KVR), built a 525 km set of tracks through rough terrain in southern B.C. in order to transport silver, mined in the region, to the coast. It was a difficult project as the tracks were forced to hug the hard rock cliffs and sharp curves and to span deep gorges, but a cleverly designed set of eighteen tall, graceful, sturdy wooden trestles completed the run. This line was put into use in 1915, becoming an iconic image of rail travel through the mountains of Western Canada. Unfortunately, changes in transportation lowered the demand for this line, beginning in the early 1960s and culminating with the last run in 1989.

Unused for nearly a quarter of a century, these tracks became part of the ambitious millennium plan to build a trail from the East Coast to the West Coast called the Trans Canada Trail (TCT). With the tracks removed, the bedding created a smooth, easy trail that reached into wilderness untouched by modern society's roads. For backpackers and bicyclers, this 525 km run found in the Myra Canyon is one of the safest and easiest to use in Canada.

But, in 2003, during one of the driest seasons on record, lightning struck dry timber and unleashed a firestorm that destroyed more than 25 000 acres of land, 239 homes, and twelve of the eighteen trestles found in Myra Canyon. Just seven months earlier, the Myra Canyon had been awarded national historic site status. After the fires, the federal government stepped in with a one-time grant to have them rebuilt. Today, this section of the TCT has reopened, and small businesses like B & Bs and local wineries are enjoying a rebirth. Backpackers and cyclists are back, enjoying spectacular scenery. More important, a piece of Canadian history lives on to tell visitors the story of our ancestors and their amazing feats, feats that helped open up a passageway across our beautiful wilderness to the coast.

It is the powerful scenic beauty of our landscape that makes Canada a sought-after destination. Rapids in Sambaa Deh Falls Park, NWT.

(Photo courtesy Canadian Tourism Commission.)

Zoos and Aquariums

While the majority of museums are publicly funded, zoos and aquariums are a mix of both public and private operation. Large zoological parks and gardens are significant tourist attractions. As attractions, **zoos** exhibit animals in enclosed areas or in a natural habitat where they can roam freely, as in the Toronto Zoo. In the past, zoos were simply a collection of animals kept behind bars and wires. However, most zoos are modern in design, creating comfortable natural settings focusing on the animals, balancing their comfort with the viewing and educational experiences of visitors. Some are also designed for the breeding of rare and endangered species. One of the newest animal parks is located at Walt Disney World and features a fully developed natural African setting that allows the animals a free and healthy life. The late Marlin Perkins, the famous curator and host of television's *Wild Kingdom*, insisted that zoos are a necessity; several species have escaped extinction because of zoos, and most zoo animals are healthier than they would be in their wild state.

Aquariums and oceanariums are both aquatic zoos. **Aquariums** are usually found inland and exhibit freshwater and saltwater fish. **Oceanariums** are located on the ocean coast and may include large fish such as sharks, as well as seals, otters, dolphins, and other aquatic life. Canada's best-known aquarium, in Vancouver, is renowned worldwide for its educational programs and creative displays. This facility also houses one of Canada's largest IMAX theatres, which brings visitors back for special film events.

Many oceanariums present special shows with trained dolphins, sea lions, or seals. These shows provide entertainment and allow the trainer to explain the habits of the animal. Zoos also sometimes host hourly shows with elephants, monkeys, or other animals. Elephant or camel rides are popular with youngsters and produce a small amount of revenue. Petting farms allow the visitor to feel, smell, and touch the animals. Generally, the more people get involved with the animals in a zoo, the longer the people will stay, the more they will learn, and—with luck—the more they will spend.

ATTRACTIONS THAT ENTERTAIN: PRIVATE/COMMERCIAL

Theme and amusement parks, carnivals and circuses, live entertainment, spectator sports, gaming, and shopping constitute the majority of private or commercial attractions. A fast-growing commercial attraction area is the family fun park. Private attractions rely on admission fees, food and beverage sales, merchandising, parking charges, and special event fees (see Table 7.1). Admission fees are often higher than those of public-sponsored attractions, which can rely on grants. Private attractions, free of the bureaucratic red tape and committee structure of public enterprises, can make quick decisions and therefore adapt faster to markets. Other than expansive and well known attractions like Walt Disney World and Disneyland, most private attractions are regional tourist draws at best and are considered one component of a larger vacation trip. However, each province now offers a wide variety of family fun parks that range from water activities to carnival rides, historic adventure to wildlife viewing. And, except for the actual visit, most everything, including "tickets to ride," can be arranged in advance over the internet.

Theme Parks

The **theme park** concept is most widely attributed to Walt Disney. Theme parks are oriented to a particular subject or historical area and combine costuming and architecture with entertainment and merchandise to create an evocative fantasy atmosphere.[6] Theme parks trace their roots back to the amusement park business. With the opening of Disneyland in California in 1955, Walt Disney transformed the generic amusement park into a place designed and connected around a single theme with wholesome family entertainment and a full day's worth of thrills and fantasy. Disneyland showed that theme parks could experience great success.

In creating Disneyland, Walt Disney wanted to realize a perfect vision of his own childhood, right down to a smaller version of the main streets found in the midwestern towns of his youth. This theme park was to have all the virtues of an amusement park with none of the vices. And it was to offer the Disney fantasy as a means of escape. It should be noted, as with many products, that tourism tends to combine categories or activities to increase the number of target markets it attracts. So a theme park meant to resemble a huge space centre with workers dressed up in spacesuits, may also include an amusement park with rides and an aquarium with all sorts of colourful undersea aquatic creatures to view.

Attractions, especially large theme parks, are among the first businesses to feel the downturn of the economy because spending money on theme parks is a luxury. Yet, experience shows that vacation travel bounces back quickly from economic slowdowns. Additionally, declines in international visitors to theme parks during slowdowns is frequently mitigated by an increase in local visitors who cannot afford more expensive travel and choose instead to stay close to home. Disney faces these problems head on and continues to entice its customers by adding new attractions and making good use of special events such as the year-long celebration in 2005 commemorating the fiftieth anniversary of their first theme park, Disneyland.

In 1991, Disney Corporation was selected to be a component of the Dow Jones Industrial Average, a group of thirty large American corporations whose business health and shareholder acceptance are used as measures of the United States' economic strength. Disney replaced USX (formerly U.S. Steel) and became the only representative of the tourism sector, signifying that recreation and travel had become a staple in the American economy. Disney's Dow Jones status also reflects the shift in focus from an industrial society to a leisure society.

Other theme parks have emulated the Disney model. Canada's Wonderland, just outside Toronto, for example, has themed areas such as International Street, with restaurants, stores, and boutiques in the style of Mediterranean, Alpine, and Scandinavian countries; the Medieval Faire, offers live theatre, rides, restaurants, and boutiques in the style of medieval Europe; and Hanna-Barbera Land features Taft cartoon characters in their well-known environs.[7]

The development of large-scale theme parks in North America has slowed considerably, perhaps because of the huge capital outlay required for large theme parks. Smaller parks are now becoming the trend; Sesame Place in Langhorne, Pennsylvania, is an excellent example. This park has live entertainment, water attractions, computer and educational exhibits, dozens of "kid-powered" play elements, and storefronts representing Sesame Street and the surrounding Sesame neighbourhood.

Water theme parks are becoming more attractive to all ages as well, and small wading pools and slides are being built for the under-five crowd. Even miniature

www.disney.go.com

SNAPSHOT

Walt Disney

He created a world of magic and laughter—theme parks, a new tourism product: entertainment that was family oriented, clean, safe, and well executed. Walter Elias Disney was born in 1901, fourth son in a family of five. His childhood was spent following the dreams of a father who never achieved the success he had hoped for, and after World War I, Disney returned to the States determined to make his living drawing cartoons.

In the early years, the family was very poor, and often Disney had only a crust of bread and a little cheese to survive on—but he also had a friendly mouse that came by to nibble crumbs. This little mouse became the most famous mouse in history. His animated self, Mickey Mouse, is the world's second most recognized figure, next to Santa. The turning point in Disney's life was when he joined forces with another cartoonist named Ub Iwerks. Ub became his best friend, and although the fame followed Disney, Ub was *the* renowned Disney cartoonist. Steamboat Willie was the first major success for the pair and the first talking cartoon film ever produced. In the next three years, they added other members to Mickey's family, including Minnie, Pluto, and Donald Duck.

In 1937, Disney produced the first full-colour animated film, *Snow White and the Seven Dwarfs*. It was a smashing success. Not all of his films went on to be successful, but many, like *Pinocchio* and *Bambi*, remain top sellers even today. In the late 1940s, bored with the film world of cartoons, Disney began to envision a family-style park where kids could come, meet all of his cartoon char-acters, and ride the river with Tom Sawyer or swirl around in the Mad Hatter's teacups.

Unable to get funding from his own company, Disney sold the new TV network ABC on his idea for a weekly "Wonderful World of Disney." Disney took the profits from his TV series and funnelled them into his new project, the family park named Disneyland. It opened in 1954, "a success facing failure," as he had neglected to foresee that not only children loved Disney, but parents did, too. The area had no possibility of expansion! Disneyland was far too small from the day it opened. Walt immediately began the hunt for new space and quietly began buying land in central Florida. Although Walt Disney died in 1966 of lung cancer, in 1972, Disney World opened in Orlando, Florida, to a huge audience.

Now that there was land on which to expand, his company slowly added new areas to the park every few years—to keep customers coming back. In 1995, recognizing the need for "hands-on" fun, the Walt Disney Company opened Disney University, where visitors learn new skills during the day (like drawing cartoons, rock climbing, or learning how to cook the Disney way) and play in the park at night. Disney's company has now opened theme parks in France, Japan, and China.

Walt Disney left a legacy of magic—and of firsts. He was a man of action who believed in himself when others did not, and he showed the world that dreams do come true. Without his creative genius and dedication to excellence, tourism would be missing a little of the magic we all know as Disney parks.

golf courses are turning "theme," with putting greens often built around a time period or scenic wonder. The success of theme parks is built on the "permission" granted to children and adults to forget the trials and tribulations of the real world and escape, momentarily, to a land of make-believe and fun.

Amusement Parks

Astroland Amusement Park in Coney Island, New York, Six Flags in several locations, and Canada's Wonderland in Ontario are a few of the larger-scale permanent amusement parks remaining in North America. **Amusement parks** have had to overcome their reputation for being run-down carnivals selling hot dogs and cotton candy, with tattooed ride operators and garbage-cluttered grounds. This image, which plagued amusement parks for many years, is one of the reasons Walt Disney designed his special theme park.

Today's amusement parks are touted as family entertainment centres with rides for the brave (stand-up roller coasters) and the not-so-brave (merry-go-rounds). One obvious trend, geared toward the computer-oriented youth of today, is to provide interactive computer games in a specially designed room that allows parents to sit for a moment and relax or get into the play themselves. Another important trend in amusement parks is to provide new, exciting rides or a new form of entertainment each year to bring back local clientele. The latest edition to the Disney U.S.A. properties, added in 2008, is an elaborate, interactive ride/game attraction based on *Toy Story*. During the ride experience, *Toy Story* characters like Buzz and Rex talk back to the audience and help riders play a variety of interactive games, competing for the highest score. The latest addition to Canada's Wonderland is one of the tallest, fastest roller coasters in Canada, which travels at speeds of 148 kph.

Amusement parks also feature live entertainment throughout the day, showcasing local and regional entertainers who usually come with a fan club of moms, dads, siblings, and friends who pay admission and increase park attendance. Nationally known entertainers are brought in to boost attendance three or four times during the summer season. Some family-style parks also offer interactive rides and activities for all ages, including the popular bumper cars and bumper boats, miniature golf, go-carts, and paintball. Petting zoos provide interaction with a variety of small and large animals. The Skytrek Adventure Park, located just outside Revelstoke, B.C., adds light adventure to outdoor activities. Included in the adult activities are zip lines, suspension bridges, canopy walks, and other physically challenging activities.

A park's largest expenditure, once it is open for business, is labour, with nearly 33% of total revenue going to the staff.[9] If a park is to stay on the leading edge of entertainment, it must invest in new rides or entertainment yearly. Clients will return if the quality of the experience meets their expectations, the attraction is clean, and the service staff is friendly, helpful, and knowledgable about the attraction.

Live Entertainment

If live entertainment is supplied by local talent, and promotion of the event remains local, the tourist draw will be minimal. For live entertainment to serve as a major tourist attraction, it must be promoted in tourist brochures and should be a regular, high-quality attraction throughout the tourism season. With competent marketing, word-of-mouth advertising will provide the extra tourist traffic.

Some communities thrive *because* of the live entertainment available to their audiences. For example, Nashville, Tennessee, with the Grand Ole Opry, has become a town somewhat dependent on country music.

Larger cities like New York, Boston, and Toronto have their Broadway-style productions, and gambling towns like Las Vegas have also been traditional places

FOOTPRINT

Disney Had It Right from the Start

"Conservation isn't just the business of a few people. It is a matter that concerns us all. It is a science whose principles are written in the oldest code in the world, the laws of nature. The natural resources of (the world) are not inexhaustible. But, if we use our riches wisely, if we protect our wildlife and preserve our lakes and forests and streams, these things will last us for generations to come."

Those sentiments were expressed by Walt Disney in 1950, before the world had come to the realization that our habits were destroying our ecosystem. Walt was honoured with many awards by early conservation pioneers like the Sierra Club for his work in helping create a more eco-conscious nation. He was one of the first people to use hydroponics to grow vegetables, and his hydroponic gardens at Epcot feed diners in his hotels and educate visitors to the gardens. Disney's Green Standard program has been developed for employees to provide suggestions on how to live a more ecologically aware life, from creating green workspaces to green dining. In alignment with Earth Day in 2008, Disney rolled out its most comprehensive internal environment standards, called Green Standards, with the goal of reducing the parks' operational impact on the environment.[8] This program is comprised of twenty distinct standards in four core areas that include workspace areas, meetings and events, travel, and dining. In 2005, Disney also released a green program focused on materials and waste management, successfully achieving results such as:

Energy conservation	- creation and use of a new paint for the hull of the *Disney's Wonder* cruise ship; the paint helps prohibit corrosion and minimizes friction with the water, which increases fuel efficiency - the first year of the program reduced energy use across Disney properties by 3%, the equivalent of 184 000 BTUs, valued at $1.8 million
Waste management	- composting of more than 2600 tonnes of animal waste generated by Disney's Animal Kingdom - since 1991, Walt Disney World (WDW) has recycled over 850 000 tonnes of material that would have gone into landfills
Water conservation	- reclaimed water at WDW has provided a savings of $2 million per year - the volume of processed water has not increased despite the growth of the park over the past fifteen years. Although the volume of water used has risen due to guest consumption, park operations uses reclaimed water to clean the streets and for cooling and irrigation, helping control the impact on the ecosystem

Tokyo Disney Resort (TDR) has been recognized as the strongest participant in the Green Standard program. They not only meet all of the standards set by the Disney Corporation, but they go further by recycling 53% of their waste products.

to go for live entertainment. Other communities have started their own local theatres, restoring old buildings and recreating the time when community theatre— plays, dancing, and singing—was all the entertainment that was available to the public.

Summer theatres, running from April through October, are found in every province. Canada's most famous summer theatre is the Stratford Shakespeare Festival in Stratford, Ontario. Sitting on the banks of the Avon River, the picturesque small town provides visitors with a peaceful reprieve from the stress of daily living, as well as a wide choice of live theatre, ranging from musicals to Shakespearean drama. The town and surrounding areas are a shopper's paradise and boast some of the finest restaurants in Canada.

Another beautiful town in Ontario is Niagara-on-the-Lake, home to the Shaw Festival—the only theatre in the world to specialize in the plays of George Bernard Shaw and his contemporaries. Nestled in wine country, twenty minutes from spectacular Niagara Falls, Niagara-on-the-Lake is the 1996 winner of the "Prettiest Town in Canada" award.[10]

Gaming

Gaming and gambling have been around for millennia, appearing in early societies including ancient China, Egypt, and Europe. Today, gambling is a popular and controversial form of recreation. In North America, there are four types of gambling: parimutuel wagering, lotteries, non-profit organization gambling (mainly bingo and raffles), and casinos. In Canada, the total revenue earned from all government controlled gambling, excluding prizes and winnings, totalled $13.67 billion dollars in 2008, a 400% increase over a sixteen-year period.[11]

Because lotteries, bingos, and raffles have limited clientele, they usually do not increase the flow of tourists into a town. Casinos and parimutuel betting, however, are a different matter. **Casino gambling** includes slot machines, roulette, craps (dice), baccarat, blackjack (twenty-one), and other games of chance. Casino gambling has stimulated such growth in Las Vegas that the city now has eight out of the ten biggest hotels in the world. Casino gambling is also a popular pastime on cruise ships, riverboats, and ferries, particularly when those vessels travel through international waters.

Casino gambling has only been widely available to Canadians in the past two decades. The development of a casino may be seen as a tourism draw; however, it is not always warmly welcomed by the community. For example, the 1996 opening of the Casino du Lac-Leamy in Gatineau, Quebec, raised some concerns: residents did not experience the full benefits of a stronger local economy and there was a high rate of personal and small-business bankruptcy in the region. Established regional bingo halls experienced a dramatic decline in business and were forced to shut their doors; these operations traditionally supported many local charities and their absence had a strong local impact. However, the casino complex has proven to be a strong attractor for visitors, and locals have begun to see more jobs as additional development and tourism revenues impact the community.

Niagara Fallsview Casino and Casino Windsor, on the other hand, illustrate how communities can immediately see benefits from a casino. Both establishments enjoy success due to their proximity to the U.S. border; the Fallsview Casino has the added benefit of overlooking the falls. The resort has over 3000 slot machines, 150 gaming tables, a five-star hotel and spa with 368 rooms, a 1500-seat theatre, and 50 000 square feet of convention space.

Parimutuel gambling is a betting pool in which those who bet on the winners of the first three places also share the stakes of the losers, minus a percentage for management. Parimutuel betting takes place on harness racing in Ontario, Quebec, and the Maritimes. People dine in the fine-food facilities at the track and watch drivers race in two-wheeled carts pulled by horses. Parimutuel betting also occurs across North America on greyhound dog races, quarter-horse and thoroughbred horse races, trotter and pacer horse races, and jai alai, a court game similar to handball.

The Kentucky Derby is the best-known horse race in North America. Part of the excitement of parimutuel betting is the atmosphere at the racetrack. Patrons can dine in exclusive restaurants while watching the event, or munch on nachos and hot dogs in the stands with thousands of other eager bettors. Betting has become a social event that lasts for an evening out on the town, or for a few days, and is an added attraction to visitors.

What effect will long-term legalized gambling have on communities in North America? Some people feel that the social problems caused by gambling, along with the rise in crime linked to gambling, have been downplayed. However, casinos have been proactive in dealing with these concerns, and many will, on request from a self-acknowledged problem gambler, bar the customer from the casino for a given period of time. It seems clear that the economic benefits often vastly outweigh these criticisms. It will be interesting to see whether gambling slowly loses its appeal or whether it proves to be an economic solution for some of our Canadian communities.

Tourists who visit Alberta make it a point to visit West Edmonton Mall, the fifth largest shopping centre in the world and the largest mall in North America. This attraction receives over 30 million visitors annually and takes up the physical space of 48 city blocks.[12]
(Photo courtesy Canadian Tourism Commission.)

Shopping

Shopping has always been popular with tourists, so it is not surprising that shopping itself has developed into an independent attraction. Tourists to Edmonton put the West Edmonton Mall on their must-see lists; a trip to Halifax is commemorated with the purchase of a souvenir. With the building of malls, shopping has become regionalized, drawing customers from as far as 500 km away. Mall shopping has become an annual or monthly event for many families. Most cities with regional shopping malls have other forms of entertainment, such as museums, theatres, amusement parks, swimming, or other outdoor recreation. Some malls are becoming the primary attraction by providing entertainment in their corridors and parking lots. Special events have become so important that many malls hire special events coordinators to arrange daily and weekly entertainment, contests, and food festivals.

Increasingly popular are **mega-malls**, huge shopping and entertainment centres with everything from retail stores and restaurants to indoor theme parks, game rooms, and small theatres. To keep people from migrating to warm climates such as Arizona, Florida, and California, cities in Canada and the northern United States are eyeing the mega-mall as a venue for year-round recreation opportunities. The mega-mall could become an enclosed city. The West Edmonton Mall is about the size of eighty-five football fields and has 110 eating places, 900 shops, and ten feature attractions, including an amusement park, skating rink, swimming pool, miniature golf course, and theme hotel. Opened in 1981, the West Edmonton Mall remained the world's largest shopping mall until 2004 and earned a listing in *The Guinness Book of Records.* It currently welcomes over 30 million visitors annually.[13]

Historic marketplaces are another interesting concept. They are often located in the historic part of a city's waterfront, remodelled to suit small boutiques, fresh produce outlets, and food service facilities. Tourists can buy regional crafts and combine a little history with their recreational shopping. Halifax, Saint John, Vancouver, Winnipeg, New York City, Boston, Baltimore, and San Francisco all have well-known historic waterfront marketplaces. Another trend in shopping is the factory outlet store. North Carolina has long been known for the bargains found in its factory outlets, which feature brand-name furniture, clothing, sheets, and towels. Many factory outlets have revitalized the small towns near which they are located.

Charter buses and tours will make it a point to stop at shopping areas such as mega-malls, waterfront shops, or factory outlets. Shopping as an attraction can be a financial boon for an entire region and will continue to provide travellers with an added site to visit.

In Practice

Identify one public, one non-profit, and one private attraction in your area. How do they differ in advertising, price, type of visitors, and service quality? What new attraction would be successful in your community? Why would it succeed? What are the risks?

One of nature's most intriguing experiences: the tide coming in at Hopewell Rocks, NB.
(Photo courtesy Canadian Tourism Commission.)

In Practice

Do a quick SWOT analysis of one of your regional attractions by identifying its **S**trengths and **W**eaknesses, **O**pportunities it could take advantage of, and **T**hreats to its continued success.

CASE STUDY

Promoting the "Yap"

In downtown Ottawa, the curious visitor to the Bank of Canada building will find a small, privately owned museum known as one of the capital's "hidden gems." The Currency Museum, located off the lobby of the original building, provides an interesting insight into Canadian currency from early times to the present. It also has an impressive collection of foreign currencies dating back to ancient times. The museum is one of the few that does not charge admission, and guided tours are available. Even *Ripley's Believe It or Not* has taken the time to explore the museum, especially to see its special exhibit—the "Yap Stone." The huge round stone is two metres in diameter and weighs about three tonnes. It was used as currency on Yap, one of the Caroline Islands in the South Pacific, although most of their coinage was slightly smaller. The Bank of Canada would like to increase the number of visitors it welcomes on a yearly basis, but this has been difficult as the museum is hard to find and has little recognition.

1. What target market do you think this type of museum might attract?
2. What services should be available to visitors?
3. How would you get tourists to take thirty minutes to check out this free museum located directly across from Parliament? Describe three different tactics you would design to increase the interest of tourists.
4. If the citizens of Ottawa were more aware of the Currency Museum, how do you think that knowledge would improve visitation to the museum?

Summary

- Attractions are a subset of the recreation and entertainment sector of tourism.
- Attractions provide a reason for visitors to travel or explore a region; they pique interest and give people cause to travel.
- Regionally, attractions add to the quality of life for the community. They can positively affect a local economy through tourism revenue both directly and through additional spending by visitors on transportation, accommodations, and food.
- Many of Canada's attractions build upon our vast natural resources, rich cultural heritage, and diversity.
- Museums, parks, and zoos flourish in most every province, celebrating each region's history and character.

- There is an ongoing balancing between preserving the past and embracing the future; this balancing act is seen in the decisions made around preserving historical sites, renovating older museums, and the development of modern galleries, casinos and mega-malls.
- Although Canada faces the challenge of changing seasons, amusement parks still thrive, including the famous Canada's Wonderland.
- Attractions, as a subsector, will need to be responsive to changing consumer demands and interests. Without well-supported attractions, destinations can lose their appeal to travellers who no longer find certain locations desirable to visit.

Questions

1. Create a table that identifies the following pieces of information:
   a) four public, four non-profit, and four private attractions in your area
   b) a brief description of their products and activities
   c) three ways in which each attraction helps fund its operations
   d) a special event each attraction has used to attract new and repeat visitors

2. a) The gaming industry is growing in all regions of North America. List the gambling options offered in your region and the type of gaming each one represents.
   b) Do you see the gaming industry as a positive influence on tourism? Defend your answer, using examples.

3. Is shopping a true tourist attraction? Defend your answer with examples.

4. Define the following terms as they relate to the attractions industry: *amusement park*, *theme park*, *UNESCO World Heritage Site*, *site-specific museum*, *children's museum*, and *oceanarium*.

Notes

1. http://icom.museum/who-we-are/the-vision/museum-definition.html.

2. www.warmuseum.ca.

3. Ibid.

4. www.ksan.org.html/village.htm.

5. M. Prentice *Tourism and Heritage Attractions* (London: Routledge, 1993).

6. Patricia MacKay, "Theme parks: USA," *Theatre Crafts*, September 1977, p. 56.

7. James M. Cameron and Ronald Bordessa, *Wonderland through the Looking Glass* (Maple, ON: Belsten Publishing, 1982), p. 71.

8. http://corporate.disney.go.com/citizenship/thegreenstandard.html.

9. *1990 Amusement Industry Abstract* (Alexandria, VA: International Association of Amusement Parks and Attractions, February, 1991), p. 5.

10. *Maclean's*, September 1996.

11. www.statcan.gc.ca/pub/75-001-x/2010108/pdf/11297-eng.pdf.

12. www.wem.ca/#/about-wem/facts.

13. Ibid.

Adventure Tourism and Outdoor Recreation

Key terms

adventure tourism
carrying capacity
Crown land
ecotourism
ecotourist

Green Plan
hard adventure
outdoor recreation
Parks Canada
recreational sports

responsible tourism
soft adventure
sustainable tourism

Learning objectives

Having read this chapter you will be able to

1. Describe adventure tourism and provide examples of both hard and soft adventure activities.

2. Outline the role played by Environment Canada and Parks Canada in this industry.

3. Discuss the issues around *ecotourism* and *sustainable tourism.*

4. Compare the two opposing views of tourism's impact on the environment.

5. Explain how tourism can negatively affect the environment and why the concept of *carrying capacity* is important to tourists, tourism businesses, and the environment.

6. Discuss how government and business can implement sustainable tourism.

When it comes to beautiful landscapes and interesting plant and animal life, Canada already has a strong image in the minds of travellers both domestically and abroad. However, more often than not, our images are dominated by ice and snow; people perceive Canada as a winter destination. Snow-capped mountains, polar bears, and huge icebergs are all familiar pictures of the Canadian landscape. Although Canada has hosted both summer and winter Olympic Games, in the last twenty-five years we have hosted the winter games twice. The media attention did not dispel the vision of Canada as a cold but interesting place. Selling Canada as a four-season destination can be difficult.

Canada is a country that must deal with distinct, often extreme seasons, and whether we like it or not, the arrival of snow cuts tourism figures dramatically. Still, our landscape provides some of the world's best all-season adventure tourism and outdoor experiences, which makes adventure tourism and outdoor recreation (ATOR) a major motivator in attracting tourists. Busy lifestyles and stress make vacations an important part of staying healthy. Our bodies and minds gain strength from relaxation and the chance to unwind. People often relax by getting away from work and their busy lives for a short period of time and doing something enjoyable. For those with a healthy lifestyle, ATOR is front and centre when vacation plans are made and customers look for attractive and interesting activities. This component of the tourism sector, which includes adventure tourism, ecotourism, and outdoor recreation, is now a trillion dollar industry worldwide.[1]

PARKS AND CROWN LANDS

Canada's National Parks System

Parks Canada is this country's steward of hundreds of key sites of natural beauty, cultural significance, and historical importance. This agency reports to the minister of the environment. "National parks are a country-wide system of representative natural areas of Canadian significance. By law, they are protected for public understanding, appreciation, and enjoyment while being maintained in an unimpaired state for future generations."[2]

The national parks system was inaugurated in 1885, when 26 km^2 on the slopes of Sulphur Mountain in Banff were set aside to be protected for future generations. Between 1887 and 1915, five more parks were established in the western regions: Yoho, Glacier, Mount Revelstoke, Waterton Lakes, and Jasper. The St. Lawrence Islands National Park was the first in Eastern Canada. Today, Canada has forty-two national parks representing twenty-four out of thirty-nine natural regions, and the Canadian government has set aside an additional sixty-seven natural regions to be held under its protection—thirty-nine land-based and twenty-eight marine-based. In addition, 12% of Crown land now falls under the protection of Parks Canada, taking it out of the hands of provincial authorities. The federal government's final goal is to establish national parks in each of the distinct ecosystems found in Canada.

www.pc.gc.ca

Mandates of Parks Canada

Parks Canada does more than just manage the national parks system; it manages, four national marine conservation areas, one national landmark in the Northwest Territories, and 167 of the over 950 nationally designated historic sites in

Canada. It oversees operation of our seven historic canal systems and coordinates the federal–provincial co-operative program for the Canadian Heritage River Systems. It directs and implements heritage tourism opportunities and programs, and it provides services to the more than 20 million visitors who use the national parks system every year. Our national parks are seen abroad as the iconic images that make Canada a unique travel destination.

In 2007, Parks Canada won two prestigious awards for the consistent quality of its products (our national parks and sites) and for maintaining a high level of praise from visitors by earning an overall 90% satisfaction rate. It was recognized as "Business of the Year" by the Tourism Industry Association of Canada (TIAC), and in London, England, received the World Travel Market Global Award.

On October 17, 2011, the province of Nova Scotia and the Government of Canada signed an agreement designing Sable Island as Canada's forty-third national park. Nova Scotia's Premier Dexter was "pleased that the island's natural and cultural values will be forever protected through its status as a national park reserve."[3] Peter Kent, the Minister of the Environment, observed that this agreement would "ensure that this iconic and valued Canadian landscape, fabled for its wild horses, shipwrecks and one of the largest dune systems in eastern Canada, will be protected."[4]

Management Plans of Parks Canada

The friction between the desire to use our national parklands and the need to protect them began with the establishment of the first national park in 1885. Today, the emphasis is clearly moving from use to maintenance and protection. This does not eliminate the parks as a destination for visitors, but it does change the way Parks Canada approaches its duties. There are many demands made on our land by big businesses, which range from logging, mining, and extracting oil to tourism ventures and environmental protection. Parks Canada must find a balance to ensure those on all sides of the issue are fairly treated.

The agency recognizes that one of its biggest challenges will be maintaining the integrity of the parks' ecosystems. Ecosystems that have integrity are defined as having "their native components intact, including the physical elements (e.g., water, rocks); biodiversity (composition and abundance of species and communities in an ecosystem, e.g., rainforest, grasslands, black bears, brook trout, and black spruce); and ecosystem processes (the engines that make the ecosystem work; e.g., fire, flooding, predation)."[5] Parks Canada must be assured that native species can handle the rates of change forecast without significant damages or loss when the areas are in use. Conservation of each ecosystem must be based on sound scientific principles, not based on specific demands. Parks Canada also recognizes that any use of the land will cause prime environmental damage. Their focus is on a system's ability to regenerate itself.

Stressors

Any event that causes the alteration to an environmental habitat or demise of a species is called a *stressor*, and the intensity is determined by the type and degree of invasion. Easily identified external stressors are the building of roads, establishment of businesses, or increased use of land by people (see the box on the next page).

Damage is also caused by the invasion of alien species. Some predators are common, such as English ivy, but others, such as the pine beetle currently destroying B.C.'s forests, are truly alien. Environment Canada estimates that the annual loss to the Canadian economy by just 16 invasive alien species is in the tens of billions of dollars.[6] In addition, the overall state of the global ecosystem is causing irreversible damage. Global warming has already changed snow and ice conditions in the far North, causing glaciers to retreat; higher sea levels and stronger storm surges are eroding shorelines. Other effects are felt, too—the change in migration habits of both birds and mammals, the loss of grasslands due to drought, and the shifting of plants and animals due to changes in habitat.

How is Parks Canada approaching this problem? If a region has shown an ability to regenerate, reversing damage may simply be a matter of changing usage boundaries. At other times, the region affected may require the reintroduction of native species (e.g., Alberta wolves have been successfully reintroduced to states like Montana and Wyoming) to stabilize it. It may mean attempting to remove a specific alien species such as the zebra mussels that have invaded the Great Lakes, but this is almost impossible once the territory has been invaded. At times, it may mean taking drastic steps, such as using fire or flooding to remove an alien species. However, it may be as straightforward as replacing wheat fields in Grasslands National Park with native prairie grasses. One thing is clear—Canada's *National Parks Act* makes maintenance or restoration of ecological integrity a first priority in park management, and that may mean slowing the use of parklands by tourists.

Major External and Internal Stressors Facing Canada's Parks[7]

Habitat loss—the conversion of land into urban centres or farmlands has seriously affected the natural habitat for many species.

Habitat fragmentation—remaining habitats are broken apart by the development of communities, travel routes, and other facilities; species are cut off from their normal environmental areas, and habitats transected by roads and rail systems create danger points that result in significant loss of wildlife.

Large carnivores—are disappearing or have disappeared due to the impact of human development and interaction within their habitat; reductions in the number of large carnivores are destroying the natural predator–prey relationships.

Air pollution—airborne pollutants affect all living creatures and alter existing habitats, especially the smaller at-risk animals that form an important part of the feeding cycle.

Pesticides—pesticides that have been used outside of the protected parks have been discovered in both the plant and animal life within the parks; high mercury and toxaphene levels continue to be found in many species.

Alien species—invasive, non-native species that attack local plants and animals spread unimpeded because they have no local enemies.

Overuse—Canadian parks are in high demand, with use exceeding carrying capacities; this results in damage to land, facilities, and water systems; careful monitoring is required to control overuse.

Provincial Parks Systems

In addition to national parks, each province has created its own protected areas— natural habitats governed by ministries such as British Columbia's Ministry of Environment, Lands, and Parks. The demands on and damage to their ecosystems are similar to parks under federal protection, and each province is responsible for the management of these lands and for the safety of its visitors.

National parks in Canada have tight restrictions on what a person using the land may or may not do, and many provinces are equally protective of their parks. British Columbia limits the number of participants who may trek the West Coast Trail in the Pacific Rim National Park Reserve and ensures that the strict rules of use for this specific land area are adhered to by hikers. Some of the more popular provincial camps now require advance registration before use. Park attendants patrol on land and water to ensure that users obey the rules and regulations, issue warnings when severe weather is approaching, and determine if weather conditions make open fires unsafe. Provincial administrations maintain all public access such as roads, bridges, and campgrounds, and often provide rest areas and picnic tables for daytime visitors. Most parks have plans detailing future development in the region, ensuring the preservation and wise use of these protected lands.

Crown Lands

Unlike in many other countries around the world, much of our Canadian wilderness is not privately owned but is designated **Crown land**—that is, land owned by the federal or provincial government. National and provincial parks are Crown land that has been set aside and protected by legislation governing use and development. Much of our Crown land, however, has no legislation covering its use, which makes it attractive to visitors who prefer fewer restrictions on their vacations. Crown land may be leased (under tenure) or purchased by private organizations such as logging companies or tourism businesses. Conflict over the use of Crown land is bound to arise. For example, a clear-cut logging operation, despite reforestation programs, will blight the landscape for many years and conflict with tourism development.

Crown land is important to ATOR because a great deal of adventure tourism takes place on Crown land. For example, British Columbia is Canada's third-largest province, covering an area of 94.8 million hectares. Of this area, 92% is provincial Crown land, 1% is federal Crown land, 5% is privately owned, and 2% is covered by fresh water. These proportions are fairly typical of provinces in Canada. Of B.C.'s Crown land, approximately two-thirds (59 million hectares) is public forest and provides the basis for much of B.C.'s recreational activity. The province has begun a series of initiatives to increase the use of Crown lands for environmentally sound economic development and community uses.

In all provinces, Crown lands form the basis of much of our outdoor recreational activities, and many hunting and fishing lodges, campsites, and resorts make good use of this land, its rivers, and its lakes. Tourism is seen as a "green" sector, meaning the protection of the land it uses is paramount to the continued quality of the tourism experience. Canada remains active at world conferences on ecology and sustainability and has a growing concern about development when considering our beautiful, untouched lands.

ADVENTURE TOURISM

Adventure tourism is commonly divided into two distinct types, with a sliding scale of intensity between the two: hard adventure and soft adventure.

Hard Adventure

Hard adventure is identified by four criteria:

a) It is usually a strenuous activity requiring training prior to the experience. People who enjoy this type of activity train daily to maintain body strength and flexibility.

b) It often requires some sort of equipment. If the activity is life-threatening, the participant will use their own, trusted equipment.

c) It requires that a person take on risk. A novice should be well prepared and travel with an experienced guide.

d) Hard adventure usually occurs in a more remote region of the land, where nature is relatively untouched and activities are more challenging as a result.

People who enjoy this type of vacation will pay handsomely for the trip, and the greater the challenge, the more satisfaction they gain from the experience. Canada has many hard adventure challenges, but the ones with the most global recognition are found in other areas around the world—climbing Mt. Everest, canoeing the Amazon, crossing the Pacific Ocean in a one-person sailboat, and treks into the cold of the deep North.

Whitewater rafting is a popular and enjoyable hard adventure challenge in Canada available throughout the country.
(Photo: VILevi/Fotolia)

Everest may provide us with a fitting example of hard adventure and a number of Canadians have successfully reached the summit. Everest, the highest mountain in the world at 8848 m, was not "conquered" until 1953, with the ascent of New Zealand climber Sir Edmund Hillary and Tenzing Norgay, a Nepalese climber. Since their success, many people continue to challenge Mount Everest, peaking throughout the year 2010 when 542 people successfully made the ascent up Everest.[8] The first severe risk a team meets is the slowly moving glacier, the Khumbu Falls, and risks increase as the air thins and climbers have less oxygen and become physically exhausted. Still, people try for the top every year. Their reason? Because it is there.

Of course, not all hard adventure means climbing a mountain. Rivers such as the Nahanni provide challenging, hard adventure activities for the enthusiast. Tourists may be flown into a rustic lodge that acts as home base, but once they are on the river, their survival depends on how well they can handle their craft, the river, and the wilderness. No soft bed awaits them at the end of the day, and meals are not catered. Accidents and injuries may be life-threatening. The tourist who chooses this type of trip feels a sense of self-discovery and accomplishment once the trip has been completed.

Canada is full of interesting opportunities: heli-skiing, ice climbing, spelunking (caving), sea kayaking, and whitewater rafting. Along the coast of Newfoundland, adventurers can paddle out to the icebergs that frequently float by the shoreline. British Columbia hosts one of Canada's most unusual winter sports—winter surfing. Surfing along the West Coast can be a challenge at any time of the year, but especially when winter storms hit. Canadians first started riding the winter waves in the 1940s, and more than 4000 surfing enthusiasts brave the frigid waves and the cyclonic winds every winter.

Soft Adventure

Soft adventure has some of the thrills of hard adventure but lacks the need to pre-train, has much of the risk factor removed, and has provided facilities to make the "adventurer" more comfortable along the way. Soft adventure may provide vehicles to move the visitor to the activity, comfortable shelter and bedding, and possibly even a cook. The scale that slides between the two activities subtracts "luxuries" and adds risk.

A climb that might be in on the outer realm of "softer" adventure is the trek up Mt. Kilimanjaro (5895 m) in Tanzania. The path is well maintained and there are stopping stations along the way for rest and refreshment. However, the mountain is high enough to cause pulmonary edema, a deadly reaction of the body to climbing too high, too fast, causing the lungs to fill with water and making breathing difficult and causing death.

Normally, soft adventure has much of the risk removed because companies who specialize in soft adventure have studiously worked to control risks to their guests. This doesn't mean that people who participate in these soft adventure activities will never get hurt, but with the proper equipment and trained leaders, soft adventure can be both exciting and safe. The CTC states that 23% of outdoor activities link to soft adventure, and the average age of participants is 18 to 44.[9]

Baby boomers are just discovering soft adventure. Some soft adventures might include cross-country skiing in Austria, visiting the Great Wall of China, swimming

Fresh Air Adventure in Alma, New Brunswick, provides guests with an open water experience atop the highest tides in the world.
(Photo: Fresh Air Adventure.)

www.gapadventures.com

with dolphins in the Caribbean, or whitewater rafting with a guide. The key to planning this type of adventure is to determine the amount of effort and risk demanded from the participant in order to enjoy the activity. Canadian entrepreneurs continue to expand adventure tourism to meet new market demands. Gone is the image of retirees shuffling off to sit in rocking chairs. This market is looking for adventure without the physical demands of hard adventure, so soft adventure looks to be a good source of income for the ATOR industry over the next twenty-five years.

Ecotourism

Ecotourism is defined as "responsible travel to natural areas which conserve the environment and improves the well-being of local people."[10] More simply stated, it teaches the participant the importance of understanding and conserving the world's ecosystems and habitats as well as maintaining the benefits of tourism within the local community. Surveys have shown that **ecotourists** are generally more mature, have post-secondary education, prefer longer trips (eight to fourteen days), and are willing to pay a higher price for this style of tourism.[11]

Sustainable tourism is "the informed partnership of all relevant stakeholders constantly assessing impacts and introducing the necessary corrective measures to ensure a meaningful experience to the tourists, raising their awareness and promoting sustainable tourism practices."[12] Sustainable tourism links all of the partners in the ecotourism experience, ensuring that the current visitor enjoys the experience without compromising the ability of future generations to do the same. Developing a sustainable product that is ecologically sound is called **responsible tourism**.

Specific criteria determine whether you are taking part in responsible tourism or not. Both the tourism supplier and consumer have responsibilities, which should include the following:

- minimizing the negative economic and environmental effects
- generating greater economic benefits for local people and enhancing the well-being of host communities
- improving working conditions and access to the industry
- involving local people in decisions that affect their lives and life changes
- making positive contributions to the conservation of natural and cultural heritage and embracing diversity
- providing a more enjoyable experience for tourists through more meaningful connections with local cultural, social, and environmental issues
- providing access for physically challenged people

Being culturally sensitive encourages respect between tourists and hosts, and builds local pride and confidence.

The best tool to ensure sustainability and responsibility, many believe, is through environmental legislation—and enforcement. The Yukon has done just that, putting in place a tough wilderness tourism licensing law that requires companies to have a permit to conduct adventure tours—one that can be revoked if a company does not follow strict *low impact camping* techniques. Low impact camping requires that every item carried into the wilderness be carried out, that every item created during the trip be carried out, that campers use only enclosed fires and biodegradable products, and that campsites be returned to their original state by smoothing out the leaves and replacing any items that have been moved during the stay. Not only is the legislation tough, but the fines are large.

www.vancouverisland-outdoors.com

Concern for the environment and a love of the outdoors have made biking vacations popular. (Photo courtesy Canadian Tourism Commission.)

Two other growing areas of interest are cultural tourism and heritage tourism. Cultural tourism immerses the visitor in the natural history, human heritage, arts, philosophies, and institutions of another culture. It also educates the visitor in the architecture, food, and folklore or religion of the culture. About 11% of our visitors can be defined as heritage travellers, and they tend to come from empty nest homes (children are gone). As with ecotourism, many of these travellers have diplomas or degrees.

Heritage tourism usually combines several activities in the trip, including visits to historic sites, museums, and events. Families will also include activities appropriate for the age of the children. Most vacations include a component that might be called "cultural tourism" because it is difficult to travel to another region and not enjoy some of their cultural/historical sites and events.

Wildlife in Canada provides many tourists with both amusing snapshots and more frightening ones. This one shows Newfoundland puffins on parade.
(Photo: Rolf Hicker Photography/Alamy.)

Risk Management

In this age of litigation, tourism companies are discovering that insurance policies alone do not provide adequate financial or legal coverage if a customer is injured or killed while under their care. A risk management program is not created just for hard adventure activities, but should be in place for all tourism endeavours. Risk management identifies all potential hazards customers may encounter and it reviews the products, services, and processes used in delivering them.

Risk management should provide historical data on past accidents or losses, and identify possible risk scenarios in the future. Each risk should then be analyzed carefully, noting frequency, possible loss ratios, the impact of the loss to the customer, and how the incident will affect public perception of the business or activity. At this point, the company should consider each risk and how a staff member should respond if a crisis arises. Included in this list should be the proper safety standards as set out by the manufacturer of any equipment used; also the staff must know the safety standards handbook created by the company and be trained to handle situations according to management's directives. Environmental risks must be minimal, and emergency plans must be tested and in place. Signage identifying all risks must be clear and readily visible, and should alert users to the following:

- the obvious dangers of the activity (e.g., whether not following all safety precautions may result in injury or death)
- any unusual dangers of the activity (e.g., high water levels)
- dangers that apply to specific consumers (e.g., whether a trail requires a high level of expertise, experience, and physical stamina)

Some might say that there is no need to worry about risk management if it is common knowledge that the activities your company provides have inherent risks. But having a solid risk management plan in place can also improve business operations, including possible reductions in insurance costs when you provide the insurance company with documented proof of your high standard of care. Many colleges and universities now offer risk management courses in their tourism programs. Risk management has become a core skill for any tourism business.[13]

OUTDOOR RECREATION

Recreational sports and **outdoor recreation** are big business in North America. If Canadians are to stay healthy and fit with outdoor exercise throughout the year, then the seasons dictate that they must engage in more than one sport. This benefits both the equipment suppliers and the tourism sector. A change of season means a tourist may return to enjoy a resort at different times of the year for entirely different purposes: hiking, playing tennis, or golfing in the summer; skiing, snowboarding, or skating in the winter.

Canada marked the new millennium with the creation of a continuous trail that joins the country from Newfoundland and the Atlantic Ocean to Nunavut and the Arctic, ending at the Pacific Ocean in British Columbia. The project has been designed and built by Canadian associations that represent many outdoor recreational activities such as hiking and cross-country skiing. The Trans Canada Trail (TCT), which is the longest trail of its kind in the world, covers 16 000 km, winds through every province and territory, and provides outdoor enthusiasts with five core activities: walking, cycling, horseback riding, cross-country skiing, and snowmobiling. The Trans Canada Trail Foundation, a non-profit charitable organization, funded the building of the trail with government grants and donations from local businesses and individuals across Canada. The trail is maintained by communities, and the shared experience of building and maintaining the trail has strengthened the tie that binds Canadians—a love of the outdoors.[14]

Winter Sports

Some winter sports enthusiasts claim Canada has the best snow conditions in the world, and that attracts European, Asian, and Australian ski and snowboard enthusiasts. We have some state-of-the-art ski jumps and skating rinks in Alberta and British Columbia as reminders of the Winter Olympics of both 1988 and 2010. These help train athletes from around the world. The West is also known for its incredible powder skiing. Powder Springs Resort in Revelstoke, B.C., has some of the best big-mountain heli-skiing in the world. The lure of virgin powder and a big drop prompt enthusiasts to pay $1000+ per day.

While skiing has always played an important role in keeping Canadians fit over the winter season, so has skating. Currently, Canada has two "rinks" vying for a place in *The Guinness Book of Records*: the Rideau Canal in Ottawa and Lake Winnipeg in Manitoba.

Of course, the most popular and authentically Canadian winter sport is hockey, which is so much a part of this country's identity that it was recognized as Canada's national winter sport by an act of Parliament in 1994.[15] Hockey is the winter sport most participated in by Canadians; from the backyard to the major professional rink, hockey even remains a popular Canadian sport right through the summer with street hockey.

Snowmobiling, dog sledding, curling, tobogganing, ice sailing, and ice climbing—this is just a partial list of sports available to keep you in shape during the winter. Give Canadians a little snow and they'll find a great way to use it! Most of our snow sports are for domestic tourists. We don't get a large number of U.S. visitors to our hills, as they have fabulous high mountains too, but Europeans are beginning to discover Canada. With temperatures slowly rising, the ski hills in Austria and Switzerland are finding snow a disappearing commodity. Many Europeans prefer the Canadian ski resorts because of their international flavour and rate them higher than U.S. ski hills for quality of snow and runs.

For the winter athlete, Canada offers some unique events, including the Raid International Ukatak in January. Four-person racing teams from around the globe travel across a 40-km course that tests both their endurance and skills. Over the five-day race, participants use snowshoes, cross-country skis, mountain bikes, and ice canoes (canoes with blades on the bottom).

In February, two major events take place: the Canadian Ski Marathon, and the Yukon Quest International Sled Dog Race. Nearly 2000 skiers take part in the ski marathon, which covers a 160-km trail from Lachute in the Laurentian Mountains to Buckingham, Quebec, just outside the national capital region. The Yukon Quest follows the historic gold rush trail from Whitehorse to Fairbanks, Alaska. It is billed as the world's toughest dogsled race, and covers 1600 km of wild winter terrain.

For tourists who might enjoy lying flat on their backs while careening down a mountainside at 50 kph to the roar of steel runners against compact snow, there is the wonderful world of the natural luge. Although it is an activity that dates back to the early nineteenth century, natural luge has been a fringe winter sport in Canada for fewer than twenty years. Unlike the modern luge used at the Winter Olympic Games, the natural luge's steel edges are kept flat on the ground and riders steer with reins and flexible foot-driven wooden levers. North America's first dedicated commercial natural luge course is at Mount Washington Alpine Resort on Vancouver Island. Ontario residents can try Rodle Mountain Luge Training Centre, located near Bancroft.[16]

Spring, Summer, and Fall Sports

Hunting and fishing play an integral part in the lives of Aboriginal Canadians and are major revenue generators for the tourism sector. About 5% of Canadians and 6% of Americans use their vacations enjoying these two sports. Hunters and fishers purchase equipment, lodging, food, and transportation. Freshwater sport fishing alone grosses over $650 million annually for the tourism sector.[17]

For the best experience, hunters and fishers know that they must travel into the remote regions of a province. Fly-in fishing camps in the northern regions of all provinces appeal to the true fisher. Deep, pristine lakes, with a wide variety of fish species, are particularly attractive to the U.S. market. Accessibility of the lake or forest region often determines the quality of the sport fishing or hunting. Hunting and fishing guides with an intimate knowledge of the area may be used to further ensure a good trip. Provinces grant licences for both hunting and fishing, placing limits on the hunting season and the number of animals that may be taken. Park rangers patrol northern highways and randomly stop those leaving the area to check that limits have been respected.

Although the popularity of fishing continues to grow in North America, hunting is fast losing its appeal with the younger market; however, hunting plays an important role in maintaining healthy numbers of wildlife, including bears, deer, and ducks. In national parks, hunting and fishing regulations are made at the federal level, and Parks Canada personnel are responsible for selling the appropriate licences and enforcing regulations.

Camping More than 14% of all Canadian vacations are camping trips, and 9.2% of U.S. travellers camp out on vacation.[20] Our parks system encourages camping by providing a number of different services. In some parks, tourists will find interpretive centres to help them understand the region's ecosystem; small stores that provide environmentally safe soaps, firewood, and other products; and sometimes huts with shower stalls. Advance reservations are advisable for camping in a provincial park, especially at popular parks in the summer. Although camping experiences vary greatly between major campgrounds with facilities and wilderness sites, gaining knowledge of the area and its dangers should be part of any pre-camp planning.

Golf In Canada, golf remains one of the most popular sports. As baby boomers age and move into retirement, more are choosing to walk the greens of a local golf course or to fashion a winter vacation around one of the golf resorts in the southern United States. About 5% of Canadian travellers and 7% of U.S. travellers pick up their clubs while on vacation.[21] About 2.2 million golfers take to the

Despite warnings, tourists are willing to take chances for that perfect picture.
(Photo courtesy Canadian Tourism Commission.)

SNAPSHOT

Bruce Poon Tip—"Do the Right Thing"

Drawing on his travels through Thailand in 1990, Bruce Poon Tip returned to Canada with a passion to create a company built around authentic and sustainable tourism. His experiences travelling through Asia influenced his vision of a kind of travel that was impactful for both those visiting a region as well as the hosts of the destination. In his heart, he knew that people would be interested in adventure-based trips throughout the world that were memorable and meaningful.[18]

From this vision, Gap Adventures was born. Poon Tip began building and leading tours to different countries, creating memorable journeys that created real connections between his customers and the people they visited. As his business grew, both increased customer demand and the depth of regional engagement jumped. In response, he established a series of Chief 'Experience' Officers in other countries, experts of their particular regions. Poon Tip's focus on environmental issues, authentic experiences, and sustainable tourism initially put him at odds with typical industry practices. He prevailed and has been continually recognized for both his strong business skills and environmental focus.[19] His company has been named in the Top 100 Employers and 50 Best Managed Companies lists, and Poon Tip received an award for being one of Canada's Top 40 Under 40. Today, his company, now called G Adventures, employs over 1300 people and continues to lead adventure tours focused on sustainability, leadership, and novel experiences.

greens in Canada every season, spending nearly $1 billion annually on equipment, accessories, and fees.

Marine Activities   Canada offers a multitude of popular marine experiences and water-based activities. Besides fishing and swimming, coastal waters provide tourists with opportunities to go whale watching, sea kayaking, sailing in tall ships, and deep-sea diving. In Canada's interior, lakes and rivers provide some of the finest fishing and river rafting in the world.[22] The Ottawa River near Pembroke, Ontario, offers excellent whitewater rafting, and rafters come from as far away as Australia and Sweden to train on the river. Sitting on the banks of the Athabasca River in Jasper, Alberta, visitors can enjoy a gentle, rolling ride while 100 kilometres upstream, tour companies guide whitewater rafts through the challenging, swift rapids of the very same river. Swimming, waterskiing, sailing, canoeing, kayaking, and boating are all part of the water experience.

Walking   The most popular exercise by far requires no equipment and can be done anywhere at any time. According to the National Sporting Goods Association, walking far outranks all other forms of exercise. Many cities have walking or bike paths. The large areas of green space that envelop the city of Ottawa, for example, provide safe, easily accessible paths for jogging, biking, and walking. In Vancouver, B.C., the path that follows the water's edge in Stanley Park provides residents and tourists with a scenic walk, as does the recently completed Harbour Passage in Saint John, NB. No matter where you vacation, walking provides you

Our winter climate is ideal for visitors who want to experience unique activities such as dog sledding. This sled is taking part in the Winterlude events held in Ottawa each year.
(Photo courtesy National Capital Commission.)

with daily exercise and the chance to meet local residents and perhaps learn more about their city and culture.

Hiking How does hiking differ from walking? Hiking is generally done in a wilderness setting and is the method of transportation used by backpackers as they move into an area, looking for good spots to set up camp. It is cheap, healthy, and always ready for people choosing to use their feet rather than a vehicle, to transport themselves. It is also very Earth-friendly.

Choosing an area for hiking is important. The obvious factor to consider in that choice is the ability of the hiker. If you are not used to exercise, you can still hike, provided you choose an appropriate wilderness path. One of the nicest and more moderate hikes in Alberta is to the Plain of Six Glaciers teahouse near Chateau Lake Louise. A hike requiring tremendous strength would be the trek along the West Coast Trail.

Perhaps a more important issue when choosing the wilderness path is the wildlife. As major predators are squeezed out of their habitats with the expansion of settlements, they become accustomed to humans and their flee instincts are dulled. Every year there are stories of humans killed by bears or cougars, and even the most experienced hiker can be at risk. Park authorities can inform you if there have been unusual sightings of predators or other dangers and help tourists to enjoy a safe trip.

Activities such as skiing can be shared by the entire family, creating a leisure event enjoyed by everyone.
(Photo courtesy Canadian Tourism Commission.)

There are many other outdoor activities that can be enjoyed by tourists that offer them the chance to enjoy the climate and the scenery and to exercise at their discretion. Most accommodations that cater to the outdoor enthusiast can provide visitors with supplies and equipment, or can direct them to shops where they can rent whatever they need.

TOURISM'S IMPACT ON THE ENVIRONMENT

Tourism is inherently a user and, in some ways, an abuser of the environment. It is a sector that makes demands on and affects the resources it uses, whether those resources are land, water, air, or any of the inhabitants therein. Tourism around the world is, or at least should be, associated with environmental concerns. Establishing tourism management practices that limit harm to the environment is becoming a top priority for the tourism sector. Some companies have adopted strict recycling policies (Fairmont Hotels is a world-renowned example). There are two opposing views on the relationship between the environment and tourism.

One view holds that tourism provides an incentive for the restoration of historic sites and archaeological treasures, and for the conservation of natural resources. The economic gain from tourism provides the means by which these areas can be restored and preserved. Tourism can also serve as an alternative to more environmentally damaging activities, such as the extraction of minerals or timber. Logging in the world's forests results in the loss of 11 million hectares a year. This deforestation increases soil erosion, landslides, and floods, and reduces the plant population needed to replenish oxygen in the air. Loss of forested land has also caused significant decreases in adventure tourism travel, which depends on forest-based amenities for its drawing power. The Pacific Northwest of Canada and the United States is scarred by clear-cutting, which decreases the scenic value and, therefore, the tourism appeal of the area. From this perspective, tourism is a friend to the environment since preserving the magnificent tree stands is an integral part of the tourism experience.

The opposing view is that tourism means overcrowding, noise, litter, and disruption or extinction of animal life and vegetation. Tourism results in the dumping of waste materials into rivers and onto beaches. Individuals, groups, and experts who hold this view are adamant that tourism development should be halted or even reversed when it conflicts with the natural environment. The Great Barrier Reef near Australia is a prime example of environmental damage by tourists who knowingly or unknowingly kill the corals by stepping on them. Some may even take the corals home as souvenirs. From this perspective, tourism is an enemy of the environment.

A major problem with environmental damage is that many tourists do not even realize they are the culprits. Planning and education are fundamental to understanding and preserving natural environments. In many cases, the local arm of the federal land-managing agency takes on the responsibility for educating visitors through interpretive programs, brochures, and campfire talks. The education process starts with managers appreciating the relationship between people and the natural environment. An important concept in understanding this relationship is carrying capacity.

Carrying capacity is the maximum number of people who can use a site with only *acceptable alteration* to the physical environment and with only *acceptable*

Mother Nature Bounds Back

The coast of Indonesia has long been a scuba diver's paradise, with coral reefs and a wide variety of exotic, tropical fish. Local fishers catch these colourful specimens and export them for sale in aquariums around the world.

Thirty years ago, the fishers were introduced to a "better" and faster way to catch these fish. If a small amount of potassium cyanide was added to the water, the fish became drugged and easier to catch. While about 30% of their catch would die from the dosage, the remaining fish seldom had any injuries and brought in good prices. Nature, however, reacts to the intrusive manipulations of people, and over the years, the cyanide has slowly killed off the living reef. Many fishers were forced to leave the business altogether. Those who stayed in the area returned to their roots, catching fish the old-fashioned way by waiting quietly and then snagging them in nets. It took longer to catch the numbers needed, but death rates dropped dramatically and the fish that were caught seemed to maintain more of their brilliance. In the past few years, these reefs have rebounded, and the beautiful, thriving reef community is once again full and healthy.

(CNN, *News at Noon*, March 26, 2008)

decline in the quality of the experience for subsequent visitors. Determining carrying capacity has become a science that requires setting goals for the area, defining acceptable levels of environmental modification, and considering the kinds of use. No two areas have the same set of carrying capacity factors. Canada has been attempting to identify carrying capacity in national parks, wilderness areas, camping areas, and front country (that is, the highly developed area consisting of road

To feel the power of whales playing alongside your boat is a thrill; to learn of their struggle to survive is an education.
(Photo courtesy Canadian Tourism Commission.)

access, visitor centres, lodging, and retail outlets). There are few available studies, but a recent survey of national parks reported that two-thirds suffered stress from the ecological impacts of visitors.

One successful approach is to limit privileges or access to more delicate park areas. For example, in order to preserve the Great Bear experience, Klemtu Tourism plans to limit the number of participants to 150 per year.[23]

Tourism's impact on the natural environment can be better understood by studying environmental components separately.

Vegetation Tourism may affect vegetation to the point of destroying the beauty of an area as well as the ability of plants to grow. For example, gathering twigs and branches to light a campfire has been a common practice at most campgrounds; however, stripping a campsite of live branches can permanently damage the trees. Also, fallen branches and twigs decay and become a good source of nutrients for the soil; when they are removed, the soil loses this benefit. To alleviate this problem, land-managing agencies now offer firewood to campers for free or for a minimal fee. Rangers selectively collect this firewood in order to minimize damage to any one area.

When they pull up a pretty flower, most tourists simply do not think that taking a small collection of flowers and plants can cause changes in species distribution. Parks Canada is trying to educate visitors by posting signs along pathways and roads with messages such as "Leave only footprints, take only pictures." Vegetation is often trampled by visitors who do not understand the nature of the plant world. Most people don't consider that their footsteps harm vegetation or prevent it from growing back. The impact on vegetation becomes more serious with intensive traffic in delicate ecosystems and terrains, and can be minimized by building trails and walkways that allow tourists access to controlled areas while limiting their access to more fragile areas.

The careless use of fire has caused long-term damage to many forests and parks. In addition to educating visitors, Parks Canada restricts campfire use during dry periods or in high-use areas. For example, some parks, such as Banff National Park and Rocky Mountain National Park, allow only small stoves in back country. Fires are simply prohibited, and the policy is strictly enforced.

Litter, besides being unsightly, can damage vegetation by changing the composition of the soil, which in turn can change the ecosystem balance. Litter may also kill animals that eat it.

Water Quality Tourism affects water quality in many different ways. Campers using sunscreen, soap, and dishwashing liquid in streams and lakes do not realize that these products introduce chemicals into the water system. Low impact camping techniques suggest the use of non-stick pans that require no chemicals to clean or, better yet, soap-free camping.

Camping has also increased the level of human waste in water, and mountain lakes are particularly vulnerable to this type of damage. These waste materials carry parasites that can harm the aquatic environment as well as the next visitor who drinks that water. Using the proper facilities provided by park management services is important, and campers in Canada's less accessible wilderness regions must learn the techniques for safe disposal of human waste. Although dumping refuse is decreasing as citizens become more aware of the damage it can cause, some careless boaters still throw drink cans overboard.

Other concerns relate to oil spills and overbuilding along oceans and lakes. Since 1979, more than 9000 significant oil- and tar-related spills have occurred in the wider Caribbean region, including the Gulf of Mexico, the Straits of Florida, and eastern approaches to the Caribbean Sea.[24] As a result, windward-exposed beaches have tar deposits. Water quality is also affected by activities such as recreational boating, swimming, and camping. Recreational boating on lakes and oceans leaves fuel and oils in the water, causing damage to aquatic plants and wildlife by depleting the oxygen level. The solution is to change tourists' boating habits, restricting the use of motorboats while allowing canoes, rowboats, kayaks, and other small muscle-powered craft.

Wildlife The impact of tourism on wildlife is great, and ranges from causing animals to become too comfortable with the presence of humans, to hastening the extinction of a species. Many animals have learned to tolerate the presence of tourists, and in communities like Jasper and Banff, wild animals such as elk and mountain sheep have the right of way on highways and in town. However, the consequences of tourism include disrupted feeding and breeding habits, destruction of habitats, altered food chains, and extinction.

Tourism disrupts feeding and breeding habits through resort expansion, over-zealous attempts to photograph wildlife, and inappropriate trail development. Tourism development reduces the size of animal habitats, putting greater pressure on the remaining habitat. This condition increases the risk that animals will compete with humans for food and water—or that humans will become a food source. Grizzly bears and cougars scavenge in campgrounds and garbage dumps, and occasionally have been known to actually stalk human victims. British Columbia and Alberta have seen an increase in bear and cougar attacks over the past few years and alert people to the dangers whenever possible. Vacationers may believe that because they are spending only a few days in the wilderness, the odds are with them. They are probably right, but being wrong may mean death or injury.

On an international scale, tourist consumption of ivory and fur, as well as animal skins, skulls, and tails has contributed significantly to the illegal killing of many animals. Among those most savagely hunted and nearly eliminated is the African elephant, hunted solely for its ivory tusks, which are made into jewellery, figurines, and piano keys. Importing and selling most ivory products is now prohibited in Canada.

Coastlines Images of sun, surf, and sand have long lured tourists to coastlines around the world. Too often, insufficient planning means that plant and animal habitats are disrupted; geological features are destroyed by excavation; water supplies are contaminated; and the natural beauty of the area is diminished. Lack of planning can harm many species; this includes draining swamps or wetland areas for development and failing to properly control sewage and garbage. Littering by tourists has turned many coastline areas into dumping grounds.

Tourism planning in coastal areas needs to consider the effects of structures such as high-rise hotels, and the over-development of beaches. Attention must be given to issues such as unstable ground, water drainage, and eroding cliffs.

Regulation of these fragile areas needs to be enforced so that visitors are able to experience coastlines in their natural form.

Mountains The human desire—or need—to leave the pressure of city life behind has put tremendous strains on mountain ecosystems. Mountain terrains are developed as ski areas, hiking and riding trails, campgrounds, and resorts. Accessing the mountains requires roadways that disrupt wildlife habitats. Utility lines are unsightly to area inhabitants and visitors. Roads, ski trails and lifts, hiking trails, and all terrain vehicle (ATV) trails all contribute to land erosion. In higher elevations where the ecosystem is extremely fragile and the slopes are often steep, the carrying capacity is small.

Deserts Once thought of as places to avoid, desert terrains are now playgrounds for tourists and local residents who travel in dune buggies and ATVs and on trail bikes. Many desert areas have been marred by noise, dust, fuel smells, and litter. This fragile environment has lost plant species, animal life, and water holes to overuse by off-road vehicles. In Canada, Saskatchewan is often considered farm country, but it is also home to desert-like areas including dunes and sand hills. A true desert can be found in Osoyoos, B.C., a microenvironment that features plant and animal life designed to survive in this barren region. The scarcity of water also serves as a natural protection system, as deserts and desert-like areas are less likely to become popular for resorts—communities that inevitably endanger the ecosystem.

In Practice

In a group of three to five people, design a carrying capacity plan for public land near your school. This land could be a national or provincial park or forest, or any other government-owned land used by visitors. Keep in mind how the area is used and what natural plants, animals, water, or ecosystems exist. Determine the number of people to be allowed at a given time and indicate what criteria you used to set this number. How will you enforce the carrying capacity?

Tourism, while often referred to as "a green industry" because it takes little from a destination, also leaves much pollution behind. In trying to help conserve and save the planet, the UNWTO declared 2002 to be the International Year of Ecotourism (IYE). Many conferences were hosted around the world that began seriously talking about changes in the ecology of the world. That year, Quebec City hosted a summit meeting to focus on the ecological damages created by the tourism industry.

Over 1100 delegates participated from 132 different countries, showing that global concern is there. The outcome was the "Quebec Declaration on Tourism," a paper that contains specific information on developing a sustainable ecotourism industry. It identified transportation, an essential industry for tourism, as one of the major problems. Scientists have determined that air travel alone is responsible for 3.5% of greenhouse gas emissions. Not figured into that number is the pollution from our cars and buses.

Consumers pay for and expect a beautiful, undisturbed landscape around their vacation "home." However, while we may look like a "green" industry, we are not. We need roads, infrastructure to support our buildings, hotels, restaurants, airports, and so on. Scientists use the term *carbon footprint* as a measure of the environmental damage incurred by the amount of greenhouse gases produced. Companies or people with concern for the environment try to make their carbon footprint as small as possible. However, if you travel a lot by plane, this is difficult. It is up to the individual purchasing the flight or trip to reduce their impact by purchasing carbon credits. Very simply stated, when you purchase a carbon credit you are buying an emission offset—the money spent could go toward planting a tree or investing in low-emission machinery, for example. Airlines and tour operators are making it easier to maintain a small carbon footprint by purchasing carbon credits when you buy your ticket.

Balancing the Negative Environmental Impact

It is certainly important that we begin to deal with climate change in a serious manner; however, some scholars argue that the purchasing of carbon credits may do as much harm as good. By allowing a company to continue to use offending equipment (such as an aircraft or a coal-burning furnace) without thought of reducing the carbon dioxide released into the air is not helping to solve the situation, even if their entire output is purchased on a yearly basis. More important is that the company use more fuel-efficient, non-carbon-producing methods of energy. Summing up some of the concerns, Julianna Priskin of Reseau de vielle en tourisme, University of Quebec at Montreal, says that relying solely on this method can cause problems:

- If the trees are destroyed by fire or natural causes, the carbon is released into the atmosphere, thus negating your "purchase."
- It is a complicated procedure, and still very much a subject of debate, to measure how much carbon dioxide a forest can absorb.
- The effectiveness of a plantation depends on the type of tree species planted. For example, pine trees and non-native trees provide no biodiversity.
- The establishment of "sink plantations" by developing countries may cause people to be displaced or lose access to traditional lands without being properly compensated.
- Planting trees does not move away from using fossilized fuels, nor does it encourage the development of renewable energy or renewable energy projects. It simply makes the person who buys the credits feel better.

She suggests that people who are concerned and travel a lot should try to reduce travel whenever possible and learn to cut their own emissions at home (a positive move for all of the family). If that is not possible, she suggests that making sure the plantation you are investing in is set for a minimum of 100 years, that it is a forest made of hardwood (or the most appropriate local) species, and that the project is one designed for this specific purpose and not simply the reforestation of an already clear area.

The environment's role in tourism—the scenic beauty of mountains, streams, lakes, oceans, and valleys—cannot be overstated. Unless the environment is treated with care and respect, there may soon be no scenic beauty to visit—we may be loving our parks, mountains, and lakes to death.

In Practice

Global warming is a confusing topic. Much of the world is beginning to understand the need for changes in how we live and do business. However, there are still some who deny global warming is taking place. They believe that global warming is a natural progression of climate change that has occurred over the centuries. What are your thoughts on global warming? In teams, take a piece of paper and divide it down the middle. On one side, list the ways in which you think global warming is occurring. On the other side, what arguments have you heard that deny this happening? If your team has concluded that global warming is a reality, what actions have individual team members taken to help slow it?

Many tourism businesses are getting into the "green" trade as they see the trend toward global warming increase. Some businesses handle the challenge very well while others just pay lip service. Hotels have formed green committees, which earn "trees" for suggesting environmentally sound practices. Once a year, the teams who have earned the most "trees" win trips to places like Jamaica or Acapulco. Competition can be fierce! The program enlists guests as well as employees in the effort to reduce, reuse, and recycle. Not only does the program benefit the environment, but the company also saves thousands of dollars yearly by

- reducing waste sent to landfill sites by 50%
- redesigning purchasing policies to ensure waste reduction at source
- collecting and recycling all recyclables—cans, glass, paper, etc.
- using environmentally friendly hotel supplies[25]

Canada's Green Plan

The **Green Plan**, created twenty years ago, was a commitment to solve Canada's complex environmental challenges and implement sustainable economic development, identifying tourism as an important partner in the plan.[26] It recommended that 12% of Canada's lands be protected space for parks, historic sites, and wildlife, still a priority for the government. Education of Canadians about the environment and how to protect it was another important piece of the puzzle. However, Canada has never received top grades for implementing positive changes. The Great Lakes is a prime example of the lack of positive movement. A recent report has identified seventeen highly contaminated sites, several where raw sewage is being dumped directly into the waters. The cost of cleaning these sites was estimated at $3.5 billion dollars. Unfortunately, funding promised by the government for scientific and technical research has not appeared. Additionally, action on environmental sustainability and protection shifts based on the perspectives of those holding political power, creating inconsistency at best.

Judging a Book by Its Cover

A major hotel located in northern Ontario promotes itself as a green luxury resort. It offers a broad variety of activities including golf and tennis, as well as saltwater indoor and outdoor swimming pools. As a concerned traveller, staying at an environmentally conscious resort is very attractive, and based on the company's provided information, you book your vacation.

Upon checking in, you notice that multiple lights are already turned on in your room to make it feel welcoming. The tennis courts are actually poured concrete slabs positioned next to the lake, and when playing at the golf course, you notice that employees are spraying the golf course fairways with chemical pesticides to maintain the grass quality. At the swimming pool, customers have free access to an unlimited number of towels. Although you were happy to see in-room garbage sorting bins, you did notice that the housekeepers were combining the various waste products when they cleaned your room.

1. As a guest, how might you respond to these observations? Would you stay and enjoy your holiday and then complain once you got home? Would you not complain at all, or would you leave and demand a full refund?
2. Why might a business allow misleading information to be advertised?
3. Conduct a search on Google around the sins of **greenwashing**. Discuss some of the sins that may have been committed in this case.

Summary

- Adventure tourism and outdoor recreation are the components of the recreation sector that are geared toward activity.
- Adventure activities typically fall into four categories: hard adventure such as mountain climbing, soft adventure such as hiking up a mountain path, unique ecotourism experiences, and outdoor recreational sports such as golfing, fishing, skiing, or boating.
- Parks Canada, an independent agency reporting to Environment Canada, maintains our nationally protected wildlife areas and historic sites and canals.
- Tourism development can affect, or "stress" an area's vegetation, water, and animal life. Some areas should not be developed because of the fragility of the terrain, but in general, if a good plan is implemented, tourists will cause minimal damage to the environment.
- Clear development goals need to be established and environmental impact studies conducted, including an understanding of carrying capacities, in order to balance the needs of commerce and visitors with the sustainability of the natural environment.
- Sustainable tourism development encourages tourism while maintaining the natural environment. Canada's Green Plan provides us with a governmental code of ethics.

- Education is the key to environmental awareness in the tourism sector. Some businesses are already working toward an environmentally safe industry.
- Environmentally friendly practices can include limiting the number of participants, switching to recyclable or reusable materials, using biodegradable soaps, turning down thermostats and lights, and developing tourism services *around* the landscape rather than destroying the landscape itself.
- As travellers become concerned about the environment, businesses will need to respond to consumer demands.

Questions

1. Parks Canada, an independent agency reporting to Environment Canada, interacts with the tourism sector in two of the eight components of tourism. Identify these two components and show how tourism illiteracy on the part of this agency could undermine the overall Canadian tourism product.

2. Tourists use both federal and provincial parks during outdoor vacation experiences.
   a) Explain the differences and similarities you might see in these parks.
   b) List all of the federal and four of the provincial parks found in your province.

3. Ecotourism is based on what four principles?

4. Is ecotourism an important part of your province's overall tourism product? Justify your answer by referring to the characteristics of ecotourists and how they relate to your province's tourism product.

5. Briefly summarize a minimum of five outdoor recreational experiences available to tourists in your region.

6. Choose four inconsistencies between the needs of the tourist and the need to protect Canadian wilderness. Explain how tourists might enjoy these regions with little or no impact on the environment.

7. Do you believe Canada is doing enough to protect our environment? Defend your answer using examples.

8. Define the following terms as they relate to adventure tourism and outdoor recreation: *hard adventure, soft adventure, sustainable tourism, carrying capacity, Trans Canada Trail.*

Notes

1. ctx_news@ctc.cct.ca, October 18, 2002 article.
2. www.pc.gc.ca.
3. www.gov.ns.ca/news/details. asp?id=20111017001
4. Ibid
5. Ibid
6. www.ec.gc.ca/eee-ias/default. asp?lang=En&n=02101A38-1#wsBF9C07E9.
7. www.pc.gc.ca/eng/progs/np-pn/eco/eco2. aspx.
8. www.8000ers.com.
9. www.parkscanada.ca.
10. www.ecotourism.org/what-is-ecotourism.
11. www.ecotourism.org.
12. *Canadian Geographic*, Travel Adventure Booklet, Winter 2003.
13. *Risk Management and Insurance Guide for the Adventure, Ecotourism and Alpine Skiing Industries*, Canadian Tourism Commission.
14. *The Trail Story*, Trans Canada Trail website, www.tctrail.ca.
15. www.canlii.org/en/ca/laws/stat/ sc-1994-c-16/latest/sc-1994-c-16.html.
16. www.tourism.gov.on.ca, Outdoor Segmentation, TAMS 1999.

17. Ibid

18. www.gadventures.com/about-us/
    bruce-poon-tip.

19. www.travelandtransitions.com/interviews/
    preview_bruce_poon_tip.htm.

20. Ibid

21. Ibid

22. *Tourism Industry Product Overview* (prepared for Tourism British Columbia and the Council of Tourism Associations of British Columbia, by Price Waterhouse and the ARA Consulting Group Inc., June 1996).

23. Nathalie Southworth, "Under the Great Bear's spell." *The Globe and Mail,* October 2, 2002.

24. Judy Crawford, "Environmental responsibility in the tourism industry," *Tourism: Building Credibility for a Credible Industry* (22nd conference of the Travel and Tourism Research Association, Long Beach, CA, 1991), p. 98.

25. Lou Cook, "Shades of green," *Lodging,* October 1999, p. 67.

26. R.W. Slater, "Understanding the relationship between tourism, environment and sustainable development," *Tourism—Environment—Sustainable Development: An Agenda for Research* (proceedings of the conference of the Canadian Chapter of the Travel and Tourism Research Association, Hull, Quebec, 1991), p. 11.

Events

Key terms

breakout room
civic event
conference
conference centre
convention
convention centre

fair
festival
fundraising event
hallmark event
Meeting Professionals
    International (MPI)

Rendez-Vous Canada
seminars
spectator sporting event
summit
trade show
workshop

Learning objectives

Having read this chapter you will be able to

1. Discuss the wide variety of events that might be hosted by a community.

2. Differentiate between a conference, convention, summit meeting, and business meeting.

3. Explain the difference between a conference centre and convention centre.

4. Identify the factors that make Canada a strong competitor for the conference market.

5. Explain both the positive and negative impacts events may have on a community.

As a subindustry, events are very important to the tourism sector. Events make good use of the products and services delivered by core tourism components, including transportation, accommodations, food and beverage, travel services, and recreation. This blending of areas makes it challenging to determine the exact labour impact of events; however, events bring together components that otherwise might work separately. This industry also creates jobs for a variety of ancillary businesses, including printers, audiovisual companies, and manufacturers of exhibits. All events are similar in general purpose and design but they are developed for different target markets with very particular needs and features. Special events and some trade shows target the general population, while conferences, conventions, meetings, and trade shows fill the needs of the business market.

Every community, no matter how small, holds events. Rural communities find that hosting a fair, festival, or sporting event brings new visitors to their town and may bring local and sometimes national recognition. Hosting an event can bring a community both full- and part-time jobs, an enhanced image, strengthened community bonds, economic growth, an expanded tourism season, and enhanced diversity of social and cultural activities. Revenues generated by events benefit not only tourism businesses, but also retail businesses and community associations.

Over the last decade, the industry of events has been volatile; gatherings, whether for business or pleasure, are reliant on the blending of various tourism sectors. In the first decade of the twenty-first century, terrorism and concerns over safety reduced the number of people who chose to fly. Because fewer people were travelling by plane, many major conferences were cancelled and meetings were restructured using a growing number of technological tools such as web-based communication. In North America, the peaceful conclusion of events such as the World Youth Day held in Toronto in 2002, the Winter Olympics of both 2002 in Salt Lake City and 2010 in Vancouver, and the 2003 Molson Canadian Rocks for Toronto concert all helped to reassure worried organizers and delegates.

Global summits, such as the G8 meetings that bring the industrial world's financial leaders together to discuss topics like international trade and globalization, have not suffered from terrorist threats but rather from activist demonstrations that turn aggressive. Whenever the leaders of the eight largest economies, also called the Group of Eight or just the "G8," meet in a particular city, they also draw activists and protestors to that city. Violence has erupted during G8 global summits hosted by Canada in cities including Vancouver and Quebec City. In 2002, Canada hosted the summit in the resort town of Kananaskis, Alberta, and was able to minimize any disruptions. They attempted to duplicate this strategy in 2010 by hosting the summit in Huntsville, Ontario; however, protestors descended on Toronto for extended protests that began well in advance of the summit. During these protests, violence erupted often, over 1118 people were arrested,[1] and Canada's normally peaceful image was tarnished.

Later in the decade, the world experienced a global economic crisis that affected the ability of many companies to operate. Unemployment rose as businesses worked to control expenses. Corporations and individuals alike had less available money to spend on travel, limiting the frequency of meetings and gatherings. Yet the need to communicate and connect with people directly has remained critical. People tend to build relationships and share knowledge and ideas best when they are face to face. Pick up any newspaper and you will find at least one story about a meeting being held in your community or on a national or international stage. Canada is well suited for such events. The Canadian dollar has proven stable throughout the recent economic challenges and Canada provides excellent convention facilities, an international appeal, a familiar lifestyle, and a wide variety of attractions.

In this chapter, we will examine two main areas of this industry: *events* and *meetings*. Events are social moments of importance recognized with some form of gathering that is not typically related to business activities. Meetings range in size, scope, and function but are focused specifically on business matters.

EVENTS

The definition of "events" is extremely broad; they can include activities lasting anywhere from a half day to a year. They may present new ideas to a new community, or be ongoing annual events. Donald Getz includes in his definition that events are "an opportunity for leisure, social, or cultural experiences."[2] Today, events have become big business for many Canadian municipalities. They are one of the most interesting ways of unifying and enhancing the tourist appeal of permanent structures such as museums, zoos, and arenas. A museum of art is an attraction by itself, but add to it an event such as a Picasso exhibit, and the museum's appeal becomes almost irresistible to locals and tourists alike.

Events can be a powerful tool for bringing information and political activism to the forefront in a world that is growing smaller by the day. For example, every two years the Roman Catholic Church brings its youth together to gain a more personal vision of the church's religious teachings. For athletes, the Olympics and Paralympics showcase the best competitors from participating countries around the world.

Events are often initiated by travel destinations in order to lure tourists to the region. Some special events attract domestic tourists and others appeal to the

A special event like Canada Day will bring close to 100 000 visitors to Ottawa.
(Photo courtesy Canadian Tourism Commission.)

international visitor. Two examples of international events are the Olympics and the World's Fair. In the past forty years, Canada has hosted two World's Fairs, or "expos," and three Olympic Games. Each province also hosts its own events, with some, such as the Calgary Stampede and the Royal Nova Scotia International Tattoo, gaining strong international reputations and becoming attractions for audiences around the world. Even events that don't enjoy such wide recognition remain an important part of a region's draw. Much like the restaurant industry serving multiple audiences, events play a significant role in entertaining both tourists and local residents.

Some events are considered *special events* because they fall outside of regularly scheduled or recurring activities.[3] One of the best recent examples of a special event sparked by political activism is the Live 8 concerts held around the world in 2005. Inspired and guided by rock musicians Bob Geldof and Bono of U2, musicians in eight countries, including Canada, held concerts to draw attention to the plight of poor African nations. Held just before the G8 meeting of world leaders in Scotland, Live 8's organizers and participants hoped to pressure G8 nations to forgive the massive debts owed by the African nations. Unlike Geldof's Live Aid concert held in 1985, which raised $100 million for poverty-stricken Ethiopia, Live 8 concerts were free and were held simply to bring awareness to the plight of poor nations.[4]

FOOTPRINT

The New Face of the Toronto Indy

On March 5, 2008, it was officially announced that the Grand Prix race hosted in Toronto, Ontario, an annual event held for the prior twenty-two years on the downtown street track, was cancelled. Even with strong support from the community and its leaders for the event, the race was caught in the merger between the Indy Racing League and Champ Car, two rival racing organizations, and lacked the financial support to continue.

Seizing this opportunity, Andretti Green Racing, whose owners include the internationally renowned Formula One racer Michael Andretti, stepped up to purchase the assets of the Grand Prix Association of Toronto.[5] Andretti Green Racing understood the positive economic impact of the annual event. It typically attracted annual attendance of 60 000 to 70 000 people between 1988 and 2005. Spending directly around the event was estimated at $50 million during the two-day event and visitors to the Toronto area spent an additional $30 million in lodging, food sales, and shopping. In addition, the event has raised $5.75 million for local children's charities. In 2009, Andretti signed an agreement with Honda Canada Inc. as the primary sponsor, rebranding the annual racing event as the Honda Indy Toronto. Although attendance at Honda Indy Toronto has not yet rebounded to the peak levels seen in 2001–02, they are making progress. According to Norris MacDonald, "you have solid TV numbers (which is what advertisers are really looking for), solid media interest and serious corporate support and commitment. What more can an event like this ask for?"[6]

Festivals

Public celebrations that centre on themes of local, regional, or national interest are called **festivals**. This broad category of events celebrates music, culture, seasons, and celebrations. Every year, Canada's capital city hosts the Canadian Tulip Festival, built around the gift of the tulips presented to Canadians by the Dutch Royal Family for harbouring them during World War II.

Many rural cities in Canada use special events as a draw to attract tourists and excursionists from other regions. Events become an important promotional tool for the area, as festivals will attract both local and national television coverage. Some of the bigger Canadian events include the Symphony of Fire in Vancouver, British Columbia; Folklorama in Winnipeg, Manitoba; and Carnaval de Québec in Quebec City. Even small festivals, such as the Port Elgin Pumpkinfest, can be fun to attend. The Pumpkinfest swells the small town of Port Elgin, Ontario (population 7000), by as many as 50 000 visitors who spend more than $1.4 million dollars in two days. The Pumpkinfest is not only an economic boon to the region, but it also helps to raise much-needed revenue for the area's non-profit groups.[7]

Quebec City's Winter Carnival proves that, even in winter, Canada has great activities.
(Photo courtesy Canadian Tourism Commission.)

Fairs

Fairs focus on agriculture or history. Legacy events, or historical fairs, recreate a certain period by providing the food and entertainment of that time. Medieval and Renaissance fairs are popular examples, and recreations of historical events, such as the final battle between Wolfe and Montcalm on the Plains of Abraham in old Quebec City, are becoming more popular.

Agricultural fairs feature livestock, produce, local arts and crafts, carnival rides, and food. Most farming communities have agricultural fairs, where 4-H, an organization that teaches young people about agriculture and animal science[8] and other groups gather to display their goods. Ribbons are given to prize-winning animals of many breeds. Some of Canada's agricultural fairs date back to the early 1840s. They draw regional tourists by featuring nationally known singers and entertainers and are usually held in late summer to allow crops to mature for competition.

These fairs are often sponsored by the local government or the community hosting the event, and it is common for a carnival to join a larger event in the community and become a drawing card for non-residents. Two of Canada's biggest and best fairs are held in Toronto. The Canadian National Exhibition (CNE), held at the end of August in Toronto, combines an agricultural fair with a carnival. The CNE is the largest carnival/fair held in Canada. In November, the prestigious Royal Agricultural Winter Fair brings in visitors from across North America. It does not have rides or a midway, but the fair hosts a variety of competitions including horse jumping and a dog show.

www.theex.com

Circuses

Circuses are magic for all ages; however, concern for the welfare of circus animals has caused the decline of this type of event. The only major traditional circus left in North America is Ringling Brothers and Barnum & Bailey's Greatest Show on Earth. Sometimes non-profit organizations, such as the Shriners, will sponsor a circus in order to raise money for hospitals and children's medical research. Circuses have transformed over the years, moving away from a reliance on animals and slapstick toward a focus on artistry and athleticism. Founded in 1984, Canada's Cirque du Soleil has gained worldwide recognition for its unique creativity and storytelling that uses tumblers, dancers, and acrobats to enthrall its audiences. Cirque du Soleil performs around the world, employs over 5000 people, and has recently exceeded $1 billion in annual revenues.[9]

Hallmark Events

Hallmark events include "major fairs, expositions, cultural and sporting events of international status which are held on either a regular or a one-off basis"[10] such as the Olympics, the Commonwealth Games, or World Youth Day. These events bring tourists from around the world to a destination and can have a huge economic impact on a community. Participants for World Youth Day in Toronto spent an estimated $110 million on tourism-related souvenirs, restaurants, and hotels.[11] However, the direct costs of staging the event were over budget by $3.5 million, which the Roman Catholic Church, as the organizing body, agreed to cover. The celebrations of the Diamond Jubilee of Queen Elizabeth II in 2012 were felt throughout the British Commonwealth in a series of royal visits, capped off with a large event in London, England.

Although events such as the Olympics draw in tourism dollars and provide the host city with worldwide exposure, the high level of required investment can be difficult for a region to recoup. The Olympic Games held in the summer of 1976 left both the city of Montreal and the province of Quebec with a debt of $1.4 billion, a debt that was finally paid off in 2006, thirty years after the games were held.

Events of this size take years of planning, require a substantial investment of tax dollars, and are seldom profitable. Even before the 2012 Summer Games begin in London, England, there were estimates that the outstanding debt could range from £9–20 billion.[12] Even Vancouver, a city that aggressively chased the money for the 2010 Olympics through partners, suppliers, and official supporters, found it challenging to break free from the incurred debt. Two years after the Winter Games, Vancouver still has outstanding debts of $434 million.[13] Calgary, Alberta, serves as an example of a host that made money on its Olympics, and the city is still enjoying financial success through increased tourism more than two decades later. Because the Olympic Games are not privately owned, their primary goal is not to make money; they are about sport and competition. For that reason, unlike a private company, profits either go into the community's pocket or are returned to the Olympic committee to be used for future events.[14]

Fundraising Events

Fundraising events are focused around raising funds for charitable organizations and have become commonplace in North America. They may be small, like a walk-a-thon to raise money for the local humane society, or they may be national, like the Terry Fox Run. In 2011, the Terry Fox Foundation generated over $22 million in revenue from Canadian donations and fundraising, an increase of 14.2% from 2010.[15] Because of cuts in government funding to hospitals and special disease research facilities, many charities now depend on these events. People have the chance to enjoy a special activity while helping to support a cause they believe in. For example, Willie Nelson helped create Farm Aid to bring together a group of country-and-western singers to raise money for cash-strapped, small, independent farms. Hurricanes Katrina and Rita sparked a number of different fundraisers across North America for the evacuees from devastated regions of Louisiana and Mississippi, raising over $3 billion in a matter of weeks.

Civic Events

Civic events focus on the activities within a city, town, or community. Communities may well have distinct events related specifically to their identity, such as around the city's founding or the celebration of a local hero. They may be directly connected in theme to national events, such as the celebration of Canada Day or Remembrance Day. This category also includes the investiture of a new prime minister or governor general, medal presentations, or the opening of a new building. Civic events may also be global, such as a New Year's Eve celebration. Each municipality, region, and country has unique civic events, and tourists often plan their vacations around these events.

Spectator Sporting Events

The largest **spectator sporting event** is the Olympics. However, hockey, tennis, golf, baseball, football, and basketball also draw large crowds. Although most spectators are people who live within a two-hour drive of the event, the regional draw of tourists to sporting events has been growing rapidly. Accommodations, restaurants, and shopping areas have noticed an increase in visitors whose primary reason for coming is to watch their favourite team. Special sporting events such as the Grey Cup, the Super Bowl, the World Series, the Stanley Cup, and the National

Basketball Association playoffs bring in thousands of loyal fans who will spend the night and are ready to spend money on food and souvenirs.

Professional sports belong primarily to big cities. Big-name teams like the Toronto Raptors or Vancouver Canucks bring both revenue and recognition to a region, but Canadian cities sometimes have difficulty supporting a professional team because of the influence of the U.S. marketplace. Players often demand large salaries and want to be paid in U.S. dollars, making it very difficult for even a good team to be profitable. The 2004–05 NHL strike did nothing to enhance hockey's image, and lack of business from hockey fans left many small bars and restaurants struggling to stay open and souvenir shops filing for bankruptcy. ESPN opted not to renew its contract with the NHL, proving that without the broad support of the U.S. television market, major contracts with television corporations disappear. Television rights are one of the big ways in which a professional sport sustains itself.

Most athletes never make it into the professional arena, but continue to show their love for their sport by forming city leagues. These amateur leagues also bring in tourist revenue as regions host national championships for a variety of sports, such as the Canadian National Skating Championship or the Tim Hortons Brier (Canadian Men's Curling Championship).

Trade Shows

Trade shows and expositions are a marketing and sales tool used by many industries to display and sell their products. Many trade shows are not open to the general public but are designed for specific audiences, small businesses, or entrepreneurs. They usually display the latest developments and products of an industry (such as computers, automobiles, boats, or home-care products). Unlike fairs, trade shows are commonly held indoors and require large convention centres to display the items. Consequently, trade shows are not generally sponsored by a public or non-profit organization but by the pertinent industry or trade association. Revenues for the use of the facility, however, go to the community.

There are approximately 11 000 trade shows held annually in North America. Vendors rent space and set up booths to display their products. Demonstrations are an important part of any trade show, and special trade show prices act as a lure for those thinking of a purchase. In the hospitality industry, there are several large trade shows. The International Restaurant and Foodservice Show in New York City, held every November, and the National Restaurant Association show scheduled for the middle of May annually in Chicago are both noted for their size and for their seminars, which feature top names in the restaurant business as well as high-profile speakers. These shows are important to the food service entrepreneur because they display the latest food products, marketing tools, and equipment for hotels and restaurants.

Many Canadian cities also hold restaurant shows. One example is the Canadian International Food and Beverage Show, held by the Canadian Restaurant and Foodservices Association (CRFA) in Toronto in February. For students, this show provides an educational opportunity that should not be missed, and special student discounts may be available. The International Travel Industry Expo is designed for travel counsellors. It displays the latest travel products, allowing participants to pick up information and make contact with a wide variety of suppliers. The Canadian Tourism Commission and the Tourism Industry Association of Canada sponsor

With new rules in place creating a faster, higher-scoring game, the NHL has been staging a comeback in Canadian cities.
(Photo courtesy Ottawa Senators Hockey Club.)

two major trade shows for the tourism sector. **Rendez-Vous Canada**, developed by Tourism Canada in the 1980s, displays Canadian tourism products for the travel trade market—travel agencies and tour operators. The show is now sponsored by TIAC and, in 2007, generated over $350 million dollars.[16] Visit Canada, still operated by the CTC, focuses on the media. Canadian tourism products are made available to travel writers, photographers, and other media representatives, allowing them to do "one-stop shopping" for tourism information.

Trade shows that are open to the general public, such as auto shows, may focus on one product or, like fall and spring home shows, may display a broad range of goods and services. The public pays an entrance fee and may spend the day looking and talking to experts. Ottawa's annual Wine and Food Show is an example of this type of show. Here, restaurants, wineries, distilleries, and breweries present samples of their products (for a small charge). **Seminars** are generally free to those who attend. Other examples are craft shows, auto/RV shows, or boating/sporting shows. These shows have proven to be highly successful over the past decade.

Trade shows generate more than $20 billion in revenue in North America every year. Large trade shows use spacious facilities like the Vancouver Convention Centre, the Metro Toronto Convention Centre, or the Montreal Convention Centre. All components of tourism benefit. For example, weeks prior to the Chicago Restaurant Show, downtown hotels are completely sold out, and restaurants are booked to capacity during the show.

CONFERENCES, CONVENTIONS, AND MEETINGS

An association or an organization is created by uniting a group of people with a common interest. Association meetings fall into two categories: conventions and conferences. **Conventions** are large meetings where delegates come together to share ideas and to achieve some form of consensus. Perhaps the best known type of convention occurs when a political party brings together delegates from across the country to elect a leader and create the party platform for the next election. Delegates to a convention usually come from varying backgrounds, so business leaders will mingle with firefighters, mechanics, consultants, and those who choose to work at home. Conventions are also held by large associations such as the Kiwanis Club or Alcoholics Anonymous. There is usually a strong element of recreation in a convention program, to reward those who have spent their time working with the organization.

Conferences are similar to conventions, except that the delegates usually come from a single industry or occupation. The Tourism Industry Association of Canada (TIAC) holds its annual conference in a different Canadian city each year so that attendees may enjoy varied venues and attractions. Delegates come from all areas of the tourism sector to hear about the latest research, to learn more about national certification programs, to exchange ideas, and to listen to leaders in tourism discuss current topics of interest. Many conferences take the time to recognize people who have contributed to the sector in a significant way. Conferences have a more educational tone to their programs than do conventions.

Summits are similar to conferences but tend to be meetings specifically arranged for high-level political or corporate leaders that have political, policy, or governance overtones. A well known example would be the G8 summit, an annual gathering of the governmental bodies for the eight largest economies in the world.

With the increased quality and availability, and low cost of internet-based communications, teleconferencing is a growing trend in the meetings marketplace. Advances in technology allow businesses and associations to bring together a group of people via telephone, satellite, or fibre-optic link. Video and web-based conferencing enable participants to see each other and interact during discussions, a technique that most people can now use with their computer through programs such as Skype. Although this type of meeting does not add to a city's tourism revenue, hotels and convention centres are beginning to provide these services in response to consumer demand.

The Association Meeting Market

Although associations may have very different reasons to exist, as a market, they share characteristics:

- Conventions and conferences usually last three to five days.
- Voluntary attendance is normal; delegates pay their own way.
- Destination sites must be carefully chosen to entice delegates to attend.
- Different cities are chosen every year.
- Accessibility is important to delegates.
- Regularly scheduled meeting dates allow delegates to plan their time in advance.
- Exhibitions displaying the latest goods are important.

There are about 80 000 associations in North America, and many plan annual conventions or conferences. Specific guest needs must be satisfied if the convention or conference is to be a success. The choice of destination is important because delegates often bring their families along, combining business and vacation. Resorts are popular choices, and both the Fairmont Banff Springs Hotel and the Fairmont Jasper Park Lodge have developed good reputations as conference sites.

However, these sites highlight a major drawback with resorts: the closest cities, in this case Calgary and Edmonton, are some distance away. Calgary, for instance, is a ninety-minute drive from Banff, forcing the delegate to either rent a car or make the last leg of the trip by bus. As members pay for their travel and accommodations, the cost of the trip is an important factor when booking the destination. Since most delegates like to try different locations every year, the organizing committee is kept busy searching out new sites. Booking a site five years in advance is not uncommon.

Meeting Sites The choice of a meeting location is as varied as the products available. The first concern a meeting planner must address is the size of the facility needed. General meeting space must accommodate the entire delegation, which may be anywhere from a couple of hundred to more than 10 000 people. **Breakout rooms**, smaller rooms available outside of the main conference room, are needed to handle panel discussions, seminars, and **workshops**, which are an integral part of a conference. The number of rooms available at a destination and the price of accommodations are extremely important to delegates because they pay their own way. Many conferences will choose destinations that offer a wide variety of attractions that families can enjoy during the day, and where delegates can relax together after the meetings.

www.mpiweb.org

Hotels today may generate 20–40% of their annual revenues from meetings, conventions, and conferences. Many have designed their properties to accommodate these groups, providing audiovisual support, portable food service, and a staff trained to deal with the logistics of a large meeting. Resorts also attract this market, offering recreational activities and a quiet, undisturbed setting. Intrawest Resorts invested over $1.2 million in renovations to their Blue Mountain Resort in Ontario to better meet the needs of the meeting planners and delegates. The problem with resorts has often been high room rates: many conferences are planned during peak season, when resorts are reluctant to reduce their rates.

Conference Terminology You Should Know

seminar	informal meeting in which delegates share information and ideas under the expertise of a seminar leader or presenter; seminars may also be conducted by a panel of experts who provide knowledge from differing sources
workshop	small-group session that focuses on activities in which participants learn new skills or techniques
breakout room	a room in which a small group of delegates participates in a seminar or workshop
Meeting Professionals International (MPI)	international professional association of meeting planners

Conference centres are facilities specifically designed for meetings that provide a functional, flexible, and focused working environment for a conference and its delegates. Because these meetings are of an educational nature, many large universities make their equipment and facilities available during the summer months to host small conferences and meetings, thus gaining revenue from rooms and services that might otherwise be unused.

One of Canada's most distinctive conference centres is in Banff, Alberta. The Banff Centre was established over sixty-five years ago as a retreat for musicians and artists. *Arts* programming is one of three distinct programming areas at the Banff Centre, which also provides conference services year-round. Many programs are focused on artists, including music, sound, theatre arts, writing and publishing. Professional development, including their leadership development programming, offers seminars and workshops designed to develop effective, successful leaders for all areas, including business, government, and Aboriginal communities.

Every year the Banff Centre is host to the internationally acclaimed Banff Mountain Film and Book Festival, and the Banff Mountain Photography Competition, as well as conferences and summits exploring specific mountain-related themes. The centre's multidisciplinary environment and the vast range of opportunities for guests to interact with nature make this conference centre unique. Together, all these components add value to the Banff Centre's conference product.

www.banffcentre.ca

Convention centres are specifically built to handle groups of more than 1000 people. They differ from conference centres in several ways: (a) they are larger facilities that do not have recreational opportunities on the premises; (b) they are usually located in big cities; and c) they do not provide guest rooms. Hotels in the area will handle accommodations, and many convention centres are linked to a hotel. For example, the Vancouver Convention Centre (VCC), located on the waterfront, is linked to the Pan Pacific Hotel.

The Banff Centre provides smaller conferences and corporate meetings with unique facilities and a beautiful setting.
(Photo courtesy The Banff Centre.)

Because building convention centres is enormously expensive, a unique partnership has developed between the tourism sector and federal, provincial, and municipal governments, which have provided funding as well as special loans. Civic centres also play host to conventions, but their primary function is to host special events such as sporting events or cultural shows and exhibits. Some civic centres work in partnership with smaller convention facilities to help the city handle a larger number of delegates. The Saddledome in Calgary provides seating for an additional 16 700 participants, expanding the convention centre's capacity of 2500; the Halifax Metro Centre (capacity 10 000) is adjacent to the World Trade and Convention Centre, with a capacity of 1300. Many cities in Canada are considering additions to their meeting spaces, and Canadians can look forward to new job opportunities as this expansion becomes a reality.

Canada's top convention centres, from east to west, are as follows:

- Halifax World Trade and Convention Centre
- Quebec Convention Centre
- Montreal Convention Centre
- Ottawa Congress Centre
- Metropolitan Toronto Convention Centre
- Winnipeg Convention Centre
- Edmonton Convention Centre
- Calgary Convention Centre
- Vancouver Convention Centre
- Victoria Convention Centre

The Vancouver Convention Centre recently completed a major expansion that tripled its capacity. (Photo courtesy Canadian Tourism Commission.)

The Corporate Meeting Market

This segment of the meeting market has slightly different characteristics from the associations market. Businesses will often hold meetings off site in order to avoid distractions and to achieve an atmosphere in which to build a more unified team. Here are the characteristics of the corporate meeting market:

- Attendance is mandatory.
- The cost of the meeting is paid for by the business.
- The number of participants is smaller than that of a conference or convention.

- The meeting is generally shorter.
- Meetings are planned as the need arises and are booked with only a few months' or weeks' notice. Since attendance is mandatory, meetings do not require visible publicity.
- The same destination may be used repeatedly, and it is often near corporate headquarters or factories.
- Exhibits are not generally part of the meeting structure.
- The emphasis is on business, so food service usually provides a working lunch: a simple buffet of cold meats, salads or sandwiches, fresh fruit, and dessert. Beverages are supplied throughout the meeting. Corporate meetings often take place in local hotel facilities. A hotel serious about this business must provide not only quality food service, but also quiet, luxurious surroundings to fit the corporate image.

SNAPSHOT

Meeting Professionals International

Founded in 1972 in Dallas, Texas, Meeting Professionals International, commonly referred to simply as MPI, developed as an organization designed to bring together meeting planners and organizers into an industry community. Meetings, conferences, conventions and trade shows were growing into an enormous business, yet those who dedicated themselves to careers in this field lacked an industry group to advocate their professional nature.

Forty years later, MPI celebrates standing as the foremost industry organization in the meetings, conventions, and exhibitions field. For people establishing a career in the meetings and events field, MPI is the primary international organization for communication, networking, and industry-recognized certification. Membership in MPI exceeds 23 000 people in over twenty countries and members who are active in over seventy-one distinct clubs or organization chapters.

Beyond the powerful networking capabilities that come from involvement in MPI, they also facilitate and support training opportunities. For those in leadership or upper-level management roles, they offer a Certification in Meeting Management (CMM) where highly experienced members come together in a five-day intensive course around strategic planning and decision making in the meetings management field. For career-focused meeting planners, MPI offers the Certified Meeting Professional (CMP) designation. This program has been offered since 1985, and evolved with the industry to train and recognize career excellence.

DIFFICULTIES IN SPONSORING AN EVENT

Clearly, events and festivals are an important component of the tourism sector, benefiting small and large communities alike. However, it would be naive to think that special events have only advantages. Disadvantages do exist, but if they are addressed in the planning stages, they can be overcome or minimized. Potential disadvantages include: (1) difficulty finding volunteers; (2) dissenting community merchants and residents who may block planning; (3) inadequate planning that may result in financial setbacks that jeopardize future events; (4) large numbers of visitors who may tax existing accommodations, visitor services, and restaurants, posing a threat to future events if they go home dissatisfied; (5) damage to the environment; and (6) difficulty attracting visitors until the event becomes widely known.

World-class events like the Calgary Stampede provide summer entertainment for visitors.
(Photo courtesy Canadian Tourism Commission.)

MANAGING EVENTS

What a challenge managing a large event can be! Organizers are doomed to fail if they don't understand the complexities of planning, organizing, and staging a special event. Many colleges and universities in Canada offer excellent training programs. Through the *emerit* national occupational training program, the CTHRC offers national certification for event coordinators and event managers at both the domestic and international levels. A career in event management requires the development of numerous skills, knowledge, and abilities, including the following:

- **Client needs and expectations.** It is important to start with a clear understanding of the purpose of the event, the needs of your client, and the projected outcomes. This means you must develop good communication and people skills.

- **Site selection and inspection.** For regular events such as the Calgary Stampede, the site is pre-selected. Sometimes the client chooses the site. As coordinator, you must become familiar with the site on many levels to ensure you have adequate registration areas, hotel accommodations, food service capabilities, restrooms, and utilities (e.g., electrical power, power distribution, water).

- **Designing the event environment.** Although this may be the creative side of your planning, your designs must meet your client's needs, the registrants' needs, and the budget.

- **Financial management.** Many events are enormously expensive to run, and keeping tight control of dollars is essential if an event is to be successful. Besides the obvious fixed expenses, a wide variety of vendors, entertainers, caterers, and staff must be paid. Add expenses for marketing and promotion, as well as flowers and decor, and you will see that insurance and good accounting skills are essential!

- **Training staff and volunteers.** Event planners work with full-time and part-time staff as well as many volunteers. Volunteers work for free but often lack specific skills or knowledge. Leadership skills are needed to get your people working as a team.

- **Scheduling.** Much of an event is scheduled well in advance, and the client is likely to take an active part. Promotions highlight the schedule of events, and the biggest concern is ensuring that the schedule is followed. A conference speaker who takes just ten minutes more than scheduled can throw the rest of the day off track, affecting both food service and programmed entertainment.

- **Catering.** Food is often the highlight of any meeting or event, and knowing what the clientele wants is very important. A conference of nutritionists will be looking for freshly prepared, nutritious food while a meeting of high school students will want pizza or hamburgers. One of the big logistical problems handled by the Compass Group during 2002's World Youth Day was ensuring that the 250 000 attendees were fed at regular meal times. An event planner must also ensure that caterers can handle special dietary needs or allergies.

- **Marketing.** Events are successful only if a smart marketing and promotion plan is in place. Successful events in the eyes of the client only happen when planners listen and understand the needs of their clients. Part of marketing is effectively communicating the event; budgets often determine the limits of promotional options, but having solid information about the clients will help planners know the most impactful modes of promotion. Many events are now taking advantage of social media tools that have relatively low costs while being personal and flexible in messaging format.

- **Finding sponsorship.** Unless a meeting's costs are being covered by a specific business, sponsorship is often critical to an event's success. The tourism sector can be slow to see the benefits of partnering with a special event, so finding good sponsorship is often challenging. Event organizers must learn persuasive techniques and be ready to show the benefits sponsorship brings to a company.

- **Legal and ethical considerations, and risk management.** As with any business, legal and ethical issues will arise. Knowing how to read and design contracts, as well as apply risk management techniques, can provide greater assurances that attendees are safe from harm. Large conventions and conferences can have very large budgets; the ethical and professional standards employed must meet any scrutiny from an outside person.

The conference service manager works at the site of the meeting or convention with the meeting planner to ensure all needs are properly met. The conference service manager understands the hotel or convention centre's functions and the responsibilities of each department. The basic responsibility is to make sure that schedules are maintained and that services are rendered according to the contract. The position involves continual coordination with the various operating departments to make certain that quality service standards are maintained. It also ensures all the elements of a convention or meeting run smoothly and efficiently from the time of the attendees' arrival, through the set-up, to billing and departures.

In addition to the public relations and service roles, the conference service manager has a sales responsibility to the host facility for rebooking the group by providing the best service and follow-through. Most conference service managers have worked in the hospitality industry where they may have gained experience in dealing with meetings and meeting planners.

CASE STUDY

Credit Refused

Amanda was a new front-desk clerk at a busy country inn. Enrolled in a hospitality management program at the local community college, she wanted to put into practice the skills she was learning in school. The fastidious innkeeper, Ms. Arnheim, kept profiles on each guest to ensure that their next stay at the inn was as good as or better than the last. Amanda was given the task of inputting guests' credit card numbers and ensuring she had collected information for the profiles. When she got to Mabel and Jane Kennedy, two delightful, grey-haired sisters, Mabel's credit card was refused. Amanda contacted the night manager, John, who made a courteous call to the two sisters, apologizing for the problem and asking if they had an alternate card they wished to use. Jane said she and Mabel planned to pay cash when they left and did not have another credit card.

John's next move was to call Ms. Arnheim to explain the problem. She told him not to worry and promised to handle it first thing in the morning. However, in the morning, the two sisters were even more adamant. Did the inn not trust them to pay their bill? They explained that they were on a package deal and would pay the total amount when they checked out the next morning. Against her better judgment, and not wishing to make a scene in the dining room, Ms. Arnheim decided to allow the sisters to continue their stay. She informed the front-desk staff that the women would settle their bill upon check-out the next day. At noon the next day, Amanda, who had been waiting for the sisters to check out, sent a housekeeper to their room to determine how much longer they would be. Imagine her surprise when the room was found empty, with no sign of the sisters or their baggage.

1. What is the root problem in this scenario?
2. As the manager or innkeeper, how would you have handled this problem? If your method is different from Ms. Arnheim's, what would the positive and negative of your decision be?
3. Should staff training include tactics for how to avoid situations like this?
4. As the innkeeper, what change to company policy would you make to ensure this did not happen again?

In Practice

Describe ten special events that might entice tourists to your region. Choose one event from your list and, in your own words, write an advertisement for your local newspaper that would help you promote this event.

Summary

- Events and conferences make up an exciting component of the tourism sector that includes gatherings for both business and leisure travellers.

- This industry encompasses a wide variety of events, ranging from local festivals to international sporting tournaments, from global summits to regional conventions.

- Festivals, fairs, and various special events draw in leisure tourists in a similar way as attractions.

- Trade shows, conferences, and meetings attract business travellers to various destinations.

- Events provide a community with jobs and can increase their presence and stature.

- Planning and staging an event requires tremendous coordination skills, lots of ingenuity, and plenty of patience.

- There have been many changes in the events area over the last fifteen years. Increased concerns over travel safety, increased costs paired with decreased available spending, and shorter booking times have forced the industry to adjust how it operates.

Questions

1. a) Define the terms *special event, festival, hallmark event, fundraising event, civic event, spectator sporting event.*
   b) Identify one example of each of the above events that has been hosted by your province or region.
   c) Describe five disadvantages to a community that hosts such events.
   d) Explain five benefits to a community that hosts special events.
2. a) Create a table that compares and contrasts a *convention*, a *conference*, and a *meeting* based on the following criteria: i) occupation of attendees; ii) number of attendees; iii) purpose of meeting; iv) location of the event; v) accessibility of the location; vi) payment of fees and costs; vii) duration of the event; viii) timing of the event.
   b) Name a recent conference and a recent convention held in your city or region.
3. Define *trade show* and list ten different annual trade shows in your region. Indicate whether each is open to the public or only to industry members.

4. More and more celebrities like Bob Geldof, Bono, and Willie Nelson are getting involved in politically oriented events like Live 8.

    a) How did the planning of these eight concerts differ from the manner in which a regular event is planned?

    b) Why do you think Canadian politicians might refuse to host an event such as the Live 8 concert in their city? Provide three reasons they might cite to back their position.

    c) What benefits might the concert have brought to your community?

    d) Do you think celebrities have the right to get involved in politics? Defend your answer.

5. Define the following terms as they relate to the events and conferences industry: *conference centre, Rendez-Vous Canada, convention centre, breakout room, seminar,* and *workshop.*

Notes

1. Adrian Morrow. "Toronto police were overwhelmed at G20, review reveals". *The Globe and Mail,* June 23, 2011.

2. Donald Getz, *Festivals, Special Events, and Tourism* (New York: Van Nostrand Reinhold, 1991), p. 44.

3. Ibid.

4. www.live8live.com.

5. www.tsn.ca/auto_racing/story/?id=237868 &lid=headline&lpos=topStory_main.

6. http://thestar.blogs.com/autoracing/ 2011/07/heres-how-many-people-watched-the-honda-indy-toronto.html.

7. Sylvia Densmore, *Staging Successful Small Town Events,* International Festival and Events Association Presentation, February 2001.

8. www.4-h-canada.ca/core/en/what-is-4-h.

9. www.independent.co.uk/news/business/ news/cirque-du-soleil-swings-to-1bn-revenue-as-it-mulls-shows-at-o2-2191850. html.

10. Hall, CM, "The definition and analysis of hallmark tourism events." *GeoJournal,* 1989. Vol 19(1), 263–268.

11. "Event's tourism boom may echo," *Toronto Star,* July 30, 2002, p. B3.

12. http://businesstoday.intoday.in/story/ london-olympics-preparations/1/24170. html.

13. www.vancouversun.com/sports/City+pu ts+million+toward+Olympic+Village+de bt/6459746/story.html.

14. www.Vancouver2010.com.

15. 2011 Financial Statements, Terry Fox Foundation: www.terryfox.org/ Foundation/_Library/docs/ 2011-03-31_Terry_Fox_Foundation_ FS.PDF.

16. David W. Howell and Robert A. Ellison, *Passport* (Toronto: Nelson Canada, 1995), p. 293.

Travel Services

Key terms

all-inclusive tour
commission
conference appointment
consolidator
consortium
corporate travel agency
escorted tour

full-service travel agency
gateway city
ground/land package
hosted tour
inbound tour
incentive travel
outbound tour

override
tour operator
tour wholesaler
travel counsellor
unescorted tour

Learning objectives

Having read this chapter you will be able to

1. Compare and contrast the roles of tour operator, tour wholesaler, and retail travel counsellor in the travel services industry.

2. Explain the steps in creating and costing a packaged tour.

3. Identify ten distinct types of tours offered in today's travel market.

4. Discuss the advantages and disadvantages of taking a packaged tour.

5. Describe the travel agency by size, clientele, and ownership.

6. Summarize the changes occurring in travel agency operations.

7. Discuss the value and role of incentive travel in today's corporate world.

Travel services comprise a major component of the tourism's sales force. Travel can be sold at the wholesale level by a tour operator or wholesaler, or at the retail level by a travel counsellor. Like most industries, travel services and tourism products have various routes, or distribution channels, through which they are processed to serve the end customer. For example, wholesaler tour operators sell packages *through* retail travel counsellors, not *to* them. They pay the retail travel counsellor a **commission** and sometimes a volume incentive, often referred to as an **override.**

Tour operators are restricted to selling travel arrangements for which they have been contracted. **Travel counsellors** can sell all types of travel anywhere, including components offered by tour wholesalers or prepackaged tours offered by tour operators. Working in travel services requires training and knowledge; more than 48 000 Canadians work in the travel services industry,[1] 74.2% of them have some level of post-secondary education.[2]

THE HISTORY OF TOURS

Tours are a relatively new concept in the history of tourism. Their beginnings can be traced back to the early seventeenth century, when noblemen from England arranged educational tours for their sons and heirs. *Le grand tour* was designed to educate sons in the ways of the civilized world. Upon completion of this tour, these educated, worldly young men returned to their lives as British noblemen.

The first recognized packaged tour was developed not by a travel agent (for no such thing existed at that time), but by a minister. Thomas Cook was a firm believer in the evils of liquor, so when the opportunity came to take his parish to a temperance meeting in Leicester, England, he arranged transportation by rail, a small picnic lunch, and entertainment for 570 of his followers. At the end of the day, after all bills had been paid, Mr. Cook discovered he had actually made a profit. The success of this afternoon was repeated many times over, so Mr. Cook left his ministerial calling to form the world's first travel agency.

Early tours were individually designed and were affordable only to the wealthy, but that situation changed with the new age of jet travel. What had been a costly

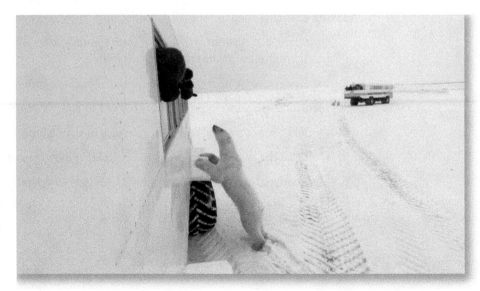

Tour operators have learned that their clientele like it live and close! (Churchill, MB) (Photo courtesy Canadian Tourism Commission.)

eighteen-hour flight or six-day ocean crossing to Europe now became a seven-hour trip. The new Boeing 707s carried a larger passenger load, so the cost of the trip was also substantially reduced. Tours suddenly became affordable for the middle class, and in 1958, more than 700 000 people took tours to Europe. By 1989, this figure had risen to more than seven million.

Taking tours is not only less expensive than booking the transportation, lodging, and attractions separately, but the cost is also known right from the time of booking. Tours are also prepaid, so the traveller need not worry about running out of money. Entrance to sights is guaranteed, because admission fees have been prepaid, and the sights have been chosen by a travel professional for their safety and appeal.

WHOLESALING

One unique method of distribution in the tourism industry is the **tour wholesaler.** Traditionally, tour wholesalers went from one travel supplier to another, booking space for their tours. They did not buy the product but acted as intermediaries between the supplier and the travel agency. Various components were "booked" and payment was exchanged when an actual purchase took place.

By the mid-1960s, however, the marketplace had changed. Most of the suppliers requested a prepurchase of the products to guarantee the low price. Tour operators became those companies willing to invest in advance, purchasing all the components of a tour prior to packaging it. There is still a distinction between these roles, although the lines have become blurred and the players may overlap. For example, Sunquest acts both as a wholesaler, selling individual products to retail agencies, and as a tour operator, selling complete tour packages, including the services of a destination representative. In contrast, the Toronto-based Holiday House sells only as a wholesaler and does not operate its own tour product.

The latest type of operator to enter the tour business is called a **consolidator**. Consolidators act as wholesalers or intermediaries between the airlines and travel agencies, and pay a commission on tickets sold. Most airlines no longer pay commissions to travel agencies, so the consolidator becomes an additional source of agency revenue. Consolidators purchase a large number of airline seats at a bulk price. They then sell these seats at a net price to travel agents, who pass the savings on to their customers.

The savings may be as great as 50%—but a word of caution to anyone planning to use one of these tickets. Each ticket has restrictions, which may include advance purchase dates, minimum stay requirements, and no itinerary changes. Furthermore, they are non-endorsable, meaning no other airline will accept them and flights may not be available every day. Most consolidators are reputable, but an agency must be cautious when dealing with a newer company. One of Canada's largest consolidators is Aventours. As long as international markets are regulated by IATA and deeply discounted tickets are not available to the travelling public, you can expect the role of consolidators to continue to expand.

There are five types of tour operators in Canada. The first is an *independent tour operator*, a category that includes large corporations such as American Express or individual operators such as Sunquest. The second type is a *travel agency*, which packages tours and sells them to its clients. The third is an *in-house tour operator*, owned and managed by a large company such as Air Canada. The fourth type of tour operator is strictly *online*. They provide no glossy brochures or sales representatives, but appeal to those travellers who are looking for savings and are comfortable with an online exchange. The final type does not sell to the public, but focuses on clubs, associations, and incentive travel groups. These tour packages must fit the special needs of the group (perhaps seniors or students) and may deal with such concerns as wheelchair accessibility or special medical equipment.

Tours are designated as either an **outbound tour** or an **inbound tour**. An inbound tour brings guests from a foreign country to Canada, generating jobs and revenue for Canadians. When Canadians travel to Santo Domingo using a packaged tour, they are outbound, and their tourism dollars are being spent in a foreign country.

Tour Development

A tour is "the services on a tourist's itinerary, usually consisting of, but not limited to, transportation, accommodation, transfers, and sightseeing in one or more countries, geographical regions, or cities. The services are entirely reserved or contracted in advance by a travel agent, a tour wholesaler, or a tour operator and are fully prepaid by the tourist."[3]

Tours are divided into two major categories: *independent tours* and *packaged tours*. Individuals or groups who prefer to create their own independent tour may do so using the services of a travel agent and a tour wholesaler. These customers choose between the assorted components offered by the tour wholesaler. Many travellers are opting to bypass the travel agency and do their own tour planning online. Using an online tour operator like Expedia.ca or Travelocity.ca, they can choose flight times, hotels, dining packages, events, and attractions they would like to see. Arrangements can be made at any time of the day or night, and the website guarantees flexibility for the purchaser.

A packaged tour, on the other hand, has a set itinerary with all of its components in place. Packaged tours may or may not have an escort and are sold to individuals as well as to groups. Once again, the internet provides customers with fully designed packages that may be booked at any time. The companies that sell this type of tour generally focus on a single travel market, or type of traveller. For example, they might target their services toward the single traveller, the economy-minded traveller, or the higher-value traveller. The budget-minded traveller would choose from tour operators like Sunquest. A higher-value traveller is willing to spend more on the trip and looks for quality sites and products to be supplied. An example of a tour operator selling high-end, unusual products would be Exodus Tours, a British-based tour operator.

www.exodus.co.uk

There are four steps in the creation of a tour: the tour idea, negotiations, costing and pricing, and promotion (Figure 10.1).

The Tour Idea Every tour has to be new once. After its first venture, the tour can be offered time and time again—if it was initially successful. New ideas, however, require creativity and the ability to listen to what people want. The idea may come from a supplier who provides a super deal for accommodations if the operator books a trip to the supplier's hotel. Or it may be an offshoot of a current trip, such as switching from a whale-watching tour to instead visiting Shediac, New Brunswick, to see the world's largest lobster and enjoy a lobster feast.

FIGURE 10.1
Tour development
stages

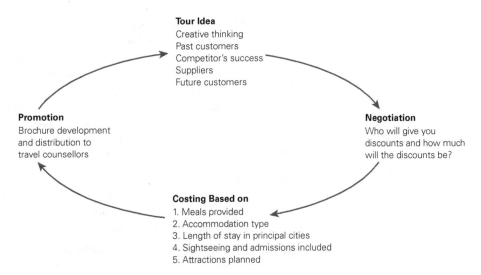

Tour Idea
Creative thinking
Past customers
Competitor's success
Suppliers
Future customers

Negotiation
Who will give you
discounts and how much
will the discounts be?

Costing Based on
1. Meals provided
2. Accommodation type
3. Length of stay in principal cities
4. Sightseeing and admissions included
5. Attractions planned

Promotion
Brochure development
and distribution to
travel counsellors

Market research is needed to determine if there is a need or a desire for the tour concept. Without consumer demand, the tour, no matter how exciting, will not be a success. Most tours are developed around a central theme or destination: for example, learning more about polar bears in their natural habitat on Baffin Island. The theme or destination is the skeletal plan, which the planner must flesh out by providing other interesting or exciting reasons for people to take the tour.

Negotiations Once the destination and other attractions are chosen for inclusion in the tour, the negotiation phase of planning begins. Are there rooms available at the right price? Is there a suitable restaurant in the area for dinner? Will the chosen attractions guarantee entry at a predetermined group rate? Will a tour guide with specialized skills and knowledge be needed for any part of the tour? What form(s) of transportation will be needed? These questions and others need to be answered before the next phase begins.

Costing and Pricing Costing is the process of determining the total cost of providing the tour for an anticipated number of customers. Pricing is the process of deciding the amount each customer should pay to cover costs, including a markup, operating expenses, and profit. In the costing stage, the direct cost of each component of the tour must be determined, such as transportation, lodging, attendance fees, and exchange rates. Then indirect costs such as promotion, the tour planner's salary, and other overhead items are added. In the pricing stage, a markup or profit on the net cost of the tour must be calculated.

Once total cost is determined, assumptions must be made about the volume or number of tour participants in order to work out the price of the tour to the traveller. Correct costing requires an accurate assessment of certain variables, especially sales—usually projected based on past experience and projected load factors. Costing is often mistaken as a simple process. However, costing out travel is a detailed and demanding endeavour, and accuracy is crucial in order for a company to reach its financial goals. Several factors will affect the price to the consumer. In each case, the operator and the travel agent should try to find the balance that best suits the target market.[4]

1. **Meal costs.** The tour operator can significantly lower the cost of the tour if the traveller pays for each meal separately. Advantages include less paperwork for the operator and perhaps greater choice for the traveller. The disadvantage is that tour participants will need to budget and pay for each meal. Many people like to pay one price and not have to worry about other costs during the trip. A tour operator who permits unlimited choice from the menu (à la carte) is offering more than an operator who arranges a set menu (table d'hôte); the tour price will reflect this.

2. **Accommodation type.** The level of accommodation significantly affects the price of the tour. An economy tour books less expensive motels, usually in smaller towns or out-of-the-way locations in larger cities. Deluxe tours are booked with the finest hotels in locations convenient for side trips, shopping, restaurants, and attractions.

3. **Length of stay in principal cities.** Usually, deluxe tours spend more time at a principal destination because a good tour should be relaxing. The pacing of a tour (the amount of free or leisure time within a tour's schedule) is an important sales feature. This free time allows individuals to pursue specific interests, explore the destination, shop, or simply relax. Driving long distances every day is not a hallmark of a deluxe tour.

4. **Sightseeing.** Itineraries that indicate "the remainder of the day is open to explore …" may be tours trying to keep costs down. Built-in sightseeing increases the tour cost. Some people prefer to have every minute accounted for; they want pampering and lots of supervision. Others prefer to make their own decisions and want more open time.

5. **Attractions.** Although the cost of the tour is higher when admission fees are included in the tour price, inclusion saves the traveller money in the long run because group discounts have usually been negotiated with the attraction manager. There is no general rule in costing a tour. Many people do not want to be nickel-and-dimed, whereas others prefer a low-cost tour that allows them to decide how much to pay for meals and amenities along the way.

Promotion The communication and promotion of tour packages have grown in sophistication. Traditional print mediums, such as bright, glossy brochures, with pictures featuring the excitement of a rafting experience or the comfort of a hotel, remain a staple of the industry. Web-based tools, including video content and social media, allow customers in engage and interact with tour companies. Without good promotional material, even the best tour products will fail to connect with their customers.

Tour Categories

There are two main types of prearranged packaged tours. It is important for the customer as well as the travel counsellor selling the tours to understand the advantages and disadvantages of each type.

Independent Tours Travel counsellors and tour operators can arrange independent tours, but as previously mentioned, customers may create their own vacation packages by using one of the many online tour companies. So why use a travel agency? An agency likely knows the reputation of the chosen tour company, the destination's political or environmental atmosphere, and can accurately provide information regarding documents and pre–trip medical advice that should be sought. They are also a link to home in case things do not go as planned. The fees charged by travel agencies can be well worth the expertise they provide when helping you meet your travel needs while moving you through the details of arrangements. Single travellers obtain all the benefits of volume discounts and prearranged, guaranteed rates without sacrificing independence and flexibility. Customers can determine departure and return dates as well as budget.

Independent tours vary in flexibility and complexity. Some tours allow the customer to choose accommodations at different hotels listed in the brochure, while others provide car rentals, which increase flexibility for the traveller. Other tours may offer fly/drive, rail/drive, rail/fly, cruise/fly, or other combinations. The keys to independent tour success are flexibility and cost savings for the traveller.

Independent tours may use more than one tour wholesaler in the creation of the package, and a distinct disadvantage of taking an independent tour is that you are on your own. There is no company representative available to help find solutions in case of a problem or difficulty encountered during the trip.

Group Tours The original group tour was based on a true group—a club or a society that wished to take a trip. In order to take part in the tour, a traveller had to be a member of the club. Today, the main difference between a group tour and an independent tour is in the cost. Group tours are usually based on a given number of participants and may be cancelled or delayed if the required number of spaces for that departure date has not been sold. There are two types of group tours: **ground/land package** and **all-inclusive**.

Ground/land package tours include the land arrangements for the purchaser: hotel, attractions, perhaps some meals, and a rental car. They do not include airfare in the price.

Upscale tour operators choose hotels of distinction such as the Fairmont Empress Hotel in Victoria, with its renowned afternoon English Tea.
(Photo: The Fairmont Empress.)

All-inclusive tours have a specific combination of features, usually including transportation, accommodation, meals, attractions, special events, and service charges (such as tips and baggage handling), and may include amenities such as free travel bags and discount coupons. These tours may be fully escorted, partially escorted (hosted), or unescorted (independent).

- Fully **escorted tours** have a *tour director* travelling with the group. The tour director is responsible for the participants' safety and enjoyment, makes sure that the tour operates smoothly, and handles any problems or difficulties. Although the director is usually well prepared to describe the sights of an area, many companies hire step-on guides when visiting a city. Step-on guides have special training and a deep knowledge of and love for their city, region, or site. This makes their presentation more responsive to the needs of the group and provides participants with reliable answers to their questions. This type of tour is often preferred by first-time travellers and can be valuable to travellers visiting countries whose language, customs, and culture are significantly different.

- In a partially escorted or **hosted tour**, the group travels from destination to destination as a group, without a company representative. At each destination, a tour director from that city greets them and stays with them throughout their stay.

- In an **unescorted tour**, the group has an itinerary and travels without any company representative.

Types of Tours

Tours may be defined by destination and by their focus on a specific country, region, or city. A trip to the Cabot Trail in Nova Scotia is a good example of a regional tour. A two-city tour might bring visitors from Buffalo, New York, to both Montreal and Quebec City, giving them a varied experience of Canada's French culture. Tours defined by purpose are even more varied. Here are some popular examples (some will be familiar from Chapter 9):

- **adventure tours:** whitewater rafting on the Clearwater River through Skull Canyon in Saskatchewan
- **religious tours:** visiting a religious site, such as Bethlehem, at Christmas
- **ethnic tours:** being immersed in a different culture, or returning to cultural roots
- **educational tours:** travelling to learn something new, whether visiting museums, historical sites, or art galleries, or enjoying a series of lectures on, and theatrical productions of, George Bernard Shaw's plays
- **soft adventure tours:** enjoying the thrill of adventure while appreciating the comforts of life, an experience provided by most safaris in Africa
- **sports and recreational tours:** golfing or skiing at a resort, or biking along the old highways of France
- **ecotourism tours:** with expert local guides, expeditions to the rainforest or other ecosystems to learn about wildlife, vegetation, and ecology
- **special interest tours:** gambling in Windsor, visiting the wineries of British Columbia, or going to see the Calgary Stampede

Special needs tours are organized for groups of people with special medical problems. For example, a group of senior citizens with emphysema would require not only medication, but also a supply of oxygen and special handling and permits to transport it, especially if crossing borders. People with physical disabilities must have hotel rooms that are fully accessible as well as attractions and restaurants that can accommodate their needs. *Incentive tours* are created for a company as a reward for employees who have done outstanding work. They are considered gifts and are not taxable.

Tours can also be defined by their duration, such as a seven-day tour or a two-week tour. The newest trend is the three-day weekend tour. This package fits into the changing lifestyle of North Americans who, according to statistics, are taking shorter, more frequent vacations.

www.crossculturalsolu-tions.org

The Travel Counsellor's Responsibility for Tours

Although tours can be sold directly to the consumer by the company that designs the tour (provided the company holds a retail licence), many tours are still sold through *travel counsellors*. Tour wholesalers provide a commission to the travel agency for each tour sold. Even though travel counsellors work for the wholesaler, they are responsible for helping potential travellers choose the right tour for them. The counsellor must understand tour requirements and provide accurate details, including those described on the following pages.[5]

FOOTPRINT

As we have noted more than once, the relationship between tourism and the environment is a delicate one. On the one hand, tourists bring in money that can go toward environmental programs and recycling initiatives. On the other hand, airplanes, cars, and cruise lines are some of the Earth's biggest polluters. What is a customer to do? Being a smart green shopper extends not only to your rejection of plastic bags and use of sustainable products, but also to the type of vacation and tour you take. Several companies in Canada have created environmentally responsible tours that guests can enjoy guilt-free. These are just some of the several ecotours available to guests wanting to see more of Canada:

- Tundra Buggy Tours—this tour was created in 1979 to take guests from Churchill, Manitoba, to the frozen tundra 30 km away to see polar bears up close. The tundra buggies travel only on existing trails so they don't upset the fragile ecosystem.

- Boreal Ecology—in Saskatchewan, guests are guided by canoe and kayak to view wildlife and the spectacular boreal forest.

- Earthfoot Trekking—guests travel by horseback into the remote wilderness of the Yukon Territory.

- Discovering Alpine Flowers—tourists hike through forests and alpine meadows to learn more about floral identification and appreciation in the Rockies.

Validity Dates Tour brochures indicate when a tour is available at the stated price, as well as the dates of departure from the gateway city for international or charter tours. It is important that the counsellor know these dates, as tour prices may change depending on the season.

Gateway City The **gateway city** is the point from which the flight will leave or where the client can join or leave the tour. Travel counsellors work with their clients, helping them plan travel to and from the gateway city.

Cultural tourism often includes a show of art or dance, helping to give the tourist better insight into the local heritage. Here an Inuit elder performs a First Nations ritual.
(Photo courtesy Canadian Tourism Commission.)

Itinerary and Amenities The schedules and particular details may or may not be explicitly stated in promotional brochures. Customers rely on the expertise of travel counsellors to research and communicate these details. The number of meals paid for in the tour price may not be obvious. Where sightseeing is "suggested" or "optional," the cost is not included in the tour. If the brochure says the tour will "see" rather than "visit" an attraction, it means travellers will view the attraction from the bus window. If the counsellor does not read the fine print critically, the client will probably be dissatisfied with the tour.

Price Tour Prices will vary depending on (a) the season, (b) modes of transportation used, (c) length of stay in principal cities, (d) type of accommodation, (e) number of meals provided, (f) sightseeing and other activities that are pre-booked, and (g) additional service charges, such as tips and baggage handling that are included. Some brochures quote their low-season price, which sounds like a good deal until the client realizes the tour takes place in the Caribbean during hurricane season! Brochures are often confusing and contain fine print that must be explained to the customer. The travel counsellor must inform the client of items included in the price, items that are optional at an additional charge, surcharges (e.g., for currency fluctuations or fuel costs), and items that must be paid for by the customer.

Name of the Tour Operator Both the client and the travel counsellor need to know the name of the operator or wholesaler for further reference. In some provinces, it is a legal requirement to name the tour operator. When problems occur, the travel counsellor should investigate in order to prevent a recurrence or should stop recommending this particular operator or wholesaler to clients.

A final concern shared by travel counsellors and travellers alike is safety. For example, disreputable operators may use equipment that has not undergone a thorough safety check, or because of economic concerns, may choose a poorly located hotel, putting the client at risk.

In summary, the travel counsellor is responsible for relaying accurate and reliable information to the prospective traveller. A counsellor who neglects to point out disadvantages as well as additional costs to the client is not providing good service—and dissatisfied customers do not return.

Regulating the Tour Industry

Canadian tour operators are regulated by many different organizations. If the tour contains an air or rail component, the tour operator must obtain approval from the National Transportation Agency prior to promoting and operating the tour. Tour operators are also licensed by individual provinces, and the interests of the purchaser are protected by provincial consumer affairs departments.

Who protects the purchasers and their deposits when a tour operator goes bankrupt? Tour operators are required to have a special type of insurance policy called a *performance bond*, which guarantees payment to all parties (clients, travel agencies, and suppliers) in case they experience financial difficulties. British Columbia, Ontario, and Quebec all require that tour operators maintain trust accounts and compensation funds, and provide the province with detailed financial statements. The tour brochure and its information are also controlled by some provinces.

The International Air Transport Association (IATA) plays an important role in the creation of international tours. It requires that every IATA-approved tour have the following components: air transportation on an IATA carrier, accommodations for the duration of the tour, and at least one additional feature (which might be sightseeing, an activity, or transfers). IATA tour brochures will also contain some very specific pieces of information:

- What is and is not included in the package
- Deposit and payment schedules
- Travel documents needed (passport, visas, health card)
- Cancellation and refund policies
- The tour operator's limited responsibilities and liability

The Advantages of Taking a Packaged Tour

Tours are becoming more popular because they offer one-stop shopping. From the colourful brochures, customers can glimpse the facilities available at their destination. If they choose a reputable firm, they can be assured that the tour's components will be of high quality. Everything is prearranged, and the customer knows that tickets and accommodations have been reserved and all the other details of the trip, including transfer of baggage, have been organized. Instead of waiting in line for tickets, prepaid tour admission ensures immediate access to sites and events.

Volume buying saves money, and travellers need extra money only for shopping. Most tours use direct flights, and ground transportation is waiting on arrival. In addition, tour companies recognize the need for some individualization and will build preferences into their packages. Finally, one of the most important

SNAPSHOT

Randy Williams

Randy Williams served as president and CEO of the Tourism Industry Association of Canada (TIAC) from 2002 through 2009. As CEO, he brought a strong voice and positive action, supported by more than three decades of travel and tourism experience, to Canada's tourism industry.

Mr. Williams began his career in accommodations, managing hotels across Western Canada. He then moved into tourism services, becoming the first president and CEO of Tourism Saskatchewan, Canada's first provincial private–public partnership for tourism marketing. He then moved into travel services as president of the Association of Canadian Travel Agencies (ACTA), transforming ACTA into a strong national organization with regional offices across Canada.

Building on TIAC's involvement in cross-border travel issues, which included founding membership in the Coalition for Secure and Trade-Efficient Borders, in 2005, Mr. Williams formed the binational Passport Coalition to address the Western Hemisphere Travel Initiative. "The Western Hemisphere Travel Initiative (WHTI) is a U.S. law that requires all travellers, including U.S. and Canadian citizens, to present a valid passport or other approved secure document when entering the United States from within the western hemisphere."[6] This was a proactive move to be involved in cross-border security issues while simultaneously understanding the negative impacts of additional barriers to travel at the border.

As president of TIAC, Mr. Williams worked to ensure that tourism was at the forefront of public policy debate. He was also a strong advocate of easily accessible visitor information services and was instrumental in the establishment of *.travel*, a sponsored top-level domain exclusive to the travel and tourism industry that will help travel consumers find the information they need to make purchase decisions on the internet.

During his tenure with TIAC, Randy Williams pushed Canada's national tourism advocate to greater heights and achievements than ever before. His dedication and expertise benefited the almost 190 000 businesses in Canada, both large and small, that depend on tourism for their livelihood.

motivators of travel is companionship, and tours ensure a trip with fellow travellers who have similar interests and needs. Many baby boomers enjoy this style of travel, and growth in the tour industry is expected to be strong.

The Disadvantages of Taking a Packaged Tour

There are some drawbacks to taking a tour. Dissatisfaction is sure to occur if the tour operator does not provide what has been promised in the brochure—a quality product. Travel counsellors and clients depend on the operator's integrity and financial stability. Because a tour is a prearranged trip, it is inflexible. Your time is not your own. When the tour moves on to the next site, so must you. Do the advantages of taking a packaged tour outweigh the disadvantages? Only the consumer can answer that question.

TRAVEL AGENCIES

The travel agency is a retail business, somewhat like a department store. It has a broad array of items for sale and is staffed by knowledgable professionals capable of guiding you through a travel purchase. The agency arranges for travel services with suppliers such as airlines, cruise ships, bus companies, railroads, car rental firms, hotels, tour operators, and sightseeing operators, and serves as a vital link between the traveller and the suppliers.

The difference between purchasing directly from a supplier and an agency is the amount and quality of personal service provided at a travel agency. Quality travel agencies understand that they must build high quality relationships with their customers. Advice and guidance on travel and travel products remain a substantial part of the job, especially with leisure travel, so the original *travel agent* title has been replaced with that of *travel counsellor*. Travel counsellors are knowledgable and persuasive about the products they sell, making them invaluable to travel suppliers. Travel agencies are firmly established as the principal distribution system for travel suppliers, and they provide the most efficient way for the consumer to sort out the ever-increasing array of travel options.

www.citc.ca

Types of Travel Agencies

Travel agencies in Canada are categorized in several ways: by size, by the services they offer, and by ownership.

Small agencies have annual sales of a million dollars or less and generally employ one to three travel counsellors. Much of their business is through word of mouth, and personal service provides them with a small but loyal customer base. Medium-sized agencies employ a staff of eight to ten travel counsellors. They rely on word of mouth too, but also invest in local promotions and advertising. They often focus on both business and pleasure travel. Larger agencies are usually highly diversified.

Competition has been so fierce over the past decade that many smaller agencies have sold out to larger, more stable firms or have become part of a merger. These agencies have departments that specialize in travel market segments, such as the corporate market or group tours. They can often compete more effectively because they can afford top-of-the-line equipment and a larger marketing budget.[7] Agencies may be full service (handling both vacation and business travel), corporate (dealing with business travel only), and specialty (handling specific products such as cruises or clients with special needs).

Full-Service Agency Most agencies fit into the full-service category and are equipped to serve all categories of traveller needs, from bus tours to wilderness tours to business trips. The business of a **full-service travel agency** is typically divided 60/40 between leisure travel and business travel or vice versa. The combination provides a more consistent customer base: business travel may be busy when vacation travel is slow. Larger agencies usually have divisions and counsellors that specialize in categories of travel such as business, international, domestic tours, or cruises. As a result, customers feel comfortable going to one full-service agency for all travel needs.

Corporate Agency The **corporate travel agency** specializes in business travel. In an effort to discourage walk-in vacation requests, many corporate agencies do not even identify themselves as travel agencies because the emphasis of their service differs. The nature of the client's business dictates when and where the travel will occur. The counsellor is responsible for finding the best-priced airfare, a convenient hotel, and a car rental. Whereas a vacation counsellor may have time to plan, business travellers often call requesting a flight, accommodations, and a car rental for the next day. Most corporate agencies charge their clients either a management fee or a per-ticket fee and change fee.

Some corporate agencies get so much business from a major client that they establish a branch in the workplace to deal solely with that client's needs. The agency becomes an integral part of the workplace, saving the client time and money, while the agency is assured of a constant customer base. Some large corporations have developed their own travel departments, which not only plan individual business travel for employees but also arrange conventions and meetings. Travel counsellors working directly for a corporation typically get higher salaries and better company benefits than agency employees.

Online travel agencies such as Travelocity, Air Miles, and Expedia have no concrete office space but run huge call centres to handle questions and help with travel problems. Booking online with these companies is very simple even for inexperienced computer users.

Specialty Agency Most agencies cannot deal exclusively with one type of travel because the people needed to fill a tour do not live in one geographic area. However, in large urban centres, some **specialty travel agencies** exist.

Some agencies may be certified cruise specialists. They represent the full line of cruise products, and their agents have had additional training on various cruise ships and on how to sell a cruise package. The wide variety of vacations available from the cruise lines, the different ships and their service styles, and the niche markets that are targeted often complicate the choice of a cruise vacation. A cruise specialist will know if the ship the client is looking at provides a product suitable for families with children, the seniors market, travellers with disabilities, or single passengers looking for fun and romance. These companies will often promote cruises with themes such as country-and-western or big-band music.

A specialty travel agency deals with a single type of travel product, such as Canadian wilderness adventures.
(Photo courtesy Canadian Tourism Commission.)

As noted in Chapter 9, adventure travel is a fast-growing segment of the travel market. Agencies specialize in arranging exotic trips to places inaccessible to the everyday traveller: a river trip down the Amazon, an African safari, cross-country skiing in the Arctic, or hiking in the Himalayas. Travel can be arranged for both the hard adventurer who prefers primitive accommodations, and the soft adventurer who wants the comforts of a fine hotel and restaurant each evening.

Senior travel is another specialty market. Planning seniors' trips may require knowledge of places with wheelchair accessibility, restaurants that will cater to specific dietary requirements, or motels with handrails in the bathrooms. To be successful with the mature travel market, tours should be designed so that clients spend less time travelling and more time at attractions and destinations.

Clients with disabilities form another specialty market. As discussed earlier in the text, travellers with disabilities make up a huge untapped market, and as baby boomers age, this market will become even more significant. Finding the proper accommodations, the right restaurants, and easily accessible attractions or events is not easy, and an agency specializing in the needs of this market while providing exciting tour opportunities will be on the cutting edge of the marketplace for tours.

Ethnic agencies focus on creating connections between immigrants or the children of immigrants and their countries of origin. Canada has welcomed people of all nations to its shores for centuries, and Canadians of all backgrounds may decide to research and visit their ancestors' homeland. Any ethnic group that has a large representation in Canada is a prime target market for a specialized agency.

Agency Operations

How do travel agencies make their money? What do they sell? Who regulates them? Travel agencies form an important distribution channel for all our tourism products. Most suppliers of tourism products pay the agency a commission on every sale. An agency's income used to come from the sale of airline tickets, but major airlines have dropped commissions entirely, forcing travel agencies to charge customers a fee for services that can include a fee for cancelling or changing a trip.

Agencies still receive commissions from consolidators, cruise lines, tour operators, car rental agencies, and railways. A smaller portion of revenue is generated from the sale of insurance policies or travel accessories (e.g., guidebooks). Travel agencies may earn additional revenue from *override commissions*—commissions paid at a higher rate once an agency reaches a set sales total over a given period of time. The increase provides an additional incentive to sell the supplier's products. Several factors are changing the way agencies earn revenue.

- After deregulation, major airlines first reduced the amount of commission they would pay on each ticket sold, and then eliminated commissions entirely. To replace this loss of revenue, many agencies now charge customers a service fee of $35 to $100 per ticket.

- The internet has become a competitor for travel agencies, providing interactive sales sites for hotels and attractions, allowing clients to book directly with the supplier. In addition, the latest in discounted last-minute sale prices are quickly put on the internet, providing the surfer with last-minute travel bargains and the supplier with additional revenue on products that might have gone unsold.

- New self-ticketing devices allow travellers to book and ticket themselves on flights, including check-in. These kiosks provide a fast alternative to using a travel counsellor. Airlines may provide this service on their websites.

- Expenses that might have been absorbed by the agency ten years ago are now being charged to the client. These include services like booking a bed and breakfast, long-distance calls or faxes, or passport applications.

With more and more opportunities for individual travellers to use the internet to research and book their own vacations, agencies must become more creative in bringing in additional revenue.

With changes in customer knowledge, involvement, and access through technology, some wonder if the travel agency business coming to an end. As with any business, technology forces changes that are sometimes difficult to adjust to, and those businesses unwilling or unable to rethink their product and its delivery are eliminated.

The travel services industry is facing a challenge over the next decade. Two factors will help it survive. First, businesses are discovering that travel counsellors do save them money. A study by Topaz International of Portland, Oregon, found that fares generated by a corporate travel agency saved the company an average of $116 per ticket. Second, purchasers using the internet often miss issues around travel, such as insurance and security, as well as the restrictive details around web fares, such as tickets that are frequently non-refundable and non-changeable. There are still many customers that prefer the personal touch of a travel counsellor, and although the way a travel agency earns revenue may change, the professional expertise and friendly service of the travel counsellor remains a competitive advantage of travel services.

Forms of Ownership

Similar to hotels and restaurants, agencies may be owned privately or operate as part of a chain, franchise, or consortium/co-operative.

Private Ownership In the early days of the travel agency, private ownership was most common, with many agencies run by families. However, changes in payment and fee structures over the last decade, especially in the airline industry, were extremely damaging to small, privately owned agencies. Today, independently owned agencies must work hard to survive in a travel world in which competition from organizations and advancing technologies is fierce. Successful agencies of this type often serve local clientele and provide a high level of service to meet the needs of their clientele.

Chain Agencies Chain agencies operate under a single corporate ownership structure and one management policy. A larger volume of business allows more vigorous promotion, more buying power, and a higher net profit than is available to independents. Some brand names, such as American Express and Thomas Cook, have gained worldwide recognition. Employees often receive better fringe benefits and more training, and have greater opportunities to focus on special skills or to rise in the management structure.

Franchises Travel agency franchises were not introduced until the 1980s, but have become popular. The benefits and the drawbacks are similar to those of any franchise system. Most customers don't know whether an agency is an individually owned and operated franchise or part of a chain. Franchises, like chains, are rigidly controlled and thus have difficulty filling the special needs of a local clientele but employees receive good training and have good job opportunities. Canada's largest franchised agencies are Uniglobe and Carlson Wagonlit Travel. Carlson Wagonlit operates both a chain and a franchise system.

Consortiums In an attempt to survive the fierce competition of the 1980s and 1990s, smaller travel agencies have formed **consortiums** or co-operatives. In this system, which is similar to hotel referral systems such as Best Western, the agency keeps its independence and personal identity but joins with other independents to get large-scale advertising campaigns, better purchasing power, and a brand name. Each member pays an initial membership fee and a continuing services fee. The central office arranges advertising and promotional activities, negotiates supplier agreements, and administers the affairs of the organization. Canada's best-known co-operatives are Advantage, GIANTS, GEM, and T-Comm.

Regulating Travel Agencies

Before a travel agency can begin operating, it must obtain an "appointment"— a form of permission to conduct business. There are two major **conference appointments** required:

1. The Air Transport Association of Canada (ATAC) represents commercial aviation in Canada. The ATAC Traffic Conference handles the Canadian Travel Agency program, as well as all matters dealing with interline standards, ticketing, and passenger and baggage processing. ATAC runs its programs by contract with IATA.

2. The International Air Transport Association (IATA) regulates the sale of international airline tickets.

To apply for ATAC and IATA certification, a travel agency must be open and operating; it must have the cash to purchase tickets directly from the airlines or it must have an agreement with a fully accredited agency to do the ticketing on its behalf. New agencies must have at least two full-time employees—a qualified management person and a qualified ticketing agent. The location must be visible to the public and clearly identified as a travel agency. It must have in place sufficient financial backing to ensure continued operation and must maintain its financial records according to the BSP accounting procedures.

Finally, the agency must show that it is actively promoting travel through some method of advertising, including brochures, flyers, direct mail, or newspaper advertisements. In addition to these regulations, British Columbia, Quebec, and Ontario all have legislation to protect the traveller, and new agencies must register with their provincial registrar. Ontario's *Travel Industry Act* includes a specific section to protect the consumer. Agencies must take out special insurance and bonding to protect their customers in case the tour operator files for bankruptcy prior to the completion of a client's trip.[8] After the bankruptcy of Jetsgo, provinces without this protection are looking at mandatory insurance to cover travellers placed in this position.

In Canada, the Canadian Institute of Travel Counsellors (CITC) works with the travel trade focusing on training and instructional materials, and ensuring professional standards are met. As with all professional organizations, the CITC has created a code of ethics that members agree to follow. Under the auspices of the CITC, the Canadian Tourism Human Resource Council has developed a new program for national certification of travel counsellors and managers based on the required skills, knowledge, and attitudes.

Marketing Travel Trade Products

Travel services assist in bringing together the four "P's" of marketing: product, place, price, and promotion. Travel agencies promote the tourism *products* of other suppliers. However, they are not considered to be a product themselves, but a channel of distribution—that is, the *place* where tourism products are sold. *Pricing* the products is not usually the agency's concern, as many products are already packaged and priced. Retail stores build in their profit margin by setting the difference between their buying and selling price. Since travel agencies cannot set the price of the products they sell, they are trying to restore profits by adding service charges.

Promotion is an important part of any business's survival strategy. Tour companies help to promote their products by supplying tour operators with colourful brochures and displays. They also have sales representatives drop by to discuss the products and provide sales help to the agents. To remain competitive, travel agencies must promote both the products they represent as well as their own services. Communication skills are important; larger chains may lean toward a focus on television advertisements while smaller, private agencies might use regional newspapers or personal messaging through email. Sales skills, including upselling additional products and closing sales, have been prized in the travel services area. However, with the increased availability of rich customer information, many agencies have moved toward a customized service approach, demonstrating their value in how well they anticipate and meet the needs of their customers.

In Practice

Many people use a travel agency only for airline ticketing. As a travel counsellor, what techniques would you use to convince a traveller that you can and should arrange the car rental, hotel, or rail ticket? What carefully chosen words would you use to sell more to your client?

INCENTIVE TRAVEL

Incentive travel is another growing area of travel sales. Originally designed as a prize for employee performance, **incentive travel** is now being used in many different ways. Incentive purchase cards such as the Air Miles card are also gaining popularity. From a business's standpoint, incentive travel creates a winning situation for all parties involved: the corporation wins with more sales, increased employee productivity, less absenteeism, and better safety records; the employees win by being treated to an exclusive trip; the incentive travel company wins by increasing sales and profits.

Incentive travel has grown because it has been shown to be a positive motivator for many employees, specifically in sales-focused work environments. Winning a trip based on performance can increase an employee's status among peers and family members, and provides the opportunity to network with other high performers within their company. Not only can a potential trip motivate extra effort, the winning employee returns feeling good and continues to work hard. By using incentive travel, companies tie rewards into their corporate culture and link personal effort with corporate objectives.

At the other end of incentive travel is the destination. Resorts, hotels, and tourism bureaus are starting to see the benefits of bringing in hundreds of people through incentive travel programs. These destinations are actively involved in persuading incentive planners that theirs is the perfect destination and offering inspection tours to make their point.

A good travel counsellor must have strong knowledge of many different tourism products, be detail-oriented, and enjoy working with people.
(Photo: Paula Kerr.)

How Incentive Companies Operate

Although it looks simple on paper, developing an incentive travel program is quite complex. Initially, the manager in an incentive house or a specialty incentive travel agency approaches the marketing manager of a company and suggests how incentive travel could help solve the corporation's problem—which could be anything from the need to sell more products to reducing absenteeism.

For example, the incentive travel manager would work out the savings for the company if absenteeism could be reduced by 50%. A portion of these savings would be put toward travel costs. The incentive company would be responsible for setting rules, promotion, program administration, and awards. Accurate records of absenteeism and tardiness over the specified time period would be kept, and letters of encouragement would be sent to participants. To motivate those who had already missed too many days, the incentive company could provide opportunities for employees to buy in (i.e., people who do not meet the quota or criteria

CASE STUDY

Adventure in Spades

Doris had just lost her husband of twenty-six years and the depression she was experiencing worried her three daughters. They felt she needed to get away; in fact, an exciting trip might lessen the grief they were all feeling. After doing internet research, the girls chose a well-known company called Tours of a Lifetime, and bought a trip that included exciting experiences and opportunities for each of them, such as bungee jumping and river rafting.

Doris agreed reluctantly, and soon found herself hiking 5 km into the mountains from the Jasper Valley. The weather was gorgeous and soon the whole tour group had become friendly. Her daughters bungee-jumped and climbed in the mountains, but Doris declined to take part. Finally, they convinced her to join them for whitewater rafting. Each raft held seven people and an experienced whitewater guide. They each wore life vests,

but their guide assured them that falling out of the raft was unlikely—and anyway, the company had guidelines in place that addressed any dangerous situations.

Doris began to relax once the trip was underway. The first three sets of rapids were small but exhilarating. As the raft headed for the fourth set of rapids, however, Doris turned to say something to the guide just as the raft bounced in the whitewater. The raft came down and Doris's ankle broke on one of the boulders that lay under the surface. The pain was excruciating. The guide steered the raft safely to shore and her raft mates carried her ashore. The ankle was cleanly broken and swelling fast. The problem they faced was how to get Doris to a medical facility. It was a ten-hour hike over backcountry in order for medics to reach their position. Doris could not even stand.

1. What initial three steps should their guide take to begin handling the situation? Why did you choose these steps?
2. Doris will have to be hospitalized. Should she get a refund on the unused portion of her trip?
3. Does Doris have a right to sue the company for negligence? Why or why not?
4. If you were the tour company owner, how would you handle this situation from your office? To avoid future accidents, what could you do?

are allowed to pay the difference, enabling them to go with their peers and fill the empty slots on the trip).

The Society of Incentive Travel Executives (SITE) publishes a newsletter and conducts training programs and seminars on how to succeed in incentive travel. Most important, SITE is the sounding board for problems and opportunities in incentive travel.

www.siteglobal.com

In Practice

Make a list of companies in your community that could benefit from an incentive travel program. What problem would you try to solve for those companies? Write down a convincing statement you would use to persuade the company.

Summary

- The selling of travel takes three basic forms: wholesale, retail, and incentive travel (a combination of the first two).
- A wholesaler/operator plans and organizes a tour package but gives the retailer (travel counsellor) the challenge of selling it to the customer.
- The travel counsellor is the retailer for every type of travel.
- The incentive travel planner organizes a trip for the employees of a company, but only those employees who meet the criteria set up by the planner will win the trip.
- Most wholesale travel is arranged as packaged tours; the tour operator decides on an attractive trip, negotiates prices with the suppliers, and sets the consumer price.
- The independent tour allows clients to travel on their own without supervision or an escort.
- The hosted tour is similar to the independent tour but has a host in each city to arrange excursions and to order tickets to attractions.
- The escorted tour provides a tour guide to accompany the group and to make sure all scheduled activities go as planned.
- A travel agency survives on the service and management fees it charges its clients and on commissions from selling various travel products to the general public. Travel counsellors can no longer collect commissions on most airline tickets, but do get commissions from cruise, hotel, and car rental bookings.
- Incentive travel is a growing field because travel is an excellent motivator, encouraging employees to work harder, sell more, or stay with the company longer.

Questions

1. Using the steps outlined in developing a tour, create a package tour of your region.
   a) Identify the type of tour and its target market.
   b) Determine whether it will be a fully escorted tour or hosted tour. Justify your choice.
   c) Explain the four individual steps you will follow as you create your tour. Use examples and list the items included in the tour.
   d) Set validity dates, a gateway city, and a suggested price.
   e) Describe four advantages for a traveller taking your tour.
   f) Describe two disadvantages and explain how you will attempt to minimize them.
   g) Identify the regulating agencies you will need to get approval from and how they will affect your final product.
2. Describe the different ownership/management styles found in the travel agency business.
3. Summarize three different changes in the travel agency business and how agencies are dealing with the challenges they pose.
4. What is incentive travel and why is it a growing part of the travel trade industry?
5. Define the following terms as they relate to the travel trade industry: *conference appointment, override, specialty agency, tour operator, tour wholesaler, consolidator, consortium, full-service agency, traveller, inbound tour.*

Notes

1. Canadian Tourism Human Resources Council, *Demographic Profile of Tourism Sector Employees*, 2006.

2. Ibid

3. David Wright, CTC, *Professional Travel Counselling*, 4th ed. (Toronto, ON: Canadian Institute of Travel Counsellors, 1998), p. 294.

4. Patricia J. Gagnon and Karen Silva, *Travel Career Development*, 5th ed. (Homewood, IL: Irwin, 1990), p. 169.

5. Aryear Gregory, *The Travel Agent*, 2nd ed. (Rapid City, SD: National Publishers of the Black Hills, Inc., 1985), p. 136.

6. www.cbsa-asfc.gc.ca/whti-ivho/menu-eng.html.

7. Wright, *Professional Travel*, p. 33.

8. David W. Howell and Robert A. Ellison, *Passport* (Toronto: Nelson Canada, 1995), p. 323.

Tourism Services

Key terms

chamber of commerce
convention and visitors
   bureau (CVB)
destination marketing
   organization (DMO)

familiarization (FAM)
   tour
site inspection

tourism information
   centres

Learning objectives

Having read this chapter you will be able to

1. Describe the five industry components of tourism services.

2. Summarize the activities of the provincial and municipal governments as they relate to tourism.

3. Explain the functions of destination marketing organizations such as convention and visitor bureaus, and the role of chambers of commerce.

4. Discuss the membership, mandate, and goals of the Tourism Industry Association of Canada (TIAC).

5. List the miscellaneous services that ensure the tourism sector in Canada remains competitive, modern, and in a positive state of growth.

People in tourism services specialize in serving the needs of the industry rather than the needs of the visitor. The tourism sector is somewhat akin to a stage production: the setting consists of landscape and buildings, and the cast is represented by the entire community—with everyone playing the part of tourism host. Behind the scenes are those who really make the production work. This support group of back-stage workers is called tourism services. A wide variety of organizations, associations, government agencies, and businesses supply these services. Because many tourism businesses are small and privately owned, they rely on this industry for help in dealing with marketing and promotions, taxation, government regulations, safety, education, and staff training. Tourism services are their link to the world of tourists.

Tourism services also include retail sales and media coverage, and the services of construction companies, financial institutions, and telecommunications and computer industries. Together, the businesses that comprise tourism services ensure that the product offered is modern and competitive and that the tourism sector as a whole runs smoothly. This chapter provides information on the inner workings of the tourism sector.

The tourism services industry can be divided into five components,[1] each handling a different tourism need:

- Government agencies
- Tourism associations and organizations
- Marketing services
- Research and consulting
- Miscellaneous services

GOVERNMENT AGENCIES

In Chapter 2, we looked at the federal government and the specific departments that play a role in Canadian tourism. The names and roles of each department are subject to change, and the following is a quick review of the most important roles played by the federal government.

Industry Canada	Responsible for the overall well-being of tourism, including economic development, research, and industry investment
Parks Canada	Responsible for national museums, national parks, national heritage sites, heritage canal systems, and heritage river systems
Canada Border Services Agency (CBSA)	Checks people arriving at the borders for proper documents and illegal goods; enforces tariffs and taxation laws
Foreign Affairs and International Trade Canada	Provides foreign visitors with visas and Canadians with passports
Transport Canada	Responsible for the development and security of our transportation systems
Canadian Heritage (CH)	Responsible for some cultural/heritage events, as well as non-professional sports (the majority of direct responsibility for national museums has been moved to Parks Canada)

As noted in Chapter 2, there are two Crown corporations that also affect the tourism scene in Canada: one is the Canadian Tourism Commission (CTC), the organization responsible for marketing Canada to the world as a tourism destination. The second Crown corporation is the National Capital Commission (NCC). It is responsible for overseeing the development of Canada's capital region—Ottawa/Gatineau.

www.canadatourism.ca

Provincial Governments and Tourism

Provincial governments have ministries or departments similar to those in the federal government although generally under a different name. The major difference is the scope of their activities. For example, most provinces have a specific department responsible for tourism: Tourism NB; Travel Manitoba; Ontario Tourism. All provinces, however, are hoping to engage in and encourage the following activities:

1. **Promote travel opportunities and increase the number of visitors to the province.** Provinces advertise their tourism products in many ways. Many set up booths at trade fairs across Canada and the United States to promote their resorts, adventure activities, attractions and historical sites, accommodations, food services, and transportation services. Should a potential visitor make a simple request for information from a provincial tourism board, they receive an amazing response with a deluge of brochures on a wide variety of fishing vacations, equipment rentals, and maps. Some provincial tourism departments are taking full advantage of social media tools to share, connect, and engage with visitors.

2. **Encourage the development of the tourism sector through market research and planning.** All provinces use strategic planning to ensure that they are developing sustainable tourism products with a significant market base. Many programs focus on existing resources: cultural heritage, recreational activities, natural attractions, and historical sites. Although Canada is one destination, each province works hard to differentiate itself from its neighbouring provinces in terms of attractions and character.

3. **Work with the province's tourism sector to continually improve the product.** Recognizing the need for skilled workers, provincial governments have helped fund tourism education councils (TECs; see Chapter 2), which provide training and certification programs for a wide variety of tourism occupations. Workers dealing directly with tourists may take a short customer service course offered in all provinces under a variety of names, including SuperHost, Alberta Best, and FirstHost. These courses cover quality service and good hospitality practices—how to handle customers in a friendly, professional, and informed manner. Provinces may also create infomercials to educate residents on the value of tourism as a revenue generator.

4. **Produce literature that promotes the six front-line components of the sector.** Provinces fund television commercials, travel videos and DVDs, and web-based content that market their regions. February through April is the most important time of the year to advertise a province's specialties. Advertising tends to focus on markets close to the province: i.e., Ontario will hear about PEI and Newfoundland, but B.C. audiences won't. Newfoundland and Labrador has had great success with

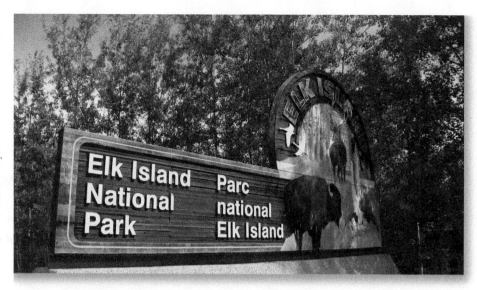

Branding has become an essential element in the marketing of a destination. The brand for Canadian tourism, developed by the CTC, is: "Canada—Keep Exploring."
(Photo courtesy Canadian Tourism Commission.)

its advertising efforts over the past number of years, tapping into their unique culture, history, and geographic beauty. Today, all provinces have their own tourism webpages and many are investing in state-of-the-art tourist information centres. Most provinces also have a toll-free number that provides advice for planning everything from weekend getaways to extended trips.

5. **Liaise with federal and municipal ministries.** Many tourism events require participation from all levels of government. British Columbia would not have been successful in its bid for the 2010 Winter Olympics had it not been able to show strong financial support from all three levels of government.

Municipal Governments and Tourism Associations

Municipal governments have similar needs and perform activities similar to their provincial counterparts. To promote their tourism products (attractions, hotels, restaurants, etc.) some cities have a tourism marketing department. Others turn to private, non-profit associations like convention and visitors bureaus (CVBs) or the local chamber of commerce.

Some cities manage a separate accommodation tax in order to increase revenues that are specifically set aside for regional marketing. This specific stream of revenue will provide an infusion of money into cities, money dedicated solely to promoting and advertising tourism opportunities in the region.

Chambers of Commerce and CVBs Recognizing the financial impact tourism has for its members, **chambers of commerce** become involved in all aspects of tourism. These groups work with the city to promote local events and attract visitors. They advertise in newspapers and magazines, on radio, television, and the internet, and produce booklets, usually in the form of a visitor's guide. These guides, which are placed in hotel rooms, offer information on attractions, festivals

Looking Beyond Trends—Seeing "Megatrends"

In the tourism industry, operators spend the majority of their time dealing with daily business, managing short-term objectives, and focusing on keeping their operations functioning successfully. Operators with foresight keep one eye on upcoming trends, and changes in consumer demands, preferences, and behaviour over a relatively significant number of years. Trends, such as alterations in eating habits and vacation patterns, can be capitalized on by tourism operators as they change their products and services to better align with future customers. Yet there exist trends of such large scope and magnitude that they are categorized as *megatrends*. Researchers, a valuable subgroup of the tourism services area, spend time searching for indicators that allow for an educated prediction of these megatrends.[2]

One megatrend that exists worldwide is the changing characteristics of the population, referred to as *demographics*. The population can be divided into two distinct groups: people in the developed areas of the world and people in the developing areas. In the developed areas of the world, including North America, Europe, and parts of Asia, there is relatively little growth in population and the average age of the population is rising. People in the developed areas have higher-than-average levels of wealth and additional free time, providing both the means and freedom to travel. The population in developing areas of the world, calculated at approximately 95% of the world's people, is growing rapidly. As these areas move forward economically, the younger people will begin to exert greater influence in the tourism marketplace.

Another megatrend is the rapid development of disruptive technologies. These are considered to be technological advances that significantly alter the way in which people move, interact, or communicate. At the time Ford developed the Model T, it would have been considered a disruptive technology as it fundamentally changed how people moved and travelled. In today's marketplace, cell phones, mobile technologies, social media tools, and advances in transportation vehicles are seismic shifts in the way business is conducted. Just a few years ago, a tourism company could expect praise or complaints from a customer in the form of a telephone call. Today, social media has provided every customer with a loud voice to praise or condemn services publicly, and businesses must be listening more closely than ever. Space travel, once the stuff of science fiction, is now in the early stages of commercial production thanks to companies like SpaceX and Virgin Galactic.

Tourism service companies have the opportunity to forecast future megatrends through research and consultation with experts situated outside of their daily operations. This information can then be communicated to operators. Those clever enough to execute business changes around megatrends have an opportunity for long-term success.

and events, shops, restaurants and bars, and transportation systems. Some guides are hardcover, and guests are requested to leave them in the room on departure. Other guides resemble magazines, and guests can take them home as souvenirs or pass them along to friends.

The fundamental mission of a **convention and visitors bureau (CVB)** is to enhance the economic stability of a community by soliciting and servicing conventions and other types of events that generate overnight stays. In addition, a CVB promotes vacation travel to the area. The CVB is the community's liaison between potential visitors and the businesses that will host them. It is a city's information clearinghouse, convention management consultant, and promotional agency, and is often the catalyst for urban development and renewal. CVBs have a sensitive and important role in leading the community's tourism sector. A dynamic and professional CVB creates a favourable image of the community for tour and meeting planners, which can increase tourism volume and profits.

Chambers of commerce and CVBs run on membership fees. Both organizations offer members co-op advertising programs and trade shows. The CVB usually coordinates these programs and sometimes charges a commission on each convention booking. Destination publications include visitor guides, maps, meeting planner guides, and brochures on attractions, hotels and restaurants, activities, and city tours. These may be sent out by direct mail, given to walk-ins, mailed to people inquiring about the destination, and given to meeting planners.

Another way to promote sales is to arrange **familiarization tours** (or FAM tours) to show off the city's charms and suitability for conventions. A FAM tour, free to the prospective client, is sponsored by city businesses. A **site inspection**, in contrast, is held for a single prospective client (usually an association) at the client's expense and is tailored to the prospect's needs and desires. While a FAM tour solicits business from associations that have not yet considered the site, a site inspection provides final details to associations that have narrowed the choice to two or three locations.

When all the marketing techniques have been employed and the association or client wants to do business, the CVB puts together a bid presentation. The presentation may be given to a single person, a select group, a board of directors, or to the entire association. The bid should answer all the client's questions, so the CVB needs to understand all the client's needs and desires. Many CVBs contact the client's previous convention sites to gather information before bidding.

Convention Services In most cases, CVBs are not designed to perform the actual convention set-up, although they can provide a wide array of assistance. Some services are performed for all associations, whereas others are part of the host city's responsibilities. The CVB convention division may provide city and site information to generate interest among association members, or it may host an event at the association's current convention as a welcome to the following year's meeting. The CVB arranges pre-convention tours to assist the client in planning the convention and may organize programs to encourage spouses to come along. The CVB may also set up a speakers' bureau to book local speakers for the upcoming convention or conference. Finally, if more than one hotel is needed, the CVB may set up a housing bureau to help with hotel reservations and confirmations.

During the convention, services range from the simple, such as welcome banners strategically placed at the airport and convention centre, to more detailed tasks such as registration and shuttle services. CVBs have a list of trained personnel who can perform many of the tedious convention duties, from typing name badges to collecting registration fees. The CVB may also be asked to provide the speaker for the opening ceremony. They can work with regions and arrange for the premier, mayor, or an other prominent person to welcome the convention delegates. Often the CVB will also provide a tourism information desk in order to increase visitor enjoyment and maximize spending while guests are in the area.

Tourism Information Centres

Tourism information centres act as gateways and provide visitors with their first impression of a province, region, or town. All levels of government fund information centres to tell tourists about the region: its accommodations, attractions, special events, food service choices, historical sites, and unique environmental experiences. In the Ottawa region, the National Capital Commission has a large information centre adjacent to Parliament Hill, open from June to September. Bilingual guides offer visitors tours of the grounds and buildings. Brochures on historic sites are also available. Provinces usually locate tourism information centres along major highways and at border crossings. These centres offer general information on the province as a whole. Information centres all across Canada are easily identified by the question mark symbol (**?**). Because information centres are usually open in the summer, the jobs are often filled by students, who can practise their customer-relations skills and apply their knowledge of the region.

In Practice

List fifteen attractions in your region. How would you promote them to tourists at a visitor centre? If you were a CVB, which ones would you emphasize to an association considering a convention? How would you promote them?

Making use of international recognition is also an important sales tool. The Rideau Canal in Ottawa, ON, was designated a UNESCO World Heritage site in 2007.

(Photo courtesy National Capital Commission.)

Judith Cabrita

When Judith Cabrita walks into a room, her energy quickly spills over into conversations. Here is a woman whose love of tourism has guided her career and life over decades of endeavours. Judith epitomizes the new tourism professional, successfully manoeuvring her career through three tourism sectors: accommodations, food and beverage, and tourism services. A native of Toronto, she is Nova Scotian at heart. Judith was educated at Ryerson University, and her tourism career began in the accommodations industry. Working first in the hotel business and then the resort business, she gained skills in a variety of different positions, including serving as the chef manager at the Voyageur Restaurant in Halifax.

Judith's next step was into the tourism services sector where she worked her way up to vice-president of a hospitality consulting group. Her continuing quest for challenge turned her career path toward education and innovation. Teaching a class for youth with special needs, she took over the management and training of these students and successfully turned their classroom into a small, profitable dining room, which provided them with valuable hands-on skills. Judith then worked as a consultant to the government of Nova Scotia, helping design and implement a hospitality curriculum. Her last position in education was served at Mount Saint Vincent University, where she held positions as industry coordinator and co-op coordinator.

"Learning is a lifetime experience" has been Judith's personal mission statement. She not only believes in education and training, but she has also used her strong convictions to improve the tourism product of Nova Scotia through the development of skills upgrading and training for the province's tourism workers.

Judith was one of the original members of the Tourism Industry Standards and Certification Committee (TISCC). In 1989, she initiated development of the Education and Training Department branch of the Tourism Industry Association of Nova Scotia (TIANS), which is now a provincial arm of the Canadian Tourism Human Resource Council. In 1995, Judith was appointed director of TIANS. Under her leadership, it was one of the most active councils in Canada. Judith strongly believes in the power of people and in investing in tourism employees by providing them with continuous educational opportunities and training based on industry standards. During her period at TIANS, she helped in the development and implementation of fourteen occupational standards for the industry, including Responsible Beverage Service and Gambling.

Ask Judith Cabrita what she believes life's most important lesson is and her quick response will be "lifelong learning." Most of her working life has focused on education and training, and she can give no higher compliment than that of a job well done. This focus on excellence has driven Judith all her life, and she has passed her energy on to those around her, helping develop Nova Scotia into one of Canada's most successful tourism destinations. In 1993, she was awarded the Canada 125 Medal, and there is a scholarship in her name—the Judith B. Cabrita Tourism Professional Scholarship. Judith's work with TIANS, the CTHRC, and occupational standards is helping the industry develop a more professional workforce—making an imprint that will last well into this century.

TOURISM ASSOCIATIONS AND ORGANIZATIONS

Because of the complex nature of the tourism sector, a variety of industry associations have developed in the past century. They can be divided into two categories: organizations that focus on marketing, and those that focus on advocacy or lobbying. CVBs are examples of marketing-oriented organizations that concentrate on selling a city and all that it has to offer. Another example of a marketing organization is the Canada Ski Council. Many special-interest groups have organizations that help promote their products, and some are linked to international organizations with the same intent. Inns of Canada promote Canadian accommodations, but it is a member of a global organization called Inns en Route. A visit to the organization's website links the searcher to inns around the world. These organizations strive to attract visitors to a destination or to encourage people to participate in a specific pursuit. They develop and execute marketing plans, design special promotions, coordinate publicity, and work with advertising agencies. Tourism advocates and lobbying organizations are more concerned with the welfare of the tourism sector as a whole or with the success of a specific industry such as accommodations, or food and beverage. Many of these associations have already been discussed in previous chapters. Nationally recognized advocacy groups in Canada include:

- Tourism Industry Association of Canada (TIAC)
- Hotel Association of Canada
- Association of Canadian Travel Agents (ACTA)
- Canadian Restaurant and Foodservices Association (CRFA)
- Canadian Culinary Federation
- Canadian Association of Foodservice Professionals (CAFP)
- Aboriginal Tourism Canada
- Meeting Professionals International (MPI)
- Association of Tourism Professionals

These associations represent their members to governing bodies and the public in general. They put on seminars, sponsor events, conduct research, and keep their members informed about all the activities within their industries. They prepare briefing papers for governments on issues such as taxation and regulations that affect their industries. They have also been instrumental in writing national occupational standards and in providing training and certification (see Chapter 2).

Tourism Industry Association of Canada (TIAC)

TIAC is a good example of a lobbying organization that has made a difference. It is a private organization, founded in 1931, and funded by membership dues. It serves as the tourism sector's national voice. Members come from all areas of the tourism sector: businesses, institutions, associations, and individuals. TIAC's mandate is to strengthen tourism by lobbying the federal government on tax issues, federal tourism initiatives, training programs for tourism workers, and legislation that promotes a proactive tourism sector.

TIAC has been issuing warnings to the federal government regarding the status of tourism for some time. The expansion of the existing and mature global tourism markets as well as exciting new markets has been great, and Canada is being left behind. Tourism impacts the lives of 1.6 million Canadians who make their living working in this industry, and the revenues it has produced yearly are being threatened by Canadian government inaction.

TIAC understands the difficult times tourism has weathered so far in the twenty-first century: the terrorist attacks on September 11, 2001, the SARS scare, the ongoing rise in the cost of fuel, and the rise in the value of the Canadian dollar. To put the dollar's value in perspective, the cost of our tourism products has gone up by 30% over the last decade solely because of the changing value of the dollar. Prices are sure to rise again as we face the fuel crisis. None of this is our doing, yet all of it hurts our industry. TIAC points out that not only is the government responsible for the well-being of the industry, but in fact it is a major shareholder as it has ownership rights in our national parks, museums, and historic sites. It is responsible for our transportation systems, our border infrastructure, and the global marketing of Canadian tourism.

According to TIAC, Canada requires some major policy reforms in order to stem the decline in its global ranking as an international destination.[3] They focus on areas including accessibility, government actions, and labour.

1. Fees, such as airport rents and the air travellers security charge, need to be reduced or removed completely. In lieu, revenues collected through municipal taxation should be redirected to cover these costs. Additionally, the excise tax currently placed on fuel should be earmarked for investment in airport infrastructure.

2. The transportation infrastructure should be planned with greater connectivity between major airports and other modes of transportation. There should also be a distinct travel and tourism infrastructure banking system set up to provide low-cost financing for infrastructure development projects.

3. Smarter border control systems and additional human resources should be added to the Canadian Border Services Agency to a) increase trust and security of travellers, b) minimize the impact of security procedures on travellers, and c) increase the efficiency of border crossing. Part of this would include changes at the Canadian Air Transport Security Authority that increase both transparency and communication with stakeholders.

4. The Canadian Tourism Commission should receive additional funding to continue marketing Canada as a tourism destination to the international marketplace. The stability of the CTC should be ensured in a longer-term design, including the predictability of funding.

5. Continue investing in tourism as a strong career option through increased investment in skills training and development, especially through organizations such as the Canadian Tourism Human Resource Council. Also encourage under-represented labour groups, such as younger people and new Canadians, to move into careers within the tourism industry.

It is short-sighted that the government minimizes the impact of the tourism industry, especially when nearly $0.28 of revenue is generated for all three levels of government for each dollar spent by tourists.[4] Many large manufacturing corporations are closing shops in Canada and moving workers to less expensive countries.

That won't happen with tourism—we need Canadian workers doing their jobs right here in Canada. The collective weight of association membership influences government policies and legislation and can create a healthy environment for workers and visitors alike. Without the strong voice of TIAC and associations that have joined with it in demanding that politicians take action now, it may be too little too late. Most businesses know it is much easier to keep a consumer than to try to find new ones, but without substantial help from the government, tourism growth will suffer.

MARKETING SERVICES

For the most part, travel is not an activity essential to our survival. Consequently, advertising and promotion need to entice the traveller. Canadian destinations compete in the global tourism marketplace, but also with each other. The tourism sector as a whole is competing not only against mature marketplaces like the United States and new marketplaces like Nicaragua and Peru, but also against other discretionary purchases, such as home renovation and consumer goods.

Canada's National DMO—the CTC

Destination marketing organizations (DMOs) promote their cities, regions, provinces, or country. Our national DMO is the Canadian Tourism Commission, or CTC, a Crown corporation that is responsible for marketing Canada as a desirable tourism destination to international visitors. They work in six core areas: direct-to-consumer advertising; media and public relations activities; assistance with overseas travel agencies; interaction with the meetings, conventions, and incentive travel market; engagement through multiple social media outlets; and management of an ongoing tourism research program. Working for a DMO is challenging and can be exciting. Workers must have good knowledge of their region and strong marketing and communication skills.

Recently, the government of Canada reduced the operating budget of the CTC by over $14 million while simultaneously expressing the importance of the tourism industry to the Canadian economy;[5] this is the lowest level of base funding (this does not include special one-time infusions) for the CTC over the last twelve years, a 20% reduction from 2011 and a 41.4% reduction from peak base funding in 2001.[6] This continual reduction in available funds translates into fewer services and less advertising, actions that have negatively affected international tourism growth.

In 2005, the CTC began to revitalize Canada's branding, giving it a new focus and catchphrase: Canada—Keep Exploring. This branding campaign has worked quite well, and the CTC continues to use it in all of its marketing materials. Of course, its key areas of concentration have evolved over time. The 2012–2016 strategic plan is focused on meeting organizational targets and objectives, including:

- Increasing demand for Canada's visitor economy
- Focusing on markets where Canada's tourism brand has a high profile and that yield the highest return on investment

The 2012 plan is focused on the new federal tourism strategy, in which the federal government has set a tourism revenue goal of $100 billion annually. To address this, the CTC has launched a program of unique, prepackaged Canadian

Marketing services use a variety of tools to sell a destination: commercials, posters, perhaps even a safari hat.
(Photo: Paula Kerr.)

experiences under the brand, Signature Experiences Collection.[7] For the period between 2012 and 2016, the CTC has also established four key priorities:

- Ensure customer relevancy and differentiate Canada
- Advance a culture of innovation and entrepreneurial development among tourism businesses
- Lead industry in international brand alignment and consistency
- Foster organizational excellence[8]

RESEARCH AND CONSULTING

Not all products appeal to all people. How do you figure out who will use your products? Will your product suit their needs? Those questions are answered through market research and analysis. Research can be done informally, simply by asking clients about their satisfaction, but many guests are reluctant to give negative responses. Tourism research firms usually focus either on tourism products in general or on specific products, providing important information to help guide decision making. Here are some of the questions that product research should answer:

- Is the product unique?
- How does the quality of the product measure up against similar products?
- Does the product have enough capacity to handle demand?
- What are the benefits of purchasing the product?
- What drawbacks have been identified with the product?
- Is the product sustainable? Easily accessible?

- What do clients expect when they purchase the product?
- What needs does the product fulfill for the client?
- What needs are left unfulfilled?

Research also provides the sector with a track record of its performance, and it measures the impact of tourism on the economy. Some companies, such as Air Canada, have their own research divisions. Others hire consulting firms. Many large multinational consulting firms, such as PricewaterhouseCoopers and KPMG International, work with the sector. The non-profit Conference Board of Canada is the lead agency responsible for research in Canada. The board's Canadian Tourism Research Institute (CTRI) concerns itself with tourism issues. Its members' mandate is to "assist their customers in the Canadian tourism sector to anticipate and respond to emerging trends in a manner that will enhance their competitiveness."[9]

Consultants in the tourism industry help support operators by trading on their specific areas of expertise. For example, if you have worked extensively in the food and beverage industry, you may be able to use your knowledge of foods to help a restaurateur create an exciting menu using colours, shapes, and good descriptive copy. Perhaps you are an accountant with a specialty in food and beverage labour cost control. Whatever your field of knowledge, being a consultant means you sell your expertise to those willing to pay for your services. Consultants may work for a large firm, such as HVS, or independent operators with an entrepreneurial spirit. When you work for yourself, you can have greater flexibility with your work hours, but you must also have a strong skill set and the willingness to take a risk—because unemployment may be just one contract away. Many consultants find that the satisfaction of being their own boss outweighs all of the risks.

www.conferenceboard.ca/ctri

MISCELLANEOUS SERVICES

Miscellaneous services are the final component of the tourism services industry. Here is a short list of some of these businesses and occupations:

- **Education and training services** for tourism are provided by a variety of institutions and businesses: high schools, colleges, and universities; private trainers; and organizations such as tourism education councils (TECs) and the Canadian Tourism Human Resource Council (CTHRC). TECs focus on front-line training—that is, training staff who deal directly with the tourist. Because tourism businesses are also interested in creating and maintaining a professional workforce, they will often provide in-house training for staff. Having an education and background in the industry provides you with expertise other applicants will not have.

www.cthrc.ca

- **Media opportunities** exist for travel writers, photographers, television personalities, and documentary writers and producers. These artists combine their love of travel with their creative or artistic abilities. A travel writer or photographer may work for one magazine (such as *Canadian Geographic*) or may freelance. Food photographers working with culinary or tourism magazines document outstanding dining experiences found in Canada. Cable television has channels dedicated solely to travel and culinary shows. Many networks include at least one travel documentary and culinary demonstration in their schedules because of the popularity of these shows.

- **Webpage designers** are indispensable to the industry. Producing compelling webpages that incorporate graphics, video, text, and a high level of interactive elements requires a specific talent and skill set. With so much of our business based on marketing through the internet, people who design and maintain—and can sell through—this medium are indispensable. Good web designers who support the tourism industry must also possess a thorough knowledge of the tourism industry, the variety of products it offers, and the different target markets the seller is focusing on.

- **Social media managers** are becoming a staple for many marketing departments. Sometimes, this is maintained in-house; however, there are a growing number of companies that contract out these tasks to individuals with excellent communication skills matched with social media savvy.

- **Duty-free shops and retail merchants** provide opportunities for travellers who love to shop. Many department stores are offering SuperHost training to their floor staff to provide good customer service.

- **Construction engineers and architects** design and build facilities for the tourism sector. Often, a firm will specialize in the construction of restaurants, cruise ships, or hotels.

- **Specialty food producers** such as farms and cheese factories (Balderson), vineyards (Inniskillin), and food distributors (Summit Foods) all help to make Canadian foods a culinary adventure.

- **Auto clubs** around the world are important to any vacationer who uses a private vehicle. Auto club counsellors design travel routes to help CAA (Canadian Automobile Association) customers avoid construction areas and bypass large cities. Counsellors must have knowledge of the region, including current highway information, regulations, and the skill to explain travel routes.

- **Manufacturers** produce items used by different businesses in the industry, such as commercial ovens, machines, furniture, and amusement park rides.

The list goes on. So many people work in and with tourism services that it is easy to see why it is known as a labour-intensive industry. The work can be fun, and the rewards—even just a warm hello or hearty thanks—make a tourism job a special event every day.

CASE STUDY

Claudia's Late Shift

When Claudia got her first job at a local fast food chain, she was thrilled. She had great bosses, good training, and enthusiastic co-workers. Claudia soon became an important part of the team when she showed maturity well beyond her age. She handled responsibility easily, never had problems with her cash register, and had a special knack for working the drive-through window. By the time she was eighteen, she was a junior shift supervisor, which meant that she made more money, but also often had to work the closing

continued…

shift. Even though company policy dictated that either a manager or an assistant manager had to be on duty with her during these closing shifts, her mother worried about her, especially when another fast food restaurant two blocks away was robbed.

Claudia, however, felt safe even late at night because either her parents picked her up or she walked the two blocks home with friends from her shift. One night, the assistant manager was called away to an emergency and left the late-shift team to close up. Claudia's parents were out of town, and her friends had other plans, so she found herself walking home alone. Though she walked quickly and was alert for danger, she did not arrive home safely. Her brother called the police when he discovered her missing and a search party was raised. Claudia was found hours later a few kilometres from her home. She had been attacked and abandoned on the side of the road.

While this is not a true story, it is based on events that have occurred in Canada recently. As a result of these events, many fast food restaurants have made efforts to change current company policies to include safety measures for employees who work the late shift.

1. What is the root problem in this case study? Is it a common problem in the fast food industry?
2. What options did the assistant manager have when she was called away to an emergency?
3. What would you have done if, like Claudia, you had been faced with walking home alone?
4. Should the fast food chain have had a policy regarding the safety of employees working the late shift? Why or why not?
5. How much responsibility should a company take for ensuring safety for its employees in situations like these?

Summary

- The tourism services industry can be broken down into five components: government agencies, tourism associations and organizations, marketing and promotional firms, research and consulting firms, and miscellaneous services.
- All levels of government become involved in the tourism sector through research, development, promotion, education, funding, and legislative and regulatory initiatives.
- Tourism associations are promoters of and advocates for the sector, providing information to members and help set the direction of tourism. Marketing and promotional firms know how to sell the sector's products; Canada's destination marketing organization (DMO) is the Canadian Tourism Commission or CTC.
- Research and consulting firms provide the industry with a wealth of information, including an analysis of current market trends and projections for the future.
- The remaining occupations that keep the sector progressing and running smoothly fall into the "miscellaneous" category and include educators, architects, construction engineers, and companies that supply the tourism sector with products such as fresh produce, cleansers, and landscaping services.

Questions

1. The government of any country plays a crucial role in the planning, development, maintenance, and promotion of a country or region.

   a) Summarize briefly the roles played by: i) the CTC, ii) your provincial government, and iii) your municipal government.

   b) List two regulations or pieces of legislation created by provincial and municipal governments that help or hurt the tourism sector as a whole, or the tourist as an individual. Explain why you believe this legislation is helpful or harmful.

2. Research your city's convention and visitors bureau and describe four different services it performs for the tourism sector in your region.

3. Tourism services provide the sector with many different support services.

   a) Choose any five services that appeal to you from this industry and explain why you might be interested in this line of work.

   b) Would you require further education to work in each of these businesses? If so, what courses would you be looking for?

4. Define the following terms as they relate to the tourism sector: *familiarization tour, site inspection, DMO.*

Notes

1. Canadian Tourism Human Resource Council, *The Student Travel Map*, 1995, pp. 102–103.

2. Global Intelligence Briefing for CEOs: Megatrends. September 2011 www.ijet.com/uploads/userfiles/file/iJET_White_Paper_Megatrends.pdf.

3. *Looking to 2020: The Future of Travel and Tourism in Canada* (Whitepaper), National Travel and Tourism Coalition, October 2010.

4. Ibid.

5. http://www.canada.com/life/Canadian+Tourism+Commission+refocuses+face+budget+cuts/6449502/story.html.

6. *Harnessing Innovation and Alignment: 2012–2016 Corporate Plan Summary.* www.corporate.canada.travel.

7. *Strategy 2012–2016*, www.corporate.canada.travel.

8. Ibid.

9. www.conferenceboard.ca/ctri.

Challenges and the Future

Key terms

code of ethics
ecotourism
ethics

risk management
sex tourism
social media

time poverty

Learning objectives

Having read this chapter you will be able to

1. Identify and explain the impact of current trends in lifestyles, travel, and technology on the tourism sector.

2. Explain how and why ethical behaviour is important in the tourism sector.

3. Identify eight challenges that the CTC has expressed about the tourism sector.

4. Explain how these challenges may either expand or contract the sector's growth rate.

5. Outline the trends and challenges in each component of the tourism industry.

Think of tourism like a snowfall. During blizzard periods, the sheer number of tourists makes life for a community difficult. Tourism can produce overcrowded streets, hour-long waits for restaurant tables, and overbooked flights and hotels to name a few. The Olympic Games is a good example of an event where all the planning in the world cannot reduce the strain on the entire community. As with a massive snowfall, the aftermath of such an event requires a tremendous amount of cleanup. At other times, Canadian snowfalls are beautiful, soft, and steady; this is the equivalent of tourism's high season, when the number of tourists is constant but workable. Attractions are busy, hotels and restaurants are full, and the crowds are friendly.

At times, the snow falls sporadically, enough to tell us that it is snowing, but not enough to bother us—the equivalent of tourism's shoulder period or the transition phase between peak and off-peak periods. The tourists are still coming, but there is no inconvenience to residents. Hotels and restaurants experience a slow cycle, and often the airlines cut back on their flights. Finally, there comes a time when no snow falls at all. Not all destinations experience a total lack of tourists, but some less-accessible resorts must close for the winter. This is equivalent to tourism's low season when prices are lower, top attractions are easier to get into, and tourists are not constantly bumping into other tourists on the street.

Snowfalls are similar to tourism in other ways: just as no two snowflakes are alike, no two tourists are alike; the impact of a snowfall is affected by external factors (winds, time of day, day of the week, amount of snow already on the ground), just as tourism is affected by external factors beyond its control (weather, economics, politics). The early years of the twenty-first century have illustrated that, despite our efforts, tourism is often deeply affected by the unpredictable factors of politics, weather and other environmental issues, and disease. Some of the unexpected and destructive events that have focused attention on and brought about concern for the tourism industry include: the terrorist attacks in New York, London, Egypt, and Thailand; the SARS epidemic in China and Toronto; and the natural disasters in Southeast Asia and New Orleans. Despite these negative effects, it is human nature to focus on the positive and hope for the best. In the majority of these cases, tourism rebounded, and as an industry, supported the stabilization of these regions.

Canadians have no choice about how much snow they get—but they do have a choice about the quality and size of their tourism industry. Political decisions made outside the direct control of tourism operators have deepened concerns for the financial stability of our tourism industry. Few experts predicted in 2007 the fast rise in value of the Canadian dollar, foresaw the rapid rise in the prices of fuel, or forecast the impact that WHTI (Western Hemisphere Travel Initiative) legislation would have on tourism in Canada. The power of political decisions, such as the Canadian government's refusal to sign a travel-based memorandum of understanding (MOU) with China, and political actions, including Prime Minister Stephen Harper's decision not to attend the 2008 Olympic ceremonies in Beijing, set up a challenging landscape for strong international tourism relationships.

Moving forward, we need to explore the directions that tourism will develop in Canada, the pressures and influencing factors on the industry, and some fundamental shifts in how we do business. This chapter examines the future of tourism.

SOCIETAL CHANGES THAT AFFECT TOURISM

Each generation develops its own style of living based on a great many different factors. The structure of family life has changed, influencing the fabric of North American society. People are choosing to marry later in life or not to marry at all. The financial need for two incomes adds stress to all members of the family. Due to widely distributed family members, people are seeking "familial people ties" by looking outside the family circle, linked via computer and cell phone. The exchange of information made possible by sites like Facebook and YouTube has helped show how many world cultures there are, and has, perhaps, made the desire for travel stronger.

Generation Y members, according to some authors, show higher levels of narcissism[1] or increased self-importance; they might be more willing to leave their jobs for an extended period of time in order to satisfy travel desires and fulfill pleasures. To this generation, money earned may have greater value when spent on pleasure than when being held as savings. In the 1950s–1970s, destinations relied on celebrity endorsements to sell vacations. This advantage has disappeared as younger generations choose a destination with little consideration of its celebrity status.

Even the boomers have not aged as experts had forecast. While some remain true to predictions—retiring to quiet lives with travel that suits their aging needs—others have grabbed their new freedom with a gusto not foreseen by the experts. They are retiring earlier and using the internet more and more to research and book trips. This new breed—some experts are now calling them "zoomers" because of their need to stay busy—want to take part in the activities found at the destination.

Not only are these zoomers interested in seeing the sights, they are looking to be challenged by travel. They feel a need to give back to society as volunteers, helping build homes, schools, water systems, and home businesses in developing countries instead of sitting on the beach. Many travellers are concerned about the ecosystem, want to better understand biodiversity, and are interested in the actions they can take to help slow climate change. They may consciously choose a "greener" mode of

FOOTPRINT

Are You a True Ecotourist?

The International Ecotourism Society (IETS) recently published the results of a survey taken in Berlin by the University of Eberswalde based on guest responses at an eco-travel show.

- Seventy-fuve percent of those surveyed said they believe tourism is a contributor to climate change.

- Only 6% of travellers said they offset their carbon footprints related to their travel experiences.

- Exhibitors agreed that they also have concerns for the environment and try to create packages that meet green standards. The cost of implementing eco-changes will determine if those changes become commonplace.

- Less than 3% of travellers said they had carbon offsetting plans in place.

- Sixty-six percent noted that their business has changed because of the impact of climate change, but seldom is anything done about it.

The IETS suggested that eco-trotters incorporate the following into their travel plans: choosing destinations that can be reached without flying, preferring travel by bus or train; using public transportation at their destination rather than renting a car or using a taxi; selecting eco-friendly hotels whose operations focus on recycling/reducing waste policies; buying locally produced souvenirs; and eating local, not packaged, food products. Travellers note that fresh, local foods not only taste better and support the local economy, but are also generally healthier.

What this survey suggests is that both travellers and tourist businesses are concerned about climate change, but are not often committed enough to incorporate major lifestyle changes.

transportation or pick tourism companies that have strong eco-conservation backgrounds. Of course, many boomers still look at vacations as times when they are looked after and pampered. They are just entering their retirement, after all.

Technology is an ever-growing part of the tourism puzzle. Ecommerce drives the industry as young people and the tech-savvy go online to research, book, and post comments on their trip choice—good or bad. Travel has been made easier with the online booking system, "ticketless travel," and machines that check people through immigration faster. Because trips are easier to book and promotions are plentiful, there has been a rise in "impulse buying," or trip deals that are just too good to turn down. And now, a bad experience can be quickly broadcast to the world, not just the next-door neighbour. Customers are just as likely to post their feelings about experiences on Facebook or Twitter as they are to engage in face-to-face discussions with service providers.

www.yelp.com

ETHICS AND TOURISM

Throughout this book, we have addressed ethical standards and why they are so important to the tourism sector. In North America, we have legislation that protects tourists from some forms of unethical behaviour. Laws against false commercial claims and laws that protect travellers when tour operators or airlines go bankrupt are just two examples. Yet how easy it is, with computer technology, to create a brochure that shows mountains in the backyard of a cute little chalet, when in truth they are 30 km away! Another marketing deception is the so-called *bait and switch*, in which a company advertises a deeply discounted price for, say, a cruise, but sets aside only a few cabins at this price. Once potential customers are on the line, a good salesperson can sell a space at a higher price.

Tourism workers have a very close relationship with tourists. Few businesses are given this type of trust, and it is important to tourism services and products everywhere that this trust is not misplaced. **Ethics** in business—understanding the differences between good and bad business practices and activities—is crucial to building and maintaining trust. The tourism product is intangible and cannot operate well without trust. The tourism worker is the fundamental link between the product and the tourist.

Tourists entrust their lives, their security, and their possessions to tourism professionals. Individuals who enter the tourism sector must accept this responsibility and serve with honesty and concern for their customers' welfare. The reward is happy clients, a profitable business, a sense of pride, and the satisfaction of a job well done. In addition, having **risk management** policies in place ensures your establishment has the highest regard for safety. The importance of these concepts, those of safety, responsibility, and integrity, are the fundamental building blocks within a **code of ethics**; these need to be instilled in employees from the very beginning of their employment, ensuring the safety and enjoyment of tourism guests.

ISSUES OF CONCERN IN THE SECTOR

Over fifteen years ago, the CTC addressed eight key tourism issues requiring the federal government's attention.[2] These issues still exist; in fact, some have been exacerbated by government action and inaction. If not resolved, the CTC believes they will likely weaken the Canadian tourism product and its future prosperity. This section will explore those key issues.

Transportation Easy, reasonably priced access to and around a country is essential if tourism is to flourish. Canada's transportation system is slowly deteriorating. The quality of highways, roads, and roadside facilities has diminished, and the refurbishment of these facilities has been both slow and expensive. Although deregulation removed the complete monopoly of Air Canada in the Canadian air system, choice is still limited within Canada to a handful of carriers, including WestJet and Porter Airlines. Air travel has become increasingly expensive as governments and the airlines tack on additional taxes and surcharges. Many airlines now charge additional surcharges for fuel, checked baggage, and simple services, such as seat selection. For example, a regular passenger travelling with Air Canada within Canada is allowed one checked bag up to 23 kg; a second bag would cost $20 in each direction. However, if that same traveller flies between Canada and the U.S., they are charged $25 for their first bag and $35 for the second.

In truth, the impact of rising oil prices has forced all modes of transportation to increase their pricing structures, and while they adjust to the new prices people think twice before taking even short trips by car. As mentioned, concern for the ecosystem is another factor. Aircrafts are big polluters, and while newer models are more eco-conscious, they are not pollution-free. Faster, eco-friendly train systems are available, but their expense will likely ensure that Canada will not invest in this technology.

In fact, Canada has been very slow to make any advancement in this area. High-speed trains between Calgary and Edmonton or Toronto and Montreal would cut down on the number of flights between these major cities, reduce pollution, and provide a comfortable journey for clients. It would take just forty-five minutes on a maglev to get from Edmonton to Calgary, normally a three-hour drive. Although there is overwhelming public support for a high-speed rail system between key city centres in Canada, the costs to construct these systems would require massive financial support from both provincial and federal governments.[3] Yet, new investment in all areas of transportation is necessary if we are to maintain our position as a world leader in tourism.

The Role of Parks, Historic Sites, and Crown Lands National parks and historic sites are important to the tourism sector because many product offerings have some natural or historic significance. However, conflicts arise when Parks Canada, for example, attempts to balance the need for better tourist accessibility with the need to preserve land, flora, and fauna for future generations. The tourism sector has raised concerns because demand for travel to our national parks is growing, while deteriorating facilities threaten the overall quality of the tourist experience. Banff National Park and Jasper National Park are perhaps the most pressured parks at present. Wilderness areas such as Nahanni and Tatshenshini-Alsek National Parks are already showing the strain of more adventure-seeking tourists.

Added to these problems, the dilemma caused by world oil supplies is encouraging some politicians and business people to reconsider using Crown land under government protection for development. The use of land tenure systems on Crown land is creating great concern among some people in Canada's western provinces. The oil sands in Alberta, while producing over a million barrels a day, are expected to quadruple output by 2020. With oil in such demand, and billions of dollars already spent to extract it, there is little thought of slowing development of this land even though the ecological effects will be felt for hundreds of years. British Columbia is also facing a major power struggle between the need to preserve landscape for tourism and the need for energy found in the coal reserves of Flathead Valley. Coal could be strip-mined from the area, destroying one of the world's last great ecological treasures. These challenges are forcing Canadians to take a stand on how Canada should be protecting its vast ecosystems.

The Evolving Role of Canada Customs and Immigration More than two million border crossings take place daily between the United States and Canada. While the European Union reduces formalities at border crossings, making travel on the continent easier, enforcement agencies in North America are moving to stricter controls that make it more difficult and time-consuming to cross our border.

The United States has expressed concern about Canada's immigration system because, in the past, several known terrorists have entered the United States through Canada. Officials are being given broad powers to ensure that anyone crossing the border has proper papers and legitimate business. WHTI legislation requires Canadian citizens travelling to the United States to carry valid passports. Over the past decade, many European countries have eased border restrictions, making travel more convenient across the continent, while the "open border" between the United States and Canada has become increasingly more challenging to cross. There is growing pressure for the Canadian government to invest in upgraded border technologies in an effort to ensure a smoother, safer border crossing for tourists while still minimizing security threats. While the NEXUS card is already being accepted, it will be years before border improvements are implemented that reduce current security concerns.

The Tax Issue Taxes have always been a challenge for tourism, as they raise the bottom-line price for price-sensitive travellers. In 1991, the goods and services tax (GST) was introduced in Canada, pushing the issue of taxation on tourism products and services to the forefront. The major area of contention focused on international tourism and visits to Canada by international visitors, classified as an export service. When established, the GST was not to be levied on Canadian exports, yet because international tourist must visit Canada to consume our tourism products, they were charged the full tax, just as if they were domestic travellers. Tourism advocates felt strongly that this discriminated against tourism products that are already costly.

In 1998, after lobbying by the Tourism Industry Association of Canada (TIAC), the government agreed to remove the GST paid by international conferences choosing a Canadian destination. Delegates must still pay GST on any purchases while in Canada, but TIAC also lobbied for remuneration rights for tourists on any GST they pay while in Canada. The program was set up in 1998, allowing visitors who kept their receipts and filled out the correct paperwork to receive an instant rebate at the border or a cheque in the mail. Over a decade ago, Ken Hine, then CEO of the International Hotel and Restaurant Association (IHRA), described the harsh tax situation that once existed in New York City and warned that Canada was quickly moving in this direction. When taxes in New York City reached a high of 21.25%, the industry was able to prove to both municipal and state governments that they were driving more business away than they were generating in tax revenues.

Consider the case of tourists visiting Ontario: they must add 13% HST (PST plus GST) to all their purchases, plus a liquor tax, and a hotel tax. In 2004, some larger city destinations developed a hotel tax of 2% to 3% that was funnelled directly into future destination-specific promotions. On top of this, there exists an entertainment tax levied on some forms of entertainment, as well as airport improvement fees, CATSA and NAVCAN charges, and numerous other municipal taxes. Increased taxes are hurting the golden goose of tourism. When taxes push tourism prices up too high, tourists simply choose other destinations that are more affordable. When the Canadian dollar was valued at 65 cents U.S., perhaps taxes were not a concern for American tourists. When the U.S. and Canadian dollars were at par, as they were in 2007, all of our markets looked at other destinations for a less expensive vacation. In 2009, when the Canadian dollar was much stronger than its U.S. counterpart, the added taxes that existed in Canada simply drove more U.S. visitors to choose other destinations while Canadians themselves travelled south.

Training of Tourism Workers Quality of service has been identified as one of the most important features consumers look for when purchasing any product and it remains one of the biggest problems faced by the tourism sector today. Because many workers have direct contact with the tourist, proper training is essential. If Canada is to continue competing in a global market, our tourism professionals must have the skills, knowledge, and attitudes (SKAs) to deliver the product effectively. Training programs developed by the tourism education councils and the sector are an important advancement. With the CTHRC's *emerit* certification process now online, getting certified is even easier. Once a business's workers are certified, an owner can display his workers' individual certificates and allow them to wear their certification pins—showing the individual's personal investment in training.

The range of scenery that Canada can offer tourists will continue to keep people coming back. From cityscapes to mountain retreats, there is something for every traveller.
(Photo courtesy the Fairmont Jasper Park Lodge.)

Financing the Future of Tourism The financial community has never perceived tourism as a sound financial investment. There are several reasons for this. First, tourism is mostly made up of small businesses, many of which have to work very hard to succeed and avoid financial hardships. Second, it is difficult to define the tourism business and its potential revenues in a financial statement, although the new NAICS system should help outline businesses as contributing to the tourism sector. Third, financial institutions have struggled with a clear vision of the tourism sector and this is a problem that continues to exist within the sector itself. As tourism moves front and centre in the world of financial investment, Canadian lending institutions and the government of Canada will need to increase their understanding of this industry and the investment strategies needed to maintain the quality of Canadian tourism products.

Aboriginal Tourism Both the federal and provincial governments, along with the tourism sector, recognize the growing demand for experiences centred on the cultural heritage of Aboriginal Canadians. All too aware of the harm tourism can bring, the sector strongly supports the development of Aboriginal tourism as long as it meets the government's requirement for sustainability. This development must enhance Aboriginal culture, respect Aboriginal lands and lifestyle, and produce viable employment for our First Nations. In the end, Aboriginal tourism, already in high demand, should help improve the quality of life, both financially and culturally, for Aboriginal Canadians.

www.greensuites.com

TERRORIST THREATS

In the past decade, the threat of terrorism has increased in many nations. Terrorist acts have plagued U.S. facilities on foreign soil, and the destruction of the World Trade Center in 2001 brought the fear of terrorism home to Americans. In the 1970s, hijackings were more common than they are today, but passengers were used as hostages, allowing terrorists to bargain for certain demands. In opposition to hijacking airlines for a particular "gain," the terrorists involved in the events of September 11, 2001 turned airplanes into weapons, causing massive destruction and loss of life.

Israel's tourism sector has suffered more than most from terrorist actions, and in Malaysia, tourists were captured and held for more than three months while their captors' demands were being considered. In Bali, two Canadian tourists died when a nightclub was bombed. Terrorism is taking a toll on tourism around the world. Although we still view our country as a safe place for travel, there is no doubt that if terrorists continue to make headlines around the world, tourism everywhere will suffer.

OTHER GLOBAL CONCERNS

Climate Change

Our climate is changing, and that is having an impact in many areas. Ski resorts in Europe, open from November through April just forty years ago, are now finding their season lasts from late December through to February. The volume of snow falling has been decreasing over time, the cold weather of the winter season begins later and ends earlier, and the quality of skiing over the entire ski season is deteriorating. Many resort areas have already started to expand summer season activities in order to stay profitable.

Rising waters may not have had a big impact on Canadian shores, but they are threatening islands with low water lines such as the Maldives. Historic cities like Venice are slowly "sinking" into the sea. Concerns are high in the Netherlands and Mexico City regarding the possibility of major flooding. Rising temperatures are also causing problems. Climates once considered "warm" are now hot, with temperatures reaching and exceeding 43° C (100° F). Warmer, dry weather is causing drought that is harming crops and spawning major forest fires across the west coast of North America. Southern European countries like Spain are seeing their first major forest fires. Hurricanes of greater magnitude and frequency batter the Caribbean islands and Central/North America. More tornadoes are being reported, and in Asia typhoons are becoming more intense. Africa is suffering from sustained drought that threatens most of the continent and its delicate ecosystems.

Weather is one of those factors beyond our control. We cannot change it, but we must be prepared for it and try to prevent any destruction that we can. Dikes, dams, and levees should be strengthened; campfires are forbidden in many parks; modern forest fire–fighting equipment needs to be enhanced in many Canadian provinces; hotels and attractions must be built to withstand strong winds; and risk management plans must be in place for evacuation of guests if their safety is threatened.

Cultural and Economic Concerns

The internet has opened up whole new areas of tourism, with one of the most disturbing being the sex trade. Tourism has increased in some developing countries where exploitation of women and children in the sex trade is tolerated, rolling out a secondary niche: **sex tourism**. Some countries such as Great Britain have passed legislation allowing authorities to prosecute British tourists who travel to these countries for the purpose of engaging in any aspect of the sex trade.[4]

TRENDS IN THE TOURISM SECTOR

Peter Yesawich, a leading expert in the field of marketing research, identified some of the trends in lifestyle, travel, and technology.[5] He reminds us that contemporary customers are better educated, have more knowledge about the products they are purchasing, and demand and expect more value for their dollar than customers of past years. The internet has made them better-informed shoppers and has given them the tools to search out the best price for the tourism products they desire.

As business becomes more competitive and as companies try to produce more for less, our society is also burdened by **time poverty**. Many people find they have less time for everything, including vacations; indeed, the average North American lunch "hour" is just twenty-eight minutes long! How well will restaurants handle the need for quicker service or the working lunch? The number of hours that most people work is increasing, while the time we allot for vacation and business trips is getting shorter. As a result, the need for efficient service is greater. Today's consumers are willing to pay more for convenience.

Happy tourists take pleasant memories of their vacation home, share these memories with friends and, we hope, return to visit again.
(Photo courtesy National Capital Commission.)

With the workweek getting longer, time at home is focused on family and family activities. Research has shown that our priorities have changed. We want more control of our lives and what we do with our time. We are concerned about our health. We want to be able to take time off work when needed, to have successful relationships, and to experience a better quality of life. These desires are becoming more important to younger generations than is personal wealth.

Over the years, North Americans have become increasingly critical in their view of government and the media. Advertising has lost much of its credibility now that customers have ways to express themselves authentically through **social media**. Consumers are more willing to complain if a product or service does not meet expectations. This erosion of trust in the marketplace can easily affect tourism because tourism is a product that is both expensive and intangible. Tourism businesses that want to succeed and thrive in the future must deliver a product that surpasses customer expectations.

Although business travel has largely rebounded a decade after 9/11, studies are conflicted about the overall trend in business travel, with some projecting a continued decline. Trips may be shorter or less frequent; they may also be extended to cover more than one objective. Technology has rapidly advanced, providing tools that offset the need for many traditional face-to-face business meetings. Safety remains a concern on many fronts. Although Canada has kept some international meetings quiet and secure, such as the G8 conference hosted in Kananaskis, Alberta, in 2002, others have erupted with lengthy riots, including the G20 summit of 2010 in Toronto. Domestic issues at events that should be celebrations, including the destructive riots in Vancouver following the final game of the 2010 NHL Stanley Cup final, put Canada's peaceful image at risk.

As branding becomes important to sales, small businesses are having more difficulty staying profitable. The growing demand for high-profile brand names is expressed by the forming of alliances and associations, and the buyout of smaller businesses by larger ones. Using a brand name provides customers with a familiar product, one that they have confidence in. Large numbers of consumers—51% to 71%—choose a brand name over an unknown name, especially when dollar values are similar.

Consumers are looking for products that are easy to purchase and use, and tourism businesses can fill this need by creating partnerships. Package deals—for example, putting accommodations together with a rental car and some entertainment and dining options—are growing in popularity. This kind of package is seen not only in the tourism sector, but in many aspects of the North American lifestyle. Consider the new mega-stores that sell groceries, clothes, furniture, appliances, and pharmaceuticals under one roof. This trend reflects the longer workweek and the erosion of personal, discretionary time.

Travel packages that provide short, relaxing holidays are expected to gain a greater share of the market. For example, hotels should be looking at strategic pricing such as Sunday-through-Thursday stays or Thursday-through-Sunday packages. This fills the need for business travellers looking to reduce the cost of their travel, and the vacation traveller who wants to take a four-day weekend.

Transportation trends include ticketless air travel; do-it-yourself, computerized check-in; and discount airlines that offer little or no service. Aircraft manufacturers are designing larger, much faster planes. Expect to see continued alliances and code sharing between the major airline companies. Trains are becoming an attractive alternative to air travel because they seem less likely to attract terrorism. With the added surcharges on an airline ticket in Canada, at least on short-haul runs like Montreal to Toronto, the train can be more affordable. VIA Rail has recognized the tourist demand for luxury train travel and has added newly refurbished cars and more service, making the trans-Canada trip more like a cruise—a total vacation package.

Cruise lines seem to be following the convention that "bigger is better." They are making cruises even more luxurious and elaborate, including facilities such as wedding chapels, bowling lanes, ice rinks, jogging paths, and surfing pools. High-end cruise lines like Crystal Cruises are focusing on "smaller is better" for upscale clients looking for fewer people aboard, luxury, and different ports.[6]

Trends in the accommodation industry include creating a more home-like atmosphere in rooms with more comfortable beds, pillows, and furniture, while providing customers with a high level of personal service (delivered through enhanced training programs for workers). The high-end customer is looking for facilities that include a gym or spa and high-speed internet connectivity. Larger hotel chains are expected to continue their partnerships with, and buyouts of, smaller properties. Furthermore, hotels are beginning to look at the airlines' surcharge strategy to keep rates low. A study by PricewaterhouseCoopers published in May 2005 reported that U.S. hotels expect to rake in more than $1.4 billion by adding surcharges such as "resort fees" (use of the parking lot, use of the pool and towels, and airport shuttle services); restocking of mini-bars (whether or not they have been used); additional fees for room service (in addition to the automatic gratuity); and even a charge for housekeeping. Hotels have lost money as more customers use the internet rather than the phone to contact customers and friends from their rooms; "free" internet may soon come with a hefty hook-up charge.

Since these surcharges are as frustrating as airline surcharges, many convention and visitor bureaus (CVB) suggest that if customers wish to avoid or at least reduce them, they should negotiate the add-ons the moment they arrive at the front desk.

Waiting until the end of the stay means they will likely not have much luck at reducing or eliminating charges for services that were not used.[7]

Food and beverage will remain a growing entrepreneurial industry. There seems to be a growing interest in how food is produced and its nutritional value, including an increased popularity in local farm co-operatives. Farmers are benefiting by tapping into local demand, especially from baby boomers, for fresh, local products, whether this is meat, produce, or wines. Smaller establishments will continue to struggle against the larger, well-known chains and must be able to reach a target market that believes that smaller is better.

Alliances and buyouts will continue to be commercially successful. Technology will play an ever-increasing role in this industry, and businesses will have to keep tight control of their food costs, using modern computers and cash systems. Menus are beginning to reflect consumers' interest in healthy eating by offering dishes that meet the standards of many diets.

www.workopolis.ca

Finally, the demand for contract food services and for food service aligned with upscale retirement homes will provide hospitality and culinary students with interesting career options.

Recreation and entertainment, the experiential components of tourism, will flourish as more baby boomers enjoy their retirement years. Attractions and special events that focus on culture and historical themes will be popular. More attractions are getting the visitor involved with hands-on workshops or seminars. Communities will expand their economic base by hosting a variety of special events to help extend their tourist season and increase revenue generation.

Special events are not just important for the tourism sector; they are also a main source of revenue for charities, and bring needed recognition to local enterprises. While the rising dollar no longer gives this country a cost advantage, Canada is still perceived as a safe and welcoming country—a perception that is sure to mean new growth in the conference and convention business.

Adventure tourism and outdoor recreation continue to have strong growth potential. Good risk management policies providing a high level of safety will be important for this market. **Ecotourism** has an ever-growing audience that supports

Our challenges for the future must include respecting the environment and creating a world in which tourism and our natural wonders coexist comfortably from one generation to the next.
(Photo courtesy Canadian Tourism Commission.)

nature and sustainability. Resorts that boast a unique natural setting will be held to a higher standard of sustainable development, and designs will have to ensure minimum harm to the environment. Boomers looking for a healthy retirement will lead increasingly active lives that include daily exercise. Golf courses and walking trails within suburban sites will become an integral part of the tourism experience.

www.tourism.govt.nz

SNAPSHOT

John Gow

With a love of skiing and the mountains, it is no wonder that John Gow set his sights high early in life. He began his career in 1964 at Sunshine Village in Banff, Alberta, as a ski instructor and mountain guide. He was soon recognized for his skill and knowledge, which were too great to leave him on the mountain. With his first promotion, he became director of ski school operations. From there he moved to director of marketing for Sunshine Village. Then he became its general manager and, finally, chief executive officer. John Gow was an integral part of the development strategies that led to Sunshine Village's great expansion (including one of the world's largest gondola systems) and its ability to operate at virtual capacity.

By 1981, John reached the pinnacle of success at Sunshine Village. His next move, along with several associates, was to purchase Silver Star Mountain Resort in British Columbia. As president of his own company, John discovered that his responsibilities included not only the day-to-day operations of the resort, but also the challenges of working alongside government agencies, planning for future expansion, and determining how to finance his ideas. How Silver Star Mountain Resort has changed under his guidance! What had once been a local ski hill has now become a major resort area in the Okanagan region and all of British Columbia. Gow added a themed village centre, hotels, restaurants and bars, shops, and special recreation facilities that satisfy the needs of both day visitors and tourists. Recently, he expanded the resort, tripling its

ski-able acreage, installing two express quad chairlifts, and increasing the vertical drop by 40%. Plans for the future include an eighteen-hole golf course, making Silver Star Mountain Resort a year-round property.

John Gow is not a man to sit around. In Banff, he became an active member of the chamber of commerce, serving on the hospitality board and the municipal council. During his seventeen years in Banff, he was a major catalyst in the construction of two housing developments, improving the quality of life for residents who lived and worked in the mountain resort area. Working with local transportation companies, he formed a partnership with the ski schools, creating a joint marketing program with ticketing and transportation facilities, which allowed them to penetrate markets in Eastern Canada, Japan, and the United States.

When Gow moved to British Columbia, he became even more active. He is currently chair of both the Pacific Rim Institute of Technology and Rendez-Vous Canada; he is also a board member of Tourism British Columbia, and past chair of TIAC.

Who is John Gow? He is an energetic man with a passionate commitment to the ski industry, to the development of the western ski product, and to tourism as a whole. His ability to work with all levels of government and industry and his vision for a sustainable and profitable future have made him one of the most respected voices in Canadian tourism. There are few who can balance life and its challenges as well as John Gow.

Travel services will remain an important piece of the tourism sector, but methods of doing business will change. How customers use travel agencies will depend more on the agencies' expertise and accountability. Tour companies will need to align many of their products with an older audience, providing well-paced, intellectually stimulating tours.

Tourism services will expand with the other industries. Customers approach service experiences with higher expectations; as better services are demanded by consumers, employees will need better customer service skills. Good trainers and quality training programs will be increasingly popular with all service industries. Good consumer research and statistics will also be required. Niche marketing will become important for smaller businesses as they work against the tidal waves of branding and big business. If brands are to remain competitive, they will have to produce more cost-effective advertising campaigns that clearly address the needs of their target markets.

www.hcareers.com

TOURISM CHALLENGES

Challenges provide opportunities for people to grow and expand their vision—and they frequently lead to greater achievement and new inventions. Some challenges are life-changing. Where would the world be if scientists did not challenge disease by searching for cures? Some challenges simply make life interesting—like walking the Great Wall of China.

As mentioned, the biggest (and most silent) challenge for tourism is the continued threat of terrorism. Although the safety of tourists has always been important, it is now a priority. The events of September 11, 2001, forced Canada to deal with the ongoing problem of fake Canadian passports and forced the government and the airlines to take additional security precautions. However, investigative reporters have identified many different lapses in security that leave us open to people intent on doing harm and promoting their cause, both here in Canada and around the world.

The rising cost of fuel is likely the number one challenge for all modes of travel. Using airport improvement fees (AIFs), airports are adding better facilities to reflect the demand for faster and more efficient services and longer runways for larger jets. Taking steps such as reducing baggage allowances, charging for checked baggage, removing food service on flights under four hours, and removing pillows (the most frequently stolen item) from airplanes illustrates how hard airlines are working to control costs. Some airlines are considering removing entertainment systems as well. Note: pillows, blankets, and meals may often be purchased from the airline.

Car rental companies will likely be stocking smaller, more fuel-efficient cars, with SUVs becoming less popular. Cruise lines face myriad challenges: too few ports, overcrowding at popular ports, and ports unable to handle the needs of the larger ships currently being built. Passenger safety becomes an issue—whether threats come from food poisoning, terrorism, or crime. A report by CNN that aired in 2007 reviewed treatment of crimes onboard a cruise ship and showed that crimes committed in international waters with no one country clearly in charge are a cause for concern. Cruise lines, unwilling to become involved, often ship the suspected perpetrator back to their own country once the ship enters a port. With no investigative personnel onboard, the crime scene is frequently not examined properly, evidence is lost, and many crimes go unanswered. The cruise industry's challenge is to alter this perception and reach the 85% of the population that has never experienced cruising.

Lodging facilities are facing many different challenges, including luring guests back and providing consistent, high-quality service. Businesses in this industry must begin to provide better facilities for the disabled and the elderly traveller, including wheelchair accessibility, ergonomically designed bathrooms, and brighter lighting. Analysts predict that over the next twenty years, baby boomers will begin to sell their homes and move into retirement communities. Already some small hotels have been converted to retirement condominiums, making good use of existing facilities such as commercial kitchens, dining rooms, exercise facilities, and meeting spaces. Resorts will need to plan for all four seasons. By adding spas, winter activities, and special events, resorts can extend revenue seasons and appeal to a broader clientele.

The food and beverage industry faces many challenges. Service and training will continue to be priorities, as will a focus on nutritious offerings. Greater competition means restaurants will need to make service a factor for the discriminating customer. Legal issues, such as lower tolerance for activities related to the effect of alcohol consumption, require restaurant operators to be creative in both their products and service. Fears surrounding changes will continue to create resistance to change; however, some changes, like the no-smoking bylaws, only cause short-term changes in business levels without the feared long-term impacts. Perhaps the most important challenge is food safety. Incidents of *E. coli* outbreaks and other food poisoning incidents continue to plague the industry. One of the best ways to ensure safe food handling is to put into place the Hazard Analysis Critical Control Point (HACCP) system.

To achieve strong growth in the recreation and entertainment industry, cities and regions must provide visitors with a greater array of attractions, event and conference facilities, and outdoor experiences. Tourists are beginning to look for unique educational experiences with hands-on activities such as weaving or wine-making or working on a ranch. A new area of growth—volunteer tourism—opens up a wide range of opportunities. Weather and other natural disasters of 2004 and 2005, such as the tsunami in Asia, earthquakes, flooding, and hurricanes, have inspired many people to travel to places where they can help other communities rebuild. In the aftermath of Hurricane Katrina, many people committed their personal time and travelled to New Orleans to help with organizations like Habitat for Humanity, building homes for residents whose houses were destroyed. Canadian leaders including Mike Holmes helped to create interest and bring attention to the building issues in New Orleans.

There also continues to be a shortage of trained and experienced event coordinators and meeting planners. The event business is growing each year as companies from many industries are recognizing the financial returns of a well-planned event. Along with the personnel issues, some cities face suprastructure challenges. Currently, Halifax is in the midst of approving the developing of a new convention centre in the city's core, one that requires both funding and community support.

Adventure tourism and outdoor recreation have also seen tremendous growth. As boomers retire, exercise and fresh air become important health issues. Baby boomers will be looking for destinations that provide a wide variety of physical activities. Young, single travellers are searching for excitement while on vacation, and finding it backpacking around the country, hiking in the mountains, and boating on our beautiful lakes and challenging rivers. Canada is well positioned to take full advantage of this trend. Canadian colleges and universities now offer a wide variety of adventure tourism courses, ensuring we have the trained personnel to meet this demand.

Use of the internet by customers is quickly eroding the travel service business. With commissions lowered or dropped altogether, travel agencies and other businesses must find new streams of revenue. That great hotelier Cesar Ritz was finding new streams of hotel revenues at the turn of the twentieth century; now travel agencies must use his techniques and find new ways to generate revenue for themselves.

CASE STUDY

The China Gem

Shannon had just graduated with her travel diploma and had the job of her dreams—acting as an escort for a large tour company. She had always loved working with people, and this job gave her the chance to see the world and get paid for it. This particular tour, "China Gems," was for retirees, and she found she had her hands full with thirty very active and talkative ladies. This high-end tour package used only five-star properties and attractions and moved at a leisurely pace for eighteen days. Check-in at the first hotel in Honolulu had gone smoothly; now they were in China. Shannon took a moment to remind the ladies of the different cultural practices they should observe. Beijing, a bustling city of ten million residents, so full of history, keeping thirty ladies on time and together would be enough of a challenge. The dinner arranged for them in the hotel restaurant had been delicious, but exotic. Some of the ladies were uncomfortable with the style, preparation, and service of the meal.

Breakfast was included in the package, and Shannon got to the restaurant early. She wanted to know if the ladies had slept comfortably and whether they were tired. If they were, she would take them to their first site, the Palace Museum, also known as the Forbidden City, and then bring them back to the hotel to rest. The ladies started arriving, and everyone seemed to be in good spirits. Then came the surprise: two of the ladies came down for breakfast in their bathrobes and with their hair in curlers. Before Shannon could reach them, they began complaining loudly about their room, the food, and the horrible coffee they had been forced to drink at dinner the night before. All eyes in the restaurant turned to them.

---

1. What do you believe is the core problem in this scenario?
2. As tour leader, what would you do first? Why?
3. Describe one positive and one negative outcome your action would achieve.
4. From the tour company's perspective, what impact do you think this situation would have on future arrangements? How might a similar embarrassing scene be avoided on future tours?
5. How might customers and staff in the dining room react to this display?
6. Brainstorm: Think of something a foreign tourist might do to upset the Canadian cultural norm.

They must be aware of niche markets (e.g., travellers with disabilities), provide services that meet customer needs in a professional and friendly manner, and be on top of changing methods of interacting with customers, including social media.

Keeping customer profiles up to date and having customers take part in sharing both data and desires will be more important than ever. Travel workers who have developed a relationship with customers, who know their likes and dislikes, know that if those customers feel comfortable and well looked after, they will return.

Tourism services, the support services for the sector, must meet the needs of the struggling tourism sector. Architects and designers must be more ecologically driven, ensuring that new products cause minimal harm to the environment. Research, consulting, and marketing firms, retail outlets, government services, educators, and trainers all must provide the tourism sector with the means to create a strong, sustainable product. The information they supply must be reliable and easily understood. The years ahead will provide many challenges for people entering the tourism business, but in the baby boomers lies a ready, willing, and able group of travellers. Opportunities no longer lie just in Canada, but around the globe.

Summary

- The tourism sector has experienced phenomenal growth over the past fifty years due to changes in modes of travel, available income, changing attitudes about travel and advancements in technology.
- There should continue to be significant growth in tourism consumption, especially over the next twenty years in North America with both the retirement of the baby boomers and the development of international markets.
- Challenges exist as the global consumer market continues to expand; destinations must pay attention to customer motivations around travel, understand economic shifts, and be ready to meet the needs and expectations of future tourists.
- The tourism sector is gearing up for a new era, and the snapshot of Canada's tourism future looks bright and exciting!

Questions

1. a) Look at the challenges identified by the Canadian Tourism Commission. Rearrange them in order of importance, as you see it.
   b) Provide a brief description of what you believe to be the five most important issues.
   c) How do you feel each of these chosen issues might best be overcome?
2. For each of the following groupings, find one positive challenge that will help the CTC redesign/update its product to reach new clientele: generational changes, ethical changes, political changes, and changes in business practices.
3. List all eight sectors of the tourism industry as studied in this text. Beside each one, explain the challenge you feel will be the hardest for that sector to overcome.

Notes

1. Jean M. Twenge, "Generation me: Why today's young Americans are more confident, assertive, entitled—and more miserable than ever before," (March 6, 2007).

2. Aditus, *The Aditus White Paper: Facts, Issues and Trends in Travel and Tourism* (Toronto: Southam, 1996).

3. Josh Visser, Trainwreck: Canada's high-speed rail failure, CTV.ca News: Monday Dec. 27, 2010, www.ctv.ca/CTVNews/Canada/20101222/high-speed-rail-101227/#ixzz1bWh3Y5Q5.

4. Christopher J. Holloway, *The Business of Travel* (Essex, London, UK: Pearson Education Limited, 2006), p. 124.

5. Peter Yesawich, "Trends in the tourism industry," Address to the TIAC Conference, Jasper, Alberta, November 1996.

6. www.cruising.org/challenges.

7. Melinda Ligos, "Hotel add-on charges can cost you more than a good night's sleep," *Edmonton Journal*, September 5, 2005, p. A13.

Tourism Education Councils
Contact Information

National: Canadian Tourism Human Resource Council (CTHRC)
Email   cthrc@cthrc.ca
Website   www.cthrc.ca
Telephone   (613) 231-6949

Alberta: Alberta Hotel & Lodging Association (AHLA)
Email   info@ahla.ca
Website   www.ahla.ca
Telephone   1-888-436-6112

British Columbia: go2—The Resource for People in Tourism
Email   info@go2hr.ca
Website   www.go2hr.ca
Telephone   1-604-633-9787

Manitoba: Manitoba Tourism Education Council (MTEC)
Email   general@mtec.mb.ca
Website   www.mtec.mb.ca
Telephone   1-800-820-6832

New Brunswick: Tourism Industry Association of New Brunswick (TIANB)
Email   info@tianb.com
Website   www.tianb.com
Telephone   1-800-668-5313

Newfoundland and Labrador: Hospitality Newfoundland & Labrador
Email   hospitality@hnl.ca
Website   www.hnl.ca
Telephone   1-800-563-0700

Nova Scotia: Nova Scotia Tourism Human Resource Council (THRC)
Email   NSTHRC@tourism.ca
Website   www.tourismhrc.com
Telephone   1-800-948-4267

Ontario: Ontario Tourism Education Corporation (OTEC)
Email   info@otec.org
Website   www.otec.org
Telephone   1-800-557-6832

Prince Edward Island: Tourism Industry Association of Prince Edward Island (TIAPEI)
Email   tiapei@tiapei.pe.ca
Website   www.tiapei.pe.ca
Telephone   1-866-566-5008

Saskatchewan: Saskatchewan Tourism Education Council (STEC)
Email   stec@sasktourism.com
Website   www.stec.com
Telephone   1-800-331-1529

Yukon: Yukon Tourism Education Council (YTEC)
Website   www.yukontec.com
Telephone   1-867-667-4733

200 km menu—All the major ingredients have been grown within 200 km of the restaurant.

Adventure tourism—Outdoor activities that present the participant with risk and challenge. Adventure tourism is divided into two types: hard adventure and soft adventure.

Agricultural tourism (agritourism)—A tourism experience that teaches travellers about the agricultural industry in Canada through hands-on farm life experiences.

Airfares—Ticket prices set according to two very broad categories: the business traveller and the discretionary traveller.

All-inclusive tour—A tour package that provides the guest with transportation, food and beverage service, entertainment, and lodging for one price. Service charges may also be included.

Allergy awareness—An increase in demand by consumers to know the ingredients used to create food products in order to avoid allergic reactions.

Allocentric—A traveller willing to take risks, and willing to go without the normal conveniences of life in order to gain a fuller travel experience. These travellers prefer to go where few people have been and are often referred to by marketers as *innovators*. They are first to try a new travel destination in its development stage.

American Plan (AP)—A hotel room rate that includes the room, plus three full meals.

Amusement park—A centre of entertainment that offers rides, shows, food, candy, and arcades.

Aquarium—An aquatic zoo that features a wide variety of fish and sea creatures in tanks for viewing by the public. It may also include marine mammals, such as porpoises.

Art museum—An institution that exhibits a variety of artwork including sculptures, oils, watercolours, and carvings.

Balanced development—A component of the integrated development theory in which one portion of the development can operate at a loss that is compensated for by a lucrative operation elsewhere in the resort.

Bed and breakfast (B & B)—Accommodation that is generally family-owned and -managed, accommodates three to ten groups per night, and includes a family-style breakfast.

Bermuda Plan (BP)—Room rate that includes a full American breakfast: juice, coffee, eggs, sausage or bacon, and toast.

Bilateral agreement—An agreement between two countries that often deals with the number of flights permitted from each country into a specific airport, the size and capacity of the airplanes, and special fares.

Bistro—A small, casual restaurant that serves fresh, eclectic food.

Boutique hotel—A luxury-style hotel designed to cater to guests willing to pay higher fees for top-level quality and very sophisticated levels of service.

Breakout room—Smaller room made available for seminars or workshops at a conference.

BritRail pass—A train pass allowing unlimited train travel in the British Isles.

Buffet house—An all-you-can-eat restaurant that offers a wide assortment of hot and cold food, to which customers can help themselves.

Bullet train—A high-speed Japanese train.

Bumped—Hotel guests who have reservations at one hotel who are relocated to another hotel because the original hotel took too many reservations. Also referred to as being "walked."

Business guest—An individual travelling for work purposes, who usually has few choices in deciding where, when, how, and how long to travel.

Cafeteria—A type of restaurant at which customers can choose their food from a serving line of different dishes, with the portions preset and served by kitchen staff.

Campground—A place where campers can set up their tents or park their recreational vehicles.

Cannibalization—A situation in which a franchisor allows two independent units to locate too near each other, causing loss of revenue for one or both.

Canadian Tourism Commission—A federal agency responsible for promoting tourism in Canada, reporting to Industry Canada.

Carrying capacity—The maximum number of people who can use a site with only acceptable alteration to the physical environment and with only acceptable decline in the quality of experience gained by subsequent visitors.

Cash bar—Alcohol service in which guests pay for their own drinks.

Casino gambling—Gambling including slot machines, roulette, craps, blackjack, poker, and other games of chance.

Catalytic development—Development of a destination in which a single developer encourages complementary businesses in and around the property.

Centralized development—A component of catalytic development; refers to the major developer who provides the basic facilities, major accommodation units, and promotion for the destination.

Certification—Industry recognition of individuals who have demonstrated competencies relating to occupational standards for a particular occupation.

Chain ownership—A single corporate identity that operates more than one property, with all properties reporting to corporate headquarters.

Chamber of commerce—A city organization that promotes industry and retail development and markets tourism to the city.

Channel of distribution—The avenues through which travel products are sold, connecting customers with tourism service providers.

Charter—A bus, plane, or ship rented for the purpose of transporting people from one location to another, usually at rates lower than regularly scheduled rates.

Children's museum—A museum that involves young children in activities to educate and entertain them; may be one component of a larger museum.

Circle trip—A type of round trip in which the routes taken to and from the destination differ.

Civic event—Event sponsored by a government organization (e.g., swearing in a new prime minister, Remembrance Day).

Clustering—Locating a variety of tourism sites and products in one area to create easy access for visitors.

Coattail development—Development of a destination that occurs naturally, without community planning. A lack of common theme often means duplication of services and a general lack of direction in the development of the destination.

Code of ethics—A system of beliefs based on the values of right and wrong in a specific culture.

Coffee house—A type of restaurant that serves a variety of coffee drinks and a limited selection of food.

Commercial food service—A division of the food service industry that serves the public and is available to anyone wishing to eat out.

Commission—The percentage of a selling price paid to a retailer by a supplier.

Common currency—Credit cards, traveller's cheques, and other currency dispensed by automated banking and currency exchange machines, which allow travellers easy access to money and credit while on vacation.

Condominium—An individually owned, apartment-style residence located in an area filled with recreational amenities; may be rented out to other travellers when not occupied by the owner.

Conference—A large meeting where delegates from the same industry or occupation come together to learn, network, and exchange ideas.

Conference appointment—Permission to conduct business with a travel agency.

Conference centre—A location specifically designed to provide an effective working environment for a conference and its delegates. Conference centres have accommodations within the complex.

Conference hotel—A hotel with conference facilities that caters to large groups, usually in the downtown area of major cities.

Confirmed reservation—A reservation at a hotel or lodging establishment that is held through prepayment or with a confirmed source of payment such as a credit card.

Consolidator—An operator that purchases a large number of airline seats every year from individual airlines at a low price, then sells them to tour operators and travel agents at discounted prices.

Consortium—A group of independent businesses that work together for a common purpose (e.g., independently owned travel agencies that promote their products through a single brand name).

Continental Plan (CP)—A hotel room rate that includes the room and a continental breakfast.

Contract caterers—Food and beverage service that is provided at establishments whose primary function is not food or beverage, such as on airlines or in museums.

Contract food service—A division of the food service industry that serves a specific clientele, not the general public; found in establishments whose main purpose is something other than serving food, such as museums, stadiums, and airlines.

Convention—A large meeting of delegates who share a common interest that typically includes either an interest in the same industry (local foods) or hobby (Comic-Con).

Convention and visitors bureau (CVB)—A municipal or private organization that promotes tourism and provides convention facilities and information services for visitors to the city.

Convention centre—A location specifically built to handle groups of more than 1000 people but that does not provide accommodations.

Corkage fee—A fee charged by restaurants for opening a bottle of wine brought to the restaurant by a customer.

Corporate rates—Reduced rates designed to encourage sales to companies.

Corporate travel agency—An agency that deals almost exclusively with business travel arrangements, as opposed to leisure travel.

Crown land—Land that is publicly owned and controlled by the government. Crown land may be owned by the province or by the federal government, but unlike protected parklands, it often does not fall under specific protective legislation. Much of Canada's wilderness is designated Crown land.

Culinary tourism—Tourism that focuses on culinary products, such as a wineries tour, a short course at a cooking school, or a series of lectures on foods of a region combined with a local food festival.

Cultural motivators—A desire to know and learn more about the music, architecture, food, art, folklore, or religion of other people.

Cultural tourism—See *heritage (cultural) tourism.*

Day rate—A hotel room rate charged between 9 A.M. and 8 P.M. (no overnight stay).

Day tour—A bus tour that lasts less than 24 hours and has no accommodation arrangements, usually in one specific region.

Demand—The need or desire for goods and services; the number of people who wish to purchase a product.

Demographics—Statistics that include age, marital status, gender, occupation,

income, and place of residence; used for understanding who the travellers are to a particular site.

Destination life cycle—The stages through which a destination moves: conception, growth, maturity, and decline.

Destination marketing organization (DMO)—A tourism organization that is responsible for creating a marketing plan for a destination and promoting it. The CTC is Canada's federal DMO, with CVBs usually representing a city or region.

Destination restaurant—A restaurant that people will visit specifically for its unique selling proposition.

Direct flight—A flight that carries a traveller from one destination to another, making at least one stop along the route.

Discretionary income—The money that one may spend as one pleases.

Discretionary time—Time away from work and other obligations.

Domestic tourist—A person travelling in the country in which he or she resides, who stays for a period of 24 hours and travels at least 80 km from home.

Double—Two people staying in one room.

Double double—A hotel room with two double beds.

Dude or guest ranch—Accommodation that is either a working ranch where guests help in the everyday work, or a luxury ranch resort for horseback riding, swimming, hiking, or tennis.

Ecotourism—Responsible travel aimed at learning more about the environment; focuses on nature-related experiences that help people appreciate and understand our natural resources and their conservation.

Ecotourist—A person who believes in responsible travel to natural areas and who aids in conserving the local environment.

Elastic demand—When demand changes significantly as a result of price changes (e.g., demand drops when price rises).

emerit—A national level skill-based training and certification program overseen by the CTHRC and provincial TECs available to over thirty tourism occupations.

Empty nest—The life stage of married couples whose children have grown and left home.

Escorted tour—An organized tour led by a professional tour guide.

Ethics—A system or code of morals of a particular person, religion, culture, group, or profession.

Ethnic restaurant—A restaurant that serves food from a specific culture, country, or region.

E-ticket—An electronic version of a paper ticket.

Eurail Pass—A discounted rail pass allowing travel by train. Certain restrictions apply. Must be purchased outside Europe. May also include other forms of transportation, such as ferry service, buses, etc. in seventeen European countries.

European Plan (EP)—A hotel rate that includes the room, with no meals.

Excursionist—Any person who travels at least 80 km from the place of residence, stays less than 24 hours, and is not commuting to work or school or operating as part of a crew on a train, airplane, truck, bus, or ship.

External locus of control—The belief that events are determined by powerful individuals, fate, or chance.

Extrovert—An individual who is outgoing and uninhibited in interpersonal situations.

Fair—A special event with a theme, such as an agricultural fair, historical fair, trade fair, or World's Fair.

Familiarization tour (FAM tour)—A free or discounted trip for travel professionals, designed to acquaint them with an area in order to help them choose a convention site.

Family life stage—Various descriptions of a person's family composition at a specific point in time that influences particular behaviours and activities.

Family Plan (FP)—An accommodation plan in which there is no extra charge for children under a given age to stay with their parents at a hotel.

Family-style restaurant—Restaurant, often located in the suburbs, that offers full, fast, and friendly service, "comfort" food, and a welcoming environment for children.

Fast food restaurant—A restaurant where customers place their own order, pick up their own food, and clear their own tables when finished. Prices are low and menu is limited.

Festival—A public celebration centred on a theme of local, regional, or national interest or importance.

Fine dining—Restaurants that provide elegant decor, high-quality food prepared from scratch, and professional, attentive service.

Fly/coach tour—A tour that combines airfare with an escorted bus tour.

Forecasting—The process of attempting to determine future demand in an area.

Foreign tourist—A person visiting a country other than the one in which he or she usually resides and staying for a period of at least 24 hours.

Franchise—A business purchased as a turn-key operation, with everything in place.

Franchise advisory councils (FACs)—Bodies that represent franchisees, providing them with a forum through which to address concerns with the franchise contract or the franchisor.

Franchisee—The purchaser of a franchise operation.

Franchisor—The company that owns the franchise rights to a product and sells it to other operator/investors.

Freedoms of the Air—Global rules regulating aircraft and airline activity and addressing rights of passage for an airplane, air traffic rights, and the granting of special rights to certain airlines under specific circumstances; also known as *rights of the air.*

Front of house—Employees who deal actively with customers, usually in a hotel or a restaurant setting.

Full-service travel agency—A travel agency staffed and equipped to answer and serve all categories of traveller needs.

Functional form—Within integrated development, adherence to a common theme.

Fundraising event—Public event that encourages people to participate in order to raise money for a specific cause or organization.

Gateway—The welcoming sign to a destination that informs tourists they have arrived; e.g., an information centre providing tourists with friendly assistance brochures and help in arrange their stay.

Gateway airport—Airport from which major international flights arrive and depart.

Gateway city—The city where a tour begins.

Green Plan—Created twenty years ago, a commitment to solve Canada's complex environmental challenges and implement sustainable economic development, identifying tourism as an important partner in the plan. It recommended that 12% of Canada's lands be protected space for parks, historic sites, and wildlife.

Greenwashing—Using the so-called "eco" label to lure unsuspecting tourists into believing that a company uses sound environmental practices.

Ground/land package—A tour that includes the land arrangements of a tour but no air transportation.

Guests—Another term for tourists.

Hallmark event—Significant occasion that brings tourists from around the world to a destination and has a huge economic impact on the community (e.g., the Olympics).

Hard adventure—Tourism activities that often take place in an unusual, exotic, or remote setting, requiring pre-training, a high level of physical activity, risk, and may require specialized equipment.

Haute cuisine—An elegant and expensive style of restaurant noted for its outstanding food, opulent atmosphere, and highly trained staff.

Heart of house—Employees who support the operation of a business but whose jobs rarely put them in direct contact with customers.

Heritage (cultural) tourism—Immersion in the natural history, human heritage, arts, philosophy, and institutions of another region or country. A trip that educates the visitor on the architecture, food, folklore, or religion of another culture. Also called *cultural tourism.*

Historic site—A place of special historical interest.

Historical museum—A museum depicting some historical event or place.

Hospitality of host—An intangible concept referring to the genuine warmth extended to visitors by the host destination.

Hospitality suite—A hotel room includes a bar and a sitting area for guests.

Hosted tour—A tour on which participants travel between destinations without a guide but are met at each destination by a host guide from that community.

Hostel—A lodge with communal washrooms and bedrooms designed for four to twenty people.

Hosts—People, communities, or regions that entertain visiting guests.

Hotel—Accommodation that provides access to guest rooms from a central lobby.

Hub and spoke—A pattern of transportation in which an airline uses one airport as the collecting point for incoming and outgoing flights. This system is also used in the motor coach industry.

Inbound tour—A tour that brings guests from a foreign country to Canada, generating jobs and revenue for Canadians.

Inbound tourist—See *foreign tourist.*

Incentive travel—The practice of using a trip as an award for performing to a certain set of standards.

Industrial tourism—Tourism that includes visits to industrial sites, such as the oil fields of Alberta or the salmon fisheries of British Columbia.

Inelastic demand—When demand does not significantly change when prices change (i.e., a large drop in price does not result in a large increase in demand).

Infrastructure—A basic system that includes facilities such as roads, sewage systems, electricity, and water supply.

Inn—Small hotel/accommodation, often using a historic building that has been renovated to meet the expectations of travellers looking for upscale but homelike accommodations. Most inns are located in the countryside rather than in large cities.

Intangible—Term used to describe the service and experience portion of tourism and how, unlike a physical product, tourism cannot be sampled prior to purchase.

Integrated development—The development of a large parcel of land by a single individual or company to the exclusion of all other developers.

Interdependency—A component of catalytic development; entrepreneurial activities of other businesses within the development succeed because the initial developer succeeds, and the initial developer succeeds because of the entrepreneurs. Each is dependent on the other.

Interline connection—Air travel between two destinations during which the traveller is forced to change airline companies in order to complete the journey.

Internal locus of control—The belief that people are in charge of what happens in their own lives.

International Air Transport Association (IATA)—A privately run international organization whose principal function is to facilitate the movement of persons and goods from and to any point on the world air network by any combination of routes.

International Civil Aviation Organization (ICAO)—An agency of the United Nations that ensures safe, orderly the development of the global air travel.

Interpersonal motivator—A reason for travel based on family and friends and the seeking of comradeship.

Introvert—A person who is more concerned with internal thoughts and feelings than the immediate expression of those ideas in public.

Isolation—A component of integrated development; a development is located away from existing settlements.

Joint venture—An arrangement between two partners, normally designed to draw together various skills sets and areas of expertise.

Landing fee—Fee charged by an airport to an airline for the right to land and use airport services.

Leakage—A community's need to import workers or goods in order to sustain its tourism industry.

"Le grand tour"—An educational tour of Europe undertaken by young English noblemen in the seventeenth and eighteenth centuries.

LGBT tourism—A niche tourism market focused specifically towards gay, lesbian, bisexual and transgendered people.

Living history museum—A museum in which people act the parts of historical characters.

Load factor—The percentage of seats filled on an airplane by paying or revenue-producing passengers.

Low-impact camping—A type of camping in which every item carried in is carried out; every item created on the trip is carried out; enclosed fires and biodegradable products are used; no souvenirs are taken from the area; and the area is left virtually untouched and ready for the next group of adventurers.

Maglev—A high-speed monorail that operates using powerful magnets (a magnetic levitating vehicle).

Management contract—A method of hotel management and operation in which one company owns the property and another company operates it.

Marketing—A continual, sequential process through which management plans, researches, implements, controls, and evaluates activities designed to satisfy both customers' needs and wants and the organization's objectives.

Marketing mix—Controllable factors that may be selected to help satisfy customer needs or wants (product, price, place, promotion).

Market match—The satisfactory situation in which the product on offer meets the needs of the target market.

Marketing plan—A written plan used to guide an organization's marketing activities for a period of one year or less.

Market segmentation—The division of the overall market into groups of people who share common characteristics or have similar needs.

Medical tourism—Travellers choose a destination to gain access to a specific medical practice.

Meeting Professionals International (MPI)—A professional association of meeting planners.

Mega-mall—A large shopping and entertainment centre offering a wide assortment of services including retail stores, restaurants, and accommodations as well as a variety of entertainment facilities such as indoor theme parks, game rooms, wave pools, minigolf courses, cinemas, etc.

Menu—A list of all the products a restaurant or other business sells.

Midcentric—In the tourist personality classification system, the halfway point between allocentrics and psychocentrics. Most people fit into this category.

Modified American Plan (MAP)—A hotel room rate that includes the room plus breakfast and lunch or dinner.

Motel—Tourist accommodation that provides free parking and access to a guest's room directly from the parking lot.

Motivator—A "promoter of action" whose purpose is to fulfill a need or want.

Motor coach package—A bus tour that lasts from three to thirty days and includes one or more of these four components: accommodations, meals, attractions, sightseeing.

Multiplier effect—the mechanism whereby the benefits of tourism dollars spread through a community, profiting businesses and residents not directly involved in tourism.

Multi-unit corporate restaurant—A chain of restaurants in which one person or company controls all the units; typically, all restaurants have similar decor, menu, and management style.

Museum—A building that displays a wide assortment of memorabilia ranging from artwork and historical or scientific items to agricultural tools or cartoons.

National parks system—a countrywide system of representative natural areas of Canadian significance, protected for public appreciation, enjoyment, and education. Operated under the jurisdiction of the federal government, national parks have strict rules and regulations that are enforced by park officials to ensure the parks are maintained in an unimpaired state for future generations. The system has forty-one established parks with an additional ten under consideration.

Natural resources—The physical means of supporting and attracting tourists, such as land and agriculture, a habitable climate, a water supply, and natural beauty.

Niche—A small, focused area of the tourism industry. For example, adventure vacation packages designed specifically for single travellers would be a niche product offering.

Niche market—A target group of customers who would match up with a niche offering.

Niche (target) marketing—Creating products to fulfill the needs of a specific segment of the total market; also known as *target marketing*.

Non-commercial food service—Often referred to as social and contract caterers, includes food and beverage services found on airlines and railways, in stadiums, museums, and department stores, and at recreational events and recreational camps.

Non-stop flight—A flight that does not stop between point of departure and destination.

Occupational standards—A code that outlines the skills, knowledge, and attitudes that an individual must demonstrate and practise to be deemed competent in a given job.

Oceanarium—An aquatic zoo that features saltwater fish and animals such as dolphins, seals, whales, and shore birds.

Online connection—Air travel between two destinations during which the traveller must change aircraft, but not airlines, in order to complete the journey.

Open bar—Alcohol service in which the host pays for the alcohol consumed.

Open-jaw trip—A type of travel in which travellers arrive in one city but depart from a different city.

Open Skies Agreement—Bilateral agreement between the United States and Canada for North American airlines that provides tourists with greater choice of carrier and types of flights.

Organically grown foods—Foods raised without the use of chemicals.

Orient Express—A historic train, noted for carrying royalty, political leaders, and the wealthy, which operated between Paris and Istanbul between 1833 and 1977. Its cars have been refurbished to their original luxury and travelling on the train is now considered a destination in itself, rather than a simple mode of transportation.

Outdoor recreation—Activities that take place outdoors, such as hiking, backpacking, canoeing, sailing, kayaking, bicycling, horseback riding, wildlife viewing, and heli-hiking.

Overbook—The practice of selling more hotel rooms, airplane seats, etc., than exist, on the assumption that not all reservations will be picked up.

Overnight/short tour—A bus tour that is two days long.

Parimutuel gambling—A betting pool in which those who bet on the winners of the first three places share the total winning amount, minus a percentage for management.

Parks Canada—Agency that oversees national parks, historic sites, marine conservation areas, heritage rivers, and national battlefields, and that reports to Environment Canada.

Partnerships—Alliances formed among various sectors of the tourism industry.

Perceived value—the customer's mental estimate of the worth of a product to them.

Physical motivator—A health-related reason for travelling to an area, including relaxation, sports participation, recreation, medical exams, or health treatments.

Place—One of the marketing Ps: the location in which a product is sold; also known as *channel of distribution.*

Planning—Organizing the future to achieve certain goals.

Pleasure guest—Someone travelling for pleasure on discretionary time and money.

Price—One of the marketing Ps: the amount charged for a product, which includes all costs and profit.

Product—One of the marketing Ps; the good or service being sold.

Product capacity—The number of facilities, the accommodations or rooms available, and the transportation system capacity.

Promotion—One of the marketing Ps: advertising and other means of generating customer interest in a product.

Psychocentric—A traveller who enjoys travel only when it is just like home; the so-called armchair traveller.

Psychographics—Information about people's activities, opinions, motives, behaviours, and interests; often used for marketing purposes.

Pub—Small casual restaurant that emulates an English, Irish, or Scottish bar, including the ambience, the menu, and the types of beverages available.

Pull factors—Tangible reasons for travel choices, such as friends, mountains, and beaches.

Push factors—Intangible reasons for travel choices, such as the need to escape, the need for culture, or a need for physical fitness.

Qualitative forecasting—The use of experts and their accumulated experience and knowledge to predict the likely outcome of events.

Quantitative forecasting—The analysis of numerical data (current and historical) to help predict the future.

Rack rate—The published full price for a hotel room.

Rapid development—A component of integrated development; refers to the speed at which development can occur because a single developer can make decisions quickly.

Recreational sports—Major sports that affect the tourism industry, including skiing, golf, tennis, and water sports.

Referral system—independently owned and operated hotels working together under a brand name in order to receive brand-name recognition, access to a global reservation system, and global marketing strategies, e.g., Best Western.

REITs (real estate investment trusts)—A company that buys hotel or resort properties, and then sells shares of the property on the stock market.

Rendez-Vous Canada—A trade show that brings together Canadian tourism suppliers and international tour operators.

Resort—A destination hotel that is usually located in the countryside, near water or the mountains. Resorts provide their guests with a wide variety of outdoor recreational activities, indoor services such as spas, pools, and workout rooms, and a variety of in-house dining experiences.

Responsible tourism—A tourism product that is both sustainable and ecologically sound.

Risk management—Policies and procedures that an operation designs to ensure the safety of both its guests and the business.

Round trip—An airline routing that originates in a city, goes to a destination, and returns to the original city.

Run-of-the-house rate—A discount rate for block bookings.

Same-day visitor—See *excursionist.*

Scheduled air carriers—Airlines that operate on defined routes at specific times, whether domestic or international, for which licences have been granted by the government or governments concerned.

Scientific museum—A museum centred on some study of science, ranging from dinosaur bones to space ships.

Secondary developers—Developers who build complementary facilities near a primary development, such as a major resort.

Sector—A distinct part of an economy (i.e., the tourism sector).

Seminar—A meeting in which participants share ideas, knowledge, and expertise under the supervision of a leader or presenter.

Sense of place—The special feeling of a destination, created by its unique feature(s), and used in marketing it.

Sex tourism—A niche area of tourism that focuses on the sex trade; associated with some developing countries and the exploitation of women and children.

Sightseeing tour—See *day tour.*

Signature item—A distinctive dish, usually associated to the chef who prepares it.

Single—A hotel room occupied by one person.

Site inspection—First-hand view of a potential conference site by the organizers to determine whether it meets the group's needs.

Site-specific—A museum located where an historic event took place.

Social media—A collection of internet-based communication tools constructed around the creation and development of user-generated content.

Soft adventure—Outdoor activities, such as hiking and snorkelling, designed to give participants the thrill of hard adventure without the risk. These activities require no pre-training, are usually less strenuous than hard adventure activities, and any equipment needed is supplied by the operator.

Spa—A hotel or resort that encourages healthy, rejuvenating activities such as massage therapy, body wraps, steam baths, aerobic exercise classes, etc. As part of the vacation package, guests often are provided with low-calorie or other specialty meals.

Spa tourism—Focuses on the overall health and well-being of the traveller.

Special event—A one-time or infrequently occurring event outside the normal program or activities of the sponsoring or organizing body.

Special interest cruise—A cruise that focuses on a specific topic of interest, usually from an educational standpoint, such as ecotourism, history, or opera.

Specialty restaurant—A type of restaurant that serves one kind of food, such as chicken or ribs.

Specialty travel agency—An agency that specializes in a particular type of travel, such as adventure travel or cruises.

Spectator sporting event—A sporting event that has audience appeal, such as professional hockey, baseball, or basketball.

Status and prestige motivators—Reasons to travel related to a need for recognition, attention, appreciation, and good reputation; same as social and ego factors.

Step-on guide—A sightseeing guide who has particular knowledge about the history, people, and events that have shaped a region and who is specifically trained to show the sights of the region.

Suite—A hotel room with one or more bedrooms and a sitting room.

Summit—An international meeting of high-level government leaders.

Supply—The amount of product available.

Surplus—An excess amount of something. For example, a surplus of hotel rooms on a particular night would mean that a hotel had more rooms available than guests that night.

Suprastructure—All of the buildings located at the destination; that is, structures that are "built up" from the ground, such as lodging facilities, restaurants, terminals, and stores.

Sustainable tourism—When tourism development and operations meet the needs of current tourists and host regions, while protecting and enhancing opportunities for the future.

Target marketing—See *niche marketing*.

Tavern—A business whose primary function is to serve alcoholic beverages.

Theme cruise—A cruise that focuses on a particular event or topic of interest (e.g., Super Bowl cruise, rock and roll cruise); also called a *special-interest cruise*.

Theme park—A family entertainment centre oriented to a particular subject or historical area, and which combines the continuity of costuming and architecture with entertainment and merchandise to create a fantasy-evoking atmosphere.

Theme restaurant—Restaurant that transports customers to a different time or place through ambience, server costumes, menu, and entertainment reflecting the theme (e.g., Medieval Times).

Time poverty—Having too much to do and too little time in which to do it.

Time-sharing—Buying a vacation segment, usually of two weeks, in a condominium unit.

Tourism—The activities of persons travelling to and staying in places outside their usual environment for not more than one year for leisure, business, and other purposes.

Tourism destination area (TDA)—A destination that has a combination of natural resources, infrastructure, suprastructure, and transportation systems, combined with a welcoming population, that make it an attractive destination for tourists.

Tourism education councils (TECs)—Organizations that work with provincial mandates to stimulate and coordinate the development of tourism training in their provinces.

Tourism illiteracy—The condition of not knowing or understanding the benefits of the tourism industry.

Tourism information centres—Operations typically run on a provincial level that provide information and assistance to inbound tourists.

Tourist court—Tourist accommodation that provides customers with a small cabin and a parking space.

Tourist destination area (TDA)—An area or region that relies on tourism as its major source of revenue and that possesses attractions and amenities that support the tourism trade.

Tourist dollars—Revenue produced by the tourism industry.

Tour operator—A company that contracts with and pays in advance for services provided by hotels, transportation companies, and other suppliers in order to create a tour package.

Tour wholesaler—A company that contracts for space with hotels, transportation companies, and other suppliers to create a tour package. Historically, it differs from a tour operator because no money changes hands until the space is purchased by a client. Today, there is no noticeable difference between the two types of operation.

Trade show—A marketing and sales tool used by many industries to display and sell their products.

Transfer—Any change in transportation, between modes or within the same mode, during a journey.

Transportation systems—The vehicles that use the travel infrastructure of a destination.

Travel counsellor—A person who has satisfactorily completed the certification process of the Canadian Institute of Travel Counsellors.

Travel deficit—The difference that occurs when the dollar amount spent by tourists choosing to vacation outside their country (outbound tourists) exceeds the revenue generated by foreign tourists (inbound tourists) who visit the country.

Trend—Current style or preference; in tourism, a popular destination or activity.

Trend analysis—The use of historical data to predict future trends.

Trip—Any travel that takes a person 80 km away from his or her place of residence for any reason, other than a commute to work or school, travel in an ambulance to a hospital or clinic, or a trip that is longer than one year.

Turn-down service—Service provided by luxury hotels, in which the bedspread is folded down and a chocolate placed on the pillow.

Twin—A hotel room with two single beds.

Unescorted tour—A tour in which the group travels without a company representative.

UNESCO World Heritage Site—A place recognized by the United Nations Educational, Scientific, and Cultural Organization for its outstanding universal value.

Unique selling proposition (USP)—The unique characteristics (physical, cultural, historic, etc.) that create a sense of place for a destination.

Unlimited kilometres—A car rental package that charges travellers a flat fee regardless of distance driven.

Upselling—A sales technique used by servers to increase the amount of a bill, by encouraging customers to purchase items not included in the cost of the meal (e.g., appetizer, baked potato, coffee).

VIA Rail Canada—A Crown corporation, created by the merger of Canadian National Railways and Canadian Pacific Railway, responsible for most of the passenger rail travel in Canada.

Visit Canada—A trade show that introduces travel writers from around the world to the Canadian tourism product.

Visitor—A generic term used for both domestic and foreign tourists.

Visitor use—The total number of tourists or excursionists to visit a destination or attraction or to attend an event over a specified period of time.

Volunteer tourism—tourism that arranges volunteer opportunities with a specific purpose or cause (e.g., building homes for Habitat for Humanity).

Walking—The practice of sending guests who have reservations that cannot be honoured to other available hotels.

Weekend rate—Special discounted rates used by hotels that rely upon corporate business during the week. These discounted rates encourage business people to bring their families in for a weekend vacation, or encourage locals to use the hotel and its services for a quick weekend getaway.

Workshop—A small group session in which participants learn new skills or techniques.

Zoo—A wildlife attraction that maintains a collection of wild animals for the purpose of information and education.

CREDITS

Photo Credits:

Chapter 1; p. 8 National Capital Commission; p. 9 Canadian Tourism Commission; p. 19 Paula Kerr; p. 24 Horseshoe Resort; **Chapter 2;** p. 36 Parks Canada / R. Garnett; p. 38 © Robert Bush/Alamy; p. 41 National Capital Commission; p. 45 Canadian Tourism Commission; p. 47 Canadian Tourism Commission; p. 50 National Capital Commission; p. 56 SteveKaiserPhotography. ca; **Chapter 3;** p. 64 John B. Kerr; p. 65 Canadian Tourism Commission; p. 71 Raymond Chan, Photomedia; p. 75 Canadian Tourism Commission; p. 76 Paula Kerr; p. 85 Paula Kerr; **Chapter 4;** p. 98 Canadian Tourism Commission; p. 107 Canadian Tourism Commission; p. 109 Canadian Tourism Commission; p. 113 Canadian Tourism Commission; p. 116 Saint John Port Authority; p. 118 John Kerr; **Chapter 5;** p. 128 Fairmont Le Château Montebello; p. 134 Canadian Tourism Commission; p. 137 Canadian Tourism Commission; p. 141 Canadian Tourism Commission; p. 142 Paula Kerr; p. 148 Paula Kerr; **Chapter 6;** p. 160 Canadian Tourism Commission; p. 161 Paula Kerr; p. 163 Matthew Honey; p. 168 Canadian Tourism Commission; p. 169 Canadian Tourism Commission; **Chapter 7;** p. 177 Mervyn Rees/Alamy; p. 182 Debbie Brady; p. 183 Mark Eastman; p. 186 Canadian Tourism Commission; p. 193 Canadian Tourism Commission; p. 194 Canadian Tourism Commission; **Chapter 8;** p. 202 VILevi/ Fotolia; p. 204 Fresh Air Adventure; p. 205 Canadian Tourism Commission; p. 206 Rolf Hicker Photography/Alamy; p. 209 Canadian Tourism Commission; p. 211 (top) National Capital Commission; p. 211 (bottom) Canadian Tourism Commission; p. 213 Canadian Tourism Commission; **Chapter 9;** p. 224 Canadian Tourism Commission; p. 226 Canadian Tourism Commission; p. 230 Ottawa Senators Hockey Club; p. 233 The Banff Centre; p. 234 Canadian Tourism Commission; p. 236 Canadian Tourism Commission; **Chapter 10;** p. 242 Canadian Tourism Commission; p. 247 The Fairmont Empress; p. 250 Canadian Tourism Commission; p. 254 Canadian Tourism Commission; p. 259 Paula Kerr; **Chapter 11;** p. 266 Canadian Tourism Commission; p. 269 National Capital Commission; p. 274 Paula Kerr; **Chapter 12;** p. 285 The Fairmont Jasper Park Lodge; p. 288 National Capital Commission; p. 290 Canadian Tourism Commission.

Text Credits:

Chapter 1; p. 16www.davidsuzuki.org/blog; **Chapter 2;** p. 32 Stanley C. Plog, *Leisure Travel* (New York: John Wiley & Sons, 1991), p. 83.; p. 37 Canadian Tourism Commission and the Government of Canada; p. 40 Canadian Tourism Commission and the Government of Canada; **Chapter 3;** p. 63 Source: www.oee.nrcan.gc.ca/publications; p. 66 USTTA, *Tourism USA* (Washington, DC: Department of Commerce, 1986), p. 20.; **Chapter 5;** p. 139 Marriott Corporation; p. 145 Canada Select Accommodation Program; **Chapter 7;** p. 184 Courtesy of Parks Canada.

INDEX

Note: **Boldface** entries and page numbers indicate key terms.